The Complete Masks of Nyarlathotep

H.P.Lovecraft
1890-1937

THE COMPLETE MASKS OF NYARLATHOTEP

Third Edition, Reset and Revised

by Larry DiTillio and Lynn Willis

with Geoff Gillan, Kevin A. Ross,
Thomas W. Phinney, Michael MacDonald,
Sandy Petersen, Penelope Love

Art by Lee Gibbons, Nick Smith,
Tom Sullivan, Jason Eckhardt

Design by Mark Schumann,
Mike Blum, Thomas W. Phinney,
Yurek Chodak, Shannon Appel

Project and Editorial by Lynn Willis
Interior & Cover Layout by Shannon Appel
Copyreading by Janice Sellers, Alan Glover, Rob Heinsoo

Chaosium Inc.
1996

The Clear Credit Box

Larry DiTillio wrote the first draft of Chapters One through Six, except as noted below. The conception, plot, and essential execution are entirely his, and remain a roleplaying classic. Lynn Willis rewrote the succeeding drafts, originating the historical background, introducing race as a theme, inserting or adjusting certain characters, writing the introductory chapter, and most of the advice, asides, incidental jokes, etc., and as an afterthought added the appendix concerning what might be done with shipboard time. In the introductory chapter, Michael MacDonald wrote the original version of the sidebar concerning shipboard travel times and costs. Thomas W. Phinney set forth the background chronology of the campaign, and created looks for many of the handouts. In the Cairo chapter, Kevin A. Ross wrote the Bast episode. Geoff Gillan wrote the game lodge episode in Kenya, Buckley's ghost in Australia, and the demon and Mr. Lung in Shanghai.

Tom Sullivan contributed a dozen or so new illustrations; his previous drawings have been rescanned for better reproduction. Apart from the maps and plans, he, Jason Eckhardt, and Nick Smith are responsible for the interior illustrations. Jason created all the small drawings of individual characters. Nick Smith painted "The Rocket Pit", which is reproduced here in black and white. The remaining drawings, mostly pencilled illustrations, are by Tom Sullivan. The front cover painting is by Lee Gibbons, while the portrait on the back cover is by Nick Smith.

Mike Blum's sketch maps were original with the first edition, and are unlikely to be improved upon. Mark Schumann updated and clarified the interior plans, based on originals by Yurek Chodak and Ron Leming, and added the repeating logo. Shannon Appel added maps for the Introduction and the Australian Chapter, and also redrew the schematic of the City of the Great Race.

Special thanks go to Alan Glover, Mike Lay, Jeff McSpadden, John B. (Ben) Monroe, and Ian Starcher for sundry important comments or other now-invisible contributions.

Address questions and comments concerning this book as well as requests for free catalogues of Chaosium books, games, and supplements to Chaosium Inc., 950-A 56th Street, Oakland, CA U.S.A.

ISBN 1-56882-069-0

Chaosium Publication 2361. Published December 1996.

10 9 8 7 6 5 4 3 2 1

Printed in Canada.

Table of Contents

INTRODUCTION

WHEREIN NYARLATHOTEP'S GRAND PLOT IS FIRST EXAMINED, AND THE MEMBERS
OF THE ILL-FATED CARLYLE EXPEDITION ARE FIRST ENCOUNTERED.

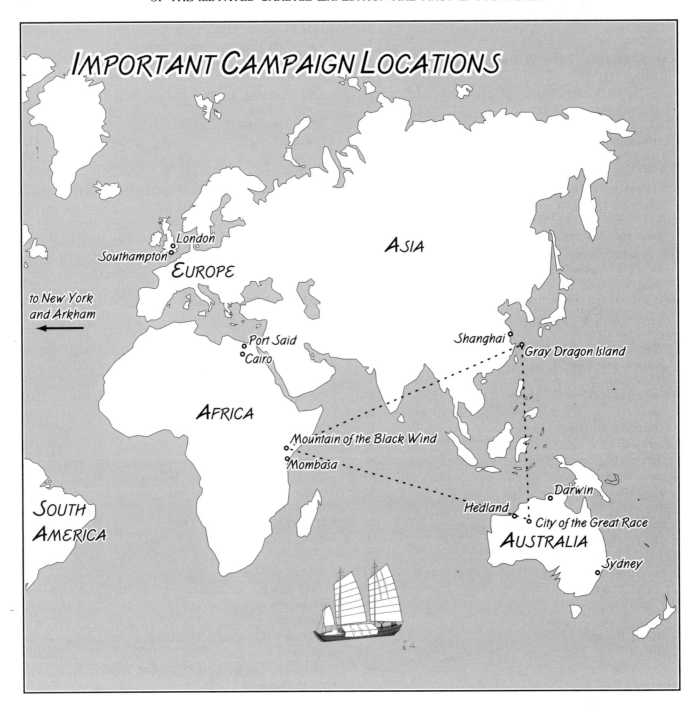

IMPORTANT CAMPAIGN LOCATIONS

*"He talked about terrible meetings in lonely places, or Cyclopean ruins... beneath
which vast staircases lead down to abysses of nighted secrets, of complex angles that
lead through invisible walls to other regions of space and time..."*

–H. P. Lovecraft, "The Thing on the Doorstep"

Masks of Nyarlathotep is a Lovecraftian exercise in horror and mystery. Set in 1925, adventures begin in New York, then move overseas to England, Egypt, Kenya Colony, Shanghai, and western Australia. Such extended globetrotting requires wit and planning by the players. Their investigators must have steady finances, good language skills, and a willingness to persevere despite governmental interference and cultist harassment. Meanwhile the keeper must bring to life different exotic locales, recreate the sensibilities of other cultures, and balance non-player-character foes and friends to allow each investigator to earn his or her own destiny—ultimate triumph, perhaps, or perhaps madness and agonizing death.

Summary of Events

In the year 1916, Kenyan cultists hold an obscene ritual dedicated to the God of the Bloody Tongue. M'Weru, a beautiful Kikuyu girl, has been priestess of the cult since her fourteenth birthday. The ritual has never caused the god to appear, but this day is different.

> *"As the priestess whirled around the fire-lit circle, chanting dim words from an ancient spell, the cult executioners busied themselves with their screaming sacrifices. As the blood flowed, a chill wind sprang up, and I felt a flash of fear: the wind had become visible, a black vapour against the gibbous, leering Moon, and slowly my terror grew as I comprehended the monstrous thing taking form. The corrosive stench of it hinted at vileness beyond evil. When I saw the great red appendage which alone constituted the face of the thing, my courage died, and I fled unseeing into the night."*
>
> –Nigel Blackwell, *Africa's Dark Sects*

Blackwell never learns that the apparition is one aspect of Nyarlathotep.

By the will of that outer god, M'Weru is sent to New York City, her mind magically infused with knowledge of the place and times. Her beauty and magnetism entrance millionaire playboy Roger Carlyle, and she uses the spell Send Dreams to align his mind to the commands of Nyarlathotep.

Encouraged by M'Weru, Carlyle forms an archaeological expedition in accordance with the dreams he receives. The people whom Nyarlathotep wants for his scheme are superior in skills and social class, but flawed in character. Three have profound desires to escape (Carlyle from his personal failures, Hypatia from her abortion, Huston from the scandalous suicide of a lover); a fourth, Sir Aubrey Penhew, wants to become a Pharaoh, a lust which only a god can satisfy. Even Nyarlathotep is not so powerful that he can change human will—he must choose from among those who are susceptible to his gifts.

In a lucid moment, Carlyle nearly redeems himself by bringing along Jack Brady, his bodyguard and confidante. Brady proves to be extraordinarily intractable to the will of Nyarlathotep, to the wiles of M'Weru, and to the wicked death plots of fanatical cultists: did a cryptic gift from his mother make Brady so lucky?

In Egypt, the expedition unlocks secrets previously shielded from Nyarlathotep. Omar Shakti, envious and powerful, gives aid—but not too much, and not without exacting payment and promises. Having broken the ward of the Red Pyramid, the expedition then encounters Nyarlathotep and his time gate, and travels back in time to dynastic Egypt, there to be tempted, seduced, and trained.

Nyarlathotep's display of magical power hooks the expedition principals. Now Hypatia has a new child stirring within her, Sir Aubrey can become an ancient Pharaoh, Huston can (as the promised ruler of Earth) indulge himself without thought for others, and Carlyle can find meaning in life through his passion for his bride-to-be, M'Weru.

(Nyarlathotep intends to keep his promises. Hypatia shall have her child, and its foul growth and birth shall destroy her. Sir Aubrey shall rule in ancient Egypt, but as the terror-ridden toady of the ominous Black Pharaoh. Huston shall lord it over the Earth, but—after the gods return—all of humanity quickly becomes extinct. Married, Carlyle shall be M'Weru's abject toy: after a jaded week she will tire of pulling him around on a leash and chucks him into a pit containing large hungry rats.)

Leaving Egypt, the Carlyle Expedition members arrive at Nairobi. Jack Brady is appalled by Carlyle's nightmarish ravings and by Sir Aubrey's power over young Carlyle. In the confusion of the expedition's departure into the Kenyan back-country, Brady drugs Carlyle and instead spirits him to the coast. Carlyle alternates between normal behavior and insanity as the two sail by Arab dhow to Durban. Using disguises, Brady hustles his charge and himself aboard a Perth-bound steamer, the first leg of a trip to Shanghai, where Brady has friends and resources. But Carlyle's health and sanity fail, and Brady places him in a Hong Kong sanitarium under the name "Randolph Carter".

Meanwhile, the expedition's bearers become sacrifices for the Cult of the Bloody Tongue, Huston and Penhew learn new spells, and pregnant Hypatia Masters is tucked away in the Mountain of the Black Wind. In the following years she slowly swells, metamorphoses, and goes permanently mad.

While their agents scour the globe for traces of Brady and Carlyle, Sir Aubrey Penhew and Dr. Huston plan, gather funds and disciples, and follow the commands of their god, preparing to open the Great Gate so that new great old ones may come to Earth. Sir Aubrey locates and breaks the ward at Gray Dragon Island. Huston becomes a high-level troubleshooter for Nyarlathotep and criss-crosses the globe.

Gavigan and the Penhew Foundation, Shakti and his cultists, Ho Fong and his minions, and many others aid the effort. By 1924, Sir Aubrey's rocket has been designed, and parts contracts are let to legitimate firms in Europe, Japan, and North America. The rocket's exploding warhead will be the ultimate boost needed to open the gate.

Except for Penhew, Nyarlathotep has chosen outsiders to

Background Events in *Masks of Nyarlathotep* (1918—1926)

Though some of the dates listed below are either conjectural or approximate, the sequence of these events is correct. Dates are all in the format Day-Month-Year.

11-01-1918	Dr. Huston first sees Roger Carlyle as a patient; Carlyle has been having "Egyptian dreams."
16-03-1918	Imelda Bosch's suicide.
18-09-1918	Carlyle obsesses about the lovely M'Weru.
03-12-1918	Carlyle pressures Huston to accompany expedition by threatening Huston with exposure.
03-01-1919	Faraz Najir writes to Carlyle.
05-04-1919	Carlyle Expedition leaves New York for England.
20-04-1919	Carlyle Expedition arrives in London.
28-04-1919	Carlyle Expedition leaves London for Cairo.
04-05-1919	Carlyle Expedition arrives in Cairo.
11-05-1919	Digs near Giza start (end May 21).
23-05-1919	Digs at Saqqara start (end May 31).
01-06-1919	Digs at Dhashur start. Carlyle breaks seal on Red Pyramid.
30-06-1919	Sacrifice at Bent Pyramid, witnessed by Jack Brady and Warren Besart.
30-06-1919	Digs at Dhashur end.
03-07-1919	Carlyle Expedition plans a "vacation" in Kenya.
18-07-1919	Carlyle Expedition leaves Egypt for Kenya.
24-07-1919	Expedition arrives in Mombasa, Kenya.
03-08-1919	Expedition departs from Nairobi on "camera safari." That night, Brady and Carlyle secretly flee.
04-08-1919	Brady and Carlyle arrive in Mombasa, then depart by ship for Perth, planning to continue to Shanghai where Brady has friends.
15-09-1919	Brady and Carlyle finally arrive in Hong Kong.
17-09-1919	Carlyle's insanity deepens. Brady hides him in a Hong Kong sanitarium under the alias "Randolph Carter."
11-03-1920	Erica Carlyle arrives in Kenya to search for traces of the expedition.
24-05-1920	Mutilated remains of the Carlyle Expedition are found.

19-06-1920	Five Nandi tribesmen executed following a short, unjust trial.
??-05-1921	Jackson Elias' book *The Black Power* is published.
13-06-1921	Sir Aubrey Penhew arrives in China to begin his task.
30-08-1921	Sir Aubrey receives the rocket plans from Huston.
07-09-1921	Shipments to Gray Dragon Island begin; deep ones contribute help.
13-03-1923	In Hong Kong, Jack Brady meets Nails Nelson.
04-10-1923	Sir Aubrey halts work on guidance system, awaiting Huston's work.
19-01-1924	Sir Aubrey resumes work.
25-06-1924	Jackson Elias departs New York City, bound for Nairobi.
23-07-1924	Elias arrives in Nairobi.
08-08-1924	From Nairobi, Jackson Elias writes to Jonah Kensington.
16-08-1924	Jackson Elias departs Kenya (Mombasa) for China.
17-09-1924	Elias arrives in Hong Kong.
19-09-1924	While in Hong Kong, Elias wires Jonah Kensington for money.
29-09-1924	Sir Aubrey completes the missile, though its warhead is still unready. Ho Fong warns him that their plans are known, presumably by Jackson Elias.
04-10-1924	Jackson Elias leaves Shanghai.
07-11-1924	Miriam Atwright replies to Jackson Elias' letter.
07-11-1924	Elias arrives in Cairo.
13-11-1924	Elias leaves Cairo for London.
25-11-1924	Elias arrives in London.
16-12-1924	Still in London, Elias wires Jonah Kensington.
17-12-1924	Elias takes passage on a freighter for New York.
13-01-1925	Elias arrives in New York City.
15-01-1925	The investigators are to meet with Elias, but arrive to find him murdered.
11-02-1925	Sir Aubrey finishes work. Rocket, warhead, and guidance system are ready. Only maintenance and the launch preparations and count down remain.
14-01-1926	Total solar eclipse occurs. Dimensional gate to be opened.

open the gate, partly because of their money, intelligence, and technical skills; partly because they are malleable to the special promises few but Nyarlathotep could keep; and partly because Gavigan, M'Weru, Shakti, and Fong will continue to be useful to Nyarlathotep, and are to be protected. If the gate ritual fails, the actual summoners risk destruction in a backlash of awful energies.

On January 14, 1926, at the same GMT second, Penhew, Huston, and Nyarlathotep's Spawn begin to intone a great ritual taught to them by Nyarlathotep. The ritual lasts for eight hours; every cultist who can get there flocks to the African, Chinese, or Australian sites, chanting and lending magic points to the spells. Mass sacrifices occur, and natural disasters—typhoons, earthquakes, tidal waves, tornadoes, volcanic eruptions, firestorms, etc.—guard the spell loci with fifty-mile-wide walls of terrible power. The continents subtly realign to a more propitious pattern. The great shifts stir Mythos creatures which dwell deep within the planet. Eldritch force shakes the world.

As the eclipse of the sun darkens the Indian Ocean, an onlooker first would see the flash from the exploding rocket, and then rippling blue waves as the atmosphere buckles back. A black rent appears in the roiling air, an interstellar blackness graced with a single red pulsing star. As the Great Gate opens wide, spheres of light hurtle through. The travelers are returning. Aldebaran and Fomalhaut send forth their children; the minions of Hastur, Cthugha, and Shub-Niggurath now join those of Cthulhu and other great old ones, to further turn the wheel toward their re-ascension of the thrones of Earth. Ships sink, farms and cities burn, and meteorites strike everywhere as the masters of the Mythos take firmer hold of Earth and the laughter of Nyarlathotep grows louder.

But, as the campaign opens, the Great Gate is closed, for about one more year.

Location of Carlyle Expedition Principals, January 1925

JACK BRADY, the one sane man who knows the plan of the Crawling Chaos, is in Shanghai. Brady has been trying to track down Penhew and Huston, and has been in peril repeatedly during the five years since the Carlyle Expedition massacre. Brady involved Jackson Elias, who in turn introduced the investigators to the campaign.

ROGER CARLYLE is in a mental asylum in Hong Kong, hopelessly insane. Brady watches over him from afar. Carlyle also knows the plan of Nyarlathotep, but is too crazy to be able to tell anyone.

DR. ROBERT HUSTON and his cultist gang are sometimes abroad, without fixed location, but they have successfully located the City of the Great Race in the Western Australian desert, and there engage in important if episodic researches.

M'WERU returned to Kenya to await the Carlyle Expedition. She is still there, leading the Cult of the Bloody Tongue.

SIR AUBREY PENHEW dwells on Gray Dragon Island in the China Sea, east of Shanghai. He presides over a local chapter of the Order of the Bloated Woman, and is busily developing the rocket and warhead that will weaken space-time and open the way for the Great Gate. Penhew is incurably insane, and maniacally capable.

HYPATIA MASTERS is a babbling shell driven insane by the entity to which she soon must give birth. She languishes in the Mountain of the Black Wind, lost to the world and to herself.

Concerning the Plot

BLOCKING THE GATE: the Great Gate might not be operable for several reasons. The likeliest is that the investigators learn the secret of the Eye of Light and Darkness, and use it to ward one of the three points of the triangle from which the gate can be opened. Unfortunately, Nyarlathotep now knows the secret of the wards: he and his servants could break those once-invincible seals in a few months or years. The Spawn could be destroyed, but in a pinch M'Weru, Nitocris, or Shakti could perform the ritual. In the Shanghai chapter, destroying the rocket makes the gate-opening spell less likely to work, yet the only effective way to stop the cultists is

ACTIVE MEMBERS OF THE CARLYLE EXPEDITION. LEFT TO RIGHT: BRADY, HUSTON, M'WERU, AND PENHEW

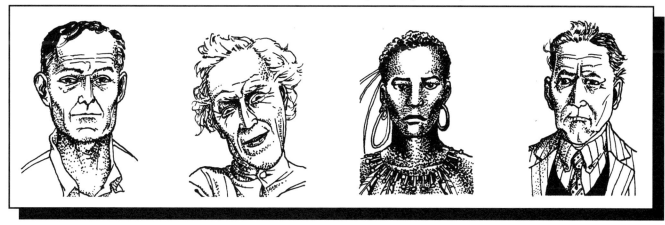

Additional Total Solar Eclipses

If the investigators stymie Nyarlathotep's plan for the early 1926 total solar eclipse, the dread god may try again during a later one. World-wide, a total solar eclipse occurs once or twice a year, though the phenomenon is rare in any one earthly location.

Here's a summary of them for the remainder of the decade, with indications of regional totality: June 29, 1927 (Britain, Scandinavia, NE Siberia, Aleutian islands); May 8-9, 1928 (SE Asia, Philippines, central Pacific, South Atlantic); May 19, 1928 (South Atlantic); April 28, 1930 (northern California, Oregon, Idaho, Nevada, western Utah—starts 10:49 a.m.); October 21-22, 1930 (South Pacific).

The yearly *Ephemeris* published by the Naval Observatory, Washington D.C., and contains more information.

to imprison or otherwise remove Ho Fong and Sir Aubrey Penhew.

If they can halt the opening of the Great Gate, give the investigators 1D20 SAN each, and another 1D20 SAN if they learn and comprehend the main elements of the conspiracy. In future adventures, of course, during another total solar eclipse, Nyarlathotep can try again.

IF THE GATE OPENS: in H.P. Lovecraft's works, Mythos activity wells in the period 1927-1934. The hypothesis prompting this campaign is that something happened in 1926 promoting or provoking such an eruption of evil. The astrological power of the total solar eclipse of 1926 is the event which allows alteration of the world fabric, and the event upon which this campaign resolves.

If the gate opens, world events occur as they did historically—the Great Depression, massive Asian floods and famines, establishment of totalitarian states across the world, erosion of personal freedoms, meteoric population increases (fodder for the gods' return), terrorism, brutality, militarism, and economic exploitation. The fall already has occurred in the world as we know it, though no one understands that this has happened. If the investigators prevent the gate's opening, world history need not change. The keeper may state with assurance that things would have been worse had the plot succeeded.

DR. ROBERT HUSTON: the keeper can maintain a mobile reserve force consisting of Huston and a small band of his cultists, as presented in the Australia chapter. They are busy there when play begins, but these wicked people have roamed the world previously, often completing despicable tasks for Nyarlathotep. They can do so again. As the keeper needs (though never in New York, the initial chapter), they may begin to shadow the investigators and to make inquiries about them. Having fairly introduced such ongoing opposition, the keeper may increase the severity of their interruptions and attacks as seems logical and

amusing. See the Australia chapter for complete statistics on Robert Huston (p. 166) and the Cultists of the Sand Bat (p. 136).

Such attacks are by no means obligatory. As written, this campaign is deadly on it own, and notorious for generating investigator corpses: *Masks of Nyarlathotep* offers many more picturesque and memorable deaths than by some thug's gun, club, or knife. If the keeper does use Huston in this way, then in compensation let each attack run a considerable chance of betraying a clue or other information leading to Huston's operations in the City of the Great Race, in Australia. Once the investigators head toward Australia, Huston and his agents should always hurry home, so that events on that continent occur as written.

Getting Started

Masks of Nyarlathotep takes many sessions to play. Though players may deduce that thwarting Nyarlathotep is the central issue, do not press them toward that end. Should Nyarlathotep's plan succeed, supplementary adventures can deal with the consequences. If the investigators foil the scheme, Nyarlathotep no doubt seeks vengeance, leading to approximately the same result.

Jack Brady is the key. By channeling the investigators to him at the strategic moment, the keeper can assure that they comprehend the design of Nyarlathotep before the ritual of the Gate takes place.

The scenarios are so designed that it makes little difference where the investigators first choose to go. The date of the eclipse does put a time limit on the campaign, but scholarly keepers can always discover "another" eclipse later in the year.

When an investigator dies or goes insane, that player should freely import or create a new character. New investigators should be connected with the places at which they first enter the game, or else adequate transit time must be allowed to bring them in by ship or train. If a party member dies in Egypt, a new investigator might be an Egyptian or an Englishman already involved with the investigators, or some other character who can logically be involved. If the player wishes, archaeologists, journalists, professors, etc., from the desired country can be abroad on business or study. Do strive to avoid a Nairobi suddenly teeming with dozens of U.S. private eyes, or a Shanghai overrun by U.S. accountants.

Always begin with the New York chapter, since it contains the initial clues. The investigators may or may not encounter the Chakota, but they must have reason to go abroad.

Should a keeper adjust the plot line, keep careful notes so that the skein of evidence can be unraveled. In New York, try to impart some of the following.

■ Some sort of cult murdered Jackson Elias.

■ This cult may have been responsible for or be connected with the infamous massacre of the Carlyle Expedition.

Oceanic Travel Times and Costs

Masks of Nyarlathotep is a long adventure that takes investigators from the fog-shrouded streets of London and the edge of the Sahara Desert to exotic Shanghai and the Australian wilds.

If the campaign is set in the modern era, a plane can move the investigators from halfway around the world in a day. If the campaign is set in the 1920s as written, travel time increases greatly, for only the steamship (or motorship) reliably spans the seas.

STREAMSHIP TRAVEL TIMES

Since the time available to foil Nyarlathotep may be posed to the players as being limited, the time needed to get from point A to point B can be important. Keepers who wish to track elapsed time may find the chart below to be of help.

The chart relates the six ports that are important in *Masks of Nyarlathotep*. The vertical column lists the departure ports. The arrival ports are cross-referenced on the horizontal band running across the top. Indexing the two gives the travel time in days (24 hours) between the two ports. The chart assumes the most favorable conditions and direct connections. Potential lay-overs for refueling, revictualing, repair, or a connecting ship are ignored. Keepers interested in such matters can routinely add three days per lay-over. (A direct sailing from Southampton to Mombasa would be rare, for instance—a connection at Port Said or Aden is much more likely.)

TRAVEL TIME, IN NOMINAL GAME DAYS

	NY	SOU	PS	MOM	DAR	SH
New York (NY)	—	4	8	12	21	25
Southampton (SOU)	4	—	3	7	16	20
Port Said (PS)	8	3	—	3	12	16
Mombasa (MOM)	12	7	3	—	8	12
Darwin (DAR)	21	16	12	8	—	3
Shanghai (SH)	25	20	16	12	3	—

Notes: the disembarkation ports for London are either Liverpool or Southampton; express trains for London are then taken. Port Hedland may be substituted for Darwin without changing the table's values.

These travel times are necessarily approximate. They assume a reputable passenger liner, a speed in excess of 21 knots, and good sailing conditions. A severe storm could add days to travel time. For instance, March through June, monsoon storms are common across the Indian Ocean and the East Indies (Indonesia), while winter gales can severely affect traffic across the North Atlantic or North Pacific. If the investigators must take a freighter or a tramp steamer (perhaps fleeing port in the middle of the night) they can expect to add days or weeks to their travel times.

COST OF SHIPBOARD TRAVEL

The cost of a ticket is a variable. Most of the factors are too petty to be applied to a roleplaying campaign. For our purposes, a simple formula determines ticket cost.

■ Cost of a one-way first-class ticket on a passenger liner: multiply the days traveled by $30. A New York to London trip is $120, London to Cairo is $90, and so forth.

■ Cost of a one-way steerage ticket on a passenger liner: multiply the days traveled by $9. A New York-London ticket costs $36, a London-Cairo ticket costs $27, etc.

■ Interpolate prices for tourist or third-class fares. Liners usually were designed to accommodate a tier of classes. Freighters and tramp steamers tended to offer a single class to passengers, if they accepted passengers at all. Some cargo ships might accept steerage or deck passengers as well, but the posher liners will not.

FREIGHTERS AND TRAMP STEAMERS

If the players opt for the much slower freighter or tramp steamer, their investigators can expect to pay a fraction of the liner fare. The exact cost is best left to the keeper and a Bargain roll by the players, but as a guide the captain of a regularly scheduled freighter might ask for a third to a half of the cost of a first-class liner ticket, and then Bargain the final price. The captain of a tramp steamer might begin at the same fare, but then haggle down with much greater flexibility. Some tramp steamer captains might even be willing to take on extra hands who are willing to work hard in exchange for passage.

A distance that a passenger liner might cover in a few days and that an eight-knot freighter might negotiate in a couple of weeks may take a tramp steamer six weeks, two months, or more. A regular freighter has a scheduled departure date, so that consigners of cargo can know when the vessel heads toward its next scheduled port. A tramp steamer charges less for carrying the same cargo, but it sails at the convenience of its captain/owner. Such a vessel might divert, detour, or stop unannounced anywhere between its port of origin and its ultimate destination, scouring backwater towns for cargo, accepting odd lots, live animals, and lethal chemicals, guided only by the force, finesse, and intuition of her captain. If a tramp steamer captain reaches a port and cannot find adequate cargo to carry his ship forward, he might discharge officers and crew and lay over until the holds fill, whenever that might be.

■ The principals of the expedition may not be dead, for no Caucasian bodies ever were found.

■ Kenya and Egypt are key points, as are London and Shanghai. Some point in Australia may be important.

Once the New York chapter has been played through, the investigators can select any of the other chapter destinations. The numerical order of the chapters represents an economical route of travel, but any sequence or order will do. The investigators might go to Shanghai first, or Kenya, or skip London entirely. Be flexible. Don't force them where they don't want to go. If a chapter of this campaign is overlooked, a well planted clue probably can draw them there later. An ultimately unused chapter can be broken into discrete adventures and played as individual games.

Chapters One through Six contain all necessary background information. Historical accuracy has been attempted, but do not represent the Nairobi or the Shanghai city maps as accurate. Loosely sketch all city locations: here is the river, here is where you docked, here is your hotel, etc. Specific locations can be added as events develop, but avoid being pinned down to precise street names, exact distances, and unnecessary geographic fiddle-faddle. The play's the thing.

Keepers may feel more comfortable with the locales after having read about London or Shanghai or New York in a good encyclopedia or guidebook. Present-day maps, histories, and rail guides can be very useful. Though much

has changed since 1925, much more has not. Seeing a photo of the British Museum or of the Great Sphinx allows a keeper to detail impressions in his or her own words, lending a conviction always more powerful than the best written scenario.

Exotic locations are fun. Play them sympathetically, but broadly and stereotypically. Scout libraries for belly-dancing music to use in the Blue Pyramid or in Cairo. "Living sound" recordings could provide atmosphere for Kenyan back-country journeys or strolls through Shanghai alleys.

It should be obvious, but sometimes is not: study the contents of this book before presenting adventures from it. Players have every right to demand that the keeper know what's going on. By understanding text and plot, keepers know what to stress, what to skip over, what to hint at, what to dismiss, what to threaten, what to paraphrase delicately, and what to leer about. Know the full meaning of every clue. When players ask questions, be able to answer without hesitation. Confident keepers make happy players. Though much of the Cthulhu Mythos is best left unknown to mortal man, that warning should not apply to campaign materials.

If you haven't enjoyed them yet, read Lovecraft's "The Shadow Out of Time", "Imprisoned with the Pharaohs" (alternately titled "Under the Pyramids"), "The Haunter of the Dark", and the other great tales from which this campaign grew. H.P. Lovecraft's special vision and narrative

NYARLATHOTEP SURVEYS HIS DOMAIN

focus must be encountered first-hand before one can appreciatively present *Call of Cthulhu* adventures.

Player Expectations

At times this campaign may frustrate your players and baffle your investigators. Clues abound. Evil is everywhere. In New York, the investigators don't know what to look for, or why to look. In England, Cairo, Kenya, Australia, and Shanghai, dangerous side-adventures lack connection to the main plot. In Cairo, the resurrection of Nitocris is peripheral to the opening of the Great Gate, and so on. Do not hesitate to adjust clues or re-motivate cultists to keep the play entertaining. The investigators are bound to run into the opposition, and then the players will get the action which balances the research and speculation central to *Call of Cthulhu*. Don't throw deranged cultists at investigators merely to cater to jaded players—the cultists will show up soon enough. Cultists such as Huston's group might pressure the investigators in a specific direction, but not often. Proceed logically, without haste. Keep your integrity (and your pleasure) intact.

Reminders

In the mid-1920s, there are no intercontinental airlines. It is headline news when an aircraft staggers across the North Atlantic. Even local phone calls must go through an operator. A connection for a long-distance phone call may take an hour or more to be established; the operator will call you back when the line has been opened. There are no intercontinental phone lines. The pace of postal delivery is often excellent across town, but leisurely at longer distances. Use telegrams for quick communication. Land travel of any distance depends on railroads. Only parts of western Europe and eastern North America have road nets adequate to lengthy automobile trips.

Travel can't be paid for by personal checks or credit card. Only local currency pays the bills, though bank letters of credit can be used to replenish funds. If the investigators neglect elementary precautions, strand them without mercy. Kindly keepers have pawnshops at hand, run by greedy proprietors. The British pound is the nearest to a universally accepted currency, but it may not be readily convertible in particular shops, even in Egypt, Australia, or Shanghai. It will be accepted in Kenya, of course. Bearers of paper money risk being charged stiff conversion fees by local shops and banks. Coins minted of silver or gold will be eagerly accepted, however, sometimes at rates remarkably favorable to the bearer.

Limit traveling investigators to that which they can carry. Force the players to think ahead. That copy of the *Necronomicon* can't be both safe at home in Boston and at hand in Mombasa. The eight-ton Hand of Ormolu (100% effective against fire vampires, if only it existed!) won't fit into the passenger compartment of any train. If investigators leave their overcoats in London, it's reasonable to require rolls to stifle night-time sneezes in Derbyshire. If investigators must flee a country without their luggage, work out with the players what is being carried and what has been left behind.

Old books and overcoats may not interest border guards, but ancient artifacts, items of obvious artistic value, precious gems and metals, drugs, and guns and other weapons get full attention. Investigators must bow to the requirements of the State, or devise ways to avoid the power of the State. Do not encourage illegal activity. If investigators are convicted in or ejected from one nation, their bad reputations should precede them at the next border.

May your investigators teeter on the brink of madness; may your players tremble when they roll the dice. Good hunting!

Characters

These are the important people in Masks of Nyarlathotep.

al-Sayed, Tewfik — London spice-dealer and high priest of the Brotherhood of the Black Pharaoh.

Atwright, Miriam — a Harvard research librarian who in the past has aided and admired Jackson Elias' researches.

Baines, Reggie — proprietor of the best Nairobi hotel, Hampton House.

Barrington, Inspector James — handling the so-called "Egyptian murders" for the London CID.

Besart, Warren — he acted as a purchasing agent for Roger Carlyle in Cairo; what he saw during his tenure with the Carlyle Expedition left him a hashish addict and almost insane.

Blackwell, Nigel — unidentified, inaccessible author of *Africa's Dark Sects*, which discusses the Cult of the Bloody Tongue among other organizations.

Brady, Jack "Brass" — bodyguard for Roger Carlyle. Always faithful to Carlyle since being saved by him from conviction for murder. In Shanghai between Elias' death and the date for the opening of the Gate.

Broadmoor, Agatha — member of the Clive Expedition, a psychic and medium hired by Clive to contact Nitocris and unknowingly aid in her resurrection.

Bumption, Sgt. Leonard — inept witness to the massacre site of the Carlyle Expedition.

Bundari — an African tribal magician of great power who can help the investigators if their quest leads to the Mountain of the Black Wind. Bundari also has a helper, Okomu.

Buckley, Bill — murdered ten years ago by the Slattery clan, his ghost still haunts the area around Dingo Falls, not far from Cuncudgerie.

Carlyle Expedition — the principal members were Roger Carlyle, Dr. Robert Huston, Hypatia Masters, Sir Aubrey Penhew, and Jack Brady.

Carlyle, Erica — sole heir to the Carlyle millions since Roger Carlyle was declared dead. She is willing to reopen the investigation in order to learn the truth about his death.

Carlyle, Roger — leader of the Carlyle Expedition and millionaire playboy. The beautiful M'Weru offers him up to Nyarlathotep, and young Carlyle is of too weak a character to withstand the Dark God. Mistakenly thought dead in a Kenyan massacre. Throughout this campaign he languishes, insane, in a Hong Kong sanitarium, placed there by Jack Brady.

Chabout, Punji — criminal and warehouse owner in London.

Choi, Mei-ling — lover of Jack Brady, and ready to give her life to protect him. For a few days she is interrogated by the sorcerer Carl Stanford.

Chu Min — leader of Firm Action, the most violent and best-armed wing of the New China patriotic league.

Clive, Dr. Henry — archaeologist and member of the Brotherhood of the Black Pharaoh, aiding in the resurrection of Nitocris.

Clive Expedition — in Egypt, it is secretly acting in behalf of Nyarlathotep. The principal members are Henry Clive, Agatha Broadmoor, James Gardner, Johannes Sprech, and Martin Winfield.

Cory, Joe — Erica Carlyle's bodyguard. A tough mug.

Corydon, Roger — Kenya's colonial undersecretary for internal affairs, who feels that no further investigation of the Carlyle Expedition is warranted.

Cowles, Prof. Anthony — from the University of Sydney, currently a Fellow at Miskatonic. He has seen amazing photos of ancient ruins in the west of Australia which were taken by Arthur MacWhirr.

Cowles, Ewa — Anthony Cowles' intelligent and beautiful daughter.

Crompton, Montgomery — in the early nineteenth century he wrote a diary since known as *Life as a God*, praising Nyarlathotep and revealing many secrets concerning the Brotherhood of the Black Pharaoh.

Dodge, Dr. David — young professor of archaeology at the University of Sydney, and an experienced hand in Western Australia.

Elias, Jackson — a globe-trotting writer specializing in exposés of death cults and other strange organizations. He gets wind of Nyarlathotep's plan, but cultists chase him down and kill him.

Emerson, Arthur — an innocent New Yorker. As an importer/exporter, he can supply the address of Ju-Ju House, which Jackson Elias intended to visit.

Efti, Nessim — bearer of the Sword of Akmallah, at the mosque Ibn Tulun.

Endicott, Col. Harry — he runs a game lodge not far from Nairobi; eventually he does battle with some new residents in the area.

Gardner, James — archaeologist with the Clive Expedition. He has a theory about an underground maze beneath the Sphinx. Potential ally to the investigators.

The Cults of Nyarlathotep

Nyarlathotep has a thousand different aspects. The investigators encounter four different cults of Nyarlathotep during the campaign. These cults' dress, rites, and names for their god also differ. The investigators must come to understand this in order to understand the central design of the campaign. At the beginning of each chapter, boxed text summarizes the new cult's activity, cult weapon, and cult characteristics, along with statistics for the average male cultist.

Those statistics are keeper templates for extra guards or attackers, when needed.

Various items of magical importance, including Mythos tomes, can be found in cult meeting-places. All cult priests know Contact Nyarlathotep and a summoning spell. If contacted, Nyarlathotep appears in the aspect appropriate to that cult (Sand Bat in Australia, for instance). Individuals will know other spells, including spells unrelated to the Mythos.

Uniformly, cult members are primitive and degenerate, controlled by intelligent and sophisticated priests. These stereotypes reflect the respective physical and magical attacks possible to them. Cultists normally try to chop investigators into hamburger. Failing that, cult priests presumably sigh and turn to their own arcane powers. Keepers may try for more rounded characterizations, but that will take more time.

Except as transplanted to New York and London, all the cults are of ancient origin and are well known in their homelands.

Brotherhood of the Black Pharaoh — an Egyptian cult worshipping an aspect of Nyarlathotep. Also found in London.

Cult of the Bloody Tongue — a Kenyan cult worshipping an aspect of Nyarlathotep. A branch exists in New York City.

Cult of the Sand Bat — an Australian cult worshipping an aspect of Nyarlathotep.

Order of the Bloated Woman — a Chinese cult worshipping an aspect of Nyarlathotep.

大胖女人

Gavigan, Edward — director of the London-based Penhew Foundation and high priest in the Brotherhood of the Black Pharaoh.

Grey, Bradley — Erica Carlyle's New York City lawyer, a partner at Dunstan, Whittleby, and Grey.

Grogan, Jeremy — madman survivor of a cult attack in the Great Sandy Desert of Australia.

Hakim — in Cairo, an ordinary thief who poses as a guide and then robs his charges.

Hetep — Omar Shakti's vicious cat-demon. It appears to be an ordinary white Persian long-haired cat.

Ho Fong — a Shanghai importer/exporter, and secret high priest of the Order of the Bloated Woman. The sorcerer Carl Stanford is staying with him.

Ho Tzu-hsi — Ho Fong's only child, she is permanently insane.

Huston, Dr. Robert — once a fashionable Jungian analyst in New York, Huston became the eager thrall of Nyarlathotep, and now leads cultists across Australia, where he has revived the cult of Sand Bat.

Isoge Taro — disguised as a factory foreman, Isoge is a Captain in the Imperial Japanese Navy, investigating rumors connecting a super-weapon with Jack Brady and the Chinese Communists.

Jermyn, Neville — descendant of Sir Wade Jermyn. Neville wants to lead the investigators on a long trek into the Belgian Congo to find the White City.

Kafour, Dr. Ali — in Cairo, the Egyptian Museum's resident expert in matters occult as well as archaeological. He is an accomplished linguist.

Kakakatak — a member of the Great Race whom Huston has physically shifted into the present. This entity can easily outsmart Huston, but only if the investigators get its full attention.

Kensington, Jonah — owner and chief editor for Prospero House, a small New York firm. He is Jackson Elias' publisher.

Kenyatta, Johnstone — known by Sam Mariga, Kenyatta is a local black leader who brings the investigators to Old Bundari. Later known as Jomo Kenyatta.

Lin Tang-yu — a degenerate and ruthless collector determined to obtain the *Seven Cryptical Books* for aesthetic reasons. He knows of the Mythos, yet does nothing to stop it.

Li Wen-cheng — a young Christian intellectual, an expert guide to Shanghai.

Lung Yun — a Shanghai astrologer who mistakes the investigators for demons from the Celestial Court.

Mackenzie, Robert B.F. — a resident of Port Hedland, he sent photos of ruins in the Great Sandy Desert to Anthony Cowles.

McChum—Real name Fergus Chum. Chinese owner of the Stumbling Tiger Bar, Shanghai. He knows the whereabouts of Jack Brady, the significance of Ho Fong, and much else.

Mahoney, Mickey — London friend of Jackson Elias and publisher of a scurrilous tabloid, *The Scoop*.

Ma'muhd — orphaned street-boy in Cairo, eleven years old, an expert guide.

Mariga, Sam — in Nairobi, an African nationalist who can direct the investigators to Johnstone Kenyatta.

Masters, Hypatia — a New York society girl, she is a member of the Carlyle Expedition, ostensibly to make its photographic record. During the campaign she is the doomed living incubator for the Spawn of Nyarlathotep.

Mu Hsien — an assistant to the curator of the Shanghai Museum with much knowledge and many contacts, among them Chu Min. Jack Brady lives in a closet-like secret room in Mu's humble home.

Mukunga — the high priest of the Bloody Tongue in New York. His temple occupies the basement of Ju-Ju House.

M'Weru — high priestess of the Bloody Tongue, seductress of Roger Carlyle, and a powerful sorceress.

Najir, Faraz — a Cairene dealer of antiquities known to Roger Carlyle and Warren Besart.

Nawisha, Abdul — proprietor of the Blue Pyramid nightclub in Soho, London.

Nelson, Bertram "Nails" — in Nairobi, a soldier of fortune who in 1923 reports seeing Jack Brady of the Carlyle Expedition, years after the supposed massacre.

Nitocris — an evil Queen of Dynastic Egypt. The Black Brotherhood attempts to resurrect Nitocris, so that she in turn may begin to create a world-wide organization.

N'Kwane, Silas — the proprietor of Ju-Ju House, New York City.

Nyarlathotep — one of the great Outer Gods, powerful and cunning.

Nyiti of El Wasta — though tragically mutilated by Mythos attacks, she and her son Unba have preserved a fragment of the warding symbol that capped the Red Pyramid.

Old Bundari — see Bundari.

Penhew, Sir Aubrey — formerly the director of the Penhew Foundation in London, he now works feverishly for Nyarlathotep, and is crucial to Nyarlathotep's plan to open the way to new Mythos influence.

Poole, Lt. Martin, NYPD — investigator of Jackson Elias' murder. He knows that in the last two years, eight other people have been killed in manners similar to Elias' death.

Randolph, Toddy — owner of the Randolph Shipping Company in Darwin and/or Port Hedland. Shipper/receiver for items significant to Huston and his cultists at the City of the Great Race.

Savoyard, Jules — captain of Sir Aubrey's yacht, the *Dark Mistress*.

Shakti, Omar — Egyptian plantation owner and high priest of the Brotherhood of the Black Pharaoh. He is never far from Hetep, his cat.

Shipley, Bertha — seemingly Miles Shipley's mother, she is actually Ssathasaa, a serpent person. The real Mrs. Shipley has been eaten.

Shipley, Miles — mad young artist and insane visionary, now collaborating with Ssathasaa the serpent person.

Singh, Ahja — a Mombasan importer and exporter who cooperates in moving Bloody Tongue artifacts and equipment.

Singh, Tandoor — Nairobi tea-seller and agent of the Bloody Tongue. He mounts several magical attacks against the investigators.

Slattery, Vern, Frank, and Jacko — the father and two sons, each seemingly more evil than the last. They eke out a living near Cuncudgerie by mining gold and robbing passersby.

Smythe-Forbes, Natalie — publisher and editor of the *Nairobi Star* newspaper.

Sprech, Johannes — archaeologist with the Clive Expedition, a cipher expert, and an enthusiastic Nazi party member.

Ssathasaa — a serpent person who has magically acquired the appearance of Bertha Shipley, Miles Shipley's mother.

Stanford, Carl — expert sorcerer, a servant of evil for centuries, presently staying in Shanghai with Ho Fong.

Starret, Dr. Horace — local Nairobi physician who participated in the medical examination of bodies found after the Carlyle Expedition massacre.

Stratton, Rev. Jeremy — vicar for the Church of England in Lesser-Edale, Derbyshire.

Torvak, Lars — drunken owner-captain of the *Ivory Wind*, a tramp freighter carrying cultist items to and from the Far East.

Tumwell, Constable Hubert — the entire police force for Lesser-Edale, Derbyshire.

Vane, Sir Arthur — his castle is on the heights above Lesser-Edale, in Derbyshire. He is a knight of the realm, and father to Lawrence and Eloise.

Vane, Eloise — daughter of Sir Arthur Vane, and unfortunate heiress to the Curse of the Vanes.

Vane, Lawrence — the male heir to the title and properties of the noble Vanes.

Janwillem Vanheuvelen — Dutch archaeologist stranded in Cairo. His theft of a Bast cult text angers the goddess and outrages her priestess.

Wassif, Nigel — anglophile publisher of the *Cairo Bulletin*, an English language daily newspaper.

Winfield, Martin — archaeologist, member of the Clive Expedition, member of the Brotherhood of the Black Pharaoh.

Wycroft, Mortimer — an outfitter in Cuncudgerie, Western Australia. An agent of Sand Bat, though not a cultist.

Yalesha — a belly-dancer at the Blue Pyramid nightclub. She loves the feel of five-pound notes on her skin.

Zehavi, Achmed — nazir of the mosque Ibn Tulun, protector of the Girdle of Nitocris. ■

☞ *Information on the ill-fated Carlyle Expedition has been widely published in the press. The following articles (Nyarlathotep Papers #3 through 10) are a sample of the most relevant stories. They should be given to the players prior to the beginning of the campaign, so that the investigators can digest these important facts.*

Nyarlathotep Papers #3

Big Apple Dateline

ROGER CARLYLE, the playboy whom everybody knows—or knows about—is quietly leaving New Yawk tomorrow to check out the tombs of Egypt! You've seen the cuties ROGER has found in the nightspots. Who can doubt he'll dig up someone—er, something—equally fabulous from the Egyptian sands?

—*NEW YORK PILLAR/RIPOSTE, April 4, 1919*

Nyarlathotep Papers #4

CARLYLE EXPEDITION EMBARKS FOR ENGLAND

Led by the fabulously-wealthy playboy Roger Carlyle, the Carlyle Expedition departed this morning for Southampton aboard the crack British steamship *Imperial Standard*.

Contrary to earlier reports, the expedition will perform researches in London under the auspices of the Penhew Foundation before continuing to Egypt next month.

Readers may recall the enormous party which Mr. Carlyle, now 24, gave at the Waldorf-Astoria Hotel upon reaching his majority. Since then, scandals and indelicate behavior have become Carlyle's trademark, but he never has become tarnished in the eyes of Manhattanites.

Members of the expedition have been reluctant to reveal their purpose in Egypt.

OTHER EXPEDITION MEMBERS

Renowned Egyptologist Sir Aubrey Penhew is assistant leader of the team, and in charge of excavations.

Dr. Robert Huston, a fashionable 'Freudian' psychologist, accompanies the expedition to pursue parallel researches into ancient pictographs.

Miss Hypatia Masters, linked in the past to Carlyle, will act as photographer and archivist.

Mr. Jack Brady, intimate to Mr. Carlyle, accompanies the group as general factotum.

Additional members may be secured while in London.

—*NEW YORK PILLAR/RIPOSTE April 5, 1919*

Nyarlathotep Papers #5

CARLYLE DEPARTS EGYPT

CAIRO (AP)—Sir Aubrey Penhew, temporary spokesman for the Carlyle Expedition, indicated Monday that the leaders are taking ship to East Africa for a 'well-earned rest.'

Sir Aubrey debunked rumors that the expedition had discovered clues to the legendary wealth of the lost mines of King Solomon, maintaining that the party was going on safari "in respite from our sandy labors."

Roger Carlyle, wealthy New York leader of the expedition, was unavailable for comment, still suffering from his recent sunstroke.

Discussing that unfortunate incident, local experts declared Egypt entirely too hot for Anglo-Saxons at this time of year, and suggested that the young American had not been well-served by his democratic enthusiasm, rumored to have led him to personally wield pick and shovel.

—*NEW YORK PILLAR/RIPOSTE, July 3, 1919*

Nyarlathotep Papers #7

CARLYLE EXPEDITION FEARED LOST

MOMBASA (Reuters)—Uplands police representatives today asked for public assistance concerning the disappearance of the Carlyle Expedition. No word of the party has been received in nearly two months.

The group includes wealthy playboy Roger Carlyle and three other American citizens, as well as respected Egyptologist Sir Aubrey Penhew of the United Kingdom.

The expedition left Nairobi on August 3, ostensibly on camera safari, but rumor insisted that they actually were after legendary Biblical treasures.

Carlyle and his party reportedly intended to explore portions of the Great Rift Valley, to the northwest of Nairobi.

—*NEW YORK PILLAR/RIPOSTE, Oct. 15, 1919*

Nyarlathotep Papers #8

ERICA CARLYLE ARRIVES IN AFRICA

MOMBASA (Reuters)—In response to clues, Miss Erica Carlyle, sister to the American leader of the lost Carlyle Expedition, arrived in port today aboard the Egyptian vessel *Fount of Life*.

Several Kikuyu-villager reports recently have been received concerning the putative massacre of unnamed whites near Aberdare Forest.

Miss Carlyle declared her intention to find her brother, regardless of the effort needed. She brought with her the nucleus of a large expedition.

Detailing agents to coordinate supply and other activities with Colony representatives, Miss Carlyle and the remainder of her party depart for Nairobi tomorrow.

Her companion, Mrs. Victoria Post, indirectly emphasized Miss Carlyle's purposefulness by recounting the rigors of the voyage aboard the Semite ship.

—*NEW YORK PILLAR/RIPOSTE, March 11, 1920*

Nyarlathotep Papers #6

IMPORTANT VISITORS

MOMBASA (Reuters)—Leading members of an American archaeological expedition arrived here on holiday from digs in Egypt's Nile Valley.

Our Under-Secretary, Mr. Royston Whittingdon, held a welcoming dinner for them at Collingswood House, where the wit of Sir Aubrey Penhew, expedition co-leader, was much in evidence.

Accompanying Sir Aubrey are two Americans, youthful financier Roger Carlyle and medical doctor Robert Huston.

The party leaves inland tomorrow, for Nairobi and hunting.

—*NEW YORK PILLAR/RIPOSTE, July 24, 1919*

Nyarlathotep Papers #9

CARLYLE MASSACRE CONFIRMED

NAIROBI (Reuters)—The massacre of the long-missing Carlyle expedition was confirmed today by district police representatives.

Roger Carlyle, New York's rollicking playboy, is counted among the missing.

Authorities blame hostile Nandi tribesmen for the shocking murders. Remains of at least two dozen expedition members and bearers are thought found in several concealed grave sites.

Erica Carlyle, Roger Carlyle's sister and apparent heiress to the Carlyle family fortune, led the dangerous search for her brother and his party. She credited Kikuyu tribesmen for the discovery, though police actually found the site.

Among other expedition members believed lost are Sir Aubrey Penhew, noted Egyptologist; New York socialite Hypatia Masters, and Dr. Robert Huston. Many bearers also are reported dead.

—*NEW YORK PILLAR/RIPOSTE, May 24, 1920*

Nyarlathotep Papers #10

MURDERERS HANGED

NAIROBI (Reuters)—Five Nandi tribesmen, convicted ringleaders of the vicious Carlyle Expedition massacre, were executed this morning after a short, expertly-conducted trial.

To the end, the tribesmen steadfastly refused to reveal where they had hidden the bodies of the white leaders of the expedition. Mr. Harvis, acting for the Colony, cleverly implied throughout the trial that the massacre was racial in motivation, and that the fair-skinned victims were taken to a secret location, there to suffer the most savage treatment.

Miss Erica Carlyle, defeated in her efforts to rescue her brother, left several weeks ago, but is surely comforted now by the triumph of justice.

—*NEW YORK PILLAR/RIPOSTE, June 19, 1920*

NEW YORK

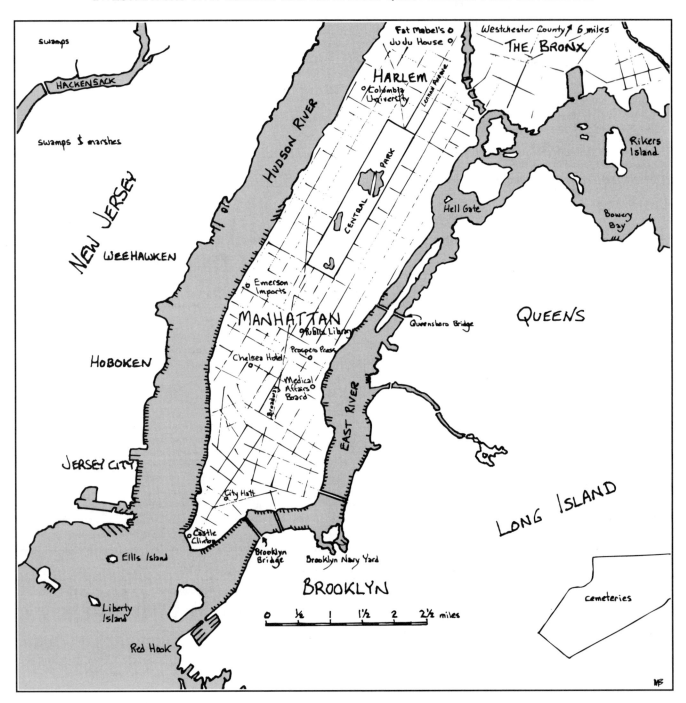

"Amongst my few playmates I was very unpopular, since I would insist on playing out events in history, or acting according to consistent plots.... The children I knew disliked them [and their] romping & shouting puzzled me. I hated mere play & dancing about— in my relaxations I always desired plot."

—H.P. Lovecraft, Letters

The Carlyle Expedition sailed from New York in 1919, led by Roger Carlyle (age 24), a millionaire playboy who inexplicably turned from the life of a wastrel to finance and head an archaeological expedition to Egypt. The principal members of the expedition were Sir Aubrey Penhew (age 54), titled, wealthy, and a noted Egyptologist; Hypatia Masters (age 27), a beautiful society girl and an accomplished photographer and linguist; Jack "Brass" Brady (age 36), mercenary soldier, weapons expert, and Carlyle's confidant and bodyguard; and Dr. Robert Huston (age 52), fashionable psychoanalyst and interpreter of dreams.

The members sailed from New York to London, to meet with Sir Aubrey Penhew. After a few weeks they departed for Egypt. Using Cairo as a base, the expedition performed several short desert excavations. An important find was rumored, but the expedition refused comment to reporters. The principal members departed for Mombasa, Kenya, and quickly went inland to Nairobi.

In Nairobi, at the beginning of August, the expedition hired twenty bearers and headed into the wilderness. They were seen often at first. The last letters from them arrived in early September, and then they vanished. In March of 1920 a Kikuyu tribesman told authorities in Nairobi of a party of whites near the Mountain of the Black Wind, a local name for one of the high Kenyan peaks. Later rumors intimated that the party had been destroyed by inhuman forces.

A search party, hired by Carlyle's sister Erica, found the remains of the expedition after ten weeks of effort. The corpses of the bearers were remarkably preserved and appeared to have been pulled apart by animals, though a coroner's report never mentions tooth marks on the bones—they had been horribly killed and torn to shreds. The encampment was totally destroyed, in no little part by the seasonal rains and undergrowth in the months since the disaster. No sign was found of the whites who had led the expedition, a fact easily established by the absence of dental work among the corpses. Despite reports to the contrary the bodies were strewn about in the open, and no effort to conceal them had been made.

Blame was quickly pinned on Nandi tribesmen. Some mention was made of a pagan cult (the Bloody Tongue) powerful in the area but authorities scoffed at the idea and did not use it in the subsequent trial. Random tribesmen were hung, the expedition members were declared dead, and the incident was forgotten, like any crime.

All this information is available to investigators, with some effort.

Starting Play

In early January 1925, one of the investigators receives an intriguing radiogram (*Nyarlathotep Papers #1*) from a ship at sea. The message is from Jackson Elias, a writer with whom the investigator has corresponded for several years. As with all handouts, keepers may find it useful to photocopy this material ahead of time, and to pass out the copies when appropriate.

JACKSON ELIAS

The investigator and Jackson Elias are good friends, though Elias rarely stays anywhere for very long. Choose which investigator receives the message—he or she can be of any profession. Elias is an author noted for studies concerning obscure religious cults. He is fascinated by the occult and the supernatural, but is a hard-headed skeptic. He tends to write about the bloodiest and most bizarre death cults he can unearth. He is not frightened easily and has a firm grip on reality.

Give the player of the chosen investigator *Nyarlathotep Papers #2*. It contains the essentials of what the investigator knows about his friend.

Once the investigator is alerted, he should put together the requested team. There should not be less than six investigators. Review the assembled team in order to scale the opposition to them. Be sure to allow enough play time for this, and allow enough game time for the investigators to assemble. If

Selected Connections for this Chapter

NP#	clue or lead	obtained from	leads to
11	letter in Elias' room	Room 410	Cairo, Faraz Najir
12	Penhew Foundation card	Room 410	London, Edward Gavigan
13	matchbox	Room 410	Shanghai, Stumbling Tiger Bar
14	photo of yacht	Room 410	Chinese junks also can be seen
15	Emerson Imports card	Room 410	New York; "Silas N'Kwane" written on back.
16	letter from M. Atwright	Room 410	Elias' Harvard researcher
17	handbill	Room 410	Prof. Cowles, Miskatonic U., Cult of Darkness
18	symbol on forehead	Room 410	Cult of the Bloody Tongue
19	*Life as a God*	Carlyle safe	Cairo, Black Brotherhood, the Bent Pyramid, Nyarlathotep
—	Insp. Barrington	J. Kensington	London
—	Mickey Mahoney	J. Kensington	London
—	Edward Gavigan	J. Kensington	London
20	letter from Jackson Elias	J. Kensington	Kenya, Carlyle Expedition
21	Elias' Kenya notes	J. Kensington	Kenya, several important contacts
22	Elias' London notes	J. Kensington	mentions a safe in Carlyle mansion
23	summary of lecture	Anthony Cowles	Sand Bat cult, western Australian ruins, Cthulhu, etc.
24	Huston's case notes	Med. Affairs Brd.	Carlyle's dreams, M'Weru, etc.
—	existence of Ju-Ju House	Arthur Emerson	Cult of the Bloody Tongue

Nyarlathotep Papers #1

What You Know About Your Friend, Jackson Elias

Jackson Elias is 38, of medium height and build, and dark-complexioned. He has a feisty, friendly air about him and, as an orphan in Stratford, Connecticut, he learned to make his own way early in life. He has no living relatives, and no permanent address.

You like him, and value his friendship, even though months and sometimes years separate one meeting from the next. You'd be upset and probably crave vengeance if anything happened to your friend. The world is better for having Jackson Elias in it.

His writings characterize and analyze death cults. His best-known book is *Sons of Death*, exposing modern-day Thuggees in India. He speaks several languages fluently and is constantly traveling. He is social, and enjoys an occasional drink. He smokes a pipe. Elias is tough, stable, and punctual, unafraid of brawls or officials. He is mostly self-educated. His well-researched works always seem to reflect first-hand experience. He is secretive and never discusses a project until he has a final draft in hand.

All of his books illustrate how cults manipulate the fears of their followers. A skeptic, Elias has never found proof of supernatural powers, magic, or dark gods. Insanity and feelings of inadequacy characterize death cultists, feelings for which they compensate by slaughtering innocents to make themselves feel powerful or chosen. Cults draw the weak-minded, though cult leaders are usually clever and manipulative. When fear of a cult stops, the cult vanishes.

[Snapshot given to you by Jackson Elias, pictured on the right.]

Skulls Along the River (1910)—exposes headhunter cult in Amazon basin.

Masters of the Black Arts (1912)—surveys supposed sorcerous cults throughout history.

The Way of Terror (1913)—analyzes systematization of fear through cult organization; warmly reviewed by George Sorel.

The Smoking Heart (1915)—first half discusses historical Mayan death cults. Second half instances present-day Central American death cults.

Sons of Death (1918)—modern-day Thuggees; Elias infiltrated the cult and wrote a book about it.

Witch Cults of England (1920)—summarizes covens in nine English counties; interviews practicing English witches; Rebecca West thought some of the material trivial and overworked.

The Black Power (1921)—expands upon *The Way of Terror*; includes interviews with several anonymous cult leaders.

All of these books are published by Prospero Press of New York City, and all were edited by owner/editor Jonah Kensington. Kensington is a good friend of Jackson Elias, and knows you well.

Nyarlathotep Papers #2

World-Wide Telegraph Service

HUDSON TERMINAL, 30 CHURCH STREET
NEW YORK, USA

HAVE INFORMATION CONCERNING CARLYLE EXPEDITION STOP NEED
RELIABLE INVESTIGATIVE TEAM STOP ARRIVE JANUARY 15 STOP
SIGNED JACKSON ELIAS

the investigators are not headquartered in New York, they will have to go there. Use Elias' publisher (Prospero Press) or his editor there (Jonah Kensington) to pick up messages.

All the investigators probably remember that the expedition perished a few years ago somewhere in Africa. This interval will also allow the investigators to research the Carlyle Expedition—all the handouts are labeled as coming from the New York Pillar/Riposte, but every newspaper that subscribes to Reuters has the identical wire copy about the expedition in its morgue files. See the handouts *Nyarlathotep Papers #3-10*, all located at the end of the Introduction, for pertinent news stories discussing the formation, achievements, and demise of the Carlyle Expedition.

Erica Carlyle, Roger's sister, lives near New York City. She can supply considerable information, as discussed later in this chapter, in the section "Erica Carlyle".

Contact

Jackson Elias calls his investigator friend on January 15, requesting that the meet him at the Chelsea Hotel, Room 410, at 8 p.m. The investigator perceives that Elias is cryptic and anxious, perhaps even frightened—uncharacteristic of him as the Elias handout should make clear. Elias gives out no information over the phone and hangs up immediately if pressed. If someone calls his Chelsea Hotel room, there will be no answer, for Elias is back on the streets, rummaging for more information about the Cult of the Bloody Tongue. Emphasize that the author's behavior is at odds with what the investigator knows of him, and try to have all the players eager to learn why the distinguished author needs such a crew of splendid investigators.

Room 410

At the Chelsea, the investigators get no answer to their knocks. Jackson Elias is inside, but his intestines have been ripped out by three members of the Bloody Tongue. The killing occurred just moments before: one cultist waits at the door to ambush anyone entering, while the others search the room. All are armed with prangas, the preferred weapon for their cult's ritual murders. Two of the killers are Kenyans, but cultist Number Two is a white New Yorker cocaine fiend of negligible skills; only he speaks English well. Each wears a shabby suit and the repulsive ceremonial headpiece of the cult.

The investigators have many options:

■ If the investigators listen before they knock, they will have their usual Listen chance to hear the murderers move about, searching for manuscripts and clues.

■ If the investigators try the door, they find that it is locked. If they then Listen at the door they hear movement only if the murderers fail their Sneak rolls.

■ If the investigators want to break down the door, any two investigators at any one time may combine STR on the Resistance Table to overcome the door's STR of 25.

■ If the investigators are able to enter Room 410 within fifteen minutes of their arrival at the hotel, the killers are present and attack the investigators just long enough to give themselves time to escape out the window and down the narrow fire escape. A captured cultist fights on until unconscious or incapacitated, successfully Grappled, or killed. Those making it to the bottom of the fire escape run to an idling black Hudson touring roadster, circa 1915, New York license NYL7, and flee.

■ If the investigators enter the room within sixteen to twenty minutes of arrival, the cultists are moving down the fire escape. The fire escape is narrow and rickety. It takes each cultist one minute to reach the bottom, and they depart the room at one-minute intervals. The fire escape can carry no more than SIZ 30 at any one time. If the limit is exceeded, the escape tumbles to the ground, and those on it sustain 2D6 damage each.

■ If the investigators enter Room 410 between minutes 21-25, they can see the killers below, running toward their getaway car. In this case, two of the six pieces of information will be found in the room (keeper's choice). At this range and in this light pistol fire at the killers has no chance to hit.

CULT OF THE BLOODY TONGUE (NYC)

Many in this cult are illegally entered Kenyans who possess forged documents to prove U.S. citizenship. In the last two years, membership has grown among degenerate circles of New York's *demimonde*. Race is no longer an important prerequisite to membership. The cult name stems from the aspect of Nyarlathotep in which the god has a single blood-red tentacle in place of a face. The cult headquarters are in a Harlem shop which retails African tribal paraphernalia. Rites occur in the enlarged basement. Silas N'Kwane runs the shop; Mukunga M'Dari is priest of the cult. Bloody Tongue assassins traditionally use the pranga (a long African bush knife) in their assaults, though at times local residents have employed guns. A cult executioner or assassin wears a hideous headpiece with a dangling red strip protruding from the forehead.

AVERAGE BLOODY TONGUE MEMBER
(Illegal Kenyan Immigrant)

STR 12	CON 15	SIZ 11	INT 06	POW 10
DEX 13	APP 04	EDU 01	SAN 0	HP 13

Damage Bonus: +0.

Weapons: Pranga* 45%, damage 1D6+2
Straight Razor* 45%, damage 1D4
* *neither weapon impales.*

Skills: Climb 60%, Cthulhu Mythos 15%, Dodge 35%, English 35%, Hide 60%, Jump 55%, Kikuyu 60%, Listen 50%, Nandi 35%, Occult 10%, Sneak 60%, Swahili 50%, Spot Hidden 35%, Track 50%.

■ If the investigators enter Room 410 after minute 25, they find Jackson Elias' corpse, clothing, and luggage. The keeper may choose to leave any two of the six clues in the room.

■ If the investigators leave the hotel after getting no response to their knocks, they read about the murder in the newspapers the next day. There is notice of a non-denominational funeral to be held the day after. If they attend, the only other person there (other than reporters) will be Jonah Kensington, who can feed them any two of the clues.

If a fight or close pursuit ensues, assume that each killer has 1D3 pieces of information on him (see *Nyarlathotep Papers #11-17*, on pgs. 23-25). Cultist One has items 11 up to 13, Cultist Two has items 14 up to 16, and Cultist Three has 1D3 of the remnants, or as the keeper pleases. Any items not taken by the cultists can be located as the list describes. The killers try to flee in their getaway car as mentioned above.

CULTIST #1, age 23, Member of the Bloody Tongue

STR 16	CON 15	SIZ 14	INT 08	POW 10
DEX 10	APP 06	EDU 03	SAN 0	HP 15

Damage Bonus: +1D4.

Weapons: Pranga 85%, damage 1D6+2+1D4
Fist/Punch 50%, damage 1D3+1D4
Head Butt 50%, damage 1D4+1D4
Kick 50%, damage 1D6+1D4

Skills: Bargain 25%, Climb 75%, Conceal 50%, Cthulhu Mythos 03%, Dodge 50%, English 10%, Hide 50%, Jump 90%, Kikuyu 50%, Listen 65%, Nandi 35%, Sneak 65%, Swahili 35%, Swim 60%, Track 10%.

CULTIST #2, age 24, Member of the Bloody Tongue

STR 12	CON 12	SIZ 12	INT 07	POW 08
DEX 13	APP 07	EDU 13	SAN 0	HP 12

Damage Bonus: +0.

Weapons: Pranga 35%, damage 1D6+2
Fist/Punch 65%, damage 1D3
Head Butt 50%, damage 1D4
Kick 50%, damage 1D6

Skills: Bargain 15%, Climb 60%, Conceal 55%, Cthulhu Mythos 04%, Dodge 65%, Drive Auto 35%, English 55%, Hide 65%, Jump 65%, Listen 75%, Locksmith 25%, Sneak 60%, Swahili 15%, Swim 30%, Track 15%.

CULTIST #3, age 26, Member of the Bloody Tongue

STR 15	CON 13	SIZ 12	INT 10	POW 08
DEX 16	APP 04	EDU 03	SAN 0	HP 13

Damage Bonus: +1D4.

Weapons: Pranga 75%, damage 1D6+2+1D4
Fist/Punch 50%, damage 1D3+1D4
Head Butt 50%, damage 1D4+1D4
Kick 50%, damage 1D6+1D4

Skills: Bargain 25%, Climb 55%, Conceal 60%, Cthulhu Mythos 05%, Dodge 65%, English 01%, Hide 55%, Jump 55%, Kikuyu 60%, Listen 75%, Nandi 25%, Sneak 55%, Swahili 40%, Swim 25%, Track 65%.

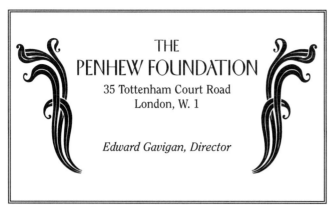

Nyarlathotep Papers #12

Nyarlathotep Papers #13

All of the next-day papers will report the murder. Most of the stories link this killing with several similar murders perpetrated during the last few years.

THE INFORMATION IN ROOM 410

ITEM. A letter, addressed to Roger Carlyle. The text is in a barely readable scrawl (*Nyarlathotep Papers #11*).

Relevance of the Information: Faraz Najir is alive and in Cairo, but his shop is no longer in the Street of Jackals. The agent mentioned in the letter is a man named Warren Besart, a Frenchman. He is still in Cairo. An interview with Erica Carlyle also turns up this information.

ITEM. A business card, elegantly engraved *(Nyarlathotep Papers #12)*.

Relevance of the Information: leads the investigators to London, to the Penhew Foundation, and to Edward Gavigan.

ITEM. A matchbox—empty (*Nyarlathotep Papers #13*).

Relevance of the Information: this Shanghai, China, bar is where Elias first met Jack Brady.

ITEM. A photograph—blurry and grainy. It shows a large steam- or diesel-powered yacht beyond some Chinese junks. Part of the name of the yacht is visible: the first three letters are DAR (*Nyarlathotep Papers #14*).

Relevance of the Information: the photo was taken along the Whangpoo River in Shanghai. The yacht is the *Dark Mistress*, owned by an "Alfred Penhurst", British registry. In the dim background is a building with a large tower. A trade envoy, banker, or agent familiar with China could identify the photo, as might a well traveled sailor or a diplomat currently stationed at some New York City consulate. The investigators might employ Library Use skills on back issues of the National Geographic (if nothing else!) to locate independently the subject of the photograph.

ITEM. A business card—printed on ordinary stock. Elias has written the name "Silas N'Kwane" in ink on the back of the card (*Nyarlathotep Papers #15*).

Relevance of the Information: it leads to an import house which supplies African artifacts to Ju-Ju House, New York headquarters for the Bloody Tongue. The importer also knows the exporter at Mombasa.

ITEM. A typewritten letter – without envelope, from Miriam Atwright, a Harvard University librarian, addressed to Elias in care of his publishers (*Nyarlathotep Papers #16*).

Relevance of the Information: Miss Atwright, of Cambridge, Massachusetts, has helped Elias with past research. She can easily be found for an interview, called on the phone, or written to in care of the University. See the section for Miriam Atwright later in this chapter.

ITEM. A small sheet of paper. Inserted in the second volume of Andrew Dickson White's *A History of the Warfare of Science with Theology in Christendom*, it marks the beginning of Chapter XIV, "From Fetich to Hygiene". It is an ordinary handbill, to be posted publicly or passed out on the street (*Nyarlathotep Papers #17*).

Relevance of the Information: Professor Cowles' lecture included a few over-exposed slides of strange stone monoliths photographed in the Australian desert. The photos were taken within a dozen miles of Dr. Huston's headquarters in the City of the Great Race. Cowles accepted a semester's fellowship at Miskatonic partly in the hope of being able to raise funds for a full-scale expedition to the site. So far his hopes have been frustrated. Though the investigators missed Dr. Cowles' lecture, they can call, write to, or visit him in Massachusetts.

ITEM. The symbol on the forehead. There is a last bit of evidence in the room available to the investigators only if they examine Elias' body. Symmetrical marks have been carefully carved into the forehead of Jackson Elias (*Nyarlathotep Papers #18*).

Relevance of the Information: the cultists cut the rune of the Bloody Tongue into his forehead. An investigator spending a full day of research in the New York Public Library, the Library of Congress, Yale, or certain Boston-area libraries can identify the mark as the rune of a cult thought to be descended from a sect driven out of dynastic Egypt. A successful Library Use roll establishes that the cult is the Bloody Tongue, and that of late it has been centered in Kenya. There is no mention of Nyarlathotep, but that god is connected to this cult in the *G'harne Fragments*, a Cthulhu Mythos tome (see *Call of Cthulhu* rulesbook) possessed by the Penhew Foundation in London, among others.

Nyarlathotep Papers #11

Cairo, Egypt
3 January 1919

Dear Mr. Carlyle,

I am informed that you seek certain knowledge of our land and can perhaps aid you in this. In my posession are singular curios which I most happily believe of interest. These I willingly send for your consideration, if a price can be agreed upon. Naturally they are ancient and must command a goodly sum. I will arrange matters to your satisfaction when your agent calls at my shop, in the Street of Jackals in the Old Quarter.

Until then I remain your most humble servant,

Faraz Najir

Nyarlathotep Papers #17

Tonight Only

"The Cult of Darkness in Polynesia & the Southwest Pacific"

a two-hour lecture with slides delivered by Prof. Anthony Cowles, Ph.D.

of the University of Sydney (Australia), and presently Locksley Fellow of Polynesian Esoterica at Miskatonic University (Arkham)

Schuyler Hall, NYU
8 PM

Tonight Only

Nyarlathotep Papers #16

Nov. 7, 1924

Mr. Jackson Elias
c o Prospero House Publishers
Lexington Avenue, New York City

Dear Mr. Elias,

The book about which you inquired is no longer in our collection. The information you seek may be found here in other volumes. If you will contact me upon arrival, I will be most happy to further assist you.

As Always,

Miriam Atwright

Miriam Atwright

Nyarlathotep Papers #14

Photograph

Blurry and grainy, it shows a large yacht at anchor surrounded by Chinese junks. Only part of the name of the yacht is visible: the first three letters are DAR.

Nyarlathotep Papers #18

Nyarlathotep Papers #15

Emerson Imports

648 West 47th Street
New York, New York
Telephone: HA 6-3900

Silas N'Kwane

Reverse of Emerson Imports card is in Elias' handwriting. Cut out, fold on dotted line, and tape or glue together.

PRELIMINARY INVESTIGATIONS

*Wherein the investigators learn new facts about
the ill-fated Carlyle Expedition, and realize that there
may be more to the massacre than was first apparent.*

By their decision at the door of Room 410, the investigators have begun to direct the campaign. The keeper now must keep the investigators on the trail. Emphasize the loss of friendship felt by the chosen investigator, the bizarre nature of the murder, and the importance with which Elias regarded his story. A remarkable new story about the famous expedition might be worth thousands of dollars. Handouts for this chapter lead to Elias' publisher and to Erica Carlyle; the New York police also know a little. The investigators always will have enough leads to get started.

Presumably they are smart enough to follow up on local leads before leaving the United States: if they found the right information, add Emerson Imports and Miriam Atwright to the leads, and perhaps Ju-Ju House and Ahja Singh as well. Researching the members of the Carlyle Expedition is rewarding but necessarily incomplete, as events prove.

The New York Police

The usefulness of this lead depends on how the investigators are related to the murder and to the police. If one or more members of the group are acquainted with NYPD officers, especially with homicide detectives, the investigators can gain all of the following information. If they are not acquainted, then successful Fast Talk rolls will be required to uncover most of it. If the investigators are present at the murder scene, speak to the police, and a Credit Rating roll succeeds, then they'll get all of the information. If the police notice the investigators running from the scene, the police will want to question them.

The detective in charge of the case is Lt. Martin Poole, a hard-nosed veteran of the force. Martin can inform the investigators that this is the ninth murder victim of this kind in the last two years. The victims had no apparent connections. They were poor, wealthy, and middle class, both black and white, and from all over the city. All the victims had the same marks on their foreheads. The marks have been linked to an African death cult, about which Harlemites have refused to speak. Known voodoo cults do not seem to be connected, nor do they use the symbol (though a red-herring adventure for the investigators might be in order here). The police are con-

LT. MARTIN POOLE

sulting folklorist Dr. Mordecai Lemming, an eccentric Manhattanite, but this fellow knows nothing of the occult.

At the keeper's discretion, Poole might mention that an old black Hudson was seen leaving the murder scene at a little after 8 p.m., and that such a car owned by a Thomas Witherspoon was stolen that evening while it was parked on Lenox Avenue.

Poole and his men assume that the murders are ritual slayings of people who somehow learned too much. Investigators find details of all of the crimes in newspaper files. They might even interview friends and families of the victims. If they do, they learn little more than that the departed had become involved with strange people.

At the keeper's option, the police may know more.

If it seems useful to make one or more of the previous murder victims significant—perhaps wealthy, perhaps a friend of Roger Carlyle's—this angle can fill any gaps of evidence that the keeper comes to perceive.

LT. MARTIN POOLE, age 43, Homicide Squad

STR 12	CON 13	SIZ 13	INT 10	POW 08
DEX 09	APP 09	EDU 06	SAN 55	HP 13

Damage Bonus: +1D4.

Weapons: .38 Revolver 45%, damage 1D10
Blackjack* 70%, damage 1D6+1D4
Fist/Punch 60%, damage 1D3+1D4
Kick 60%, damage 1D6+1D4
Head Butt 50%, damage 1D4+1D4
* *carries it in his hip pocket.*

Skills: Bargain 45%, Credit Rating 40%, Drive Automobile 60%, Fast Talk 75%, Law 50%, Library Use 25%, Listen 55%, Oratory 25%, Persuade 30%, Psychology 30%, Spot Hidden 40%, Track 15%.

Erica Carlyle

Miss Carlyle is presently at Carlyle House, her Westchester estate. The investigators can easily find her by reading the society column of any local paper, by phoning and Fast Talking representatives any of the numerous Carlyle companies or offices, by interviewing any of the same and proving themselves with successful Credit Rating rolls, by talking to any knowledgeable newspaperman, and so on. She is 26 years old and the sole heir to the Carlyle fortune since Kenyan courts declared Roger Carlyle dead, and the New York state courts concurred.

Interviewing Erica Carlyle will not be easy. She is busy and is not interested in discussing the Carlyle Expedition.

Though she would never say so, she detested her brother's excesses and believes him better dead—even his death, she has said privately, was too bizarre to be decent. While he was alive, Roger nearly ruined the Carlyle interests (transport, munitions, import/export) by draining them of operating capital. He also mistreated Erica, and gave her no say in financial matters. She was nearly impoverished for a while. Since gaining control, Erica has managed the estate well, and the Carlyle interests flourish. Management and stockholders are also heartily glad that Roger Carlyle is gone.

Investigators might attract Miss Carlyle's attention by implying that Roger Carlyle is alive (though the investigators have no reason to think so). If the investigators attempt to write a critical story about the Carlyle Expedition, they might attract her attention or that of an agent, and provoke some effort to stop its publication. Investigators might attempt to crash a party or benefit that she is attending, or one or more might pose as businessmen at work on a deal which requires a meeting with her. Alternatively, they might try to gain employment in her household, or try to make friends with those who are employed there. Staking out the estate might work, though she may not leave the grounds for a week at a time—her representatives and her private phone lines take care of her leg work.

Forcing the investigators to figure out ways to get into communication with this wealthy, beautiful, and somewhat willful woman might be very enter-

ERICA CARLYLE

taining. The keeper can force Credit Rating rolls at disastrous percentile reductions, have the investigators thrown out of swank clubs by enormous men wearing tight tuxedos, have Carlyle's private detectives obtrusively tail the investigators, and so on. At Miss Carlyle's request, the local police will always hold the investigators on charges of mopery (a handy vague charge with which beat policemen could arrest nuisances whenever they want).

Miss Carlyle refuses to be questioned in public places or on the run without an introduction. If the investigators have been able to prepare her in some way, or if the players roll Fast Talks at half normal chance or less, then she may listen. If one of them can think of something original to say, the chance improves. Erica Carlyle does not want to discuss her dead brother, but she will if her position is threatened, if her business empire is compromised, or if her personal interest is piqued.

The Westchester County estate is half an hour north of New York City, on the Hudson River. Motoring investigators catch an ominous glimpse of Sing-Sing Prison not too far away. The Carlyle estate consists of an elegant three-story mansion and five acres of superb grounds, all guarded by a twelve-foot-high iron fence topped with sharpened finials. There are always two armed gatekeepers. More armed men with guard dogs routinely patrol the grounds. One or more bodyguards accompany Miss Carlyle when she ventures off the estate. Numerous faithful and capable servants staff the house.

Such protection is not unneeded. Shortly after Roger

Carlyle's supposed murderers were hung in Nairobi, cultists tried to break into the library of the Westchester estate, seeking items of great interest to them (detailed in the library, below). Erica Carlyle would naturally press charges against any person who broke into her estate (each ten minutes of lurking in the mansion carries an accumulating ten percentile chance for discovery), but a successful Fast Talk roll might stay her hand—she likes feisty, well spoken people.

Erica's bodyguard is a huge man, Joe Corey, who carries a proportionately huge .45 revolver in a shoulder holster and brass knuckles in a special pocket up his left sleeve. In public he remains close to her, ready at any time to brush off opportunists, elbow photographers, or roust mashers. He was an enforcer for a mobster whom Erica once bested in a deal; the gang-leader disappeared just before Joe went to work for Erica.

Erica's chief confidant is Bradley Grey, a partner in the law firm of Dunstan, Whittleby, and Grey, West 57th Street, New York. His name is frequently mentioned in newspaper reports concerning the shift of control of the Carlyle fortune to Erica. A successful Idea roll while studying those articles suggests the importance of Grey's connection to her.

BRADLEY GREY

Bradley Grey did not like Roger, and he knows virtually nothing about M'Weru's influence on Roger. Grey is discreet, but tends to panic if publicly embarrassed or compromised. If he thinks the investigators have something of value to tell, or if the investigators somehow otherwise convince him to do so, he will arrange a meeting with Erica, though it may take a week or so.

ERICA CARLYLE, age 26, Millionaire Businesswoman

STR 08	CON 12	SIZ 08	INT 17	POW 13
DEX 11	APP 16	EDU 16	SAN 65	HP 10

Damage Bonus: -1D4.

Weapons: Fencing Foil 70%, damage (tip off) 1D6+1-1D4
.22 Revolver (in purse) 40%, damage 1D6

Skills: Accounting 70%, Bargain 75%, Credit Rating 95%, Debate 65%, Drive Automobile 35%, English 85%, French 45%, German 50%, Italian 60%, Law 35%, Oratory 50%, Persuade 60%, Psychology 35%, Ride 60%, Swim 30%.

JOE COREY, age 37, bodyguard to Erica Carlyle

STR 17	CON 15	SIZ 16	INT 12	POW 08
DEX 14	APP 09	EDU 08	SAN 50	HP 15

Damage Bonus: +1D6.

Weapons: Fist/Punch 85%, damage 1D3+1D6
Kick 75%, damage 1D6+1D6
Head Butt 75%, damage 1D4+1D6
.45 Revolver* (in shoulder holster) 65%, damage 1D10+2
Baseball Bat 65%, damage 1D8+1D6
* *always carries twelve extra bullets.*

Skills: Bargain 55%, Dodge 85%, Drive Automobile 95%, Fast Talk 65%, Jump 65%, Listen 50%, Mechanical Repair 50%, Locksmith 30%, Psychology 60%, Sneak 50%, Spot Hidden 55%.

BRADLEY GREY, age 41, Counselor to Erica Carlyle

STR 09	CON 10	SIZ 09	INT 17	POW 11
DEX 10	APP 14	EDU 18	SAN 45	HP 09

Damage Bonus: +0.

Weapons: Kick 10%, damage 1D6
Fist/Punch 10%, damage 1D3

Skills: Accounting 70%, Bargain 50%, Credit Rating 85%, Debate 85%, Drive Automobile 30%, Fast Talk 50%, French 60%, Latin 25%, Law 90%, Library Use 70%, Oratory 80%, Psychology 40%, Ride 10%, Yachting 10%.

ERICA'S INTERVIEW

From the beginning Erica knew that Roger's African expedition was much more than just another of his foolish whims—she believed that some secret fascinated and worried him. That Negro Woman (her way of referring to M'Weru) caused Roger's obsession. To Erica, Roger's entanglement with a colored woman only indicated how depraved his tastes had become. After the Negro Woman came to rule Roger's life—Erica has no idea how Roger came to meet her—Roger Carlyle began to have strange dreams in which something seemed to call to him and beckon that something be done. Roger would scream and wake up, but absolutely refused to discuss the dreams beyond that.

Erica Carlyle recommended that Roger visit Dr. Robert Huston, just then the lion of Erica's social set. She believes that Huston talked Roger into the expedition, and feels guilty about that, but feels that it was the Negro Woman who caused Roger to lose his grasp of reality. Young Carlyle would disappear for days, then suddenly turn up wild-eyed and crazed, saying only that he had been to Harlem.

Roger said that the Negro Woman was queenly, a priestess, and that she held secrets which he must have. For a while Erica encouraged the African expedition, supposing that when there Roger would see that the Negro Woman and her tales were mumbo-jumbo. Miss Carlyle knows neither M'Weru's name nor the name of her cult.

Erica Carlyle now believes that the Negro Woman drove her brother over the edge to insanity.

ERICA'S ADDITIONAL TESTIMONY

Smart investigators ask about the other members of the Carlyle Expedition. Miss Carlyle unfortunately knows very little.

■ *Sir Aubrey Penhew*: Erica knows nothing of him, and does not know why he accompanied the expedition. "Perhaps Sir Aubrey needed money—everyone else around Roger certainly did."

■ *Dr. Robert Huston*: a suave and handsome man whom Erica had found extremely sensitive and perceptive. Huston supposedly went with Roger in order to continue treatment of him.

■ *Hypatia Masters*: Erica had met her occasionally and was unimpressed. Roger dated her a few times, inconclusively. She was a good photographer; perhaps that was the reason she went along.

■ *Jack "Brass" Brady*: he was fanatically loyal to Roger, and someone whom Roger could always trust. In California, Carlyle's lawyers had saved Brady from certain conviction of murder. This occurred while Roger spent a semester at USC (having before then been thrown out of Harvard, Yale, Princeton, Miskatonic, and Cornell in succession).

THE CARLYLE MANSION LIBRARY

As an afterthought, Erica mentions that toward the last Roger constantly read several old books. She glanced through one (*The Pnakotic Manuscripts*). What she read frightened her, for it seemed to substantiate Roger's crazy actions. Roger kept those books in a hidden safe in the mansion library. Unknown to Roger, Erica knew of the safe and figured out its combination, which she jotted down on the flyleaf of Poe's collected poems. She has not thought to open the safe since Roger left for London. She has had installed a new and nearly invincible vault in the mansion's offices.

The investigators may also learn of Roger Carlyle's books through the notes left by Jackson Elias in the possession of Jonah Kensington. If they bring up the matter directly, Erica will deny it for a while, for it will occur to her that the old volumes may be of considerable value to collectors, and she will want to have them appraised (as well as to investigate the investigators). If the investigators

Nyarlathotep Papers #19

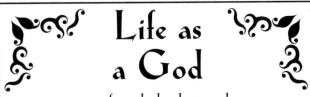

Life as a God

excerpt from the handwritten diary of Montgomery Crompton

Its angles were magnificent, and most strange; by their hideous beauty I was enraptured and enthralled, and I thought myself of the daylight fools who adjudged the housing of this room as mistaken. I laughed for the glory they missed. When the six lights lit and the great words said, then He came, in all the grace and splendour of the Higher Planes, and I longed to sever my veins so that my life might flow into his being, and make part of me a god!

try to secure the books through illegal means, they must gain access to the library, locate the safe's hiding place, and be able to open the little STR 60 wall safe. They are exposed to the Carlyle estate security precautions. If they are smart, they hire a professional safecracker to do the job. Have such people ready to hire, but let the investigators come up with the idea.

To make it easier for the investigators to rob the library, inform them of a large party at the mansion, hosted by Erica. They can roleplay through the party, find a way to clear guests from the library, lock its doors, and proceed. Such exploits could be wonderful fun. To search the library books, have the players make halved Luck rolls for their investigators every twenty game minutes. If one is successful, someone happens upon the volume of Poe and the combination it holds (R15, L14, R13, L12).

In the library are easy chairs, tables and reading lamps, ashtrays and spittoons, an elaborate High Victorian iron fireplace, a magnificent teak and slate billiards table, and several thousand volumes protected within unlocked glass cases along the walls. There are leather-bound complete editions of Trollope, Dickens, Bulwer-Lytton, Mrs. Radcliffe, Francis Parkman, Ralph Waldo Emerson, the earlier works of George Washington Cable, and other fosterers of culture during the previous hundred years. Another section contains books on the occult, but all are ordinary investigations and surveys of traditional magic. On the north wall of the library is a large case filled with old reference works in English and French. Oddly, a fat edition of Poe's collected poems—the one in which Erica wrote the safe's combination—is tucked among these volumes. Behind Poe is a small panel which can be pulled open. Behind the panel is a button: pushing the button, the entire case slides aside several feet to reveal the safe behind. Within the safe are four books.

THE PNAKOTIC MANUSCRIPTS: in English translation, +10 percentiles to Cthulhu Mythos knowledge, costs 1D8 SAN to read, x2 spell multiplier.

SELECTIONS DE LIVRE D'IVON: French commentary on Latin original by Gaspar du Nord, +6 percentiles to Cthulhu Mythos knowledge, costs 1D6 SAN to read, x2 spell multiplier. Contains the spells Contact Nodens and Eibon's Wheel of Mist.

PEOPLE OF THE MONOLITH: in English, +3 percentiles to Cthulhu Mythos knowledge, costs 1D3 SAN to read, no spells within. This is a rare volume, however, since it is hand-bound in the skin of a chthonian. Give the reader's player a chance equal to the investigator's Cthulhu Mythos for his investigator to notice this.

LIFE AS A GOD: in English, +4 percentiles to Cthulhu Mythos knowledge, costs 1D6 SAN to read, no spells within. The only copy of a handwritten diary by Montgomery Crompton, an English artist who came to Egypt in 1805 and became a minor priest of the Brotherhood of the Black Pharaoh. The work is bound in human skin. Crompton was insane by the time he wrote this diary, which narrates all manner of unspeakable acts committed for the Pharaoh of Darkness. In particular the diary mentions the Black Pharaoh's throne room (see *Nyarlathotep Papers #19*).

The quote refers to the secret sanctum of Nyarlathotep within the capstone of the Bent Pyramid in Egypt. If the investigators read this passage and find the sanctum, remind them of this description. Crompton always refers to Nyarlathotep as the Black Pharaoh, or the Pharaoh of Darkness.

In the diary are graphic descriptions of murders, sacrifices, and so on, all of which mention the short, single-spiked clubs which the cult uses for ritual murders.

Keepers may withhold some or all of the information within *Life as a God* until the investigators reach London or Egypt, and then present it as something remembered from the diary which before seemed to have no significance (until, for instance, the investigators are confronted with a short, single-spiked club).

Jonah Kensington

Kensington owns and is chief editor for Prospero House, a publisher of books having occult or fantastic themes, fiction and non-fiction alike. The offices of Prospero House are located on Lexington Avenue near 35th Street. This modest concern does not aim for best-sellers, an almost unheard-of concept by the end of the millennium, but rather for books which deserve to be published because they will interest

JONAH KENSINGTON

select readers for generations to come. Investigators may make an appointment or just drop in— Prospero House is friendly and informal. Kensington was a friend to Elias, as well as the editor of all of Elias' books, and will want to talk to anyone investigating Elias' death. At the keeper's option, the investigator who was a friend of Elias may already know Kensington.

Kensington believes that the police theory of cult murder is correct. Elias was always infatuated with blood cults. His editor thinks that either some old enemies at last caught up with the courageous author, or else that Elias' new project was even more important (and dangerous) than Jackson Elias himself had believed. Elias, he says, had been persuaded that a blood cult had massacred the Carlyle Expedition, but that not all of the principals of the expedition had been killed. If asked for more information, Kensington requests the Elias correspondence file from his secretary, and reads from it the following letter.

ITEM: A letter from Jackson Elias to Jonah Kensington. (*Nyarlathotep Papers #20*)

Relevance of the Information: augments Jackson Elias' character and intentions, states clearly that members of the Carlyle Expedition may be alive, and that Elias has dug up evidence contradicting testimony admitted during the inquest and trial in Kenya.

Kensington received the notes, and then got a wire (from Hong Kong) asking for the advance, which was sent imme-

August 8, 1924
Nairobi

Dear Jonah,
Big news! There is a possibility that not all of the members of the Carlyle Expedition died. I have a lead. Though the authorities here deny the cult angle, the natives sing a different tune. You wouldn't believe the stories! Some juicy notes coming your way! This one may make us all rich!

Blood and kisses,
J.

P.S. I'll need advance money to follow this one up. More later.

Nyarlathotep Papers #20

diately. Then Elias was not heard from until the middle of last month (Dec. 16, 1924), when he wired from London. Elias' telegram was very excited and a bit crazy-sounding. He said he'd been to China, to Africa of course, and to London for a few days, where he'd dug up a lot of stuff. Elias said he'd seen unbelievable things, and mentioned a plan or conspiracy of monstrous, world-wide proportions. He said that there was a timetable, and that he needed to find the missing pieces, but wouldn't or couldn't explain more. The wire ended, saying that he would soon be in New York. Elias took passage on a freighter, the *Phalarope*, the next morning.

Arriving in New York a few days ago, Elias left more notes with Kensington. They were so bewildering and fragmentary that the editor concluded that either Elias had gone over the edge and needed six months in a sanitarium, or else that the author so little trusted anyone that he'd hidden all the data in his head so that it would be undetectable. Kensington is not eager to show the later notes to the investigators, because he believes that their strangeness reflects on Elias' sanity and upon his integrity as a writer, and potentially upon Prospero House. Kensington may let someone who is not a writer or an editor see the material, since his embarrassment for Elias will be correspondingly less if the reader is not a peer. Alternatively, the investigators can break in and steal the notes (which are in that same Elias correspondence file)—a simple matter in this unguarded building where editors and authors come and go constantly, and work at odd hours.

Kensington says he always thought Elias' work exposed the author to much too much danger, though he could never persuade Jackson Elias to do less personal research. He is very grieved at the loss. If the interview is within a day or two of the murder, Kensington informs the investigators of the time and place of Elias' funeral. (If they are congenial, Kensington could well finance their investigation for up to $1000.) If Kensington understands that the investigators might decide to go to London, he will give them two names—Mickey Mahoney, editor of *The Scoop*, and Inspector James Barrington of Scotland Yard, both of whom Elias mentioned in conversation.

The Bloody Tongue does not know that Kensington has Elias' notes, though it would be a simple deduction if they happened to think about it. If they find out they will kill Kensington and destroy the notes. This could easily occur if the investigators mention Kensington's involvement to someone who belongs to the cult, such as Edward Gavigan, in London.

ITEM. The Nairobi notes of Jackson Elias. Sheets of plain paper covered on one side only with Elias' neat printing, and paper-clipped together into sets by Jonah Kensington. (*Nyarlathotep Papers #21*)

Relevance of the Information: the first set of notes arrived by mail from Nairobi. They are reasonably well-organized, and seem in many ways complete, yet are remarkable for the absence of conclusions, connections, and clearly-defined themes. The hand is strong and bold. Implicitly, the investigators must go to Kenya to get the information at which Elias only hints. Consequently, only summaries of the notes are provided here, to give the players leads and lines of research, but not conclusions.

ITEM: The London Notes of Jackson Elias. This set of notes embarassed and alarmed Jonah Kensington. The pages are folded and stitched together to form a small quarto volume of forty pages. Frequently a page or a dozen pages are blank. Sometimes a single word is repeated for several pages. Most entries are written with agitation and can barely be read. (*Nyarlathotep Papers #22*).

Relevance of the Information: all the words are clearly in Elias' hand. The following quotes represent what can be gleaned from this text: "Many names, many forms, but all the same and toward one end... Need Help... Too big, too ghastly. These dreams... dreams like Carlyle's? Check that psychoanalyst's files... All of them survived! They'll open the gate. Why?... so the power and the danger is real. They... many threads beginning... The books are in Carlyle's safe... Coming for me. Will the ocean protect? Ho Ho no quitters now. Must tell, and make readers Believe. Should I scream for them? Let's scream together...". A copy of these notes exists in the player handouts for this chapter, though keepers may wish to coach players through Elias' terrified handwriting.

JONAH KENSINGTON, age 48, Owner / Editor in Chief of Prospero House

STR 10 CON 12 SIZ 10 INT 15 POW 10
DEX 06 APP 13 EDU 14 SAN 75 HP 11

Damage Bonus: +0.

Weapon: red correction pencil, of no combat value

Skills: Accounting 60%, Anthropology 25%, Bargain 35%, Credit Rating 55%, Debate 50%, Drive Auto 25%, English 90%, French 65%, Greek 54%, History 67%, Latin 33%, Library Use 50%, Occult 50%, Oratory 35%, Photography 20%, Psychology 75%, Read Acutely 88%.

Miriam Atwright

In person or over the phone, an interview with her establishes that Elias sought a book called *Africa's Dark Sects*. The book mysteriously disappeared from the Widener library several months before Elias sought it. By "mysteriously", she means that one day it simply vanished. "There was an unspeakable odor in the collection the day we noticed the *Sect*s book was missing." Miss Atwright admired Jackson Elias and will help the investigators if they ask. Her library can

MIRIAM ATWRIGHT

The Nairobi Notes of Jackson Elias

Sheets of plain paper, each covered on one side only with Elias' neat printing, and paperclipped together into sets by Jonah Kensington. They are reasonably well-organized, and seem in many ways complete, yet are remarkable for the absence of conclusions, connections, and clearly-defined themes. The hand is strong and bold.

SET ONE of the Nairobi notes sets forth the offices, officials, and tribes which Elias visited, searching for material concerning cults and cult rituals. Nothing conclusive was learned, though Elias discounts the official version of the Carlyle massacre.

SET TWO describes his trip to the massacre site. He notes particularly that the earth there is completely barren, and that all the tribes of the region avoid the place, saying it is cursed by the God of the Black Winds, whose home is the mountain top.

SET THREE is an interview with a Johnstone Kenyatta, who says that the Carlyle murders may have been performed by the cult of the Bloody Tongue. He says that the cult reputedly is based in the mountains, and that its high priestess is a part of the Mountain of the Black Winds. Elias is politely skeptical, but Kenyatta insists upon the point. In quotes, Elias records that regional tribes fear and hate the Bloody Tongue, that tribal magic is of no protection against the cult, and that the cult's god is not of Africa.

SET FOUR follows up on the Kenyatta interview. Elias confirms from several good sources that the Bloody Tongue exists, though he finds no firsthand evidence of it. Tales include children stolen for sacrifice. Creatures with great wings are said to come down from the Mountain of the Black Winds to carry off people. The cult worships a god unknown to folklorists, one fitting no traditional African pattern. Elias in particular cites "Sam Mariga, rr-sta."

SET FIVE is a single sheet reminding Elias that the Cairo-based portion of the Carlyle itinerary must be examined carefully. He believes that the reason which prompted Carlyle's Kenyan sidetrip is on the Nile.

SET SIX is a long interview with Lt. Mark Selkirk, leader of the men who actually found the remains of the Carlyle Expedition, and a Kenya hand since the Great War and the fight against the resourceful von Lettow. Importantly, Selkirk says that the bodies were remarkably undecayed for the length of time which they lay in the open—"almost as if decay itself wouldn't come near the place." Secondly, the men had been torn apart, as if by animals, though what sorts of animals would pull apart bodies so systematically he could not guess. "Unimaginable. Inexplicable." Selkirk agrees that the Nandis may have had something to do with the episode, but suspects that the charges against the ringleaders were trumped-up. "It wouldn't be the first time," he says cynically. Finally, Selkirk confirms that no caucasians were found among the dead—only corpses of the Kenyan bearers were scattered across the barren plain.

SET SEVEN is another single sheet. Elias ran into Nails Nelson at the Victoria Bar in Nairobi. Nelson had been a mercenary for the Italians on the Somali-Abyssinian border, and had escaped into Kenya after double-crossing his employers. Nelson claimed to have seen Jack Brady alive (March of 1923) in Hong Kong, less than two years before Elias was in Kenya and long after the Kenyan court declared that Brady and the rest of the expedition were dead. Brady was friendly, though guarded and taciturn. Nelson didn't press the conversation. From this report Elias deduced that other members of the expedition might still live.

SET EIGHT discusses a possible structure for the Carlyle book, but is mostly featureless, with entries like "tell what happened" and "explain why."

identify the rune carved in Elias' forehead. It is ancient, thought to have been an offshoot of an unnamed cult driven out of dynastic Egypt. She can make the identification over the next week in spare minutes while she works, or an investigator can do it in a single 12-hour day with her help.

The investigators learn that the cult is that of the god of the Bloody Tongue, and that the cult is centered in Kenya. They do not learn that the cult worships an aspect of Nyarlathotep, though that information exists in the *G'harne Fragments*. The Penhew Foundation in London possesses an excellent copy.

Prof. Anthony Cowles

Because of his beautiful young daughter, Ewa, most young men in Arkham can offer exact directions to Professor Cowles' bungalow on Pickman between West and Garrison, to Cowles' office in the Liberal Arts Building, or to Cowles' favorite lunch spot (Grafton Diner, near the Boston and Maine train station), so fixedly are their wistful eyes drawn and held by her graceful form and style. Cowles himself is of no interest to any of them. The normal academic routes of phone, letter, telegram, or even inter-office mail reach Cowles less quickly, but the investigators are always able to communicate with the scholar within twenty-four hours.

Nyarlathotep Papers #22

The professor is friendly and open. Unfortunately, he knows little. He never met Jackson Elias. He never consciously saw the man. He has no knowledge of Elias' life. He has read several of Elias' books in connection with Polynesia and New Zealand, and recalls a few details of the works if an investigator recites titles.

Cowles collects tales about strange doings, a hobby which more than once has gotten him into troubles with University officials, who see him as keeping bad company. Cowles believes sorcery exists and has an open mind about things like monsters and underground cities, though he always wants proof. He is a large eccentric man with a brilliant red beard. The keeper may introduce the beautiful Ewa, but the daughter has no necessary role in this campaign, and no picture for her is supplied.

PROF. ANTHONY DIMSDALE COWLES, age 46, University Professor of Anthropology

STR 10	CON 12	SIZ 11	INT 17	POW 14
DEX 11	APP 12	EDU 18	SAN 78	HP 12

Damage Bonus: +0.

Weapons: Fist/Punch 35%, damage 1D3
20-Gauge Pump Shotgun, 2D6/1D6/1D3

Skills: Aboriginal Lore 65%, Anthropology 60%, Archaeology 45%, Bargain 25%, Credit Rating 50%, Cthulhu Mythos 03%, Dodge 35%, Drive Automobile 50%, English 90%, Fast Talk 55%, Greek 35%, History 35%, Latin 20%, Law 15%, Library Use 80%, Listen 50%, Natural History 30%, Occult 15%, Oratory 60%, Persuade 45%, Pidgin English 10%, Polynesian Cultures 35%, Psychology 45%, Ride 25%, Spot Hidden 30%, Swim 30%.

MISS EWA SEAWARD COWLES, age 20, Student and Dutiful Daughter

STR 13	CON 14	SIZ 10	INT 16	POW 14
DEX 15	APP 18	EDU 16	SAN 80	HP 12

Damage Bonus: +0.

Weapons: Fist/Punch 55%, damage 1D3
Kick 40%, damage 1D6
.45 Revolver 40%, damage 1D10+2

Skills: Anthropology 40%, Arabic 15%, Archaeology 20%, Astronomy 20%, Bargain 25%, Climb 50%, Credit Rating 40%, Dodge 45%, Drive Automobile 30%, English 90%, Fast Talk 35%, Jump 40%, Library Use 30%, Listen 45%, Martial Arts 50%, Medicine 20%, Photography 25%, Pidgin English 20%, Polynesian Cultures 70%, Ride 70%, Spot Hidden 70%.

A voluble man, one or two questions can keep him lecturing for an hour. If suitably flattered or Fast Talked, Cowles gladly summarizes his recent lecture at NYU.

ITEM. The main points of Prof. Anthony Cowles' recent New York University anthropology lecture. (*Nyarlathotep Papers #23*).

Relevance of the Information: establishes that an Australian death cult of the Sand Bat once existed, and links this cult to evidence of the Cthulhu Mythos.

The professor has heard of Cthulhu and R'lyeh, and finds certain disturbing parallels between the tales of the Sand Bat and Cthulhu. Some Polynesian legends discuss them also, though the tales are different. Cowles has read the *Ponape Scriptures*, "a most disturbing and disgusting tome." However, the University of Sydney copy of the *Ponape Scriptures* was lent to a John Scott of Boston, Mass., and was never returned. (John Scott is a villainous character appearing in the first *Call of Cthulhu* campaign, *Shadows of Yog-Sothoth*, later part of an omnibus volume, *Cthulhu Classics*.)

While he is a man of great curiosity and some personal courage, Cowles has a career to pursue and a contracted fellowship to complete. Neither he nor his daughter can spend many hours helping the investigators, and will not volunteer to join them. The Cowles family are reliable, and would be good U.S. contacts if the investigators need help while abroad. They have more Credit Rating in Sydney than in Arkham.

They'll return to Sydney in seven months, within the frame of this campaign, and so might participate in the Australian chapter. A Prof. David Dodge is tending their house, and he would be of even more use during an expedition into the desert than Cowles.

Since the death of his wife, Cowles has watched over Ewa with some intensity, something she understands but feels hampered by. She has decided to move from her father's home when she reaches 21, accepting any out-of-town teaching job she can find. Each loves the other, and would seek vengeance if the other came to harm.

Main Points of Prof. Anthony Cowles' NYU Lecture

ONE A bat cult once existed among the Aboriginals of Australia. It was known across the continent, and the god of the cult was always known as the Father of All Bats. Adherents believed that by making human sacrifices to their god they themselves would become worthy enough that the Father of All Bats would appear to them. Once he was enticed to appear, he would conquer all men. Sacrifices were run through a gauntlet of worshipers who struck the victims with clubs embedded with the sharp teeth of bats. The teeth were coated with a substance derived from rabid bats. The poison was quick-acting, but victims apparently went mad before they died. Leaders of the cult reputedly could take the forms of bat-winged snakes, enabling them to steal sacrifices from across the land.

Cowles believes that this cult became dormant or extinct hundreds of years ago. Its former existence is the reason that he became interested in Jackson Elias' books about present-day cults.

TWO An Aboriginal song cycle mentions a place where enormous beings gathered, somewhere in the west of Australia. The songs say that these gods, who were not at all like men, built great sleeping walls and dug great caves. But living winds blew down the gods and overthrew them, destroying their camp. When this happened, the way was open for the Father of All Bats, who came into the land, and grew strong.

THREE Cowles shows the investigators a set of four over-exposed glass slides. Each shows a few sweating men standing beside enormous blocks of stone, pitted and eroded but clearly dressed and formed for architectural purposes. Dim carvings seem to decorate some. Billows of sand are everywhere. Though he did not bring the book with him, Cowles says that the discoverer, one Arthur MacWhirr of Port Hedland, kept a diary in which he records several attacks on the party by Aboriginals. MacWhirr reportedly records deaths to victims from hundreds of small punctures, reminiscent of the earlier bat-cult.

FOUR Cowles tells finally of a tale he collected from near the Arafura Sea in northern Australia. In it Sand Bat, or Father of All Bats, has a battle of wits with Rainbow Snake, the Aboriginal deification of water and the patron of life. Rainbow Snake succeeds in tricking and trapping Sand Bat and his clan into the depths of a watery place from which Sand Bat can only complain, and is unable to return to trouble the people.

Nyarlathotep Papers #23

Emerson Imports

The company is in a long, narrow, building. There are loading docks at both ends. The building is a warehouse piled high with freight, with a small set of offices upstairs at the front. Mr. Arthur Emerson, a man in his fifties, recalls the visit of Jackson Elias, and expresses condolences when he is told that Elias is dead.

Elias had been checking importers to find connections with Mombasa. Emerson is the U.S. agent for the Mombasan exporter Ahja Singh, whose only known U.S. account happens to be Ju-Ju House, 1 Ransom Court, New York City. Emerson says that he is sure Elias intended to visit Ju-Ju House. If they ask, he tells the investigators that Silas N'Kwane manages Ju-Ju House. If the investigators ask his opinion, he responds that those people are "darky foreigners and bad to boot", and adds that he told Elias the same thing. After the investigators leave, Emerson may decide to inform the police about Elias, his destination, and the investigators, if the keeper so wishes. See p. 37, "Horror at Ju-Ju House" for more information on this establishment.

THE CARLYLE EXPEDITION PRINCIPALS

*The investigators may look deeper into
the histories of the Carlyle Expedition members,
and perhaps uncover a few surprises.*

There were five important members in the Carlyle Expedition: dashing Roger Carlyle, Dr. Robert Huston, Sir Aubrey Penhew, beautiful Hypatia Masters, and tough-guy Jack Brady. The following entries summarize the pertinent data about them which the investigators can easily obtain or may already know. While the keeper is free to photocopy these summaries and hand them out, the summaries are more conceived as information to be included in other interviews, perhaps with Erica Carlyle, the police, or other characters.

Deeper research reveals more incident, but not more meaning. On a purely biographical level, all researches about the principals finish as dead ends in which their public personas and private personalities match believably. Make sure that the players know of the general lack of written information concerning people during this era. Historic objections to documentation of citizens in the United States was first muffled by World War II and then by the Cold War that followed it. To emphasize, most of this information would be passed on in conversation, not by the Library Use skill.

Roger Vane Worthington Carlyle

No police record; no military service. Always wealthy, always neglected and ignored by his father. Young Carlyle craved attention. His lawyers evaded a paternity suit against him when he was 17. Roger underwent short treatments for alcoholism when he was 18, and again when he was 20. Miraculously, he graduated from Groton, but was allowed gentleman's resignations from a succession of excellent universities (Harvard, Yale, Princeton, Miskatonic, Cornell, and USC) in the next three years. When his parents died in an automobile crash, Carlyle seemed to take stock of himself and for the next year gained the general approval of his peers, retainers, and relatives. But he slipped back into his old ways when his sprightly sister (who had not neglected her studies) showed a better grasp of family affairs.

His lack of character seemed confirmed when Carlyle fell under the influence of a mysterious East African woman, a self-styled poetess with the nom de plume of Nichonka Bunay. Rumors of debaucheries and worse circulated among police, journalists, and others whose business it is to know the backgrounds of public personalities. Roger Carlyle began to drain great sums of money from family interests, which prompted vicious arguments between himself, Erica, and their executives. In person Carlyle remained forthright and friendly, and was a popular figure at glittering New York night spots. In the

months before he left for Egypt, Carlyle seemed to withdraw and become more serious. But though Carlyle might have been maturing, the goals of the expedition remained nebulous and secretive, even to those who should have known.

The first Carlyle, Abner Vane Carel, was transported to Virginia in 1714, having been convicted of "unwholesome and desperative activitie" not otherwise characterized by Derbyshire authorities. Abner was the illegitimate and discredited son of an undistinguished Midlands nobleman. Abner's son Ephraim moved to New England, adopted "Carlyle" as a more gallant surname, and made sound investments in lumber and textiles, the basis of the family fortune to come. The Carlyle interests amassed huge profits during the American Civil War, and far-sighted management further expanded the financial empire in the half-century thereafter.

Dr. Robert Ellington Huston

No police record; no military service. The youngest of three sons, his father was a Chicago M.D. who as a young man was reputed to have been caught up in the utopianism of the early plains, and to have belonged to several deviant sects. Robert Huston graduated with honors from Johns Hopkins. After three years he threw over his circulatory-ailments practice (and his wife), and went to Vienna to study first under Freud and then under Jung. Huston was among the first Americans to undertake this esoteric and controversial study of the mind, which dealt so much with sexual behavior that no respectable person could talk about it. Huston's seemingly salacious and dangerous past, along with his elegant manners and sardonic wit, made him much in demand when he returned to New York City. There he established a practice in psychoanalysis catering to the very wealthy.

Huston enjoyed fame and notoriety. His fees were whispered to be $50-$60 dollars per visit, this at a time when a college professor might make $4000 a year. Women found him suave, handsome, sensitive, perceptive, and sexy. Among his patients was Roger Carlyle. Though Huston supposedly went on the expedition with Roger Carlyle in order to continue treatment, Huston had just broken off an affair with Miss Imelda Bosch, who had then committed suicide. Roger Carlyle helped hush up the scandal, perhaps in return for Huston's company on the expedition. There also were rumors that Carlyle did not want Huston at large while Carlyle was far away in Egypt. Carlyle may have believed that Huston's ethics were not strong enough to resist revealing explosive material about his young patient.

After Huston was declared dead, his records were turned over to the Medical Affairs Board of the State of New York. Controversy about this reached the newspapers. If the investigators ask, they will learn that the records have not been destroyed, because nobody has gotten around to authorizing the destruction. In those records are all of Huston's notes concerning Roger Carlyle.

THE CARLYLE RECORDS

Dr. Huston's files were carefully boxed, marked, and stored at the Medical Affairs Board, in a room adjoining the secretary's office. Adjudication finally determined that these records were in fact medical in nature, though old-line doctors resisted the notion for several months. These therefore are confidential records. Only Huston's heirs, the patients, or a doctor showing good cause can gain access easily. A Mr. Adrian Ferris, secretary to the board, controls all such files. Ferris is a tough cookie, impossible to Fast Talk, though an investigator who is a practicing physician in the State of New York can get by him with a successful Credit Rating roll.

The offices of the Medical Affairs Board are on Park Avenue at 61st Street. There is always a guard on duty in the lobby. A watchman passes the offices once every hour between 6 p.m. and 6 a.m. Assume that the investigators have D50+10 minutes until his next round. The Board offices are in Suite 1002. If needing statistics for the watchman, use one of Erica Carlyle's guards at her estate.

The files contain only a few relevant excerpts: with a successful Idea roll, any investigator reading the files perceives that the more Huston grew to know Carlyle, the less Huston was willing to put on paper about him. As desired, the keeper should add other information, including the apparent coincidence of Imelda Bosch's suicide.

HUSTON'S FILE FOR ERICA CARLYLE

Though there is a handout for Roger Carlyle's file, not enough exists to warrant anything for Erica. Her file notes a few innocuous consultations for which he charged her an outrageous $90 each, and establishes that she was troubled by her relations with her brother, Roger. Huston believed Erica to be of remarkably fine character, and notes that he not often saw such capable adjustment to the problems of living. He suggested to her that he would be glad to talk to Roger.

HUSTON'S FILE FOR ROGER CARLYLE

ITEM. Dr. Huston's file for Roger Carlyle: a simple manila file folder headed Carlyle, Roger V.W. It contains minor interview notes for about twenty sessions over the span of a year. (*Nyarlathotep Papers #24*)

Relevance of the Information: represents the best glimpse possible into Roger Carlyle's mind as he departed for London and then Cairo.

Visct. Pevensey, Sir Aubrey Penhew

Limited service as a Lieutenant with the Yorkshire Guards, 1901-1902, breveted as a Colonel in British Army Intelligence, 1915-1916, and then retired because of injury. Police records list only that young Sir Aubrey was caught pinching a policeman's helmet in 1898, while at Oxford. Penhew's public life is easily followed in *Who's Who*, *Burke's Peerage*, etc. With the inevitable nimbus of black sheep and blackguards down through the centuries, the Penhews trace their nobility from the time of William the Conqueror, when Sir Boris Penhew acquired great holdings in the west of England. With the exception of one Sir Blaize, who was beheaded for treason and black magic (his crimes nearly cost the line its titles and properties), the Penhew prosperity and prestige has been undiminished for eight centuries.

Sir Aubrey graduated with honors in classics from Oxford, but spent the next several years in Egypt, surveying and performing exploratory excavations amid the then little known wonders up-river, to the First Cataract and beyond. As his official biography notes, Sir Aubrey is credited with founding several important branches of Egyptology, and for several important archaeological discoveries, particularly at Dhashur. Nearly as important, the Penhew Foundation, set up by Sir Aubrey, has underwritten many important researches at home and abroad, and is responsible for the education of many brilliant but penniless scholars.

Sir Aubrey has title to several famous stately homes, as well as mansions in London, the Cotswalds, Monaco, and Alexandria (Egypt), and townhouses in Paris, Rome, and Athens. He is incontestably wealthy, and reputedly made new fortunes from his American holding companies during the Great War.

Though a public figure, Sir Aubrey's private life is little known. He is a bachelor, without family or heirs other than the Penhew Foundation. His Egyptologist peers hold him in high respect.

Miss Hypatia Celestine Masters

She has no police record or record of public service. She is heiress to the Masters armaments fortune, the dark antecedents of which have been chronicled in the muckraking *Masters of Corruption* by Nikolai Steinburg. Miss Masters' grandfather, Aldington Masters, held onto and increased the holdings by leaving most decisions to a series of chief executives who uniformly made intelligent, far-ranging, and profitable moves. George, her father, also adopted this relaxing way of life, spending his time doting on his daughter. Hypatia attended Swiss and French academies, showing facility for languages. Her great interest proved to be photography. Several of her shows earned good reviews and enthusiastic attendance. A daring streak in her led to an incautious affair with a Catholic Marxist, one Raoul Luis María Piñera, at City College of New York. With a successful Luck roll, a close friend (Olivia de Bernardesta) confides that Hypatia was pregnant by Raoul, had the baby aborted, and fled the country with Carlyle rather than face her lover.

Miss Masters dated Roger Carlyle several times, but apparently only as a friend. Her presence on the expedition might have been Carlyle's gallant whim. No one actually knows why she was invited or why she accepted.

Jack Oriel "Brass" Brady

His police record lists assaults and barroom brawls, petty theft, loitering, gambling, mopery, public drunkenness, and an acquitted murder charge. As a Marine sergeant, Jack Brady served in China and later on the Western Front in France, earning a Bronze Star and other commendations. He is rumored to have been a mercenary in Turkey just after the war, and to know Turkish and Arabic as well as several Chinese dialects. In the Oilfield, California, fight he apparently throttled his opponent to death before onlookers could pull him off, suggesting great strength or perhaps excellent technique.

The Oilfield murder piqued the curiosity of Roger Carlyle, who just then was being expelled from USC. After an hour-long interview, the two forged an intimate alliance, amazing everyone who knew Roger Carlyle, for the youth had never made any strong friendships. Carlyle summoned the best legal minds in the country for the defense, who proceeded to blow to pieces the seemingly open-and-shut case offered by the county prosecutor and eclipsing the testimony of seven eye-witnesses. Brady was acquitted on a variety of technical grounds. From that time, Jack Brady and Roger Carlyle rarely were separated—at times Brady was Carlyle's bodyguard, and at other times was his spokesman. For the expedition, Brady acted as general foreman and manager, and by all accounts performed well.

Brady's nickname comes from a brass plate about four inches square which he carries over his heart. The plate is described as covered with strange signs and inscriptions. Bullets twice have dented it. Brady has said that his mother, a recluse in Upper Michigan, had The Eye, and that she made this plate to guard her impetuous son.

Nyarlathotep Papers #24

```
First Meeting Jan. 11, 1918
Reference: Erica Carlyle
Closest Relative: Erica Carlyle

        At his sister's insistence, Mr. Roger Vane Worthington Carlyle visited me
this morning.  He deprecates the importance of his state of mind, but concedes
that he has had some trouble sleeping due to a recurring dream in which he
hears a distant voice calling his name.  (Interestingly the voice uses Mr.
Carlyle's second given name, Vane, by which Mr. Carlyle admits he always thinks
of himself.)  Carlyle moves towards the voice, and has to struggle through a
web-like mist in which the caller is understood to stand.
        The caller is a man--tall, gaunt, dark. An inverted ankh blazes in his
forehead. Following the Egyptian theme (C. has had no conscious interest in
things Egyptian, he says), the man extends his hands to C., his palms held
upward. Pictured on his left palm C. discovers his own face; on the right palm
C. sees an unusual, asymmetric pyramid.
        The caller then brings his hands together, and C. feels himself float off
the ground into space.  He halts before an assemblage of monstrous figures,
figures of humans with animal limbs, with fangs and talons, or of no particular
shape at all.  All of them circle a pulsating ball of yellow energy, which C.
recognizes as another aspect of the calling man.  The ball draws him in; he
becomes part of it, and sees through eyes not his own.  A great triangle
appears in the void, asymmetric in the same fashion as the vision of the pyra-
mid.  C. then hears the caller say, "And become with me a god."  As millions of
odd shapes and forms rush into the triangle, C. wakes.
        C. does not consider this dream a nightmare, although it upsets his
sleep. He says that he revels in it and that it is a genuine calling, although
my strong impression is that he actually is undecided about it. An inability to
choose seems to characterize much of his life.

September 18, 1918.  He calls her M'Weru, Anastasia, and My Priestess.  He is
obsessive about her, as well he might be--exterior devotion is certainly one way
to ease the tensions of megalomaniacal contradictions.  She is certainly a rival
to my authority.

December 3, 1918.  If I do not go C. threatens exposure.  If I do go, all pre-
tense of analysis surely will be lost.  What then will be my role?
```

HORROR AT JU-JU HOUSE

*Wherein the investigators directly confront
Nyalathotep's minions in New York,
the Cult of the Bloody Tongue.*

This establishment is in Harlem, at 1 Ransom Court—a dirty alley off of 137th street, east of Lenox Avenue. This short alley opens into a 20-foot-square court. The only doors from the court are those of Ju-Ju House, and of the back door of an abandoned pawn shop (which fronts on 138th Street). On meeting nights, 1D4 cultists sprawl in the court, posing as winos and acting as guards.

Crumbling tenements surround the court and many windows overlook the place. If the investigators interview the residents (who will be reticent or hostile if the investigators make no efforts at friendship), they learn that once a week strange people and foreigners go into the shop very late at night. Odd noises are occasionally heard at those times. A small present—cash, food, a carton of cigarettes—will be sufficient to allow the investigators to watch the shop entrance for a few hours from a neighboring window.

Investigators who choose to use the empty pawn shop as an approach will have to get through the boarded-up front door (STR 17), then through the back door which is chained from the inside and padlocked from the court side (STR 35). From within the pawn shop, the locked door may be opened slightly to allow a narrow view of the Ju-Ju House entrance.

Entering Ju-Ju House

The shop-front on the court consists of a display window and a glass door. Both are curtained, so that the interior of the shop cannot be seen. In the display window are pieces of African art (genuine, by a successful Anthropology or Archaeology roll). Shop hours are 9 a.m.—5 p.m.; it is closed only on Sundays. Statistics for cultists and entities within Ju-Ju House appear at the end of the Ju-Ju House section.

SILAS N'KWANE

The shop interior is a mere fifteen by twenty feet, and only Silas N'Kwane tends it. He is a spry 73-year-old, clever and perceptive, though long insane from associating with the cult. He will never reveal cult secrets, and actually knows little beyond the existence of the Chakota. He will fight if he must, preferring to attack from the rear. With the benefit of a successful Spot Hidden roll, an investigator notices a key hanging on a leather thong around his neck.

The place is dirty, dusty, and piled with African tribal artifacts and bric-a-brac-devil masks, leather-headed drums, stuffed model giraffes, carved wildebeasts, dull hand weapons intended for display, ivory warthogs, and so on. The shop has an oppressive, uneasy feel to it, especially if the investigators break in at night. A successful Occult roll points out that certain fetishes are traditional components of African ritual magic. None of these souvenirs are of use to the investigators without knowledge of African traditions. No pieces related to the Cthulhu Mythos can be seen.

There is a 25% chance that 1D3 innocent customers are present when the investigators arrive, and a 45% chance that 1D4 cultists are within shouting distance. If the investigators are all Caucasian, black customers may be suspicious of apparently slumming white men.

Into the Depths

There are no clues in the street level of Ju-Ju House, but there is an entrance to a lower level—a trap door beneath the rug behind the shop counter. Anyone who lifts the rug sees the inset steel handle of the trap door. Lifting the trap door and laying it back on its hinges reveals a set of stairs barely wide enough for one person. The steep stairs lead downward nearly twenty feet. These stairs end in a corridor fifteen feet long, which in turn stops at a stout door. Walls, ceiling, and floor of this corridor are stone. The ceiling is eight feet above the floor. Cut into the stone slabs are arcane tribal symbols (a successful Anthropology roll identifies them as Kikuyu tribal signs symbolizing evil). A kerosene lantern hanging from the center of the corridor will be lit if this is a meeting night, but otherwise the corridor is pitch black.

The door at the end of the corridor is oak reinforced with iron strips. Cut into the wood are more symbols, this time unidentifiable. The door is STR 30. Two investigators can match STRs against the door at the same time. If rites are in progress, this door is unlocked. The key to the deadbolt lock hangs around the neck of Silas N'Kwane. However, the hinges of the door are on the outside. The door can be taken off its hinges and pulled aside in twenty minutes or so.

The Basement

Beyond the door is the sacrificial chamber, with a fifteen-foot ceiling. All surfaces are of dressed stone. A successful Cthulhu Mythos roll shows that the obscure cult symbols here are related to the great old ones. Torches in wall niches light the ceremonial chamber. A curtain shields a small alcove where Mukunga the priest meditates upon the joys of serving his god. Four zombies wait in the alcove.

At the center of each wall are large African drums, accompaniment for the rituals.

Two long, stout poles jut from the entry door wall. Leather thongs dangle from the poles. The thongs hold the wrists of victims to be sacrificed. Such ceremonies are held monthly. At least two victims must be dedicated to the god of the Bloody Tongue during each rite.

In the center of the room is an eight-foot-diameter pit, covered by a thick stone block. A large pulley lifts the heavy block, which is so heavy that STR 25 is necessary to shove it aside.

THE CHAKOTA

At the bottom of the fifteen-foot-deep pit is what the cult knows as the Chakota, the Spirit of Many Faces, worshiped as a spirit subservient to the god of the Bloody Tongue. This dismaying entity is described in the section "Entities of Ju-Ju House" later in this chapter.

While in place the stone block silences the crying voices of the Chakota, but once it is lifted or moved aside horrible shrieks fill the room. Once the stone block cover is removed, the Chakota expects to be fed within ten minutes. If it is not, its faces redouble their wails, costing 1/1D8 SAN loss to hear.

GUARDS OF THE SACRIFICIAL CHAMBER

Four zombies watch over the chamber. Mukunga the high priest created them for that purpose. All are mutilated vic-

tims of cult murders. With their intestines dangling and their foreheads incised with the cult rune, they cost an investigator 0/1D8 SAN to encounter, together or singly. If Mukunga is absent, they attack whoever enters the chamber, but pursue no further than the base of the stairs. The keeper may choose the actual moment of attack.

During rites, the zombies flank Mukunga as bodyguards. When not needed, they stand within Mukunga's meditation alcove. Statistics for the zombies are at the end of this chapter. Mukunga made the zombies by means of the Create Zombie spell, as recorded in *Africa's Dark Sects,* a book present in this chamber.

ITEMS WITHIN MUKUNGA'S ALCOVE

The alcove is six feet square, and curtained from the sacrificial chamber. Along each side wall of the alcove stand two zombies, making a total of four.

Most of the small items described below are wrapped together in a leopard's hide and placed against the back wall, well out of the way. The priest's robe and the lion's claws hang on a peg on the rear wall. If Mukunga is present, he carries the scepter.

THE HIGH PRIEST'S ROBE: a long feathered shawl of shimmering color. A successful Natural History roll identifies flamingo and kingfisher feathers, likely from East Africa.

THE LION'S CLAWS: claws from a lion fixed to glove-like garments so that they may be worn, one for each hand. The construction is sturdy enough that these two ritual items might be used as weapons (see Mukunga's statistics).

AFRICA'S DARK SECTS*:* the book is the stamped property of the trustees of Harvard University. In English, +6 percentiles to Cthulhu Mythos knowledge, costs 1D10 SAN to read, x2 spell multiplier. Recently published (but only thirteen copies exist—authorities managed to burn the rest). This book contains one rulesbook spell, Create Zombie.

THE MASK OF HAYAMA*:* an African devil mask apparently carved of wood, though a successful Botany roll establishes that it is built of no wood known on Earth. The mask represents a combination of four Outer Gods. It was hewn by a Congolese high sorcerer who led a Cthulhu cult; a successful Archaeology roll establishes its Congo origin. See a nearby box for the special properties of the Mask of Hayama.

A BURNISHED COPPER BOWL: etched with unrecognizable runes and signs. A successful Cthulhu Mythos roll identifies this ancient bowl as used in conjunction with the spell Send Dreams. That spell is detailed in an Arabic scroll possessed by the Penhew Foundation in London. Though the bowl appears to be made of copper, its substance is alien to earthly science. The cultists know it as the "copper from above."

A CARVED SCEPTER: African in origin, carved of baobab wood and inset with runes, perhaps recognizable to someone who knows Egyptian hieroglyphics. The runes mean Nyambe, Thy Power Mine. The scepter grants ten additional magic points to anyone grasping the scepter and calling on

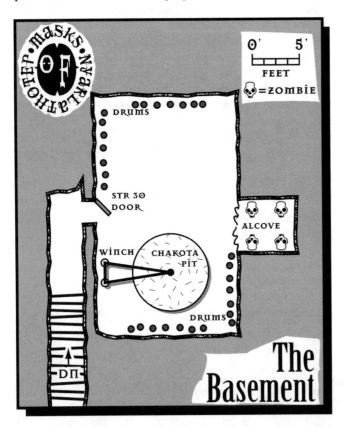

DRUMS

STR 30 DOOR

WINCH   CHAKOTA PIT

= ZOMBIE

ALCOVE

DRUMS

0'   5'

FEET

The Basement

The Mask of Hayama

No straps, ties, or handles hold this carved African mask to the face. If someone presses it to the face, it adheres like a living thing and clutches the wearer—a disturbing effect, even to watch. The wearer cannot remove the mask, and neither can other investigators pull it free. As the mask stays on, the wearer ceases to struggle. After fifteen seconds the pupils expand to fill the eye sockets. At that point and for the following thirty seconds, the wearer has an all-too-clear vision of one of four gods, and must make a SAN roll.

The mask then drops from the face of the wearer. Used in conjunction with a Call or Contact spell for one of these gods, the mask also falls away when the spell concludes.

There are benefits to wearing the mask, if the wearer survives with his or her Sanity intact. For the first time each god is viewed through the mask, increase the wearer's Cthulhu Mythos by 1D10 points, in addition to any Cthulhu Mythos gain due to insanity. Secondly, donning the mask while casting any of the spells Contact Nodens, Call Azathoth, Call Shub-Niggurath, or Call Yog-Sothoth effectively opens a more direct line to that god. In game terms add 25 percentiles to the chance for the spell being cast to succeed.

The Mask of Hayama is a prized Mythos artifact. Cultists will kill for it.

MASK VISION TABLE

1D4	God	Success	Failure
1	Nodens*	no roll	no roll
2	Azathoth	1D10 SAN	D100 SAN
3	Shub-Niggurath	1D10 SAN	D100 SAN
4	Yog-Sothoth	1D10 SAN	D100 SAN

* as noted in the Cairo chapter, the Mask of Hayama can help investigators foil the resurrection of Nitocris.

Nyambe. These points will dissipate in one hour if not used. Once used, the scepter cannot provide more magic points until the next sunrise. Nyambe is a western and southern African name for the supreme god. The scepter is not a Cthulhu Mythos artifact.

A HEADBAND OF GREY METAL: Cthulhu Mythos runes are scratched in it. A successful Cthulhu Mythos roll determines that the headband is some sort of protection device having to do with Nodens. When worn, the headband protects against nightgaunts. No nightgaunt can hurt the wearer of this headband unless the wearer first hurts a nightgaunt.

Rites of the Bloody Tongue

Though cult meetings are weekly, sacrificial rites are held once per month, with 2D20+10 cultists attending.

Monthly rites require at least two sacrificial victims. Usually the victims are kidnapped from other portions of Harlem on the day of the sacrifice, and brought to the shop not long before rites start. If an investigator has been kidnapped for that purpose, he or she arrives earlier in the day, captive within a packing crate. The rest of the cultists begin arriving shortly after 1 a.m., and rites begin about 1:30 a.m. Anyone watching dozens of cultists enter tiny Ju-Ju House realizes that there must be a connection to another room or to a basement, in order to hold all the people

Neighbors might be able to give the investigators a good idea when ritual nights occur. Friendly manners also might yield a phone call to the investigators the next time the neighbors notice a lot of people entering late at night.

During rites, the court goes unguarded. Most cultists enter the shop between 1-1:30 a.m. A 75% chance exists that 1D6 cultists will enter after the investigators have, if the investigators enter during that time. The chance lowers to 10% if the investigators enter after 1:30 a.m.

As cultists reach the basement corridor, they doff their clothes, putting on only the grotesque Bloody Tongue headpieces. They chant and dance for hours, until Mukunga determines that a proper frenzy has been reached. He then carves the foreheads of the sacrificial victims, and pronounces an invocation which distinctly includes the name Nyarlathotep. The stone cap is raised from the Chakota pit, and the screaming victims are hurled to their doom. To attest his or her faith, occasionally a cultist will jump with the victims, and be consumed as a willing sacrifice.

During the rites, Mukunga wears the feathered robe. He uses the lion's claws to mark victims with the cult rune. He'll also attack with these claws if investigators interrupt the rites. If physical efforts fail to kill or capture intruding investigators, Mukunga can summon a Hunting Horror (only Mukunga can do this, and he can summon only one per night).

With the noise and frenzy, investigators opening the door of the sacrificial chamber enough to peek in will not be noticed. Even if they open it all the way they won't be noticed for 1D3 minutes.

As might be imagined, the cult frowns upon uninvited guests, and all of the cultists will pursue intruders, hoping to capture and sacrifice them to their bleak god. Cultists have no weapons in the sacrificial chamber, and have a hard time sorting out their clothes quickly enough to find personal weapons among their garments. If the chase leads up into the shop, they grab from the stock of spears, knives, and clubs available there. The chase might then continue until the investigators are killed or caught, or until they escape. Keep in mind that a howling mob of naked cultists chasing dapper investigators down the middle of Lenox Avenue probably attracts the attention of the police.

Ju-Ju House Entities

In order, they are the Chakota, Mukunga, the six zombies (two of them spares for the keeper), the cultists, and Silas N'Kwane. Keepers who need more cultists can appropriate the three killers from Room 410, or generate more using the sample statistics from the Bloody Tongue box at the beginning of this chapter.

CHAKOTA, the Spirit of Many Faces

STR 36	CON 36	SIZ 36	INT 0	POW 36
DEX 03	MOV 4			HP 36

Damage Bonus: n/a.

Weapons: Bite 30%, damage 1D3 per face, 1D8 faces per target. Wails of the Chakota, damage 1/1D8 SAN but only when hearing them the first time.

Armor: the Chakota is immune to firearms, clubs, and knives, but fire, magic, and electricity can harm it. If all the mouths are covered, it can suffocate in earth or water.

Skills: none.

Sanity Loss: 1D3/1D20 Sanity points to see the Chakota.

ATTACKS: roll to bite for each face. A successful bite clamps down on the victim, holding him beside the Chakota. The victim's player may make a STR against STR roll on the Resistance Table, but at an automatic cost of one point more

SILAS N'KWANE PUTS ON A HAPPY FACE

of damage per set of clamped teeth. Assume that each bite has STR 1: total the bites and use that sum to roll against on the resistance table—do not use the Chakota's bodily strength. For each successful attack, remove one hit point from the target.

As the keeper decides, allow only one target at a time or up to three targets as the situation demands. The Chakota seeks to devour the first target before turning to the second, but each victim takes only half a dozen or fewer rounds to ingest.

DESCRIPTION: the Chakota is composed of dozens of human faces set into a thickly cylindrical, worm-like mass of sickly, purple-veined muscle. The faces weep, shout, and cry out with great woeful feeling. The Chakota is somewhat mobile, but cannot escape its pit. It is about six feet high and three feet in diameter.

The faces of the Chakota are those of its victims. Each new victim's face appears about two hours after ingestion. The Chakota kills by biting and devouring with its myriad faces. There is no significant limit to the number of victims the thing can claim, for its bulk can constantly grow. An investigator seeing on it the face of a person known to him or her may experience double or even triple Sanity loss. Anyone bitten by the Chakota automatically loses 1D10 SAN. No Sanity roll is possible.

MAKING A CHAKOTA: a Chakota's characteristics are a function of the number of its faces. Each face yields 1 STR and one SIZ point. The CON of the thing equals its STR. The DEX is always 3, and its Move is always 4. The Chakota in the pit has 36 faces. If it ate two investigators, then it would have 38 faces.

The Chakota is created by a magical ritual involving a willing person who is consumed in the process, and whose face becomes the first face of the creature. At first the cultists must help the new-made thing feed, but soon it takes care of itself.

Mukunga, High Priest

This tough customer relishes smiting the foes of his god. Mukunga knows the location of the Mountain of the Black Wind, knows what lies within its temple cavern, and knows something of Nyarlathotep's grand design. But Mukunga will never reveal this information unless forced by magic. If close to death, his last act will be to contact Nyarlathotep and pray for vengeance from the god (the god has a 1% chance of agreeing to do this). Mukunga contacts Edward Gavigan if he learns that the snoopy investigators are headed toward London, but only after Mukunga no longer has a chance personally to mete out justice to those blasphemers. Mukunga knows vaguely of the Chinese cult to Nyarlathotep, but has no way to alert it if the investigators decide to go first to Shanghai, and knows nothing of Huston's activities in Australia and elsewhere.

A dock-worker by day, Mukunga lives in a shabby East Side room on 129th Street. In that room is a sleeping mat, a few clothes, and many Kenyan carvings. Most of the carvings have mystic significance, as a successful Occult roll shows. Mukunga sometimes practices stalking unsuspecting strollers in Central Park. He may be found in Fat Maybelle's, a sleazy bar at 139th Street and 6th Avenue—a place popular with native Africans. Though rarely seen there, Caucasians are perfectly welcome. Regulars there know Mukunga, and say that he has the power, the ju-ju. They're right.

MUKUNGA M'DARI, age 36, High Priest of the God of the Bloody Tongue (New York City Branch)

STR 16	CON 20	INT 13	POW 17	SIZ 15
DEX 13	APP 17	EDU 0	SAN 0	HP 18

Damage Bonus: +1D4.

Weapons: Fist 85%, damage 1D3+1D4
Pranga 75%, damage 1D6+2+1D4
Large Club 75%, damage 1D8+1D4
Lion's Claw 75%, damage 1D4+1D4 per hand
Switchblade 65%, damage 1D4+1D4 (carried when wearing European-style clothing)

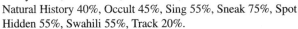

Spells: Bind Byakhee, Contact Nyarlathotep, Create Zombie, Dread Clutch of Nyogtha, Dread Curse of Azathoth, Mindblast, Power Drain, Shrivelling, Summon/Bind Hunting Horror.

Skills: Bargain 50%, Climb 70%, Conceal 55%, Credit Rating 07%, Cthulhu Mythos 26%, Dodge 85%, English 35%, Hide 65%, Jump 75%, Kikuyu 30%, Listen 65%, Nandi 90%, Natural History 40%, Occult 45%, Sing 55%, Sneak 75%, Spot Hidden 55%, Swahili 55%, Track 20%.

SILAS N'KWANE, age 73, Manager of Ju-Ju House

STR 06	CON 17	SIZ 08	INT 15	POW 13
DEX 10	APP 09	EDU 06	SAN 0	HP 13

Damage Bonus: -1D4

Weapon: Pranga 30%, damage 1D6+2-1D4

Skills: Anthropology 15%, Archaeology 10%, Bargain 60%, Credit Rating 23%, Cthulhu Mythos 11%, Dodge 35%, English 45%, Fast Talk 45%, Hide 65%, Kikuyu 70%, Listen 35%, Nandi 20%, Occult 50%, Sneak 50%, Spot Hidden 65%, Swahili 20%.

EIGHT AVERAGE BLOODY TONGUE CULTISTS

	1	2	3	4*	5	6	7	8
STR	12	10	14	14	15	11	09	11
CON	15	13	12	17	11	12	14	18
SIZ	12	14	10	08	09	12	14	13
EDU	06	04	03	05	05	02	01	04
APP	10	09	06	04	09	13	12	06
SAN	0	0	0	0	0	0	0	0
INT	13	08	14	10	10	15	10	11
DEX	17	15	13	11	10	10	09	08
POW	10	10	11	15	12	11	13	09
HP	14	14	11	13	10	12	14	16
DB	0	0	0	0	0	0	0	0

* born in the United States.

Weapons: Pranga 45%, damage 1D6+2
Small Knife/Razor 45%, damage 1D4
(if American) .22 Revolver 30%, damage 1D6

Skills: Cthulhu Mythos 05%, English 35%, Hide 60%, Jump 55%, Kikuyu 35%, Listen 50%, Nandi 35%, Occult 10%, Sneak 60%, Spot Hidden 35%, Swahili 35%, Track 15%.

The Zombies

The SAN cost to see one is 1/1D8 SAN. If the zombie was known in life to the investigator and is still recognizable, the investigator loses an additional 1D4 SAN whether the Sanity roll succeeds or fails. A hit by an impaling weapon does only 1 point of damage to a zombie. Damage from other physical weapons is half that which is rolled.

THE ZOMBIES

	1	2	3	4	5	6
STR	18	22	21	12	09	24
CON	19	07	13	19	06	10
SIZ	12	09	08	09	09	08
POW	01	01	01	01	01	001
DEX	12	11	10	08	06	4
HP	16	08	11	14	08	09
DB	+1D4	+1D4	+1D4	—	—	+1D4
MOV 6						

Weapon: Bite 30%, damage 1D3

Aftermath

Armed mostly with clues, motivation, and a small inkling of the vast conspiracy which confronts them, the investigators now may sail to England, Egypt, Kenya, Australia, or China to learn more and perhaps to stymie the plans of the Dark God. Keepers with novice player-groups might want to suggest that their investigators choose an at-home coordinator to receive reports, to store magic items and tomes, and perhaps to raise new funds—this is the person who'll always pay for collect telegrams from Katmandu, and always make sure they reach the right person. He or she also might handle news of investigator deaths or commission new investigative teams. Have the players generate the character, and make sure they explain and justify that character's appearance, resources, and why the investigators trust him or her. One player should own the character, and play him or her if need be. At the end of an adventure, the keeper should get a summary of wires, packages, etc., sent to and from the coordinator. In this chapter, Professor Cowles, Miss Miriam Atwright, Jonah Kensington, or Erica Carlyle all would be suitable, for instance.

With this line of communication defined and established, if novices thereafter casually dispatch their investigators into horrors so overwhelming that the keeper either must destroy the entire party or sacrifice his or her own integrity in order to save the campaign, the choice is clear. Placidly watching the carnage mount, the keeper is secure in the knowledge that he or she has created a way to restart the campaign at the point which death stopped it, has accounted for everything which the players already know, and may have imparted a salutary lesson about caution as well. In this campaign, incautious investigators will die. ■

LONDON

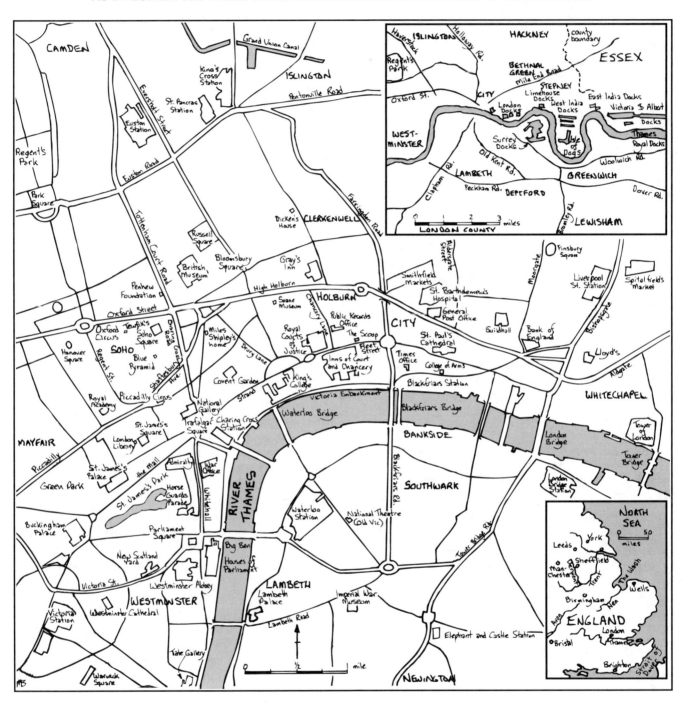

"He wondered at the vast conceit of those who had babbled of the malignant Ancient Ones, as if They could pause from their everlasting dreams to wreak a wrath upon mankind. As well, he thought, might a mammoth pause to visit frantic vengeance on an angleworm."

–H.P. Lovecraft, *"Through the Gates of the Silver Key"*

London is the nearest and perhaps the most logical place for investigators to travel to first: Elias was last there. The Carlyle Expedition first went there. London's scholarly resources are vast, and its rulers also rule Egypt, Kenya, and China in important ways. Most happily, London's natives for the most part are friendly, and its street signs are in English. A Chaosium publication, *The London Guidebook*, is a useful supplement for the city.

Here the shadows of Chapter One become more substantial. The investigators again find themselves beset by a cult, one other than the Bloody Tongue but perhaps one connected to it. Clues again point to Egypt, Kenya, Australia, and Shanghai. Along the way, anomalies exist such as a werewolf, a mad artist, and a respectable administrator who has odd friends. Keepers should remain flexible so that they can emphasize the fun. Give the players the feel of London—the fog, the coal smoke, the seeping chill of night, the crowds and the enormity of the daytime bustle, the bohemian atmosphere of Soho, the magnificent museums and galleries, the threatening byways of Limehouse, the frightened villagers of Lesser-Edale, the luxurious hedges of country estates behind which the most pagan and monstrous rites are held.

Mickey Mahoney, owner/editor of *The Scoop*, can steer the investigators toward several encounters, though it is likely that the investigators will find trouble on their own.

Except for the Brotherhood, most menaces can be avoided or escaped by the investigators. Expect a few deaths or cases of insanity. Once the investigators interview Edward Gavigan, the eyes of the Brotherhood will be upon them.

In New York, most of the time was spent in gathering information. The episodes in England involve several deadly encounters. Allow the investigators to make their own choices, but do not fail to present them with the opportunities. Two clues lead to adventures which are horrible enough, but unrelated to the unraveling of the Carlyle Expedition disappearances and to Nyarlathotep's cruel plans for our planet.

About London

For generations, London and its suburbs have comprised the greatest city known to man. Approximately 7.5 million live in greater London. Not only the largest, London is also the wealthiest city in the world. In later generations, New York will overtake the sprawling city on the Thames, but just now London is queen of civilization. The Great War inter-rupted the rate of building, but that has since renewed itself despite labor unrest. The irregularly-shaped County of London is approximately 11.5 by 16 miles, with an area of about 116 square miles. It is ridiculously easy to hide in the swarm of streets and buildings.

The district of Soho—a locale traditional to prostitutes and advertising men, and convenient to the seats of government—is mentioned several times in the text, but is not identified on the London map. It is roughly bounded by Oxford Street, Regent Street, Charing Cross Road, and Piccadilly.

The wealthiest portions of the city are north of the Thames: the West End, most of Westminster, with extensions into Chelsea, Kensington, Paddington, and Marylebone. Within Westminster rest the palaces and governmental offices commonly thought of when the word London is mentioned. The most fashionable addresses include Mayfair (just east of Hyde Park), Belgravia (south of Hyde Park), Kensington (west of Belgravia), and Chelsea (to the south of Belgravia and Kensington). The actual City of London is about one square mile north of the Thames, within London's medieval walls. It is there to which the rail terminals funnel, to the commercial heart of the British empire.

Further north, the districts are predominantly artisan or middle class.

The mean streets of the East End—Stepney, Bethnal, Green, Limehouse, Shoreditch, etc.—form a distinct and abruptly contrasting poverty, a state also normal along the south bank of the Thames from Battersea to Greenwich. A writer of the time noted that "even in the richest quarters, in

Selected Connections for this Chapter

NP#	clue or lead	obtained from	leads to
12	business card	Elias' murder scene	Edward Gavigan, Penhew Foundation
—	reference	J. Kensington	Inspector Barrington
—	reference	J. Kensington	Mickey Mahoney
25	Mickey Mahoney	*The Scoop*	Miles Shipley
—	painting by Miles S.	upstairs of house	portrays Nyarlathotep and cultists of Bloody Tongue
26	Mickey Mahoney	*The Scoop*	Derbyshire Monster
27	Mickey Mahoney	*The Scoop*	Inspector Barrington, "Egyptian murders"
—	Edward Gavigan	surveillance	Tewfik al-Sayed, Misr House
—	find secret panel	Gavigan's office	secret room in the Penhew Foundation basement
—	packing crate	Penhew Foundation	Ho Fong, Shanghai
—	packing crate	Penhew Foundation	Randolph Shipping Co., Australia
—	Blue Pyramid Club	Insp. Barrington	Tewfik al-Sayed
—	Penhew Foundation	Insp. Barrington	Tewfik al-Sayed
—	Tewfik al-Sayed	Gavigan, Barrington	Brotherhood of Black Pharaoh, Mirror of Gal
—	cultist movement	Yalesha the dancer	truck to Misr House, in Essex
—	cult ceremonies	surveillance	Gavigan possibly in English cult
—	Penhew Foundation	surveillance	truck to Limehouse and Punji Chabout
—	Chabout's warehouse	freighter *Ivory Wind*	crate to Ho Fong, Shanghai
—	Gavigan's ledger	Misr House	Shanghai, Australia, Egypt, New York, etc.
29	Gavigan's letter	Misr House	Sir Aubrey Penhew, Jack Brady

Westminster and elsewhere, small but well-defined areas of the poorest dwellings occur..."

Further south of the Thames, the districts become progressively more middle class and suburban.

Mickey Mahoney

If Jonah Kensington did not give Mahoney's name to the investigators, the investigator who was Elias' friend can remember that Elias frequently told stories about Mahoney, who is a logical London contact. Mahoney is a grubby Irish journalist who publishes *The Scoop*, a weekly tabloid. Mahoney delights in printing stories about gory murders, sex scandals, and weird happenings. He is a cigar-smoking, red-haired, 43-year-old—cynical and tough. The offices of *The Scoop* are on the third floor of a shabby building in Fleet Street, not far from Ludgate Circus. Mahoney is greatly saddened by Elias' death, having long known of it from the press wires. He is anxious to help, but will quickly sour on the investigators if they seem incompetent to him.

BROTHERHOOD OF THE BLACK PHARAOH (LONDON)

Originally composed of Egyptian servants, now depraved Indians, Arabs, and Caucasians make up nearly equal portions of the membership; the cult is small and the hierarchy is still mostly Egyptian. The name of the cult comes from an Egyptian form of Nyarlathotep, who in dynastic Egypt was whispered to be a dark or invisible ruler who was, like night, both everywhere and nowhere.

The Brotherhood here serves the Penhew Foundation. Sir Aubrey Penhew accompanied the Carlyle Expedition. The cult uses several outdoor locations in England for its rituals. It has two important leaders in London—Edward Gavigan, the director of the Penhew Foundation, and Tewfik al-Sayed, who runs a small spice shop not far away in Soho. Both are intelligent, dangerous, and insane. The cult's characteristic ritual weapon is a short club with a single spike embedded in it; in payment for certain crimes, cultists will attempt to break their victim's bones with the club before driving the spike into his or her heart. They never leave an identifying rune on the body of the victim. The use of guns by this cult is very rare. The Brotherhood does not accept women as active members. Lately a cult artist from New York has sculpted an ankh with a broken or bent top; perhaps the Bloody Tongue and the Brotherhood are drawing closer together.

AVERAGE BROTHER (London)

STR 10	CON 12	SIZ 08	INT 08	POW 07
DEX 09	APP 05	EDU 03	SAN 0	HP 10

Damage Bonus: +0.

Weapons: Cult Club 50%, damage 1D8
Butcher Knife 30%, damage 1D6
Fist/Punch 30%, damage 1D3

Skills: Arabic 45%, Bargain 15%, Climb 45%, Cthulhu Mythos 04%, Drive Automobile 40%, English 20%, Fast Talk 25%, Hide 70%, Listen 50%, Pick Pocket 15%, Sneak 35%, Spot Hidden 50%, Track 10%.

While he was recently in London, Elias visited Mahoney, promising a story about an evil cult operating in London. Elias hinted that the cult might be well connected. Mahoney never got the story, but would love to have it, and will offer to pay the investigators up to fifteen English pounds for it. Of course Mahoney wants any sort of odd or gruesome story, and also pays well for photos of cute models in their knickers (with such accompanying stories as "Her Cornish Holiday"). A true professional, Mahoney cares about truth unless not caring brings more cash.

MICKEY MAHONEY

Elias never mentioned the name of any cult, nor mentioned anything about his evolving suspicions. Elias browsed through *The Scoop*'s files, and Mahoney says the investigators are welcome to do the same, but he recalls that the author seemed interested by only three stories. Those stories are quoted at the beginning of later sections. They are all unsigned— Mahoney says that he himself may have rewritten them from wire or stringer copy, "to give 'em that little extra whoosh!"

Each of these three leads represents a discrete adventure. "The Derbyshire Monster" is a red herring, with almost no meaning other than in itself. "Slaughter in Soho" deals directly with the Brotherhood of the Black Pharaoh. "A Serpent in Soho" has to do with the Cthulhu Mythos, but otherwise does not relate to the themes of this campaign.

Mahoney does not know if Elias followed up on any of these. Elias seemed rushed and desperate, and he soon left for New York (because he had been found out by Gavigan, though Mahoney does not know this). As far as Mahoney knows, the Penhew Foundation and Edward Gavigan are completely above-board.

Mahoney knows the city intimately, and knows the real worth of many people. If the investigators require the services of an expert safecracker, want to contact an underworld boss, or want to know if Inspector Barrington is an honest bloke, Mahoney is their man.

If the investigators have been followed to *The Scoop* and if their subsequent activity proves harmful to the cult, the Brotherhood will send three ritual killers to murder Mickey Mahoney. The keeper may turn this into a scene if he or she wishes—perhaps it happens like Elias' death, with the investigators on the premises.

MICKEY MAHONEY, age 40, Cynical Journalist

STR 11	CON 13	SIZ 08	INT 14	POW 09
DEX 10	APP 14	EDU 13	SAN 55	HP 11

Damage Bonus: +0.

Weapons: .303 Enfield Rifle 55%, damage 2D6+1
Fist/Punch 60%, damage 1D3
Kick 50%, damage 1D6
Head Butt 45%, damage 1D4

Skills: Accounting 65%, Bargain 55%, Debate 65%, Drive Automobile 55%, English 50%, Fast Talk 75%, History 35%, Libel Law 95%, Mechanical Repair 55%, Occult 10%, Psychology 60%.

THE PENHEW FOUNDATION

*Wherein the investigators visit an important clearing-house and museum
for Egyptologists, meet the Foundation's esteemed director,
and perhaps learn more than they wanted.*

Probably the investigators come to England to follow the trail of Carlyle and Elias in London. If their tracks do not provide to be sufficiently alluring, plant more material to tempt the investigators to come—the London episodes are not to be missed. The Penhew Foundation and its director, Edward Gavigan, are logical targets for investigator scrutiny.

An interview with Mr. Gavigan will not be difficult to obtain, particularly if Jackson Elias is mentioned. Gavigan would love to know what the investigators know about Elias, since Gavigan is high priest of the Brotherhood of the Black Pharaoh in the British Isles.

The Penhew Foundation is in central London, at a Bloomsbury address north of Oxford Street and west of the British Museum, roughly between Regents Park and the Thames. It is a High Victorian building, of fewer stories and greater ceiling height than the buildings to either side, and of altogether grander scale and elegance of detail. Within, its appointments are opulent. It is of two stories and a basement (in British terms a basement, ground floor, and first floor). A doorman waits at the door; a burly secretary waits just inside. This is the sole public entrance. A careful man, Gavigan keeps guards at the public door whenever it is unlocked.

An intelligent and polished man in his fifties, Gavigan is superbly dressed, and greets the investigators in a magnificently paneled office. As a touch of fashion, he wears a wristwatch, still a relatively new item of personal adornment. Though Gavigan epitomizes the highly successful Londoner, he was poor as a young man, and spent many years scheming and dealing his way into Sir Aubrey's confidence. He likes material life as much as he enjoys being empowered by gods. His statistics occur with the rest of the cultists at the end of this chapter. Gavigan is a formidable sorcerer.

A strong, modern floor safe, its door slightly ajar, gleams in one corner. Gavigan's greeting is friendly and open. He acknowledges that Mr. Elias spoke to him concerning Sir Aubrey's participation in the Carlyle Expedition. Gavigan expresses sadness at the news of Mr. Elias' death. He met with him just once. He agrees to try to recapitulate the conversation.

(On a successful Psychology roll, one chink in Gavigan's armor appears: the investigator notices that Gavigan's face twitches when asked about Elias' activities in London, though he denies all knowledge.)

Gavigan says that Carlyle obtained information, apparently from a mysterious African woman, concerning a shadowy time in Egyptian history about which Sir Aubrey had long been interested. In this ancient time a sorcerer was reputed to have ruled the Nile valley. Alas, Gavigan smiles, the information proved to be a hoax. In Egypt, the African woman disappeared with the expedition's ready funds, in the amount of some 3500 British pounds. "We are gentlemen of the world, are we not? Carlyle counted the lost money as insignificant, but he was deeply affected by the defection of his lover."

Fearing the heat and disappointment of Egypt would seriously affect her health as well as Carlyle's, Hypatia Masters suggested that the party spend the summer months in the relatively cool Kenyan uplands, affording her a wonderful opportunity to use some new lenses to photograph African wildlife. Once there the group injudiciously entered dubious territory, and paid for it with their lives. The vast share of the expedition records were lost there as well, for Sir Aubrey (always loyal to Carlyle) took them along to work on, while matters were still fresh in his mind. "Wherever he is, there they are," Gavigan says, and closes the topic of the expedition as well as its records.

If the investigators suggest that Sir Aubrey must have sent letters of interest to the foundation, Gavigan

EDWARD GAVIGAN

agrees, but says that they concern much about young Carlyle. It would be unethical to show such documents to outsiders.

The expedition did turn up some interesting artifacts from other periods, and was able to dig a large number of test trenches to help begin Sir Aubrey's systematic study of Dhashur. They also found some secondary sites in the wastes to the west of the Giza pyramids. The Egyptian government loaned some of the artifacts to the British Museum, and some of the lesser pieces were bought for the Penhew private collection. Most of the items are still being catalogued for the Egyptian Museum in Cairo, but Gavigan is eager to show the investigators the lesser miracles which were brought to England. If the investigators express interest, he shows them endless inscribed shards, broken pots, noseless statues, and bas-reliefs of sleek cats and ladies wearing thin linen, perhaps for the rest of the day, or at least until he is sure that the investigators have nothing left to tell him. Egyptology and archaeology rolls find nothing to fault him for, but he is irritatingly dull.

Gavigan acknowledges that the foundation is the sole heir to the Penhew family fortune and estates, but he will be insult-

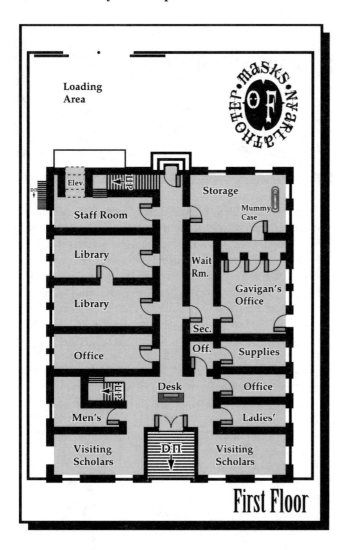

First Floor

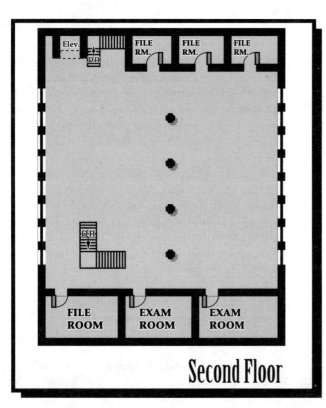

Second Floor

ed by such prying, and the interview will then soon conclude abruptly. Research shows that Gavigan is independently wealthy and without personal interest in the Penhew fortunes.

Surveillance

Though he believes the investigators are a threat, Gavigan is subtle and will not immediately hurl cultists at them. He has the investigators followed. Occasionally have the players roll Spot Hiddens for their investigators, or keepers may make a hide roll for the tailing cultist every few turns—if failed, the investigators notice the person doing the tail.

If the investigators seem about to reveal cult secrets, or to expose the cult's headquarters, then attacks begin. Investigators might also be attacked if the cult learns that the investigators possess Mythos artifacts or tomes, such as the Mask of Hayama or *Africa's Dark Sects*. Such assaults will be more to gain possession than to kill investigators. The investigators' hotel rooms certainly will be ransacked and plundered.

If they watch Edward Gavigan for a few days, the investigators discover that he makes nocturnal visits to the seedy Soho shop of Tewfik al-Sayed. The first such visit is the night of his interview with the investigators. If the investigators tail him, have their players roll Hides and make Spot Hiddens for discovery, as above. Tewfik's shop is only a fifteen-minute stroll from the Foundation. An Englishman in habit, Gavigan walks. If Gavigan spots the tail, he'll go instead to one of his clubs, the Diamondback, up Tottenham Court Road. This club has no relation to Mythos activities, but the food is excellent, and the card-playing ability of several members remarkably low. Sated and seventy pounds richer, Gavigan returns smiling to his Mayfair flat that night.

If later on the investigators break into that flat, they find nothing of interest except good whiskey, fine furniture, dynastic Egyptian bric-a-brac, and excellent clothing.

The Penhew Foundation Building

The building is well designed and sturdy; the building is guarded around the clock. A high iron fence surrounds the building. A delivery entrance in the back is wide enough for heavy trucks. It is usually padlocked with two stout chains across it. All exterior doors have STR 50. Interior doors have STR 30.

When the investigators enter or leave the Penhew building, they may notice suspicious-looking men lounging about. Some are English, others possibly Hindu or Arabic. If the player of the investigator with the highest Luck roll succeeds with the roll, the men are delivering or picking up items at the rear of the building. If the investigators wish, they can tail the lorry to the Limehouse docks. The same procedure for tailing can be applied here, but this time if the investigators are spotted 1D8+3 crazed cultists ambush them in a dark Limehouse alley.

Foundation Staff

The Egyptian collection is open for viewing from noon to 4 p.m., Monday through Friday. During that time, two guards are stationed in the exhibit hall. A doorman is on duty at the front from 8 a.m. to 6 p.m., Monday through Friday. A secretary/guard sits at the desk just inside the main entrance from 8:30 a.m. to 5 p.m., Monday through Friday. At all other times, only a single watchman patrols the building, making a single round every hour. He is mainly there to guard the collection against fire, burst pipes, or storm damage. Normal office hours for the foundation are 8:30 a.m. to 5:30 p.m. Lesser staff have a half-hour for lunch beginning at noon.

Including Gavigan, eight secretaries, librarians, and specialists work at the Foundation. There are a total of five guards and watchmen employed. A single workman opens and closes the delivery gate, moves items to and from the exhibit hall, and does miscellaneous repairs for the building. A cleaning woman works from 5 p.m. to midnight, nightly.

Only Edward Gavigan, the night watchman, the cleaning woman, the secretary/guard at the front desk, and the workman are cultists. The rest are normal subjects of the Crown, doing their part for King and country, and are well versed in Egyptology, fund-raising, and associated legal technicalities.

The Exhibit Hall

Nothing in the exhibit hall has to do with the cult of the Black Pharaoh or with the Cthulhu Mythos. The file rooms at the front and back are filled with flat-file drawers containing countless carefully evaluated and catalogued artifacts from dynastic Egypt. A librarian will bring requested artifacts to one of the examination rooms, but the visitor must be a accredited scholar. The examiner is locked in while making his or her study of the requested artifacts. When finished, the scholar knocks to be let out, and the artifacts are returned to their cases or files.

The windows of the exhibit hall are broad and tall, with ventilator openings at the tops via mechanical arms. The surfaces are finished in marble; the ceiling is twenty feet high. Glass cases, mummies, statuary, etc., fill the hall in tasteful rows.

The Main Floor

Here the main business of the foundation is carried out: evaluating scholars and granting them funds, negotiating permits and exceptions with Egyptian authorities, arranging itineraries and schedules, and acting as a physical and informational repository for things Egyptian, especially Egypt before the Ptolemies. Though the foundation is legitimate,

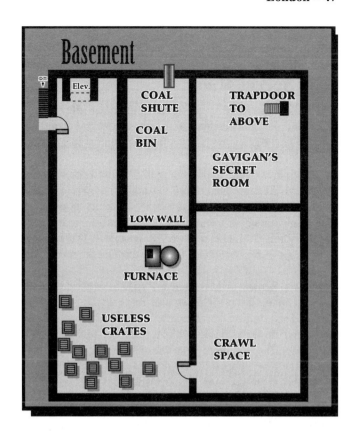

Gavigan finds it convenient cover for his activities for the Brotherhood of the Black Pharaoh. On this floor, only Gavigan's office, his closets, and the storage room will be of much significance to the investigators.

The rest of the floor consists of offices, work rooms for visiting scholars, and associated conveniences. The library strictly concerns things Egyptian. Given a successful Library Use roll, investigators have one chance every hour to learn that there really was some sort of mysterious, sorcery-wielding ruler early in the history of Egypt.

Gavigan's office contains no suspect material. The unlocked safe does contain a packet of one hundred consecutively numbered five-pound notes drawn by Gavigan from his London bank. If the investigators began to watch Gavigan immediately after the interview, they saw him go to the bank and return to his office. No mean chess player, Gavigan has decided to tempt the investigators to steal the easily identifiable money if they return to rifle through his office.

In the north wall of Gavigan's office are several closets. A hidden panel (Spot Hidden minus 20 percentiles to notice it) opens the back of the center closet, which allows Gavigan to enter the storage room without being seen. In the storage room are many boxes and crates, old furniture, and so on. There is also an empty mummy case in poor condition lying on its back on the floor. A successful Spot Hidden or Track reveals that a section of a circle relative to the mummy case is less dusty and somewhat worn. If one or both eyes on the sarcophagus are pressed twice, an electric motor slides the case aside to give access to a set of steep stairs leading to a secret room in the basement. A control button beside the stairs closes the opening. The mummy case can be moved manually (STR 50). Up to six people can help move it. Moving it manually breaks the mechanism.

The Secret Room

The room is enclosed by foot-thick concrete on all sides and is essentially independent from the rest of the building, rather like a box within a larger box. The enclosed stairs are the only entrance.

There are several small, not well disguised connections. An electrical cable leads from the main fuse box. Hot and cold water pipes pass through, as well as a connection to the building's boiler for steam heat. There is also an air-intake pipe leading from the roof to the basement—it, coupled with an air-pump, circulates fresh air through the room. Any successful skill roll for Operate Heavy Machinery, Electrical Repair, or Mechanical Repair identifies the outside air intake pipe for the secret room if the rear of the building is studied—or identifies the utility connections cemented through the coal bin wall if the investigator is examining the basement from the inside. The keeper may always call for Spot Hiddens.

In this room Gavigan prepares and casts Mythos spells. The room contains the materials for casting them, dubious tomes detailing many spells, a comfortable study area, seating for small meetings, a three-day supply of tinned food and water, a revolver and a box of bullets, a couple of false passports, a bundle of used five-pound notes, candles and matches, changes of clothes, and similar emergency supplies.

ARTWORK: Natural to a man in Gavigan's line of work, there is a small gallery of art—ancient icons, statues, paintings—but this collection depicts various Mythos deities and servitors. The paintings are mainly on masonry and stucco-like surfaces carefully separated from the original walls. Over the decades, expeditions underwritten by the Foundation have brought them back to be appreciated and to stymie the lines of research which their continued presence might have instigated. Most are obviously Egyptian or proto-Sumerian; a successful Archaeology roll shows everything to be extremely old. A successful Cthulhu Mythos roll reveals that all the art is of the Mythos. The wall art is not magical, but in sum is grotesque enough to require a Sanity roll (0/1D4 SAN). The pieces depict byakhee, chthonians, ghouls, shantaks, sand dwellers, and fire vampires. If they meet such creatures later on, investigators recall that such creatures were depicted here.

THE BLOATED WOMAN: Several small wooden crates are stacked about the secret room. All but two are open and empty. The larger closed one is stenciled Ho Fong Imports, 15 Kaoyang Road, Shanghai, China, in English and Chinese. In smaller letters are the words "attention honourable Ho Fong." Within the crate is a corroded brass statue of Nyarlathotep in the awful Bloated Woman form. Sanity rolls must be attempted upon viewing it (0/1D6 SAN). The statue is SIZ 20 for lifting purposes. Proximity of three yards or less to this statue adds ten percentiles to the chance of success for the Contact Nyarlathotep spell.

THE BLUESTONE CTHULHU: the smaller wooden crate is stenciled Randolph Shipping Company, Port Darwin, Northern Territory, Dominion of Australia. In smaller letters are the words "Personal to Mr. Randolph." Within the crate is a 16-inch-high representation of a fat humanoid figure whose evil-looking head is fringed by tentacles. Previous experience or a successful Occult or Cthulhu Mythos roll identifies the form as that of Cthulhu. If the small statue is touched, the investigator feels an odd tingle pass through his arms and torso. Unless the point becomes significant, the keeper should not inform the player that his investigator's magic points have just increased by ten. These extra magic points will stay for 24 hours and then disappear, unless spent before then.

THE BOOKCASE: Within the fine walnut case are several glass-protected shelves of books and scrolls. Quickly recognizable are volumes in German, French, Russian, Latin, and Spanish. Two are in English. Some are mere insane glosses praising various gods or talking about the most abstruse theological questions, such as how many non-believers the Dark God will eat in his first mouthful. There are a few useful Mythos tomes: the *G'harne Fragments*, *Book of Dyzan*, and the *Liber Ivonis*, all as per the *Call of Cthulhu* rules. The keeper may have the investigators discover whatever additional tomes he or she finds pertinent. A passing comment in the Fragments reveals that Nyarlathotep is the god of the Bloody Tongue. If this is a surprise to the investigators, consider a small Sanity charge for the information.

There are fifteen scrolls, all very old. Ten are poems of praise to Nyarlathotep which are used in cult rituals; three in Arabic, four in Latin, two in Medieval French, and one in Old English. The remaining five scrolls contain one spell each:

■ Summon Byakhee (Egyptian hieroglyphs)

■ Summon Hunting Horror of Nyarlathotep (Egyptian hieroglyphs)

■ Bind Dimensional Shambler (Arabic)

■ Dread Curse of Azathoth (Arabic)

■ Send Dreams (Arabic). A bowl made of "copper from above" is needed for this spell, such as the burnished copper bowl found in Mukunga's alcove at Ju-Ju House in New York. Gavigan does not own such a bowl.

Reading each scroll costs 1/1D6 SAN. Naturally the reader must understand the language of the scroll.

SMALL ORNATE CHEST: it is fashioned of carved sandalwood, and inlaid with silver depictions of dimensional shamblers. In the box are two silver daggers, already enchanted and usable for the Summon Dimensional Shambler spell. On the shelf with this is an eldritch jumble of dried bat-wings, pickled toad-eyes, wyvern claws, and so on.

SMALL STONE JAR: it contains five applications of the Powder of Ibn Ghazi, and rests next to the small ornate chest.

A Serpent in Soho

Jackson Elias noticed the lead — he was lucky not to have followed up on it!
In retracing his steps, the investigators expose themselves
to a cold intelligence of dangerous strength.

This adventure is not part of the overall plot of *Masks of Nyarlathotep*, though it easily could be integrated. As in the "Monster of Derbyshire" later in this chapter, this adventure is intended as a red herring, to keep the investigators (and the players) guessing. A campaign exclusively concerned with cults and evil gods will be too predictable to satisfy anyone. This adventure can be played in any of the campaign locations by ignoring the news story handout and changing the family names and backgrounds.

ITEM. A news story from *The* (London) *Scoop*. (*Nyarlathotep Papers #25*)

Relevance of the Information: establishes Shipley's connection with the Mythos, but draws the investigators into perilous proximity with Miles Shipley's mother, now a serpent man.

Along with the accompanying story, *The Scoop* also printed a reproduction of a lurid monster sizing up an unfortunate damsel, but the transfer to newsprint drained the reproduction of any sanity-shaking impact. None of the investigators recognizes either the monster or the lady. No Sanity roll is needed after viewing the photo.

Both photo and story were prompted by a small, unsuccessful show which Shipley gave for his work. The artist's home address is on file: 6 Holbein Mews.

The story of Miles Shipley has nothing to do with Nyarlathotep's machinations. It is a chilling footnote to the Cthulhu Mythos. In 1923, Shipley met a stranger in the Rose & Crown pub. This man swore that he could show Shipley scenes to paint which no artist before had ever captured. Since the stranger was a high sorcerer of the serpent people, he was as good as his word.

Using hypnosis and doses of the Plutonian drug, he sent Shipley's consciousness back in time to the era when the serpent people were powerful. Shipley saw their basalt cities, visited their temples, watched their blood rites, and witnessed their gory wars. As he feverishly painted picture after picture of the hellish sights, Shipley's sanity slipped away, even as his paintings grew in power and impact.

In return for such a gift, the high sorcerer (Ssathasaa in his own sibilant speech) wanted a safe place in which to live and eat a hearty meal or two each week. Miles' home became the place, and human flesh would make up the meals. Miles' aged mother, Bertha Shipley, comprised the first meal. Miles killed her, and Ssathasaa ate her and took her form—a kindly old woman of about age 70. It is as her that Ssathasaa lives at present.

Miles is now incurably insane and addicted to the Plutonian drug. He rarely leaves his house, except to hunt down meals for his muse. These meals have been Bertha's old friends, or prostitutes with whom Miles first sleeps and then murders. He is careful not to be noticed with these unfortunate victims. Since his paintings are his entire life, he talks only about them—or sizes up someone as a possible meal for Ssathasaa.

The House in Holbein Mews

The Shipley home is a two-story brick building in need of repair. Every window is locked shut and tightly curtained. There are front and rear entrances (STR 35); interior doors are uniformly STR 15. Front and rear windows are barred (STR 30 each).

Breaking and Entering

A skylight with a handle can be seen at the top of the house from the street; flanking buildings are deserted and offer easy access to the Shipley house roof. Of normal glass and easy to break through, the skylight can be lifted up, but is padlocked and chained from within. Because of the chain, the skylight frame can be lifted only a fraction of an inch—not enough room to pick the padlock or to cut the chain. Smart investigators brought glass cutters and suction cups. There is a 50% chance that Shipley is painting in the garret. If the investigators break the glass, make Listen rolls for Ssathasaa and Shipley to hear the noise. Subtract ten percentiles if they are upstairs, and subtract twenty percentiles if they are on the ground floor. They hear nothing if both are in the basement.

It is impossible to break in through the doors or windows without making racket enough to warn Ssathasaa, and Shipley if he is not painting.

Ssathasaa suns in the garden 15% of the time, and enjoys laying there day or night if just after a meal. But check the garden only if the investigators try to enter through the back on a sunny day.

Knocking at the Door

Ssathasaa always answers the door, hiding any suspicious materials and coming to the door in Bertha Shipley's guise. He carries a knitting basket—he wields a deadly knitting needle. If the investigators convince him that they want to buy a painting, and can show cash, then they will get in, for the pair

MILES SHIPLEY

survive with this money and that which they take from their weekly victims. Depending on the story, the investigators may need successful Credit Rating or Fast Talk rolls to convince Ssathasaa—and (perhaps with reduced chances) to convince Shipley, who has become acutely paranoid.

Aleister Crowley, the infamous occultist, has been a customer, as have several members of the Bloomsbury set (though these latter would never mention such art to their friends).

Gaining entry, the investigators will be led to the garret to inspect the paintings. Both Shipley and Ssathasaa accompany them. Shipley is egotistical about his own paintings, and loves

Nyarlathotep Papers #25

Shocking Canvases Bring Recognition

Local Artist's Monstrous Scenes Mock "Surrealists"

NOW COLLECTORS CAN BUY savage scenes which rival or surpass the worst nightmares of the Great War, but which are far more exotic than that grim business.

London artist Mr. Miles Shipley's work is being sought out by collectors, who have paid up to £300 for individual paintings.

This correspondent has seen dozens of the works of artist Miles Shipley, and finds them repulsive beyond belief. Maidens ravished, monsters ripping out a man's innards, shadowy grotesque landscapes, and faces grimacing in horror represent only a fraction of Shipley's work.

Withal their repellent content, these works are conceived and executed with uncanny verisimilitude, almost as though the artist had worked from photographs of alien places surely never on this Earth!

The artist reportedly is in contact with "other dimensions" in which powerful beings exist, and says he merely renders visible his visions.

Mr. Shipley is a working-class man without formal artistic training, who has nonetheless made good where thousands have failed.

Art critics say that Shipley provides an English answer to the Continental artistic movement of "surrealism," whose controversial practicioners have still to convince John Bull that the way in which a thing is painted is more important than what is painted.

A tip of the hat to Miles Shipley for exposing those frauds!

—*THE SCOOP*

praise. No Psychology roll is needed to understand that he is mad. His trembling body and screeching voice betray him. Unless they somehow have alerted Ssathasaa, they will not be shown The Painting in the Closet (see a little further below).

After they have purchased a painting (£75+1D50), or state that nothing quite pleases them, the investigators are shown out. As they walk away, a successful Idea Roll suggests that the Shipley house smelled like the reptile house at the zoo.

Watching the Shipley House

If the investigators stake out the Shipley house, there is a 20% chance that night for Shipley to leave and bring back a prostitute. This chance increases by ten percentiles each succeeding night until Miles actually does go on his merciless errand. When he returns, he and his companion enter through the back garden; to see them, investigators must be lurking on both sides of the house.

A successful Spot Hidden from Shipley notices the stake-out. Shipley pays off his date and alerts Ssathasaa, who decides what to do. Investigators always make good meals.

The Garret

It is a bare room with sloping ceilings. Dangling kerosene lamps light it. Beneath the skylight (painted black, since Shipley can no longer stand natural light) is an easel. The canvas on it bears a few pencil sketches toward a new work. A table to the left holds brushes, paints, palettes, etc. The door leading downstairs is always locked from the outside; Shipley carries the key. It can be unlocked from the inside the room without a key.

Against the walls lean finished paintings. Play fair: tell the players that every painting is hard to look at because of its insane subject matter, but keep the method of determining SAN loss secret until they have finished any inspection. If the investigators are cautious, none of them should not take a disastrous Sanity loss. There are four tiers of finished canvases ranked along one wall. Each tier contains 1D4+3 paintings. Determine and record the actual number of paintings in each tier. Though of various dimensions, all the canvases are gruesome and weird. Seen close up, in malevolent color and true size, each costs the viewer 0/1D3 SAN. Be fiendish: allow the investigators to inspect the mind-shattering canvases at their leisure and absorb the unspeakable images, then count up the number of paintings viewed by each, and have each player make the appropriate number of Sanity rolls after the investigators have finished viewing.

Of particular interest to the investigators is a painting which shows the Mountain of the Black Wind in Kenya, over which rises the monstrous form of Nyarlathotep in his Bloody Tongue aspect. Near a temple-like building, tiny human figures lift their hands imploringly toward the god. Each figure wears the headpiece of the cult of the Bloody Tongue. The painting looks like Africa, and the investigators will recognize the headpieces if they have seen them before. Miles beheld this scene from a time hundreds of years ago, while under the influence of the Plutonian drug.

The Painting in the Closet

In the north wall of the garret is a padlocked closet, to which Shipley has the key. The door is STR 15, and the hinges are on the outside of the door as normal with all closets. Shipley never willingly opens this door. Within are an easel and a canvas covered by a sheet. The painting on the canvas is Shipley's masterpiece, showing a swampy area infested with serpents. A small island in the center holds a stone altar. If the painting is adequately lighted, the images quickly appear to become three-dimensional. In the space of one minute the waters of the swamp start to ripple, the serpents wiggle, and the altar glows. If viewers look away when the effect begins, and do not look back, they will be safe.

If viewers continue to look at the painting, each is then subject to a POW vs. POW match on the Resistance Table. The attacking Power is 10, plus one point for every minute that the painting is studied after it becomes three-dimensional. After one minute of study of the 3D images, for instance, the Resistance Table match would rise to POW 11. Any investigator overcome by the attack finds himself in the painting, standing beside the stone altar: he or she has been transported back in time to an ancient bastion of the serpent people. The transported investigator loses 4/1D20+4 Sanity points.

Other investigators viewing the transportation see their comrade fade from the room and reappear in the painting. Each witness to a transportation loses 0/1D8 SAN. If the transportee remains in the picture's field, the other investigators can see him or her, and what next happens to their friend. If they continue to watch, they'll soon be transported there as well.

The investigator in the painting cannot see back into the garret. There is no way back. The painting has become the world, and all about him stretch the swamps and skies of a long-vanished Earth. It is now the era of the dinosaurs. After an investigator is sent through the picture, there is a 50% chance every thirty minutes that 1D8 serpent people emerge from the waters at the island's edge. If the transported investigator moves off the island (swimming 50 feet through water infested with venomous serpents), his or her player must successfully roll 1D6 dodge rolls or the investigator is bitten and dies. If he or she makes it to the boggy shore, the chance of the serpent people showing up remains the same. Victims of the painting are probably lost for good, perhaps killed by the serpent people as sacrifices.

The painting in the closet can serve as several adventures in itself, and keepers should feel free to expand upon the serpent realm. The best scenario involves the investigators finding a gateway back to their time, but in an inconvenient place.

The Painting in the Closet is magical, but it is only canvas and oil paint on stretchers. It can be destroyed just as any canvas might be. If it is destroyed, the gate to the Serpent Realm is also destroyed. Destroying the painting after the fact in no way affects the fate of previous victims. Once they understand the one-way properties of the painting, the investigators may even find it a useful weapon. Ssathasaa commissioned the painting specifically to send enemies to his people as sacrifices—and as an escape route should he need it. The magic involved took two years to complete.

Ssathasaa will use the painting against the investigators if he perceives them to be a threat.

Upstairs

The four rooms and their scant furnishings are perfectly ordinary. Nothing is of interest on this floor unless the keeper desires it. No door here is ever locked.

The Ground Floor

The rear door leads to a small garden enclosed by a nine-foot-high brick wall of recent construction. There is a kitchen, a short hall with a bedroom off of it, and a parlor. A door in the kitchen leads to the basement, and that door is always locked. One room, the bedroom, is of significance.

The door to the bedroom is locked 80% of the time. Shipley has the key. In the bedroom closet, hidden behind a hatbox on the top shelf, is a small lacquered box containing a syringe and a small vial filled with ten doses of the Plutonian drug. If taken without intention, such as a hypnotic suggestion to go to a particular era, the drug randomly sends back the user's mind through time, perhaps to a time of the Hounds of Tindalos, while the user's body drops senselessly to the floor. The drug is a dull green. The syringe has been used so often that the proper dosage is represented on it by a dull green residue within the tube. The needle is dull and painful to Shipley, but he persists. One dose lasts 1D3 hours; larger doses last proportionately longer. There is no way to know what the drug does unless one is told or already understands its effects. Ssathasaa makes the drug from rare, expensive ingredients.

The Basement

This large room is cluttered with ordinary junk. The boxes and broken chairs are so stacked that a clear path leads to the south wall of the basement, behind which is a secret room. The wall opens if anyone presses hard at its center; a successful Spot Hidden notices the door seam.

Inside, many mystic symbols are inscribed on the walls of the small room. Shelves cover one wall, holding jars filled with strange substances used in magic and in making the Plutonian drug. If investigators know how, there are enough Plutonian drug ingredients here to make two gallons of the stuff. There are also grimoires and tomes in many tongues, and they hold spell-casting information; none are in English; most are in serpent tongue. No specific Cthulhu Mythos spells exist in them. At the keeper's option, they may contain more spells than those presently listed for Ssathasaa.

Against another wall is a deep stone tub with a stone lid. In it rest butchered leftovers from Ssathasaa's latest meal. Uncovering the severed head of the anonymous woman costs 1/1D6 SAN. The smell of the snake pit is strong in this room.

About Ssathasaa

The serpent priest wants to remain undetected, wants to keep Shipley painting scenes from the Serpent Realm, and wants to create a gate through which his folk can enter the future. If the investigators pop up and start asking questions, he feigns the ignorance of a gentle old woman and tells them to be off, naturally knowing nothing of what the investigators want to know—the literal truth, in fact.

Ssathasaa has but two forms. When he deals with humans or while he suns himself in the garden, he takes the form of Bertha Shipley. In the house and in his secret basement room, he goes about as a serpent man—scales, claws, a long crocodilian snout, and a fat reptilian tail.

He can switch from human form to serpent man form in about 20 seconds; only if he is surprised will the investigators detect his actual monstrous nature.

For him to appear as Bertha Shipley involves a ritual lasting several minutes. If Ssathasaa is damaged while in human form, the shock of the hit reverts him to his original form—he then will attack all witnesses. In human form, his characteristics appear to be those parenthesized in the accompanying statistics, but his actual physical characteristics, skills, knowledge, and self-identity always remain those of Ssathasaa.

His shadow, always that of a serpent person, betrays his true nature. Consequently he never goes abroad in daylight and rarely enters brightly lit places. Though they are cold, he loves the London fogs, for they dispel precise shadows. The keeper may allow players a Luck roll each; if successful, the investigator glimpses Ssathasaa's shadow. If the sorcerer believes that the investigators know of his existence, he will try to destroy them.

SSATHASAA, semi-immortal, High Priest of the Serpent People (a.ka. BERTHA SHIPLEY of Soho, and looks about age 70)

STR 10 (04)	CON 11 (08)	SIZ 09 (08)	INT 19 (09)	POW 35 (09)
DEX 17 (05)	APP n/a (09)	EDU 30 (06)	SAN 0	HP 10 (08)

Damage Bonus: +0 (-1D6)

Weapons: Knitting Needle 75%, damage 1D3 (can impale)
Bite 35%, damage 1D8 + poison POT 11

Armor: 1-point scales

Spells: Call Azathoth, Call Hastur, Call Yog-Sothoth, Contact Yig, Consume Likeness, Deflect Harm, Dust of Suleiman, Mesmerize, Mindblast, Power Drain, Voorish Sign.

Skills: Arabic 50%, Bargain 65%, Brew Plutonian Drug 95%, Conceal 75%, Cthulhu Mythos 45%, Dodge 95%, English 95%, Hide 75%, Jump 65%, Knit 05%, Natural History 90%, Occult 95%, Serpent Tongue 95%, Sneak 85%, Swim 70%, Throw 55%, Track 60%.

MILES SHIPLEY, age 37, Insane London Painter

STR 13	CON 14	SIZ 12	INT 13	POW 10
DEX 15	APP 06	EDU 10		SAN 0	HP 13

Damage Bonus: +1D4.

Weapons: Meat Cleaver 65%, damage 1D6+1+1D4
Butcher Knife 45%, damage 1D6+1D4
Fist/Punch 35%, damage 1D3+1D4

Skills: Anatomy 65%, Cthulhu Mythos 15%, Occult 35%, Paint Picture 85%, Pen-and-Ink 65%, Sketch 80%, Serpent Tongue 20%.

THE DERBYSHIRE MONSTER

Gruesome monsters and horrible screams haunt a once-cheerful English country village.
The authorities are baffled. Should the investigators take a hand,
make new allies, and put matters right, or run from the terrors of the night?

If *Call of Cthulhu* players are told that their investigators face merely a werewolf, probably collective sighs of relief ripple around the room—werewolves, though deadly enough, are small potatoes compared to Mighty Cthulhu and his monstrous minions. To keep up the tension and to forestall the effective preparations which can easily eliminate werewolves, strive to be vague enough to convince the players that the events might be Mythos-related. This adventure frequently talks about monsters or beasts, not werewolves, as a way to remind keepers of this point. The villagers can aid the mood: eyewitnesses are seldom reliable, and they might say that they saw a thing with wings, or some shambling hulk as opposed to the wolf-that-walks-as-a-man.

Emphasize that the bodies of victims were "torn to shreds", and try to ignore the pathologist report which merely cites lacerations and bites from a large animal. Finally, though he connects to vital information, the vicar of Lesser-Edale can also be a red herring: this man spends his nights poring over presumably ancient volumes of lore, and don't forget that he is corresponding secretary for the Derwent Valley Order of the Golden Druid. The word "druid" should be enough to make any investigator twitch.

Reaching Lesser-Edale

Via the Midland railway, Derby (say *Darby*) lies some 130 miles north of London. Beside Derby flows the river Derwent. To the north of Derby is the valley of the Derwent, within which the events of this adventure take place. Investigators may entrain for Derby from London's St. Pancras station, about three quarters of a mile north of the British Museum and the Penhew Foundation offices. The station is adjacent to Kings Cross, near Euston.

Lesser-Edale can be reached from Derby via motor omnibus leaving Derby at 7:52 a.m., 2:12 p.m., and 9:40 p.m., or by hired car. Hikers from Derby need nearly six hours to arrive in Lesser-Edale.

The valley of the Derwent is one of the most beautiful regions in England, and its upper reaches frequently are compared to the Lakes district. The day that the investigators arrive, they find the limestone cliffs and outcrops, the lovely wooded vales, and the splendid waterfalls refreshing after the dank mornings and dangers of London. The countryside is immaculately green, and the fences well-tended. This afternoon has turned showery. Many locals have gathered in the pub.

ITEM. Clipping from *The Scoop*, summarizing the recent murders in and around Lesser-Edale (*Nyarlathotep Papers #26*).

Relevance of the Information: lists who was murdered, and names possible witnesses to these murders.

Lesser-Edale

The village of Lesser-Edale is as beautiful as its setting. There are about thirty homes in the village (including two which still have thatch for roofing), the Laughing Horse pub, the Pitchlock Modern Mercantile store, a small modern church (beside the foundations of the Elizabethan-era church unfortunately burnt in 1906), and a veterinary clinic serving the upper valley and adjacent vales. Bus service from Lesser-Edale to Derby is at 6:35 a.m., 9:20 a.m., and 4:00 p.m.

All statistics for the inhabitants of Lesser-Edale are found at the end of this short adventure.

CONSTABLE TUMWELL

The atmosphere in the Laughing Horse is friendly and curious, for not many visitors from the United States come this way. Constable Tumwell stops by while the investigators are there. He is a steadfast fellow, though not all that competent. His mustaches have been dampened a bit by the downpour. He sloughs off the murders as done by a wild dog, which he strongly believes he killed with his shotgun. "Gone off to die in the hills. We ha'nt been troubled since, thank God." Two of his friends tease him, implying that he wasn't nearly so sure when the big-city detectives came out to study the killings, nor when the inquest was held.

A general discussion ensues if the investigators are willing to pay for drinks all around; if not, Fast Talk or Oratory skills might keep the villagers talking. Most fear that the monster will return, and affirm that they still hear howls at the full moon. Full moon, they remind the investigators, is just one night away. One man swears he caught a glimpse of the thing—"No dog be a-walkin' round on his back paws, Hubert," he says to the constable, "and no dog e'er ripped bone fra bone in such a way as done to poor Lydia." Hubert Tumwell has little reply to this, and a successful Psychology roll shows that his concern for the truth has gotten confused with his concern for his job and reputation.

If the investigators decide to interview the families of the victims, their players must successfully make Persuade or Fast Talk rolls at half or less of their investigators' percentages—one investigator per family. Harold Short was a bachelor, and is still recovering at his brother's home in Norfolk, but eyewitnesses in the Osgood and Parkins families are available.

Edith Osgood says that her husband heard a noise in the barn and went out to investigate, taking his shotgun with him. A moment later she heard him fire, then scream. Peering out, she saw a hairy hunched-over form race away. It was as tall as a man, and ran howling into the woods. Her children cling to her skirts and say the same thing.

The horse-dealer John Parkins did not see the murder of his daughter. He found her body after coming home from the Laughing Horse. He is convinced that Lawrence Vane, son of Sir Frederick Vane, had something to do with it. A neighbor (Tom Corty, who has nothing to add to this testimony) saw Lawrence Vane near the Parkins house the night of the murder. Corty said that young Vane looked upset, and was hurrying from the direction of the Parkins house. Tumwell and his superiors questioned Lawrence, and declared him innocent of involvement, but Parkins feels the authorities were protecting the Vane family from scandal. Bitterly he

Nyarlathotep Papers #26

POLICE BAFFLED BY MONSTROUS MURDERS!

Inhuman Killer Shot But Still Alive?

VALLEY OF THE DERWENT RESIDENTS, shocked several months ago by two murders and a serious assault on a third victim, are still without explanation or perpetrator of the dreadful attacks.

At that time, Lesser-Edale farmer George Osgood and resident Miss Lydia Perkins were torn to shreds in apparently-unrelated murders on consecutive nights. On the third night, wheelwright Harold Short was nearly killed but managed to drive off a grisly creature which he swore to be man-like but not human.

Constable Tumwell, also of Lesser-Edale, believes that he shot and killed the beast on the night Mr Short was attacked. Other residents of the region have claimed to have seen the thing since.

Reportedly, Lesser-Edale endures to this hour the bizarre wailings of the beast on nights near the full moon.

Readers of *The Scoop* are reminded of their esteemed journal's long-standing Danger Protocols, and are advised that the picturesque cloughs surrounding The Peak have been declared by *The Scoop* to be a Zone of High Danger!

Residents of the Midlands are advised to remain indoors at night, and to report all mysterious happenings to the police and to *The Scoop*.

—*THE SCOOP*

declares that the Labour party must correct such class injustice, and spends several minutes lecturing the investigators about political power and an oppressive ruling class. A successful Psychology roll suggests that Parkins has been somewhat unhinged by the loss of his daughter.

The Vicar, the Right Reverend Jeremy Stratton, also caught a glimpse of the thing, but will be difficult to question for the reasons discussed below.

The Curse of the Vanes

Sir Arthur Vane is a country gentleman, 67 years old and very proud. His handsome son Lawrence is 23, and also proud. Having attended Oxford, Lawrence has only recently returned. Since the monster struck soon after Lawrence came back, some villagers agree with Parkins that Lawrence is the criminal. But Eloise, Lawrence's sister, is actually to blame. A soft-spoken 21-year-old, she has unknowingly inherited the curse of the Vanes, and now turns into a werewolf on the nights of the full moon.

The story passed down for generations of Vanes is that Lady Evangeline Vane had a young witch burnt at the stake. For the death of her daughter, the mother of the dead girl put the Mark of the Beast on all the daughters of the Vanes. For centuries since then, when a blood-daughter of the Vanes reached the age of 21 she became a werewolf. The family kept the secret, locking up women during the full moon or slaying outright any female babies born to Vane women. Then, for four generations, no Vane daughters were born, and the curse was forgotten. Now the evil is abroad once more. Sir Arthur has pieced together enough of the family records to understand something of what is happening, and has shown this information to Lawrence. Tom Corty spotted Lawrence when the brave young man was searching for his sister.

The Vanes have resided in the valley for nearly seven centuries. They were titled in the reign of Charles II as a reward for Wellington Vane's skillful handling of certain royal indiscretions. The family lives in the keep of a medieval castle otherwise fallen or in bad repair. A few servants, all old and loyal, also live in the keep. They know that something odd happened after Eloise Vane's 21st birthday, but out of love and respect for Sir Arthur Vane they have kept silent.

Only Sir Arthur and Lawrence know that Eloise is a werewolf. They lock her away in the castle dungeon on the three nights of the full moon. It is Eloise's howls from the depths of the castle dungeon that the villagers hear. Sir Arthur Vane will allow no inquiry by outsiders. It is family business. An emissary from the King might move him, but little less than that. Investigators can get Lawrence's attention through successful Credit Rating or Persuade rolls.

The Vanes have kept to their castle since the murders. There is a 25% chance that Lawrence will appear in the pub while the investigators are in town—roll each day. He comes into the village to keep up appearances and thereby suggest to the residents that everything is all right with the Vanes. A sophisticate, he is contemptuous of the local gossip, though

What's in a Vane?

Sharp-eyed keepers no doubt notice that the Vane family in this adventure shares a name with Abner Vane Carel, the felon who was sent to the American colonies in 1714, and whose family later became the rich and powerful Carlyles of Massachusetts and New York. Abner was the illegitimate son of Sir Joshua Vane, a man of otherwise severe probity. Roger Carlyle is a cousin, many times removed, to the present-day Vanes. This remarkable coincidence has absolutely no significance in the present scenario or in the campaign, though keepers should make use of it as they wish, perhaps as another red herring.

Eloise's sudden ruin has softened his pride. If he talks to the investigators, he assures them that the villagers are stupid, that the constable knows his business, and that the Vanes have nothing to hide. A successful Psychology roll shows that Lawrence is keeping something back.

A Visit to Castle Plum

To talk at length to any of the Vanes, the investigators must enter Castle Plum, two hundred feet up on a stone bluff above the town. A winding road leads from the town to the castle entrance. A longer road up a nearby vale also leads to the top of the bluff, somewhat further back, and from there it is a short walk to the tumbled walls and towers of the ancient fortress.

SIR ARTHUR VANE

Intelligent investigators get a villager to introduce them to the Vanes, or wangle an invitation from Lawrence, or leave their cards and a message with the servants, or contrive some other way to preserve decorum while getting what they want. In a few days or a week, they'll be able to talk with one or more Vanes.

LAWRENCE VANE

If they are stupid, the investigators will rush up to the castle like cowboys, and bang endlessly on the great door of the main hall (immobile since the day that Charles I was hung, to this day held to have been a portent from God). After some minutes a servant will approach from the side of the hall, and lead the investigators to the door commonly used for the last 270 years. There either Lawrence or Sir Arthur will austerely question them, decide that such noisy people are not to be trusted, and dismiss them. No investigator questions will be answered.

If the investigators manage to prove their courage, discretion, and intelligence to the Vanes, Lawrence will seize upon the chance to explain the true facts of the situation in return for investigator aid. Lawrence is in as desperate position as his sister, for in peril are both his present family and any family he might father in the future.

Eloise Vane remains at all times within the castle walls. She is a sweet girl, soft-spoken and thoughtful, but terribly distracted. A successful Psychology roll shows that she suffers greatly. She does not know that she is a werewolf, but she does know she has evil dreams every month, terrible dreams in which she witnesses ghastly happenings, though later events are vague to her. Family members and servants watch her constantly, so the investigators must be ingenious in order to question her. She walks about the flower gardens on fair afternoons; if her chaperone can be distracted, the investigators can speak to her then.

ELOISE VANE

THE MAIN HALL

The fine wood paneling was cleaned and refinished just before the Great War, and several new high windows cut in, so that the beautiful hall has a lighter, more airy feel than it had originally. Nonetheless, the Vanes spend almost no time in it. If the investigators achieve an interview, it will be in chambers, or perhaps in the library, a lamentable Gothic wing added in the 19th century.

In past centuries the dungeon was a normal tool of ruling families. To find it, one merely follows the butler through a stout oak door (STR 60) to the wine cellar. In one wall is a locked iron door (STR 90); the key hangs high on a hook beside the door. There is no electricity in the basement, so candles, lanterns, or electric torches are needed. The wine cellar is suitably filled with dusty old bottles of exquisite claret, made in the old style to bloom slowly and to last fifty or more years.

A long flight of steps lead the investigators into the eerie silence of the warder's room and the torture chamber, where are another iron door (STR 90) and individual cells. Iron doors of that strength close each cell. In each cell are individual shackles and rings set into stone walls five feet thick. Some light filters in through the bars of ventilation windows set fourteen feet above. These bars are quite old, and weakened (STR 20) by exposure. If Eloise is held in a cell, it is the cell marked Eloise on the Castle Plum plan, strewn with clean straw in anticipation of her need.

A routine concerning Eloise has evolved. On the afternoon of the full moon, she is always drugged and then transported to her cell by her father and brother. The servants are restricted to their rooms at these times. When Eloise begins to bay, they are happy to stay there.

If and when the investigators learn enough, they may confront the Vanes or perhaps try to sneak into the castle, no doubt at the full moon. Perhaps they see father and son carry the unconscious Eloise to her cell. Sir Arthur and young Lawrence generally sit in the library with brandy and cigars to await the end of the nightly ordeal. Then they carry Eloise back to her bed. She becomes a werewolf at midnight and remains in that state until the moment of sunrise.

Eloise at Large

If the precautions fail, Eloise escapes her cell, to wander abroad in wolf form and search out victims. She attacks wandering investigators if they are out and accessible. Probably she will not enter a building, though she might smash through the glass and grab someone who stands next to a window.

As a werewolf, Eloise is a traditional half-human, half-wolfish monster. Only silver weapons or other silver projectiles can harm her. A heavy natural blow (ordinary fire from a point-blank shotgun) startles her and drives her off, though she will not be hurt. Harold Short, the wheelwright, drove her off by a smart blow from a silver candlestick (he was lucky—this usually will not be effective). Silver is available in the village, in coin and utensil form. The investigators must negotiate to get it, and find a way to transform the metal into effective weapons. The local blacksmith can melt down the metal and forge knives and spear tips of it, but he has no bullet molds, and he is sure to spread gossip about silver bullets. Gunsmiths in Derby, Sheffield, or Manchester can easily do the job.

If the investigators attempt to kill the werewolf, they will have to deal with Sir Arthur and with Lawrence Vane, both of whom wish Eloise to live, and have hopes of curing her condition. If Eloise is killed without witnesses about, then murder charges may be in order, since a dead werewolf

---

About Castle Plum

It is not true that Castle Plum is so called because it fell into the hands of Edward III "liketh an Plum" when its rebellious former baron neglected to secure the gates.

Originally the castle defended the important lead mines of the area, and lead in Latin is Plumbum. For more than five centuries the region shortened the castle's name to "plum". The mines are long since exhausted, but those cramped, convoluted, and easily collapsed tunnels and shafts remain. Some of the mines are adjacent to the dungeons of Castle Plum: when Eloise in wolf form howls in her unhappy prison, the villagers hear her cries because the winding tunnels carry her echoes beneath the town. But only the vicar of the town or some specialist in local history might guess this. The mine entrances have been bolted and buried for more than two centuries and the story is lost to the people.

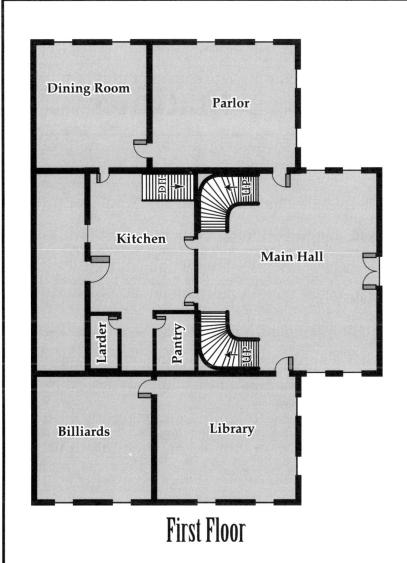

First Floor

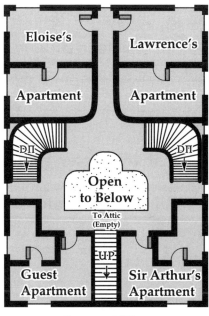

Second Floor

CASTLE PLUM

0' 10' 20'
FEET

Cellar

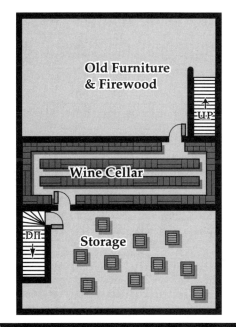

Dungeon

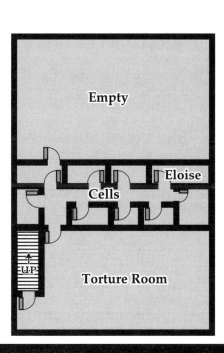

always makes a final transformation to return to its ground state. The slaughter of a young woman of good family cannot go unpunished.

ABOUT THE CURSE

The curse of the Vanes is clearly magical in origin. The effect of the curse is not transmitted by bite. Silver and fire will damage or kill this werewolf, but nothing else has more than momentary effect. Seeing a lycanthrope in bestial form costs 0/ 1D8 SAN. See the rulesbook for supplemental werewolf information.

The Vicar of Lesser-Edale

The Right Reverend Jeremy Stratton is a widower in his late sixties. He has been vicar of Lesser-Edale for thirty years.

REV. STRATTON

After the murder of the two victims, Stratton began to translate an old journal written by a long-dead vicar of the village. Some of the journal was in English but a portion was in classical Greek. That portion dealt with the Vane family curse, and Vicar Stratton has been translating it ever since. He is not competent in Greek, but can satisfactorily plod along and finish the work. He has gotten far enough to know that something strange happens to the Vane women after their 21st birthday, and he is smart enough to link this with the monster. He and Sir Arthur are good friends, and the vicar does not wish to ruin his friend's life, nor to fuel the village rumors concerning the Vanes. Stratton hopes to find a way to lift the curse, but when he finishes his translation, he'll know that the earlier vicar had no solution either.

In all of this he practices the utmost discretion. If the investigators can get the reverend to talk to them (successful Persuade roll only, half-normal chance of success), they will not learn about the journal, but a successful Psychology roll reveals that the reverend is keeping something from them. By spying upon him, the investigators might see the reverend working on his translation. If they want to steal it, the key to the desk drawer within which the journal is locked always rests in Stratton's pocket but the STR 5 drawer is easy to pry open.

The vicar, it is easy to learn, is corresponding secretary for the Derwent Valley Order of the Golden Druid, an association which the Reverend Stratton helped to form while up at Cambridge. The order is devoted to collecting information about and artifacts from pre-Roman Britain, and is absolutely above-board, though the investigators should be free to make up their own minds about this group. The order publishes a quarterly journal about spearheads, costumes, old customs, and such, and once yearly holds a midsummer-day gathering and picnic at some local ruin, if the landed proprietor grants permission.

Sarah Bright, an elderly lady who keeps house for the reverend, knows nothing about the journal, but she does know that the Reverend Stratton has been acting queerly since the murders. He has taken to locking himself in the rectory at night, where he stays for hours. He is also praying much more often than he once did. Lesser-Edale is so small that everyone else knows this too.

Statistics

HUBERT TUMWELL, age 43, Constable for Lesser-Edale

STR 12	CON 13	SIZ 10	INT 08	POW 06
DEX 10	APP 08	EDU 09	SAN 75	HP 12

Damage Bonus: +0.

Weapons: .303 Enfield Rifle 60%, damage 2D6+1
12-Gauge Shotgun 50%, damage 4D6/2D6 damage
Nightstick 40%, damage 1D6

Skills: Bargain 40%, Credit Rating 22%, Drive Automobile 20%, First Aid 60%, Law 25%, Police Practices 35%, Psychology 45%, Ride Bicycle 65%, Spot Hidden 50%, Track 20%.

REVEREND JEREMY STRATTON, age 67, Vicar of Lesser-Edale

STR 07	CON 10	SIZ 08	INT 14	POW 08
DEX 07	APP 09	EDU 17	SAN 50	HP 09

Damage Bonus: -1D4.

Weapon: none.

Skills: Accounting 15%, Anglican Theology 75%, Archaeology 15%, Bargain 35%, Druidic Ritual 20%, First Aid 60%, Greek 11%, History 25%, How Things Were at Cambridge 85%, Latin 15%, Law 15%, Library Use 35%, Medicine 25%, Persuade 25%, Preach Sermon 35%, Psychology 30%, Sing 15%.

AVERAGE TOWNSFOLK

	1*	2	3	4	5	6	7	8
STR	12	09	08	14	13	10	13	15
CON	10	08	09	12	15	12	12	18
SIZ	11	13	14	10	11	12	11	09
APP	13	12	13	09	07	11	10	13
INT	14	09	11	12	09	10	14	07
POW	12	06	12	17	13	10	12	11
EDU	08	09	11	10	05	06	03	07
DEX	16	15	13	12	11	10	08	08
HP	11	11	12	11	13	12	12	14
SAN	60	55	50	70	35	40	55	15

Damage Bonus: +0.

Weapons: Torch 15%, damage 1D6 (10% chance for additional 1D10 damage from fire)
* *Number One has a 20-Gauge Shotgun 25%, 2D6/1D6 damage.*

Skills: Bargain 40%, Climb 50%, Credit Rating 30%, Electrical Repair 10%, Fast Talk 20%, First Aid 30%, Hide 25%, Jump 35%, Listen 40%, Mechanical Repair 40%, Natural History 35%, Operate Heavy Machinery 15%, Psychology 15%, Ride 25%, Sing 10%, Sneak 25%, Spot Hidden 45%, Swim 25%, Throw 35%, Track 20%.

LAWRENCE ARTHUR PONSONBY VANE, age 23, Firstborn Son and Heir

STR 10	CON 16	SIZ 14	INT 16	POW 10
DEX 15	APP 10	EDU 16	SAN 55	HP 15

Damage Bonus: +0.

Weapons*: 12-Gauge Shotgun 50%, damage 4D6/2D6/1D6
Fencing Foil 50%, damage 1D6 (with tip removed)
Fist/Punch 60%, damage 1D3

* *Lawrence will fight to protect his sister; but otherwise goes
unarmed.*

Skills: Accounting 50%, Bargain 15%, Credit Rating 60%, Drive
Automobile 70%, Family History 70%, Fast Talk 15%, French
75%, Greek 35%, History 35%, Law 50%, Library Use 40%,
Listen 55%, Persuade 55%, Psychology 20%, Ride 55%, Spot
Hidden 35%, Track 25%.

**SIR ARTHUR GORDON FITZHUGH VANE, age 67, Knight of the
Realm**

STR 06	CON 08	SIZ 11	INT 15	POW 07
DEX 10	APP 12	EDU 16	SAN 35	HP 10

Damage Bonus: +0.

Weapon*: 20-Gauge Shotgun 25%, damage 2D6/1D6

* *Sir Arthur uses his weapon for grouse hunting. He will fight
only to protect his children.*

Skills: Accounting 60%, Bargain 30%, Credit Rating 90%, Fast
Talk 20%, Greek 10%, History 55%, Latin 37%, Law 65%,
Library Use 25%, Natural History 35%, Occult 15%, Persuade
40%, Psychology 25%.

**ELOISE GWENDOLAK ELDREDA VANE, age 21, Heiress to the
Curse of the Vanes**

STR 05	CON 06	SIZ 07	INT 12	POW 10
DEX 09	APP 13	EDU 12	SAN 20*	HP 07

Damage Bonus: -1D4.

Weapon: none.

Skills: Art (Song) 45%, Credit Rating 65%, First Aid 30%,
French 50%, Library Use 40%, Listen 35%, Natural History 55%,
Psychology 45%, Ride Horse 55%.

* *when Eloise's Sanity reaches zero, she understands that she is a
werewolf, and revels in the feeling.*

ELOISE in Werewolf Form

STR 25	CON 14	SIZ 12	INT 05	POW 12
DEX 16	APP 01	EDU 0	SAN 0	HP 13
MOV 12				

Damage Bonus: +1D6.

Weapon: Bite 45%, damage 1D8
Claw 35%, damage 1D3+1D6

Armor: 1-point skin plus 1 HP regeneration per round.

Skills: Listen 70%, Scent 65%, Spot Hidden 50%.

*Eloise kills without compunction in this form. A good look at her
beast-form shows it is female.*

SLAUGHTER IN SOHO

*After talking with the police, the investigators may choose a night
on the town for a little relaxation. If they tip their hand to the wrong man,
they'll need more than relaxation.*

This episode continues the line of clues and evidence which began with the interview of Edward Gavigan at the Penhew Foundation. Like the other London adventures, several encounters in this episode can be fatal.

Inspector Barrington

If the investigators talked with Jonah Kensington, he referred London-bound investigators to Inspector James Barrington of Scotland Yard. If the investigators bypassed Joshua Kensington and arrived in London anyway, the first thing that they see is a newsboy hawking *The Scoop*, flashing the front-page headline of the article below, and shouting, "Egyptian murders again!" at the top of his lungs. If the investigators visit Mahoney at *The Scoop*, he also supplies Barrington's name, and says that Elias interviewed Barrington.

Inspector Barrington is a methodical man in his early fifties. He has been investigating the series of murders for nearly a year. His predecessor on the case disappeared mysteriously and never has been found; Barrington assumes that he was assassinated, and dearly wants to apprehend the murder or murderers. The Egyptian murders—so called because

seventeen of the dead were native to Egypt—are a sore spot with the Inspector. Mentioning the murders automatically gets an interview with him.

Barrington wants to know the investigators' purposes in London, and warns them about illegalities committed through

JAMES BARRINGTON

excessive zeal. This experienced professional is not likely to reveal directly anything about his own clues, though the investigators may find later on that he actually gave them quite a bit of data if they impressed him as fresh, responsible bloodhounds useful to his ongoing chase. He will admit that Elias talked to him briefly. See the nearby box "Leads Possessed by Inspector Barrington" for other possible gleanings from the Inspector.

The Inspector also tries to learn everything that the investigators know. If they babble about horrid monsters and gods beyond space and time, he humors them but never thinks of them as desirable allies.

Find statistics for the Inspector and for a clutch of his bobbies on p. 71.

Leads Possessed by Inspector Barrington

(1) Jackson Elias told him that the murders were ritual killings by the Brotherhood of the Black Pharaoh, an Egyptian death cult. Barrington interviewed Edward Gavigan of the Penhew Foundation about this; Gavigan denied that the cult has any modern-day equivalent or that the method of murder imitated those of the ancient cult. Gavigan implied that Elias was a sensation-seeking profiteer.

(2) A favorite Egyptian nightspot in London is the Blue Pyramid Club, in Soho. Many of those who were mur-

dered had frequented the club, but police stake-outs learned nothing.

(3) Before dying, one victim reportedly cried out "Hotep!", an ancient Egyptian word meaning "rest" or "peace", according to Edward Gavigan.

(4) A spice dealer, Tewfik al-Sayed, was interviewed. He had once guided an Egyptian expedition for the Penhew Foundation. Tewfik also denied that the Brotherhood of the Black Pharaoh still existed. A police tail learned nothing.

ITEM. News clipping from *The Scoop* (*Nyarlathotep Papers #27*).

Relevance of the Information: establishes that serial killings are occurring in London, and suggests that the man to contact is Inspector Barrington of Scotland Yard. Barrington can supply connections to Egypt, Jackson Elias, and the Penhew Foundation.

The Blue Pyramid

The club is in Soho. It features belly dancers, Egyptian food, and Egyptian singers. Abdul Nawisha, a fat, taciturn man, owns the place. He is not a cultist, but he knows of the cult and will not cross it in any way. If the investigators try to question him, he has his bouncers throw them out. But he is a busy man, and the club is packed with gesticulating, shouting customers; it takes half an hour before Nawisha can see the investigators.

Nyarlathotep Papers #27

SLAUGHTER CONTINUES!

Scoop Offers Reward!

AN UNIDENTIFIED FOREIGNER was found floating in the Thames this Tuesday, the 24th victim in a series of bizarre slayings.

Though Inspector James Barrington of the Yard had no immediate comment, sources exclusive to *The Scoop* agreed that the victim had been beaten severely by one or more assailants, and then stabbed through the heart.

This series of murders has continued over the space of three years, to the bafflement of our faithful Metropolitans. Must we hope that Mr. Sherlock Holmes, though reported by Mr. Doyle to be in retirement, will one last time rise to the defense of our majestic isles?

Readers of *The Scoop* are reminded that this esteemed journal has a standing reward for information leading to the apprehension and conviction of the perpetrators, in an amount now risen to £24 with the latest death. Be on guard!

—*THE SCOOP*

Meanwhile, they can watch the floor show, which consists of several attractive young ladies in scanty costumes cavorting about. At the Blue Pyramid, they dance around the tables and expect patrons to tuck pound notes as tips beneath the straps and belts of their belly-dancing costumes. This makes the evening more interesting for everyone concerned. If the investigators have asked leading questions, Yalesha, one of the dancers, whispers that she has information and wants to be met at midnight down the street. She'll whisper even more urgently if an investigator gives her a fiver.

Surely no investigator refrains from collecting on such an investment. When they meet, Yalesha says she is fearful of the Brotherhood. Her boyfriend was killed by them, and she wants revenge. She knows little, but once a month an old truck appears around midnight in the vicinity of the club. Up to two dozen Blue Pyramid customers climb in, led by a man named Tewfik al-Sayed. They all go to somewhere out of London, she thinks (true: they go to Gavigan's Essex estate). If the investigators stake out the club, they see the same thing a few nights later.

YALESHA

The club closes at 1 a.m. No one stays late to clean up. The front and back doors are STR 15 each. There is room for two to force a door at the same time. Inside the club they find liquor, cigarettes, an icebox full of Egyptian munchies, a gramophone, and 200 scratchy recordings of Middle Eastern hits. The place is well kept and entirely aboveboard.

ABDUL NAWISHA, age 53, Owner and Manager of the Blue Pyramid Club

STR 14	CON 16	SIZ 15	INT 15	POW 8
DEX 10	APP 06	EDU 06	SAN 50	HP 16

Damage Bonus: +1D4.

Weapons: Switchblade 60%, damage 1D4+1D4
Small Blackjack 65%, damage 1D4+1D4

Skills: Accounting 60%, Arabic 80%, Bargain 50%, Cthulhu Mythos 01%, Drive Automobile 45%, Electrical Repair 15%, English 46%, French 24%, Gamble 65%, Listen 60%, Pick Pocket 50%, Psychology 60%, Sneak 35%.

BOUNCERS AND PALS at the Blue Pyramid

	1	2	3	4	5	6
STR	10	15	13	16	14	12
CON	15	14	10	12	11	15
SIZ	17	15	16	10	12	13
APP	06	03	07	09	10	10
INT	05	09	08	12	11	06
POW	15	05	10	09	09	07
HP	16	15	13	11	12	14

Damage Bonus: +1D4.

Weapons: Chair Leg 65%, damage 1D6+1D4
Fist/Punch 65%, damage 1D3+1D4
Blackjack* 50%, damage 1D6+1D4
Switchblade 50%, damage 1D4+1D4
Head Butt 50%, damage 1D4+1D4

These men are expert in the use of blackjacks. If a skill roll suc-ceeds, match the actual damage done against half of the target's CON on the resistance table. If the damage rolled overcomes that amount, the target falls unconscious, and still takes the rolled damage in hit points.

Skills: Climb 40%, Dodge 38%, Hide 40%, Jump 45%, Listen 50%, Sneak 30%, Spot Hidden 45%.

YALESHA, age 19. Entertainer at the Blue Pyramid

STR 09	CON 10	SIZ 08	INT 10	POW 11
DEX 17	APP 15*	EDU 08	SAN 73	HP 09

APP 18 in dancing costume.

Damage Bonus: +0.

Weapons: none.

Skills: Arabic 70%, Belly Dance 95%, English 45%, Flirt 80%, Sing 55%.

The Shop of Tewfik al-Sayed

It is a small, neat, two-story building on Ardour Street in Soho. People of all sorts patronize the spice shop. The shop is ordinary, it smells nice, and Tewfik's spices are of good quality. The shop is open 9 a.m. to 5 p.m., Monday through Saturday. On the second floor is Tewfik al-Sayed's small flat.

The front doors are of STR 20 each. The back door (STR 35) opens into the shop. Tewfik is the owner of the shop, and the only employee.

After Tewfik closes for the day, half of the time he can be found at the Blue Pyramid. If he is in his flat, the front upstairs windows will be lit until about midnight. If he has gone to the Blue Pyramid, he returns in 1D3 hours—at 10 p.m., 11 p.m., or midnight.

Tewfik's statistics are at the end of this chapter, along with the other cultists.

THE FLAT

Entering the building through the front, the door to the left leads up to his flat. Tewfik's living room and bedroom are furnished with couches, pillows, incense burners, rugs, low tables, a hookah, and hanging lamps, all in muted shades of yellow and blue. A sizable oil heater keeps the Egyptian rooms at Egyptian temperatures. In a prim glass

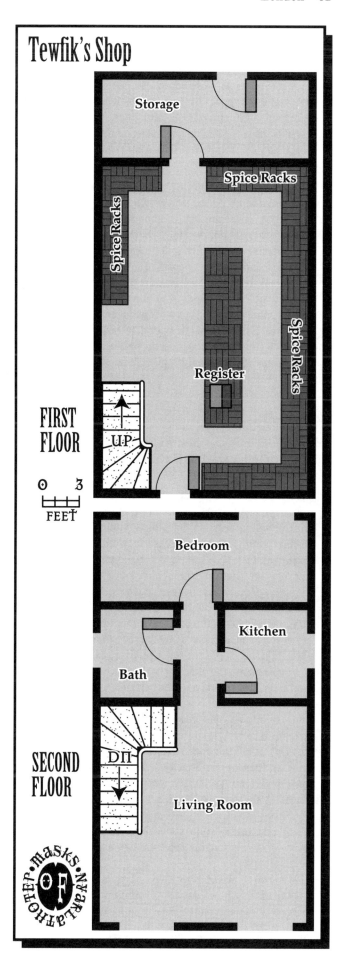

The Mirror of Gal

The Mirror is a scrying device and a powerful weapon of attack. To employ its powers, the user must have a supply of the substances within those sandstone vials hidden in the secret drawer of Tewfik's desk. Some manuscripts term the red syrupy substance *obra'an*, and the blackish powder *gabeshgal*. Both are rare.

AS A SCRYING DEVICE: use the obra'an to draw an inverted ankh on the glass, which then will shimmer and become translucent, at the same time extracting 1D3 magic points and 1 SAN from the user. Whatever the user concentrates upon while creating the inverted ankh then appears in the glass—a particular person or thing, a place, a fish-and-chips stand, etc. If a place or thing from the Cthulhu Mythos appears, the user and any viewers are subject to applicable Sanity rolls. In regard to other planes of existence, the Mirror has unlimited range, but on Earth it has a range of 200 miles. The Mirror of Gal reveals only one locale, person, place, etc., per use. It holds the image or viewing area for 1D20+10 minutes, or until the user removes concentration. A new or continued image requires a new ankh and a new sacrifice of magic points. As a scrying device, the Mirror only views—one cannot hear, smell, touch, etc., through it.

AS A WEAPON: to attack with the mirror, the target must have been made visible in the mirror. Then the black powder gabeshgal is applied within the loop of the ankh until no image is visible within it. At that instant the target with be beset by intense fear. The user may sacrifice additional points of POW to harm the target. The attack is resolved on the Resistance Table, with a POW vs. POW roll, but each point of POW sacrificed by the attacker counts for 10 points on the Resistance Table. If the target is overcome, he takes 1D6 hit points in damage for every point of POW energizing the attack. The damage done appears on pathologist reports as "heart strain."

If the target fights off the attack no damage is done, but the target feels a momentary brush of extreme terror. One application of the powder permits one attack; as many attacks as desired may be made so long as the attacker's POW holds out, the black powder is available, and the image remains visible in the mirror. The black powder evaporates after each attack. Whether or not successful, each attack also costs both the user and target 1D10 SAN. Only one person at a time can use the mirror for an attack.

While it is possible to attack Mythos deities with the Mirror, such an attack is unlikely to succeed because of the amount of POW required.

case stand statuettes of Egyptian gods. Prominently, piously displayed on a table in the living room is an open copy of the Koran.

On one wall of the living room is an ornate mirror with a golden frame. The frame is subtly asymmetric; strange figures have been worked into it. This is the Mirror of Gal, an ancient Mythos artifact for which any member of the Brotherhood would gladly kill or die. Its remarkable properties and uses are discussed in a nearby box.

A locked (STR 10) roll-top desk dominates the living room. A cursory search within it reveals only shop records, invoices, account books, paper, pens, etc. If the searcher's player makes a successful Luck roll, the investigator pulls the center shelf, hears an audible click, then sees a large hidden drawer open lower down on the right side of the desk.

A Spot Hidden also discovers the large space shielding the hidden drawer, but does not reveal how to open the drawer. The wood is of STR 20, and can be cut away to open the drawer.

In the drawer are two sandstone vials with caps, a folded silk robe, a black inverted ankh on a metal chain, a crumbling papyrus scroll, a black skullcap embroidered with inverted ankhs, and a pair of scepters made out of a black metal. Each item is further described below.

THE ROBE, THE SKULLCAP, AND THE METAL ANKH: robe and skullcap are of black silk cut for a person of Tewfik's size. Each is embroidered with the inverted ankh of the Brotherhood. These are priestly garments, but neither is magical nor has added significance. The metal ankh is symbolic and does not have powers or properties, through the alloy itself is alien and would puzzle any metallurgist.

THE SCROLL: it is filled with Egyptian hieroglyphics decipherable by an Egyptologist. At his option, the keeper may allow translation through a successful Archaeology roll. Arabic will not translate hieroglyphics. The scroll contains a spell, Body Warping of Gorgoroth, the properties of which are discussed in the *Call of Cthulhu* Lesser Grimoire.

THE TWO SCEPTERS: each is about a foot long, cast or grown from an unidentifiable alien metal. One has a crook at one end; the other ends in the inverted ankh. Properly used, the scepters have considerable power. See their properties in a box near the end of this chapter, titled "The Two Scepters".

THE SANDSTONE VIALS: these two red-brown sandstone vials contain respectively a syrupy red substance and a black powder flecked with odd, rubbery crystals. A successful Chemistry or Physics roll identifies neither substance, though either roll establishes both substances as new to science. The contents of the vials are used in conjunction with the Mirror of Gal, hanging on the living room wall and discussed in a box nearby. There are fifteen applications of the red substance and eight applications of the black powder.

OTHER LEADS

*Wherein a terrifying monster, a warehouse full of criminals and evidence,
and a long sea voyage may
await the investigators.*

The Thing in the Fog

If Gavigan has begun to fear the investigators, he may set cultists on them, or he may unleash the Thing in the Fog. See an accompanying news clipping, "It Almost Had Me!", for an account of the Thing's attack by a victim who luckily escaped. If investigators survive such an encounter and describe the incident to Mickey Mahoney, he'll recall this earlier report and show it to them. If they go to Brown's Resident Clinic for the Insane in Glasgow, or if they telephone the clinic, they learn that these days Groot says but one word, "Gavigan", over and over again. No one can explain the name's significance.

The larvae of the Thing are sometimes obtained by servants of the Great Old Ones and brought to Earth to smite enemies.

The Thing attacks by inserting its pliable tentacles into the nostrils and mouth of the target. The target only can escape the insertion attack by running away from the Thing and receiving a successful STR vs. STR resistance roll. The Thing resists with STR 5 for each tentacle that has hit the victim. The attack of the Thing cannot be seen or deflected—it only can be felt. The Thing attacks only in lightless places.

The target notices a characteristic odor of burning hair when the Thing closes to within 25 feet. Investigators trying to hit it as it attacks may instead hit the victim—for the Thing is only fog, insubstantial in Earthly terms.

Bright light, such as from a flashlight, is the only defense against the Thing. Alan Groot's article in *The Scoop* doesn't mention it, but a bobby happened along, heard Groot's gasps, and turned his electric torch in that direction, driving off the creature. The bobby glimpsed the Thing, but refrained from reporting what he saw. Though the Thing is insubstantial, it can be seen momentarily in bright light—a sparkling gray cloud with thin, whip-like tentacles reaching out up to 35 feet. Attacked by light, it will try to flee into some lightless area. The light from a match or cigarette lighter is inadequate to deter this terrible enemy.

If cornered by bright light, or trapped in the sun when thick fog suddenly lifts, the Thing returns to its native dimension, from whence it cannot return. The transition takes ten minutes. Were the Thing to find some place perpetually dark, such as a deep sewer or a cave, the Thing might stay on this plane for some time. Apparently it is immortal in Earthly terms, with no need to feed. Its motives or instincts are mostly unknown.

Though Alan Groot escaped the Thing, the story concludes by noting that Groot at present is in a Scotland asylum—investigators may not be so lucky!

ITEM. A clipping from *The Scoop* (*Nyarlathotep Papers #28*).

Relevance of the Information: should forewarn the investigators, especially the detail of the scent of smoldering hair. If Mahoney had written the piece more carefully, all the information that the investigators need to chase away the Thing would be in the article. As it is, the detail about the light is in Mahoney's notes, but never saw print.

THE THING IN THE FOG, an Other-Dimensional Life From

STR 30	CON 30	SIZ 30	INT 01	POW 25
DEX 18	MOV 10			

Damage Bonus: n/a.

Weapons: Six Tentacles of Mist, 50% each

Note: does increasing choking damage each round, up to six victims simultaneously. First round attack does 1 point damage, second round does 2 points, third round does 3 points, and so on.

Armor: none needed, since the Thing is insubstantial, and nothing material can harm it. Bright light can drive the Thing from this plane, and it then cannot return, but even the brightest light does not actually harm it.

Skills: Hunt for Victim 65%.

Sanity Loss: if seen, 1/1D10 SAN. Automatically lose 1D8 SAN upon the Thing's first successful attack.

The Limehouse Docks

If the investigators keep watch on the Penhew Foundation, they see a truck leave. It goes to Limehouse, a grim and dirty part of London where the nights are reputedly thick. Gambling houses, derelicts, opium addicts, exotic restaurants, cheap housing, and shifty residents abound. Members

Nyarlathotep Papers #28

"IT ALMOST HAD ME!"
by Alan Groot, Victim

It was like turning suddenly, knowing something was there, only to find nothing — a nothing possessing hideous life! The dank water smell of the cloying fog was replaced by a foul scent of smouldering hair which somehow reached out and filled my lungs, driving itself deep into my body. I began to choke. It meant to kill me. I cannot describe the terrible feeling of invasion by those foggy tendrils. And still I could see nothing!

— excerpt from longer article ghost-written by Mahoney months before the investigators arrive.

of the small African and Asian communities live here, especially Chinese, Japanese, and East Indians. Only bribes, Fast Talks, or threats get residents to talk about the warehouse where the truck unloads: they say only that goods often leave the warehouse in the dead of night, and that the workers there are tough customers.

From this Limehouse location the Brotherhood often ships statues and other Mythos artifacts overseas. Punji Chabout owns the building. He is not a cultist, but he finds acceptable the money they pay him to keep their dealings secret. The warehouse is close to several docks, convenient for late-night loading of suspect items. Several (1D4+4) Lascars watch over the building at all times. They'll try to knife snoopers and then drop their bodies into the Thames.

Many of the goods in Chabout's warehouse are illegal (stolen merchandise, weapons, explosives, drugs) and more are occult- or Mythos-related. Literally tons of evidence wait here. If the investigators can get the London police to take a look, the law will find leads to many crimes, in consequence boosting the investigators' credibility with Barrington.

The truck from the Penhew Foundation unloads one large crate. Chabout signs for it and stores it in the warehouse. That night, several degenerate-looking sailors from the *Ivory Wind* claim the crate, move it to the nearby ship, and stow it below. Watching investigators see everything. The crate contains an unimportant Mythos item—a statue, a painting, an altar stone, or whatever the keeper desires.

Chabout always carries a knife and a garrote, but he is dangerous only if he believes the investigators are a threat—he'll try to have them murdered in that case. Chabout knows about the Cthulhu Mythos, but doesn't believe in what the Brotherhood professes. Except for the money he might lose, he is unconcerned about people uncovering Brotherhood secrets. Chabout is personally fearless, and will not hesitate in taking on superior odds in a fight.

Quicken Fog-Spawn
a preparatory spell

The ritual Quicken Fog Spawn, making a larva grow, is known to Gavigan, who has it in a Hebrew scroll in the workroom of his Essex mansion (1D10 SAN loss to cast, INT x2 to learn, +1D2 Cthulhu Mythos).

The spell requires a larva, and the spell must be cast within dense fog through which no bright light can penetrate. A drop of the caster's blood must be smeared on the larva, and 25 magic points and 2 POW points expended. As the larva smokes and evaporates, the unseen Thing then grows. The creature may be mentally commanded by the caster to move in any direction and to kill as the caster chooses. But the caster must remain within 200 feet of the Thing, or it will go free; the caster can sense its approximate location while it is under control. Control lasts for three hours, or until the fog lifts or day breaks. After three hours, the Thing will wander aimlessly through the night, killing those it catches.

PUNJI CHABOUT, age 39, Shady Owner of a Shady Warehouse

STR 10	CON 16	SIZ 08	INT 14	POW 08
DEX 13	APP 12	EDU 05	SAN 60	HP 12

Damage Bonus: +0.

Weapons: Garrote 65%, conditional strangulation damage 1D3 per round, STR vs. STR to dislodge
Head Butt 65%, damage 1D4
Fighting Knife 60%, damage 1D4+2
Fist/Punch 60%, damage 1D3
Kick 45%, damage 1D6

Skills: Accounting 35%, Bargain 50%, Bluff 90%, Credit Rating 05%, Criminal Insight 45%, Cthulhu Mythos 02%, English 50%, Order 75%, Hide 70%, Hindustani 75%, Law 10%, Listen 65%, Persuade 35%, Pick Pocket 50%, Sneak 50%, Spot Hidden 50%.

LASCARS at Punji's Warehouse

	1	2	3	4	5	6	7	8
STR	08	15	10	12	13	11	09	10
CON	12	13	11	12	11	16	10	15
SIZ	09	07	09	09	09	10	12	08
APP	06	04	03	07	08	03	06	05
INT	06	08	09	05	07	05	09	12
DEX	16	14	13	13	11	11	10	09
POW	12	10	08	10	06	13	07	08
HP	11	10	10	11	10	13	11	12

Damage Bonus: +0.

Weapons: Fighting Knife 75%, damage 1D4+2
Fist 65%, damage 1D3
Head Butt 60%, damage 1D4
Kick 40%, damage 1D6

Skills: Climb 40%, Dodge 40%, English 15%, Hide 55%, Hindustani 35%, Jump 45%, Listen 50%, Loiter 75%, Sneak 50%.

The *Ivory Wind*

This dilapidated freighter is captained by Lars Torvak, an alcoholic Norwegian. The ship is of Chinese registry. Its home port is Shanghai, to which it is bound. The crew is mostly Chinese, but keepers could add other nationalities as seems fitting. Torvak's relation to the cultists is extra-curricular—they give him side money to transport crates and goods to China for them. He puts false addresses on the crates and leaves them off the cargo manifest.

LARS TORVAK, age 43, Drunken Captain of the *Ivory Wind*

STR 16	CON 13	SIZ 14	INT 12	POW 07
DEX 10	APP 10	EDU 08	SAN 06	HP 14

Damage Bonus: +1D4.

Weapons: .30-06 Rifle 50%, damage 2D6+3
Fist 45%, damage 1D3+1D4
Fighting Knife 35%, damage 1D4+2+1D4
Kick 30%, damage 1D6 +1D4
Head Butt 30%, damage 1D4+1D4

Skills*: Accounting 25%, Arabic 30%, Bargain 40%, Cantonese 25%, Drink Self to Sleep 90%, English 40%, French 40%, Navigate 70%, Norwegian 65%, Operate Heavy Machinery 40%, Mandarin Chinese 25%, Pidgin English 15%, Pilot Ship 65%, Pilot Small Boat 50%, Psychology 45%, Sailing 50%, Pilot Small Boat 60%, Swim 70%, Threaten 70%.

* Torvak is drunk 75% of the time; halve relevant skills if drunk.

If the investigators watch the ship for a few hours, they'll see Torvak getting a few quick drinks in a nearby bar. If they

LARS TORVAK

demonstrate a reason for him to talk (easy money or physical force works best with Torvak), he will talk, but he hasn't much to say. Most of the cult shipments go to the Shanghai importer Ho Fong. There have been a lot of crates lately. If the investigators sneak aboard the ship and are discovered, they'll be in risk of their lives, though there are no cultist crewmen. Torvak fears imprisonment and loss of his ship. If he has to, he'll kidnap intruders and drop them overboard when far at sea.

If they get Torvak to open some of the crates for them, a few hold statuettes and other Mythos trinkets, but most contain oddly crafted valves, struts, strange hand-wired electrical boards, and monstrous and baffling radio tubes. A handful of physicists (Physics 90% or better) could identify the uses of some of the components (the valves have to do with reaction motor control, for instance). Most of the parts are baffling. Some pieces are machined from titanium alloys that have never been seen outside of a lab. All of this gear is spare parts for Sir Aubrey's 'engine of destruction', as discussed in the Shanghai chapter.

The *Ivory Wind* is an older merchantman, of about 7,000 tons displacement, designed to haul general cargoes. On this particular run to China, her holds are half full. The forward crew's quarters have been abandoned. Since no respectable person would take passage on this ship, the crew now occupies the staterooms originally intended for paying passengers. It is possible that investigators with sufficient food and water could skulk in the forward part of the ship for most or all of the voyage to China, without discovery.

The ship's route includes stops in Marseilles, Malta, Port Said, Aden, Bombay, Singapore, and Saigon. The voyage could take from six weeks to three months.

SAILORS OF THE *IVORY WIND*

	1	2	3	4	5	6	7	8
STR	09	10	11	13	09	08	12	10
CON	12	09	10	11	07	09	15	11
SIZ	15	10	13	13	09	13	11	11
APP	14	11	09	09	10	07	08	12
INT	07	13	09	08	06	10	09	11
DEX	15	13	13	12	12	11	10	10
POW	03	08	04	05	10	10	10	09
HP	14	10	12	12	08	11	13	11

Damage Bonus: +0.

Weapons: Fighting Knife 50%, damage 1D4+2
Small Club 30%, damage 1D6

Skills: Cantonese 25%, Climb 65%, Mandarin Chinese 25%, Dodge 40%, Pidgin English 10%, Hide 35%, Jump 55%, Listen 50%, Operate Heavy Machinery 40%, Sneak 35%, Spot Hidden 50%, Swim 30%, Throw 50%.

The Investigations of Jackson Elias

Elias busily accumulated leads, two of which (Miles Shipley and the Derbyshire Monster) he was unable to explore. Edward Gavigan had tabbed Elias as dangerous, and forced the journalist to flee the country. Many people remember talking to Elias. All recall him as being distraught, upset, or frightened. Only Edward Gavigan can detail all of Elias' movements while in England.

RITES OF THE BROTHERHOOD

*Through North Sea marsh and gloom, both the respectable and the suspicious flock
at regular intervals to a secluded island. Will the investigators also risk
that narrow road which winds into the darkness?*

The Brotherhood of the Black Pharaoh holds regular rites thirteen times yearly, always at the dark of the moon. In the UK, the most important gathering of this kind occurs at Edward Gavigan's country estate in Essex, in the midst of the marshes at the edge of the North Sea. Driving there takes about an hour and a half. Reach the area by rail in about an hour, departing from Liverpool Station.

The foundations of the estate's mansion, built in the 17th century, have since settled into the boggy ground. The subtle distortions of its architecture and the wild aspect of its poorly kept grounds lend the place a gloomy and foreboding air, a place of impalpable menace. The whole of the island estate is some thousands of acres. A moat of marsh and slough separates the island and manor from productive inland fields upon which Gavigan collects rent. Locate this fictitious estate at The Naze, about seven miles southwest of Harwich.

In Arabic, Misr means "Egypt". The mansion formerly was owned by enthusiastic occultists who littered house and grounds with Egyptian bric-a-brac. The UK Brotherhood thought it a great coup when Gavigan finally wrested away control of Misr House.

It is the manor that the cultists from the Blue Pyramid club visit. The investigators, if they follow those cultists' truck, must exercise caution once the truck turns onto the long lane leading to the manor. If the investigators are spotted, the cultists will want to use them in that night's ritual.

Entrances to the Estate

A six-foot-high stone fence marks the outer border of the estate, not far from the main highway. There is an iron gate at the entrance, with a telephone link to the manor. During rituals, 1D4+2 guards lurk at the gate. At other times, only a single gatekeeper waits. The guards never unlock the gate until they understand the visitors' business and until Misr House tells them to admit strangers. Except on ritual nights, the STR 30 gate is kept locked. On ritual nights the gate is left open until midnight, and then is locked—no one is admitted after then, nor is there anyone in the manor to answer the phone during the ritual.

Inside the gate, the narrow road follows along the top of a levee, raised nearly five feet above the fields (centuries of tilling have left the fields far below sea level). Great dikes protect the land from the sea. The island, mostly unfarmed for generations, is relatively higher. A turnstile bridge ostensibly rotates on its center column to allow small boats to pass. Gavigan installed it as part of the island defenses. It takes a successful Spot Hidden to notice that the bridge can be opened and closed. If an investigator vehicle makes it across the bridge, the cultists can lock open the bridge, trapping the vehicle on the island.

The sea offers better and safer access. Cultists have no associated deep one colony here, though the investigators shouldn't know that—keep them jumpy with lots of fog, strange ripples, bulgy-eyed guides, mysterious splashes, and so on. Any kind of boat can be rented at Walton-on-the-Naze, Clacton-on-Sea, Ipswich, Harwich, etc., and operator-guides can be found. Let the Lovecraftian names of some of these cities give the investigators pause.

If investigators hire too large a craft with too many crew, make the sloughs too shallow for entrance. Force the investigators into awkward, vulnerable rowboats so that they confront the cultists without an intervening screen of fearless British seamen.

The Manor House

Whenever he is at the manor, ten cultists act as Gavigan's valets, butlers, maids, groundskeepers, cooks, and companions. They are mostly Egyptians or Chinese, illegally in England. On dark nights, Gavigan brings replacements ashore from the *Ivory Wind*, using the small motor launch anchored not far from the bridge. He also uses this watery route to send messengers abroad.

These cultists never leave the island. They speak poor English and are loyal to Gavigan, their high priest. During rituals, some guard the gate to the road, armed with switchblades. All keep their ritual clubs and robes in their rooms; many prominently wear inverted ankhs as pendants, jewelry, etc. A search of the mansion yields enough evidence of the cult to land the whole crew in prison if the local authorities know the significance of the cult.

The interior of the manor is unremarkable, except that it is dirty, and lacks the furniture and comfort one might associate with a man of Gavigan's standing. In the great hall, two bricks in the fireplace can be pulled forward—a successful idea roll will be enough to find them. The one on the right side opens a door to a narrow stairway leading to a small, dank room without windows—a priest hole, where the builders hid Catholic priests during the time of Cromwell.

The movable brick on the left side causes the left portion of the fireplace to slide aside, revealing another set of narrow stairs leading down. These stairs connect to the dungeons and Gavigan's workroom. Priest hole and dungeons are unconnected.

To close, the secret doors must be pushed shut. Within the walls, obvious handles reopen the doors. Successful Spot Hiddens might also detect the doors, but they would have to be directed at the massive fireplace. The doors cannot be locked from either side; each can be pried open by successful Resistance Table rolls against STR 30.

The kitchen also communicates with the basement of the mansion, but the dungeon and basement are separated by very thick stone walls.

The Cells

The stairs from the left-hand fireplace door descend to another door, this one of iron (STR 60). The door is not locked. Within is a small room and a corridor. A number of stone-and-iron cells open from the corridor; each cell is complete with great iron rings set into the walls as anchors for shackles.

Gavigan keeps sacrificial victims in these cells. The investigators have a 50% chance to find 1D4 captives here, all of whom will die within a few weeks. These unfortunates know only that they have been kidnapped and imprisoned. If a Luck roll can succeed for the investigator with the highest Power, one prisoner is an Egyptian who knows details of the U.K. branch of the Brotherhood—he is to be killed to be stopped from talking. This man can supply the investigators with information about Gavigan's plans, what will happen to the captives, and even the general layout of the estate and the number of cultists likely to be present.

Gavigan's Country Workroom

The corridor concludes in what was once the torture chamber. The room still serves that purpose upon occasion (boot, rack, tongs, pincers, etc.), but mostly now it is Gavigan's country sorcery shop. Browsing investigators find materials and information of five types.

STATUARY, PAINTINGS, JEWELRY, ETC.: all of this is Mythos-related, and literally is piled throughout the room. Much of it Gavigan coveted and won by slaying the previous owners. Most of it deals with the Black Pharaoh. A bust of the Black Pharaoh enables investigators to recognize the god if they see him in human aspect—both successful Idea rolls and Spot Hidden rolls must be made for such recognition, however. Some of the jewelry might help the investi-

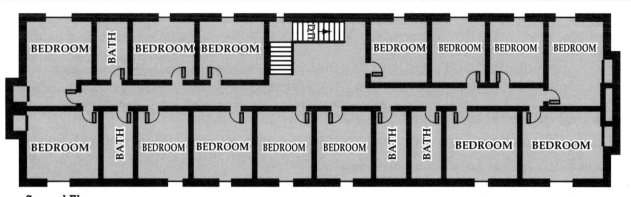

Second Floor

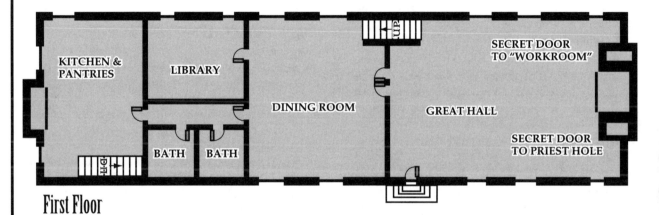

First Floor

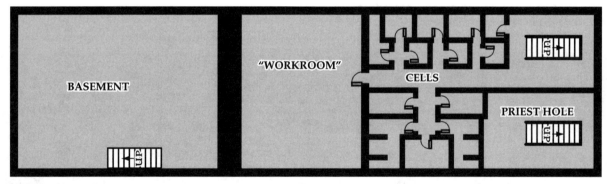

Basement

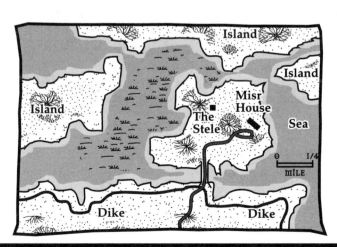

The Neighborhood

Misr House

> *Dear Aubrey,*
> *Elias has been dealt with in New York. You must stop Brady. It is stupefying that he has evaded us for so long. This man may become an obstacle to our Great Lord. If you wish, I will ...*

Nyarlathotep Papers #29

gators pass as cultists: there are lots of inverted ankhs, rings with the sign of Cthugha, twin scepters like Tewfik's, etc. Keepers may decide how much is here and whether it is intrinsically valuable. The mere quantity of this stash should dismay the investigators, showing that the cult is powerful and numerous. Every investigator automatically loses 1D3 SAN after evaluating Gavigan's hoard.

A FAT LEDGER: on a table adjacent to his desk, Gavigan records everything he ships abroad, with addresses of recipients and notes of what was shipped. More than any other volume, this book holds the key to the destruction of Nyarlathotep's organization and plans. Reading the past three years' entries shows many shipments to Ho Fong in Shanghai, more to Randolph Shipping in Darwin, Australia, and many more yet to Egypt, New York, Tokyo, Rio de Janeiro, Odessa, Calcutta, and Los Angeles. Mythos tomes and magical artifacts are unlisted; they're rare enough to remember, and hand-carried by cult couriers. A typical ledger entry: *4/9/25 -invoice #32121, 60cm statuette of Yig, solid gold* — to Ho Fong Imports, Shanghai.

ITEM. An unfinished letter, in Gavigan's hand, dated yesterday, written in black ink on excellent cream-colored rag paper. The letter is unfinished (*Nyarlathotep Papers #29*).

Relevance of the Information: connects Gavigan with the murder of Jackson Elias. Suggests that Sir Aubrey Penhew is still alive, and presently located near Jack Brady. If Brady is alive, it may be that Roger Carlyle still lives.

BOOKS AND SCROLLS: nearly one hundred rare and intriguing occult books are here, though none concern the Cthulhu Mythos—Gavigan keeps those in his secret room at the Penhew Foundation offices, thereby protecting them from Tewfik, his rival. At the keeper's option, these volumes may contain some of the spells which Gavigan knows. The languages of the books and scrolls include Arabic, Hebrew, French, German, Frisian, and Spanish.

INGREDIENTS FOR SPELLS: in jars, tubes, wooden boxes, tins, bags, sacks, and pouches are herbs, roots, pickled organs, strips of skin and hide, powdered blood, pressed flowers, vari-colored dusts, powders, and sands, and other special aids for magic-working. A successful Occult or Idea roll indicates that the materials are magically connected; successful Botany and Zoology rolls can identify the contents of some containers.

On a shelf are two one-inch-long metal vials. Each bears the Elder Sign. Within each is a single, tiny, brittle larva—potential Things in the Fog. A Frisian scroll elsewhere in the room contains the spell Quicken Fog-Spawn.

Some spiny, diseased-looking plants grow in pots here. No one can classify these plants; a successful Botany roll reveals that all the plants are unknown to science.

THE DEATH RITUAL

The Rites

Rites, whether the monthly rites of the dark of the moon or the more-frequent sex rites, are held outdoors around a large Egyptian stele (marked on the accompanying map). The stele bears many hieroglyphics. (A stele is a four-sided column which tapers to a rounded point and which bears inscriptions.) This one is made from dark stone brought from another world. The hieroglyphics are a poem of praise to the Black Pharaoh. Iron shackles embedded in the stele hold the wrists of sacrificial victims, usually four in number, one for each side of the stele.

Rites occur at night, when the color black is strongest. Torches light the proceedings. Skulking investigators must get fairly close to see more than confused motion and fluttering flames. Robed cultists dance to music played on Middle Eastern instruments—flutes, small drums, ouds, finger cymbals, etc. Gavigan and Tewfik usually attend all the rites to set good examples. They wear priestly garb, and each carries the twin scepters, which grant considerable defensive powers. The Brotherhood's rites are more formal and more complex than those of the Bloody Tongue, but they are no less barbaric.

A *DEATH RITUAL* is held every lunar month. In this rite victims are slowly and methodically beaten to death, at last put out of misery by a final spike through the heart. When the last sacrifice dies, 1D3 shantaks alight in the midst of the cultists. These faithful vie to mount one per monster and be carried off to Azathoth and the dread court of the Outer Gods. Needless to add, no one ever returns from such a journey. Cultists who miss the trip content themselves by consuming the corpses of the sacrifices. Once the bones are bared, Shrivelling spells splinter and destroy the remains.

These rites are gruesome and terrible to witness even from a distance. Investigators lose 1/1D6 SAN for the rites and another 0/1D6 SAN for the shantaks. Disturbing a death ritual attracts the wrath of every cultist. The rank and file heft their short spiked clubs, while Gavigan and Tewfik cast spells.

A *SEX RITUAL* may happen every week or so at the whim of the priests. In it, humans captured by the cult are ravished by 1D8+1 lesser other gods specially dispatched by Nyarlathotep for this despicable celebration. The purpose of the rites is to change human society by founding new cults of minor gods, ones which will owe their existence to the minions of the Crawling Chaos.

The preliminaries are short, for the foul gods are unwilling long to delay perpetrating obscene and sickening acts upon their victims. Captured men and women are shackled to the stele and staked to the ground nearby. Female cultists dance around them in a lustful frenzy, while male cultists dutifully wait. Once the other lesser gods are satiated, they return to their plane of existence. Though these deeds do not immediately cause the death of anyone, viewers cannot fail to be appalled. Witnessing the ritual costs 1/1D6 SAN, and each arriving lesser other god costs 1/1D20 SAN. After the lesser gods depart, the male cultists may do as they wish.

THE EGYPTIAN STELE

There is a 5% chance that a female victim bears a child with a bizarre physical impairment characteristic of the rapist god. Such children may grow up to become priests in cults of the Outer Gods. Their mothers' memories of the events are erased magically, though ever after the mothers are subject to terrible nightmares. Cultists favored by the priests are sometimes allowed to participate and to remember every disgusting detail. Captured investigators with high APP are likely to suffer such violation. Interrupting a holy sex rite invites death. The other lesser gods will join in the hunt 50% of the time.

To reward their obedience, Nyarlathotep grants his priests increased Power and (sometimes) knowledge, and advises them concerning enemies of the cult. Obviously chosen by the god, they have little trouble having their commands carried out. It is only between priests that friction exists.

Conclusion

As with the cult gathering in New York, the keeper always chooses when a rite of the Brotherhood is held. Unlike the cramped Ju-Ju House site, Gavigan's estate is large enough to permit investigators to watch without risk. If the investigators go to the authorities with their improbable tale, remember that Edward Gavigan is a respected gentleman and, without evidence, that the investigators will sound like madmen. After all, what is an occasional wild party if the participants are discreet? Toning down the story and bringing hard evidence (rescued abductees, ritual robes and objects, the location of one or both of Gavigan's secret rooms, a police representative who witnesses the scene, etc.) greatly enhances the investigators' chance to be believed.

If the Brotherhood learns they have been identified, their vengeance should be swift and brutal, including magical and physical attacks aimed at obliterating these blasphemers.

Statistics

EDWARD GAVIGAN, age 55, Director of the Penhew Foundation and High Priest of the Brotherhood of the Black Pharaoh

STR 13	CON 17	SIZ 13	INT 18	POW 23
DEX 16	APP 14	EDU 18	SAN 0	HP 15

Damage Bonus: +1D4.

Weapons*: 12-Gauge Shotgun 50%, damage 4D6/2D6/1D6
Cult Club 50%, damage 1D6+1D4
Sabre 30%, damage 1D8+1+1D4

* Gavigan, as well as Tewfik, has a pair of magic scepters. See the boxed comments nearby, "The Two Scepters."

Spells: Call Azathoth, Call Yog-Sothoth, Cloud Memory, Contact Chthonian, Contact Ghoul, Contact Nodens, Contact Nyarlathotep, Contact Sand Dweller, Dread Curse of Azathoth, Eibon's Wheel of Mist, Elder Sign, Enchant Knife, Enchant Whistle, Mind Blast, Powder of Ibn-Ghazi, Power Drain, Quicken Fog-Spawn, Send Dreams, Shrivelling, Steal Life, Summon/Bind Byakhee, Summon/Bind Dimensional Shambler, Summon/Bind Hunting Horror, Summon/Bind Servitor of the Outer Gods, Voorish Sign.

Skills: Accounting 30%, Anthropology 20%, Arabic 95%, Archaeology 60%, Astronomy 40%, Bargain 65%, Credit Rating 85%, Cthulhu Mythos 39%, Drive Automobile 50%, Egyptian Hieroglyphics 88%, Egyptology 90%, French 85%, Greek 70%, Hide 20%, Hindi 55%, Latin 80%, Law 50%, Listen 55%, Occult 75%, Persuade 55%, Pidgin English 20%, Psychology 50%, Ride 55%, Sneak 25%, Spot Hidden 35%, Swahili 25%, Throw 60%.

TEWFIK AL-SAYED, age 44, Spice Dealer and High Priest

STR 08	CON 13	SIZ 10	INT 13	POW 20
DEX 18	APP 10	EDU 09	SAN 0	HP 12

Damage Bonus: +0.

Weapon*: Cult Club 70%, damage 1D8

* The Mirror of Gal is Tewfik's main power and greatest responsibility. He would be frantic if it were stolen. He also has a pair of magical scepters.

Spells: Body Warping of Gorgoroth, Contact Nyarlathotep, Mindblast, Power Drain, Steal Life, Summon/Bind Servitor of the Outer Gods, Voorish Sign, and others as the keeper wishes.

Skills: Accounting 60%, Arabic 80%, Bargain 50%, Climb 60%, Credit Rating 50%, Cthulhu Mythos 40%, Cult History 20%, Dodge 70%, English 65%, Egyptian Hieroglyphs 50%, Fast Talk 35%, Hide 50%, Jump 50%, Listen 75%, Occult 20%, Sneak 70%, Spot Hidden 60%, Throw 50%.

BIGGER-THAN-AVERAGE CULTISTS of the Brotherhood

	1	2	3	4	5	6	7	8
STR	14	13	09	13	12	12	11	13
CON	12	12	11	13	09	08	09	10
SIZ	13	13	16	12	14	14	14	13
APP	06	07	04	05	09	10	03	04
INT	17	14	14	11	10	11	09	12
EDU	02	03	05	02	01	01	01	08
DEX	13	13	13	13	12	12	12	11
POW	08	09	10	10	09	06	07	03
SAN	01	02	01	05	01	08	01	01
HP	13	13	14	13	12	11	12	12

Damage Bonus: +1D4.

Weapons: Cult Club 50%, damage 1D8+1D4
Fist/Punch 35%, damage 1D3+1D4
Butcher Knife 30%, damage 1D6+1D4

Skills: Bargain 15%, Climb 50%, Cthulhu Mythos 11%, Dodge 35%, Fast Talk 40%, Hide 50%, Listen 50%, Locksmith 20%, Sneak 40%, Throw 40%.

SIX SERVITORS OF THE OUTER GODS

	1	2	3	4	5	6
STR	14	15	13	17	20	13
CON	17	18	14	22	13	20
SIZ	21	22	23	16	20	20
INT	26	21	19	24	27	17
POW	19	16	21	22	17	24
DEX	10	19	18	17	15	15
HP	19	20	19	19	17	20
MOV 07						

Damage Bonus: +1D6.

Weapons: Six Tentacles 45%, damage. each round 2D3 tentacles attack, each tentacle doing damage equal to twice the creature's damage bonus.

Armor: invulnerable to physical weapons; magic weapons and spells do normal damage; regenerates 3 HP per round until dead.

Spells: 1D10 spells of the keeper's choice.

Skills: Cthulhu Mythos 70%, Grapple 100%, Hide 100%, Listen 100%, Sneak 100%, Track 100%.

Sanity Loss: 1/1D10 SAN.

SIX SHANTAKS, Ready to Fly

	1	2	3	4	5	6
STR	38	39	44	42	39	43
CON	16	10	14	17	15	12
SIZ	41	43	43	44	39	39
INT	06	06	03	04	04	02
POW	10	10	14	09	18	08
DEX	12	11	07	07	07	06
HP	29	27	29	31	27	26

MOV 6/30 flying

Damage Bonus: +4D6.

Weapon: Bite 55%, damage 2D6

Armor: 9-point hide.

Skills: Hide 01%, Listen 05%, Spot Hidden 50%.

Sanity Loss: 0/1D6 SAN.

The Police

JAMES BARRINGTON, age 55, Chief Inspector, London CID

STR 10	CON 12	SIZ 13	INT 15	POW 10
DEX 09	APP 11	EDU 15	SAN 85	HP 13

Damage Bonus: +0.

Weapons: Nightstick 65%, damage 1D6
38 Revolver 60%, damage 1D10
Fist/Punch 50%, damage 1D3

Skills: Bargain 70%, Bluff 60%, Credit Rating 55%, Drive Automobile 35%, Fast Talk 45%, First Aid 60%, Forensic Medicine 19%, History 25%, Law 30%, Library Use 55%, Listen 80%, Persuade 25%, Pharmacy 15%, Psychology 60%, Sneak 30%, Spot Hidden 75%, Track 15%.

The Two Scepters

Ending in a crook and an inverted ankh respectively, the two scepters magically assist in two ways. Once daily, if held crossed in front of the body, they add 1D20 magic points to the holder's magic points so long as the scepters remain crossed. Unused magic points gained in this way disappear when the scepters are uncrossed. Use the magic points either for spell-casting or for resisting a spell. When so used, the scepters glow.

The scepters also absorb 1D10 points of magical damage while crossed in front of the body—every time a damaging spell is cast at the holder. For example, if three Shrivelling spells were cast at the holder, the scepters would absorb 1D10 points of damage from each, each rolled separately.

Tewfik and Gavigan each own a pair of scepters.

EIGHT STEADFAST CONSTABLES, James Barrington's Trustworthy Officers

	1	2	3	4	5	6	7	8
STR	16	15	17	16	13	13	14	18
CON	14	18	17	15	13	14	12	18
SIZ	16	17	15	16	18	13	14	12
APP	10	11	12	13	14	13	12	17
INT	11	12	14	13	11	12	14	16
EDU	10	12	09	10	11	08	08	09
POW	10	12	13	15	11	12	12	18
DEX	14	14	14	13	13	13	13	12
HP	15	18	16	16	16	14	13	15

Damage Bonus: +1D4.

Weapons: Nightstick 75%, damage 1D6+1D4
Fist/Punch 45%, damage 1D3+1D4
12-Gauge Shotgun 30%, damage 4D6/2D6/1D6

Skills: Bargain 30%, Climb 60%, Drive Automobile 25%, Fast Talk 40%, First Aid 40%, Hide 20%, Jump 40%, Law 10%, Listen 55%, Psychology 25%, Sneak 25%, Spot Hidden 50%, Throw 50%. ■

NINE LESSER OTHER GODS (The Sort Who Might Show Up for the Sex Rites)

	Dhyighash	Shinjh	Pr'ktha	Yko	Nour	Urafty	Thahash	Glagga	L'ysh
STR	59	40	38	47	40	49	49	55	39
CON	21	88	47	45	71	88	52	64	87
SIZ	59	70	78	128	62	64	120	96	88
INT	0	0	0	0	0	0	0	0	0
POW	96	100	70	36	58	80	62	28	43
DEX	15	14	12	11	10	10	09	08	07
HP	40	79	63	87	67	76	86	80	88
Move	01	05	07	01	07	03	06	04	03
D-Bonus	+6D6	+6D6	+6D6*	+10D6	+6D6	+6D6**	3 at 5D6ea.	+8D6	+7D6

* Sets victim on fire, flames doing 1D6 per round until god is dispelled; fire otherwise cannot be extinguished.
** Does no real damage unless damage equals or exceeds victim's SIZ—then victim is swallowed whole.

Servant	Hunting Horror	Servitor of Outer Gods	Servitor of Outer Gods	Servitor of Outer	Star Vampire	Servitor of Outer Gods	Servitor of Outer Gods	two Shantaks	Hound of Tindalos

CAIRO

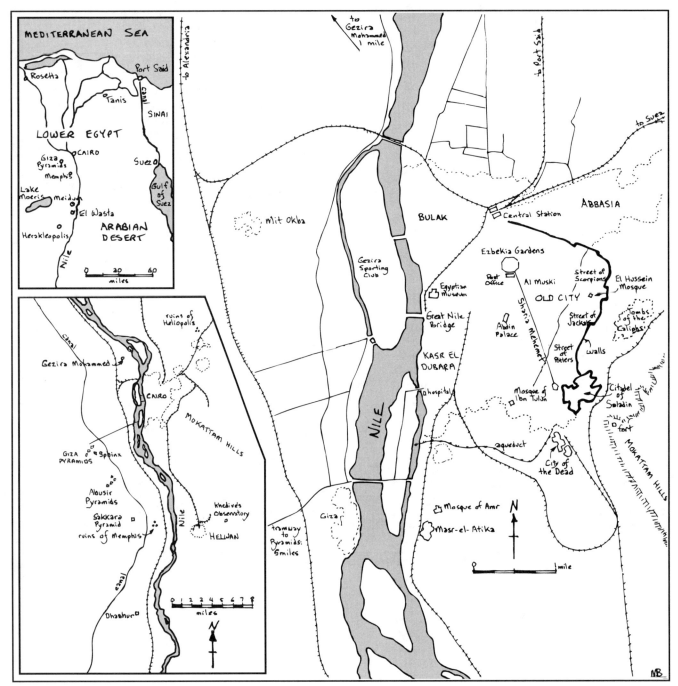

"It was sunset when we scaled that cliff, circled the modern mosque of Mohammed Ali, and even looked down from the dizzy parapet over mystic Cairo — mystic Cairo all golden with its carven domes, its ethereal minarets and its flaming gardens... Far over the city towered the great Roman dome of the new mesum; and beyond it — the awful Yellow Nile that is the mother of eons and dynasties..."
—from "Under the Pyramids", a story ghost-written for Harry Houdini by Lovecraft

airo is the pivot-point of this campaign. Investigators who survive the dangers in Cairo and environs know Nyarlathotep's intentions, and perhaps even know what might be done about them. Many non-player-characters in this chapter can be of invaluable use if the investigators befriend them. Cairo offers teeming masses, exotic customs and costumes, ruins, mystery, disease, danger, political intrigue, and fabulous wealth. The Egyptian cultists are powerful, and keepers can expect blood and Sanity points to flow freely.

This may be the first time that the investigators have been in a truly foreign environment. Strictly enforce the language and cultural barriers in this chapter—these real-world obstacles contribute greatly to feel and play-style. Browse through a modern guidebook to Egypt such as Fodor's, and read some of the descriptions of Cairo and Egypt contained in any encyclopedia. An elementary Arabic phrase-book supplies dozens of useful Arabic exclamations, pattern sentences, and isolated nouns and adjectives with which to amaze your players and confound their investigators. A Chaosium supplement, *The Cairo Guidebook*, offers much 1920s information about the city, its people, certain adjacent areas, and things Egyptian in general.

If the investigative team arrived here from Shanghai, Kenya, or Australia, some of the information in this chapter may be redundant, particularly if Jack Brady already has been found. But plenty of juicy information and spine-tingling researches remain to be savored.

Clues, information, and adventures are more tightly locked together here than in the New York and London chapters. The best single reason to go to Cairo is the letter from Faraz Najir to Roger Carlyle, which Jackson Elias somehow obtained and which the investigators may have found on Elias' corpse in that grim New York hotel room. They may also know the name of Warren Besart, the Frenchman who acted as Roger Carlyle's agent in Cairo. The most logical reason to go to Cairo is that both Carlyle and Elias did. If the investigators have already stopped in London, they have noticed already the connection with things Egyptian there.

Obvious sources of information in Cairo are the English-language newspapers. The keeper is advised to steer the investigators toward the *Cairo Bulletin* as a starting point no matter from what part of the world they arrive.

JACKSON ELIAS IN CAIRO

Elias stopped in Cairo for a remarkably short time, and apparently was interested only in confirming a few facts. Mythos minions were hot on his trail, and he could not risk staying in such a cult stronghold.

Brotherhood of the Black Pharaoh

If the investigators tangled with the Brotherhood in London and if the investigators escaped with some of the cult's artifacts or books, the Egyptian Brotherhood learns of this before the investigators arrive. They deploy cultists against them, attack them, dog them, rifle their rooms, and so on. Otherwise the Brotherhood completely ignores them until their activities affect the cult.

Egyptian and British authorities deny that the Brotherhood of the Black Pharaoh exists. The police meet such tales with laughter. However, the fact is that the Egyptian authorities do know of the cult, but are under strict orders not to impart such information to foreigners; official confirmation of a murder cult reflects poorly on the ability of Egyptians to govern themselves. If the investigators supply good information to the police, they will act on it, but they may not admit doing so.

Hiring A Guide: An Option

While the concierge at the investigators' hotel will gladly arrange for guides, all of his guides seem to have commit-

Selected Connections for this Chapter

NP#	clue or lead	obtained from	leads to
11	Najir's letter	Elias' murder scene	Faraz Najir
—	Black Pharaoh, Besart	Faraz Najir	Omar Shakti
—	rumored important item	Faraz Najir	Mosque of Ibn Tulun, Achmed Zehavi
—	address of Najir's shop	police, officials	Faraz Najir
30	letter from "A.P."	Omar Shakti	existence of Aubrey Penhew
—	artifacts exported	Shakti's log book	Ho Fong Imports in Shanghai and Randolph Shipping, Australia
—	cultist gathering	surveillance	from Shakti to Giza Sphinx
—	"agent" in Najir's letter	Erica Carlyle	Warren Besart
—	address of W. Besart	police, French Emb.	Warren Besart
31	Carlyle in Egypt	Warren Besart	the Collapsed Pyramid
—	two who aided Besart	Warren Besart	Nyiti and Unba in El Wasta
31	Msngr. of Black Wind	Warren Besart	Cult of the Bloody Tongue
—	interview	Dr. Ali Kafour	Black Pharaoh information
—	interview	Dr. Ali Kafour	Red, Bent, and Collapsed Pyramids
—	interview	Dr. Ali Kafour	Brotherhood of B.P., Nitocris, Carlyle Exp., Nyarlathotep
—	Carlyle Exp. in Egypt	Nigel Wassif	gossip, Kenya plans, Black Pharaoh, Clive Expedition, Dr. Ali Kafour
—	caverns under Sphinx	James Gardner	Nitocris' resurrection
—	existence of Nitocris	Gardner, Broadmoor	Need for Crown, Girdle, Necklace
—	interview	Achmed Zehavi	Girdle of Nitocris
—	two at El Wasta	Warren Besart	Eye of Light and Darkness
—	Bent Pyramid	Warren Besart	Nyarlathotep: Kenya, China, Australia

ments which make it impossible for them to stay on the job for more than a few hours at a time. On the streets, two poten-

HAKIM THE GUIDE

tial guides persist in offering themselves to the investigators. One, Hakim, is about 20, is strong and confident, and speaks passable English. If there are female investigators, he flirts with them. The other is a beggar boy, Ma'muhd, about eleven or twelve years old. He is quick, facile, a superb liar, and also speaks passable English.

These guides are for campaign needs. If the investigators act like yokels, sic Hakim on them. If they need to make some progress, bring in Ma'muhd. Let the investigators flounder, if they want—the keeper controls the clock and the calendar, after all.

ABOUT HAKIM

Hakim intends to lure the investigators to a quiet alley where several accomplices lounge. There they will rob the investigators at knife point. Hakim promises all kinds of information and services, but he merely wants more money than he has. If the investigators do not resist, the men hastily rob them and disappear. If they meet resistance, the robbers anger and try to slay these inconvenient foreigners.

BROTHERHOOD OF THE BLACK PHARAOH

This is the central branch of the cult. It is a large and powerful organization here. Membership is eclectic, but with a high proportion of Sudanese. The chief priest of the Cairo cult is Omar Shakti, a wealthy cotton farmer and landowner. Rituals are held in the desert, often near the pyramids at Sakkara, or in caverns beneath the Great Sphinx at Giza. Since Egyptian police and British political operatives keep careful watch on religious activity in Cairo, the cult stays well hidden there. Favored weapons include short swords, daggers, and garrotes, as well as the short spiked club.

AVERAGE EGYPTIAN BROTHER OF THE BLACK PHARAOH

STR 12	CON 14	SIZ 11	INT 11	POW 10
DEX 10	APP 06	EDU 01	SAN 0	HP 13

Damage Bonus: +0.

Weapons: Cult Club 55%, damage 1D8
Dagger 50%, damage 1D4+2
Garrote 20%, damage 1D3 choking per round; STR vs. STR to break free
Short Sword 35%, damage 1D6+1

Skills: Arabic 55%, Archaeology 05%, Astronomy 05%, Conceal 15%, Cthulhu Mythos 08%, Dodge 35%, English 15%, Fast Talk 35%, Hide 75%, Law 15%, Listen 55%, Occult 20%, Sneak 60%, Spot Hidden 45%.

ABOUT MA'MUHD

An orphan, he has lived by his wits as long as he can remember. He knows of no family or relatives. For several years he has each night watched over the flowers and fruits in a minor nobleman's garden, and in return gotten a place to sleep and a simple meal every day. But now his employer is dead, and a daughter of the nobleman has chased away the dirty beggar boy. Ma'muhd has been weighing the possibilities of prostituting himself, and has flirted several times with a notorious procurer in order to gain a meal. Now, see-

MA'MUHD

ing some hapless foreigners bumble through the city, he sees that if he could help them, they could make his life more secure.

Ma'muhd doesn't know as much as he thinks, but he is quick-witted, daring, and knows or knows of hundreds of useful Cairenes. He knows the Old City well (police often chase him from some of the districts nearer to the Nile), and knows from whom he can get reliable answers—formidable knowledge. He serves the investigators faithfully and well, but he likes to spend his money. Every time the investigators give him coin, he disappears until it is gone. He spends his earnings at the rate of four piastres an hour (24 hours a day) on food and clothing—a level of luxury he can scarcely comprehend. If the keeper wishes, he can also have the knack of turning up when he's needed.

Ma'muhd knows that as yet he is remarkably unscarred by his existence, but realizes that he is living on borrowed time. If the investigators make a fuss over him, he will strive with every ounce of his being to make them keep him with them forever and ever. Unfortunately, the desperate company kept by *Call of Cthulhu* investigators may bring Ma'muhd to his doom nearly as quickly as impoverishment on the streets of Cairo. Probably the happiest fate available to Ma'muhd would be to be adopted or protected by Nigel Wassif (a character in this chapter), a relationship which keepers may recognize from Kipling's Kim. The investigators risk their lives for the sake of such innocents—Ma'muhd personifies a small portion of their great burden.

HAKIM and His Three Brother Thugs

	Hakim	2	3	4
STR	12	11	10	12
CON	10	11	09	07
SIZ	13	12	11	12
APP	14	08	09	11
INT	12	12	08	09
EDU	03	02	01	01
DEX	11	11	10	10
POW	09	08	11	10
SAN	40	50	35	45
HP	12	12	10	10
Damage Bonus	+1D4	—	—	—

Weapons: Kick 60%, damage 1D6+1D4

Fist/Punch 55%, damage 1D3+1D4

Switchblade 50%, damage 1D4+1D4

Garrote 25%, damage 1D3 per round, remove by STR vs. STR
    Resistance roll

Head Butt 15%, damage 1D4+1D4

Skills: Bargain 25%, Fast Talk 35%, Climb 50%, Dodge 30%,
English 15% (Hakim only), Hide 40%, Jump 40%, Armed Assault
35%, Sneak 30%, Spot Hidden 40%.

MA'MUHD, age 11, Beggar Boy

STR 08	CON 14	SIZ 07	INT 16	POW 12
DEX 15	APP 13	EDU 03	SAN 90	HP 11

Damage Bonus: -1D4.

Weapon: Kick and Scream 60%, damage 1D6-1D4

Skills: Arabic 45%, Bargain 45%, Climb 70%, Dodge 85%,
English 15%, Fast Talk 30%, Listen 45%, Psychology 10%,
Sneak 70%, Spot Hidden 50%, Throw 30%.

About Egypt and Cairo

Cairo is the greatest city in Africa, and one of the great cities
of the world. With a population of about 850,000 in the mid-
1920s (one in ten of whom are foreigners), it is the capital of
the oldest continuously identifiable culture in the world—
the dynasties of north and south Egypt stretch back to 3100
BC, 5000 years before the investigators touch foot to the
desert. Guarded effortlessly by the desert and the sea, the
heritage of Egypt is unparalleled in architectural achievement, cultural sophistication, and in stability. Only China
rivals it.

Cultures now designated Naqaba I and Naqaba II long
predate the dynasties, but little is known of them even yet.

A second great period of achievement came after
Alexander's conquest and the establishment of the Ptolemies.
By blending Egyptian science and Greek philosophy, Alexandria became the intellectual capital of the Mediterranean
world.

A third period of greatness came with the Islamic conquest. The Fatimids built (in 968 AD) a new capital city, El
Kahira ("The Victorious"), a name later corrupted to Cairo.
Liberal Fatimid trade policies reestablished Egypt as a great
power. Egypt shared in the brilliant Arabic culture of the era
and, during the rule of the Mamluks, became once more the
unrivaled political and cultural center of the eastern
Mediterranean and of the Middle East.

After the Arab conquest, the native Coptic dialects of
Egypt gradually were replaced by Arabic, except that the
Bohairic dialect is preserved for religious purposes by the
Coptic Christian minority. (The written characters for this
remnant are mostly drawn from Greek, though a few
Demotic Egyptian characters also survived.)

The caliphs and khedives of Arabic Egypt built architectural wonders as great as those of the ancient dynasts.
Palaces and mosques litter Cairo and its vicinities, some of
them the finest examples of their kind in the world. It has
been written that one may satisfactorily study Arabic architecture and architectural ornament without ever leaving the
city of Cairo.

EGYPT IN THE 1920s

A British protectorate for about forty years, Egypt regained
most of its internal independence in 1922, but the British
reserved four areas of discretionary powers concerning imperial communications (including the Suez Canal), the Sudan,
the defense of Egypt and the Canal, and the protection of foreign interests and of minorities. Implicitly such reservations
are far-removed from independence, and unrest with the
British presence was ongoing. Removal of the protectorate
status occurred after the revolt of 1919, led by Saad Zaghoul.
This tumult served well to shield the dubious investigations
of the Carlyle Expedition from public scrutiny.

British garrisons remain at the Suez canal. Armed British
intervention within Egypt is a normal occurrence.

Such intervention and interference prompts general
resentment toward foreigners. A particularly sensitive area is
the removal of ancient artifacts and treasure from Egypt by
foreign archaeologists. In consequence, the Egyptian national government strictly polices such activity. The investigators will not get much help from Egyptian authorities when
it comes to the removal of Mythos items from the land of the
Nile. Surreptitious removal is a criminal offense, and applicable charges will be pressed. The British may decide to
intervene if the charges seem unfounded, but will do nothing
to aid common criminals. The United States ambassador and
consuls will not do more than weigh the facts presented in
court, or write courteous letters.

Many residents of Cairo and Port Said, especially members of the middle and upper classes, speak some English.
The overwhelming majority of the country speaks Arabic
and nothing more. Fast Talks and Persuades have no effect
when presented in a language which cannot be understood.
Players also may need to attempt Anthropology, Archaeology, History, and Law rolls to help their investigators
through the beautiful and exotic city of Cairo.

The dominant religion of Egypt is Islam. Coptic Christians
also exist in some numbers. Investigators may commit offens-
es to custom or to belief through ignorance—when entering a
mosque they may, for instance, neglect to remove their shoes,
or they may continue to talk. Rude investigators tromping
about and shouting questions must risk being corrected,
shouted out, or physically removed by angry Muslims.

Investigators must obtain visas and register as aliens at
their point of entry to Egypt. They will have to re-register in
Cairo. Both activities require valid passports. Cairo registra-
tion is done at the government house known as The Mug-
amma, located in Midan Tahrir (Liberation Square).

CAIRO IN THE 1920s

The investigators will arrive by ship either at Port Said (at
the north end of the Suez Canal) or at Alexandria. From
either port they may entrain for Cairo, an easy part-day distance, some one hundred miles from the Mediterranean at
the apex of the Nile Delta. Just north of it the Nile divides
and flows independently to the Damietta (east) and the
Rosetta (west) mouths.

Rail coaches are separated into several classes. Fares are
paid in Egyptian pounds and piastres; there are one hundred

piastres to the pound. For game purposes, treat the Egyptian pound and the British pound sterling as interchangeable. (United States paper dollars may or may not be acceptable, at the keeper's need—silver dollars, especially Mexican silver dollars, which have trickled around the globe, are acceptable.) The train arrives in Cairo at Central Station, about a mile from Ezbekia Gardens. Taxis are available. The best hotels, such as Shepheard's, can recommend short-term guides.

Ezbekia Gardens is a park of about twenty acres. It is a major center of the city, a little like Central Park in New York. The main post office is on its south side, the American consulate on the north. On the west side are most of the European-style hotels in the city, and to the east are financial institutions such as the stock exchange. Further to the east are excellent shops, but these soon conclude at the Old City.

Within the Old City are the narrow alleys and crowded markets so stereotypically Middle Eastern. The Old City also contains most of the classic Arabic architecture, though normal homes and shops are simple two- to four-story, flat-roofed buildings made from white-washed mud brick and tile.

Other than a few thoroughfares, Cairo's streets are notoriously crowded, obstructed, occupied, and otherwise inaccessible to motor cars. Trams connect many parts of the city. A tourist tramway also bridges the Nile and ends at the Giza pyramids, to the west of the city.

South of the Old City is the windswept wilderness of the City of the Dead, where only rock, sand, tombs, and mausolea exist. Investigators may want to explore such an eerie and dread place.

Along or toward the east bank of the Nile, in the district Kasr el-Dubara, are most of the governmental buildings, palaces of the nobility, and detached residences and expensive flats. Not far south of the Great Nile Bridge is the British consulate general.

A NOTE ABOUT STREET NAMES

Streets in Egypt are designated "sharia"—for example, Sharia Muhammed Ali—in the same way that Americans use "boulevard" or "avenue". Squares and plazas are designated by "midan"—for example, Midan Talaat Herb. Both designations appear in the text. Certain streets, such as Street of Jackals, are translated into English. When they are, such streets are fictitious and may be presumed never to have existed.

Small Problems

The heat is greatest June to August, with daily highs well over 100 degrees F. for months at a time. The nights are not much cooler. Rainfall is erratic and negligible, little more than an inch a year, usually in March or October. In the desert, khamsin (dust storms) occur roughly from March to June. If investigators decide to run, remind them of the heat. In the heat of the day, even villains are reluctant to move.

Most of Cairo is shockingly poor. Beggars abound. There are con-men, but most genuinely lack arms, legs, noses, untwisted spines, etc. Investigators with medical training can easily diagnose rickets and advanced cases of syphilis as they move through poor neighborhoods. Schistosomiasis is endemic.

Beggars see a lot, though, and are easier to find than police. Street people can give directions and other information if the investigators can speak even a little Arabic.

There are numerous personalities in Cairo with whom investigators may find reason to speak. Some are detailed in this section. It is most likely that investigators will begin their trip to Cairo by visiting Faraz Najir, a correspondent of Jackson Elias.

Faraz Najir

The Street of Jackals is in the Old City, one of those "narrow alleys redolent of aromatic secrets" imagined by Lovecraft. Finding it is no easy task. No complete street maps for Cairo exist in this period (the city has nearly doubled in population in the last twenty years). There is a phone book, but so few phones exist that the listings are useless as a research tool. Business registers and tax rolls (all in Arabic) are inaccessible to casual browsers. A competent Arabic-speaking guide leads them to the street in half an hour. By themselves, the investigators need a day or more.

Unfortunately, once they find the Street of Jackals, they learn that Faraz Najir's former shop is now a burned-out, rubble-strewn hole in the ground. Locals invoke Allah each time they pass the spot, and no one in this enormously crowded quarter will rebuild on the site. Stories say that, five or six years before, a hideous demon descended on the shop and set it aflame. This is true: the demon was a fire vampire summoned by the Brotherhood of the Black Pharaoh, a pun-

ishment meted out because Najir sold cult artifacts to Roger Carlyle. Police unfamiliar with the event say merely that a fire occurred, and then shrug their shoulders.

But all is not lost. If the investigators question other shopkeepers on the Street of Jackals, there is a 75% chance that someone knows that Faraz Najir was horribly burned but survived, and has since opened a new shop in the Khan el-Khalili, an ancient marketplace off the Sharia Muezzeddin Allah. Since these retailers now think that Faraz is accursed, skillful Bargains, Fast Talks, and Psychology rolls, and liberal offerings of money are needed to pry out what they know. A competent interpreter-guide is vital if no investigator speaks Arabic.

If the investigators respectfully ask for help from the authorities (perhaps someone at the Egyptian Museum, the Egyptian foreign ministry, or the American or British consuls), the respondee remembers that all such dealers of antiquities must be licensed by the government, and that Najir's name and address therefore must be on file somewhere or other. One of the places proves to be police headquarters, "not far away", where help is always available to well dressed European gentlemen. The address is the Street of Potters, again somewhere in the labyrinth of the Old City.

The Shop of Faraz Najir

In the midst of a dozen pottery shops is a door and window clearly marked "Faraz Najir" in Arabic, "Curios" in English, and "Magasin des Antiquites" in French. Several stories of tenements tower above, but Najir lives in the back of his crowded store. His stock is mostly tourist garbage. The shop holds nothing of an occult or Mythos nature, nor anything of interest to the investigators. Najir handles the shop alone. One side of his face bears ugly and extensive scars and welts.

At first mention of the Carlyle Expedition, Najir's eyes bulge, and he shoos the investigators out of the shop, and locks and shutters his doors and windows for the day. He now believes in the power of the Brotherhood, and will not cross them again. If the investigators persist, he takes a beautiful bejeweled scimitar from a case and shakes it at them, cursing loudly in Arabic about their relation to diseased camels. If they persist, Najir shouts for help, crying out that these accursed foreigners are robbing him. A sullen, hot-eyed crowd of local residents steadily grows.

If the investigators stick around too long, they'll be mauled by gouges, kicks, and spittle for an incidental 1D4 personal damage each. Their clothing may be torn. Wallets, passports, money, letters of credit, rings, and pocket watches may disappear.

But shopkeepers respect money. If the investigators come back later, they'll see Najir enter Fishawi's coffeehouse, located near the entrance to the market and adjacent to the El Hussein Mosque. Faraz goes to Fishawi's each day and enjoys a glass of mint tea before devoutly walking to El Hussein for evening prayers. He has become a pious man since his brush with death. If the investigators stave off his angry fear by offering pound notes, Najir calms himself. Each pound offered increases by one percentile the percentage chance that Najir agrees to talk; starting chance is 0%. Play the point subtly, but don't let the investigators give up on their best lead in Egypt.

Investigators may come to believe that the mosque itself is a better place to confront Najir. The keeper may encourage them in this belief, but interrupting believers in mid-prayer is bound to create resentment, possibly a disturbance, and may cause the detention of the investigators for their own protection.

Information from Faraz Najir

When Faraz Najir agrees to talk with the investigators, he sets up a meeting in a small room of the El Hussein Mosque, feeling most safe on ground sacred to Allah. He'll set the

FARAZ NAJIR

meeting for the lunch hour (1-2 p.m.), when all Cairo shops close. Najir meets the investigators at the side of the mosque, and leads them through several short hallways to a quiet room. Despite the presence of holy ground, keepers may use Najir to feed false information to the investigators.

Roger Carlyle, according to Najir, sought information about the reign of the Black Pharaoh, a reign supposed to have been ended by Sneferu, first pharaoh of the Fourth Dynasty. Najir had come into possession of a number of items related to the Black Pharaoh, including an ancient scroll detailing the entrance to a hidden room in an unnamed pyramid, within which the Black Pharaoh was supposedly entombed; a bust of the Black Pharaoh (which now rests in Edward Gavigan's secret workroom in Essex, England); a small drum (a tambour) bearing odd symbols supposedly of mystical power; and a strange circlet with a large zircon which was said to be the crown of the Black Pharaoh and to be the key to his triumph over death.

With Carlyle's agreement, Najir sold the items to Carlyle's agent, Warren Besart. Najir had stolen the artifacts from the house of Omar Shakti, high priest of the Egyptian Brotherhood of the Black Pharaoh.

Najir says that the Brotherhood is rumored to be involved in the recent theft of a mummy from the Clive Expedition, currently in Egypt. He has also heard that the Brotherhood wants an item located in the Mosque of Ibn-Tulun, but he does not know what it is or why the Brotherhood wants it.

This is all that Faraz Najir knows, though he tries to squeeze more money from the investigators before he divulges the name of Omar Shakti or confesses that he stole the artifacts from Shakti. Najir will then be of no more help. If the Brotherhood is tailing the investigators when they contact Najir, then they will shortly thereafter kill Najir, since he obviously did not learn his lesson.

Najir does not reveal that he wears around his neck another Mythos artifact, a necklace of silver and jet with a large opal in the center that protects from hunting horrors. Any hunting horror attacking a person wearing this necklace must succeed in a magic point vs. magic point roll on the Resistance Table each time it attacks. Failure indicates that the hunting horror cannot attack that round. Najir wears this beneath his djellaba: only a successful Luck roll and a successful Spot Hidden enables an investigator to spot it.

FARAZ NAJIR, age 45, Cairene Antiquities Dealer

STR 07	CON 16	SIZ 09	INT 14	POW 13
DEX 09	APP 04	EDU 06	SAN 11	HP 13

Damage Bonus: -1D4.

Weapon*: .38 Revolver 29%, damage 1D10

*Najir's revolver is illegal, but his experiences have left him barely sane and quite paranoid. He wears the .38 revolver beneath his djellaba, and will use it when he believes himself in danger.

Skills: Accounting 50%, Arabic 90%, Archaeology 30%, Bargain 75%, Credit Rating 20%, Cthulhu Mythos 10%, Egyptian History 60%, English 30%, Fast Talk 65%, French 30%, Hide 55%, Law 15%, Listen 55%, Occult 25%, Persuade 45%, Psychology 30%, Spot Hidden 65%.

Omar Shakti

A few miles north of Cairo along the west bank of the Nile lies the largest of Omar Shakti's cotton plantations. Shakti has a home in the nearby small town of Gezira Mohammed. He is wealthy and cultured, reputedly a lesser son of a fine family long powerful in Egypt. This powerful sorcerer controls the Brotherhood of the Black Pharaoh, and has the direct advice and aid of Nyarlathotep.

Though Egyptian, British, and French dispatches occasionally mention Shakti, in every such instance pertinent files and their cross-references have been destroyed by fire within a few months. Incidental tax records and property deeds exist, but no dossier ever compiled on Omar Shakti has long survived. The Cairo underworld occasionally whispers of him, but no more often than it refers to hundreds of other Cairo-area businessmen. Publicly, Mr. Shakti is an honest citizen, an astute businessman, and of impeccable manners.

Visiting Omar Shakti

Mr. Shakti's fields plainly yield cotton and bear no hint of Mythos-related activity. A successful Psychology roll does note that the workers (all Brotherhood members) are quieter and more sullen than most fellahin. On a Spot Hidden roll of half or less normal percentage, an investigator glimpses what appears to be an inverted ankh hanging around the neck of one worker.

Shakti suavely greets the investigators. If they have a cover story, he'll show them around. He is rotund and genial. He looks a robust fifty-five years old but is much, much older. He speaks English fluently, as well as other languages, including Mandarin Chinese. Usually he carries his cat, Hetep, with him; the cat has an unusually attentive air about it.

While offering mint tea and honey cakes in his well appointed parlor, Shakti denies any unusual knowledge of the Black Pharaoh or Queen Nitocris, adding that though he knows many legends of his land, he puts his faith in Allah and not in ancient stories. He aids the Penhew Foundation because every right-thinking Egyptian is eager to understand and preserve the wonders of this ancient land. He was sorry that Sir Aubrey met a violent fate in East Africa. Of course, he admonishes, magic, monsters, and desert ceremonies are tales for fellahin, not for educated gentlemen such as are his guests.

Investigating Shakti

OMAR SHAKTI

Shakti's large house holds nothing of interest except in the safe in the study. The safe is actually a thick steel cabinet secured by a key lock (STR 45 lock and front door, STR 50 all other sides). Shakti always carries the key except when he sleeps, at which time the key rests in the drawer of the night table beside his bed. The lock can be picked, however, and a prybar can force open a door or side panel.

Within the safe are business records, 250 Egyptian pounds, and a log book which lists five years of shipments: all are Egyptian artifacts sent to Ho Fong Imports, 15 Kaoyang St., Shanghai, or to Randolph Shipping Co., Port Darwin, Australia.

ITEM. An unsigned receipt stuck in the log book (*Nyarlathotep Papers #30*).

Relevance of the Information: if the investigators already have seen Sir Aubrey Penhew's handwriting, a successful Idea roll identifies it as written by him. A fine scarab brooch is listed as being sent to Ho Fong, in Shanghai, two months earlier. The note paper from A.P. is fresh, though undated. This evidence suggests that Aubrey Penhew is alive.

If the investigators stake out the plantation, they can easily follow the desert pilgrimage of the plantation workers on the last night of the waning moon (1D6+1 days later). The cultists number several hundred by the time they reach the

Nyarlathotep Papers #30

My Dear Omar,

The scarab is magnificent. If the matching pieces could be found, I would be most appreciative.

A.P.

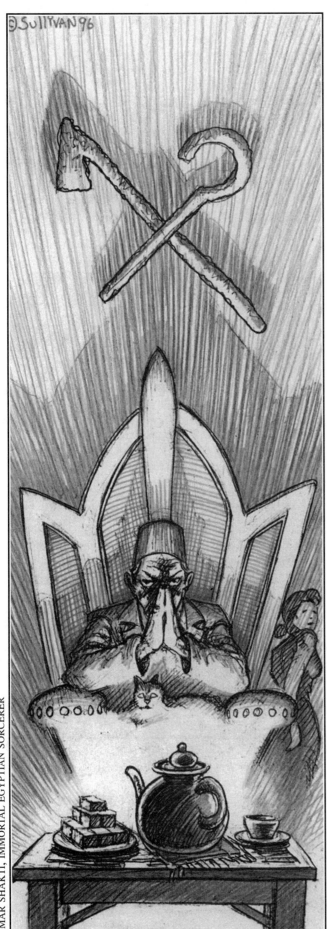

OMAR SHAKTI, IMMORTAL EGYPTIAN SORCERER

Sphinx at Giza. To join this parade the investigators must acquire white robes inscribed with inverted ankhs, which the cultists wear. Local residents do not mention these parades, nor do they speak of Omar Shakti. Major ceremonies are held at the summer and winter solstices, in Meidum.

Shakti keeps cult activities out of the public imagination, but he will risk using his considerable powers to avenge overt attack or midnight burglary. Shakti can easily rid himself of corpses. He will not want to call in the police unless he must. Without good evidence, local or national authorities make no move against Shakti. The British will never act concerning such minor internal matters.

Statistics

OMAR SHAKTI

By far the most potent adversary whom the investigators can meet in this campaign, Shakti is cunning, ruthless, and as powerful as a minor god. The investigators should try to avoid him, or else to kill him without warning. This sorcerer is several thousand years old; he has been reincarnated many times, and has seen more of history than anyone of human origin. Should he be killed, it is likely that the gods of the Mythos will raise him again, for he has always faithfully served them, Nyarlathotep in particular.

Shakti likes life as a human being. Keepers are advised not to abuse the power he possesses, but to be relentless if investigators persist in confronting him. He disdains mere weapons, though he does keep a revolver in his house. If he is killed, Shakti immediately crumbles into dust, requiring a 1/1D6 Sanity roll for viewers.

OMAR SHAKTI, appears about age 50, Wealthy Plantation Owner and High Priest of the Brotherhood of the Black Pharaoh

STR 13	CON 25	SIZ 10	INT 20	POW 33
DEX 17	APP 16	EDU 10	SAN 0	HP 18

Damage Bonus: +0.

Weapons: Cult Club 95%, damage 1D8

Scepters: Shakti has magical scepters similar to those of Edward Gavigan and Tewfik al-Sayed, except that Shakti's add 5D20 magic points for spell-casting or for resistance to attacks. He can call his scepters to his hands so long as he can see them, and only he can wield them. Tied to his life force, they crumble if he dies.

Spells: all spells in the rulesbook's Greater and Lesser Grimoires, plus others as the keeper wishes.

Skills: Accounting 65%, Arabic 95%, Aramaic 70%, Archaeology 80%, Bargain 90%, Cantonese 70%, Classical Greek 98%, Coptic 90%, Cthulhu Mythos 45%, Debate 85%, Demotic Egyptian 80%, Dodge 90%, Egyptian Hieroglyphs 95%, English 90%, French 95%, Hebrew 98%, Hide 35%, Hindi 80%, History 85%, Latin 98%, Law 65%, Linguist 70%, Listen 70%, Mandarin Chinese 90%, Occult 95%, Persuade 90%, Pharmacy 95%, Psychology 90%, Sneak 95%, Spot Hidden 90%, Swahili 45%.

HETEP

Omar Shakti's pretty white cat is more than something to hold in his lap. In one combat round it can transform itself into a cat demon which walks on its hind legs, looking something like a horrible, hairless, wrinkled lion. Its tongue attack is usually made while in pretty-white-cat form. Shakti can speak to and understand messages from the cat, and it is always near to him if not actually carried by him. If slain, the mummy of a cat dead for over a thousand years is left behind (lose 0/1D3 SAN to witness this). Sanity loss from seeing the cat-demon form is an automatic 2/1D6+1 SAN.

HETEP, Cat Form

STR 03	CON 04	SIZ 01	INT 15	POW 22
DEX 16	APP 13			HP 03

Damage Bonus: -1D6.

Weapon*: Tongue Attack 75%, damage is asphyxiation as per Drowning rules

Skills: Arabic 30%, Climb 85%, Coptic 30%, Demotic Egyptian 30%, English 30%, Hide 95%, Jump 95%, Sneak 95%, Track 75%.

HETEP, Cat-Demon Form

STR 21	CON 20	SIZ 12	INT 15	POW 25
DEX 18	MOV 09	HP 16		

Damage Bonus: +1D6.

Weapons*: Tongue Attack 75%, damage is asphyxiation as per Drowning rules
Claws 50%, damage 1D6+2+1D6
Bite 35%, damage 1D6+1D6

Skills: Arabic 30%, Climb 60%, Coptic 30%, Demotic Egyptian 30%, English 30%, Hide 75%, Jump 75%, Sneak 80%, Track 75%.

* The tongue attack consists of a surprise whiplash of about six feet of scratchy tongue which loops around and begins to choke the throat of the target. Hetep usually then transforms to demon form while it continues the choke, reels itself onto the horrified victim's torso, and rips out the target's stomach with its claws. It takes a STR success on the Resistance Table to slip free from the tongue. The tongue also can be severed by five points of damage from an edged weapon, but someone other than the victim must do the job.

MORE DESPICABLE CULTISTS

	1	*2*	*3*	*4*	*5*	*6*	*7*
STR	11	12	11	10	09	10	12
CON	09	07	09	10	11	10	18
SIZ	11	13	10	13	13	11	12
APP	07	08	09	08	06	09	06
INT	10	12	11	13	13	13	11
EDU	02	01	01	01	02	05	01
DEX	12	10	10	13	13	12	11
POW	04	07	07	08	10	11	09
HP	10	10	10	12	12	11	15

Damage Bonus: +0.

Weapons: Cult Club 35%, damage 1D8 plus chance to impale
Short Sword 35%, damage 1D6+1
Fighting Knife 30%, damage 1D4+2

Skills: Arabic 35%, Cthulhu Mythos 11%, Hide 35%, Listen 45%, Sneak 40%, Spot Hidden 45%.

Warren Besart

The investigators can find Roger Carlyle's former agent by asking at the French Ambassador's office or at Main Station, a fictitious police station adjacent to Ezbekia Gardens. Both show Besart's current address as The Red Door, Street of Scorpions, in the Darb el-Ahmar (the Red Alley). The Red Alley is another part of the Old City, a bazaar located along Sharia Muezzeddin Allah The investigators must explain why they wish to find Besart: the keeper must decide how reasonable their explanation sounds, and whether or not a bribe or arm-twisting helps matters along.

The sole red door along the Street of Scorpions opens into a clothing shop owned by Abou Udhreh. Besart hides in a small room in the back. Abou denies that Besart lives there; that is their agreement, for Besart does not want to be located. A successful Psychology roll shows Abou to be lying—Abou even glances at a curtained archway at the back of the shop which leads to the door of Besart's tiny room.

The investigators may stake out the shop, or bull their way into the back room. Abou will not resist a group of determined people, nor does he much care about the fate of Besart. If the investigators stake out the shop between after 8 p.m., they see Besart sally out to eat.

Besart wears a djellaba with the hood pulled over his face, but a successful Spot Hidden or Anthropology roll establishes that his shoes are European, that he is excessively tall for an Egyptian, that his djellaba is different from Abou's, and that his stride somehow differs from those walking near him. When Besart's face can be seen, it is sunken and pale, with a scruffy blond beard.

Besart's days are spent smoking hashish in order to dispel the terrible sights he witnessed while working for Carlyle. He is functionally insane because of what he witnessed, and only intimidation starts him speaking. Otherwise he runs. When caught, he snivels, and is reluctant to shout or to resist strongly. He lets the investigators lead him back to his filthy room.

The room is tiny, nearly filled by a foul bed, two filthy cushions, and a worm-eaten low table. The keeper should leave some doubt in the players' minds about Besart—is his tale true, a lie covering even more sinister events, or the worthless fantasy of a drug addict? Besart can be bribed with hashish or other drugs.

Besart's English alternates from precise to incomprehensible. Sometimes he lapses into French, or gutter Arabic. At other times he pauses to puff on a small, acrid-smelling pipe. A successful Pharmacy or Natural History roll identifies the smoke as a poor grade of hashish. Occasionally Besart completely forgets what he was saying. Near the end of his tale he begins to sweat profusely. Yet his voice is empty of emotion, as though his soul had long since fled.

ITEM. The statement of Warren Besart, as spoken by him in the privacy of his shabby room on the Red Alley (*Nyarlathotep Papers #31*).

MAD WARREN BESART

Relevance of the Information: establishes Besart's role as Roger Carlyle's agent, and gives valuable clues concerning the expedition's tenure in Egypt.

Whether or not the investigators agree to give Besart cash for more drugs, he tells them that the woman who told him of the evil ceremony was named Nyiti, and her son was Unba. They lived in El Wasta, a Nile town south of Meidum, easily reached by train, car, and steamer.

WARREN BESART, age 35, Nearly Mad Hashish Addict

STR 04	CON 08	SIZ 12	INT 13	POW 10
DEX 07	APP 06	EDU 15	SAN 05	HP 10

Damage Bonus: -1D4.

Weapons: .32 Revolver* 35%, damage 1D8

Kick 35%, damage 1D6-1D4

* Besart has long since pawned his firearms.

Skills: Accounting 45%, Arabic 55%, Archaeology 55%, Bargain 55%, Cthulhu Mythos 11%, Drive Automobile 30%, English 55%, Evaluate Hashish 65%, French 75%, Law 30%, Psychology 30%.

WHAT BESART SAW IN THE DESERT

The climax to the orgiastic ritual in the desert was the appearance of the Black Sphinx, a fearsome entity of great power. Investigators will not likely survive such an encounter. Besart's final memory, of a desert army of sphinxes waiting to attack, may be verifiable. The contours of the Great Sphinx at Giza are very like those of yardangs, wind-carved land forms which occur in many deserts, and which can sometimes be found in striking and suggestive groups, like great crouching beasts. Insane or shaken investigators might stumble into such terrain, to their players' infinite horror and the keeper's amusement.

Nigel Wassif

The *Cairo Bulletin* is an English-language weekly owned by the anglophile journalist, Nigel Wassif. Its offices are conveniently just across the square from whatever hotel in which the investigators stay, and its back issues are just what they need to learn about the Carlyle Expedition while it was in Egypt. In his early forties, Wassif is well fed, and has slicked-down hair and a pencil-thin mustache. His clothes are excellently cut and conservative. He is always very clean, and remarkably alert to the social implications of a situation. In some ways he is dense and unseeing, and his paper unperceptive in its general reporting, though it impeccably covers debuts and fancy-dress balls.

Wassif can be used in a fashion similar to that of Mickey Mahoney in the London section of this campaign, but where Mickey is cynical and brash, and makes no bones about the poverty of his upbringing, Wassif obsequiously strives for exquisite taste in the pages of the *Bulletin*, and lavishes care on his gossipy "Events" column. He is the illegitimate son of an Egyptian noblewoman who died at his birth. He believes that his father was an English nobleman. In conversation he implies that he is of royal blood, though he never makes a particular claim. A lot of influential Cairenes believe him, mostly because Nigel Wassif so thoroughly believes it himself.

He has long had access to the highest levels of the Egyptian aristocracy and government, and his excellent English and French, his suave manners, and his unimpeachable discretion have opened the doors to him among all the foreign social sets in the capital. Only one British functionary in Egypt knows that Wassif is an intelligence agent for King George V. If the investigators make a polished and intelligent appearance at the *Bulletin*, Wassif may mention them in routine dispatches. If they are rude, loud, or otherwise uncivilized, he will not, and this potentially valuable alliance for the investigators will never occur.

Information from *The Cairo Bulletin*

All the information in the *Cairo Bulletin* is available in any respectable Cairene newspaper.

The best item in the *Bulletin* is a photo showing Sir Aubrey, Roger Carlyle, Hypatia Masters, and Dr. Robert Huston emerging from a dinner in their honor at the Turf Club, two days after their arrival in Cairo. Carlyle is blond and handsome; Huston is darker and plumper, with a somewhat worried smile; Sir Aubrey is white-haired, tall, and distinguished; Hypatia Masters is blond and beautifully gowned. A man in a tight tuxedo in the background may be Jack Brady, but as a mere employee he is unidentified.

Bits of data in the society and news sections of the *Bulletin* weave a single story. The expedition arrives in Cairo in May of 1919, avowedly to survey for and excavate concerning the Third Dynasty of Egypt, a shadowy period. After investigations near Giza, work shifted first to a Saqqara site and then to Dhashur. Since the specific digs seemed unrelated to known Third Dynasty locations, specu-

Nyarlathotep Papers #31

Warren Besart's Statement

"A lawyer contacted me. I agreed to act as purchasing agent for Mr. Roger Carlyle of the United States, who was represented to me as a wealthy American. On written instructions from Mr. Carlyle, I purchased certain artifacts from Faraz Najir, an antiquities dealer, and illegally shipped them out of Egypt to Sir Aubrey Penhew in London. I know the artifacts were ancient, but nothing more.

"When the Carlyle Expedition came to Egypt, I arranged for all their equipment and permits. Their main site was at Dhashur, in the area of the Bent Pyramid.

"One day at Dhashur, Jack Brady came to me and told me that Carlyle, Hypatia Masters, Sir Aubrey, and Dr. Huston had entered the Bent Pyramid and then vanished. Brady was excited and suspected foul play, since the diggers already had fled the site and work had come to a stand-still. We did not know what to do, so we drank.

"The next morning, Carlyle and the others reappeared. They were excited by some tremendous find, but what it was, they would not say, nor did I learn, for Sir Aubrey was a fiend for secrecy. All of them had changed in some inexplicable way, and a way not for the better; I did not ask further.

"That evening, an old Egyptian woman visited me. She said that her son had been one of the diggers. She said the diggers had fled because Carlyle and the others had consorted with an ancient evil, the Messenger of the Black Wind. She said that she could recognize that the souls of all the Europeans but Brady and myself were lost. If I wanted proof, I should go to the Collapsed Pyramid at Meidum at the time when the moon is slimmest—the night before the dark of the moon. God help me, I went!

"I took one of the trucks, pretending to leave for a night in the pleasure quarter of Cairo. But instead I drove the twenty miles south to Meidum, and secreted myself where she advised. There in the midnight blackness I saw Carlyle and the others disport themselves in obscene rituals with a hundred madmen. The very desert came alive, crawling and undulating toward the ruins of the pyramid. To my horror, the stone ruins themselves became a skeletal, bulging-eyed thing!

"Strange creatures emerged from the sands, grasped the dancing celebrants, and, one by one, tore out their throats, killing all until only the Europeans (and one other robed celebrant) remained.

"Something more loomed out of the sand, the size of an elephant but with five separate shaggy heads. Then I realized what it was—but it is madness to speak it! I saw it rise and in a great ravening swallow as one all the torn corpses and their hideous murderers, leaving alive only five people amidst the stench of the blood-soaked sands.

"I fainted. When I recovered, I wandered into the desert. There further horrors awaited me. Stumbling up a rise before dawn, I saw beyond hundreds of dark sphinxes, rank upon rank drawn up and waiting for the hour of madness when they will spring to devour the world! I fainted again, and this time I left the world for many months.

"A man found me; for two years he and his mother cared for me—me, a man mindless and returned, I came back to Cairo. But I began to dream! Only hashish helps now, or opium if it can be found. My supply is low again, and my life is intolerable without it. Will you gentlemen please contribute? Only strong drugs keep me from insanity. Everything, gentlemen, everything is lost. There is no hope for any of us. Everywhere they wait. Perhaps you will join me in a pipe?"

lation arose about secret purposes of the expedition, and the Black Pharaoh was mentioned several times. Later, rumor persistently maintained that the expedition had made an astonishing find.

In July of 1919, the expedition suddenly embarked for Mombasa, ostensibly on holiday, and in fact Roger Carlyle was frequently reported to be sick just before this time. As spokesman, Sir Aubrey indicated that the summer was too hot for Carlyle, and also implied that the impending seasonal flood of the Nile would cover an important site for several months. Several photos show Hypatia Masters with her camera ("Miss Masters Prepares for a Camera Safari in Kenya"), but a successful halved Spot Hidden roll reveals that the background of one of the photos contains part of a calendar page for May—photos which Wassif then ran in July were actually taken during the first few days after the arrival of the expedition, and are no evidence of her later appearance. Wassif will shrug, but not remember using earlier photos, for that is common newspaper practice. Miss Masters also "fell ill" in June, and had not yet recovered when the group departed for Kenya. Wassif does remember that the Carlyle Expedition "was simply horrid" in keeping visitors away from its sites, including the press.

NIGEL WASSIF

He also recalls that the principals of the expedition had dinner several times with Omar Shakti, a wealthy cotton plantation owner whom Wassif finds repellent and whose private reputation is unsavory. Wassif will not say it to strangers, but he knows Shakti to be connected to the Brotherhood of the Black Pharaoh, an organization he fears and feels to be a great shame of Egypt. If the investigators prove to be reliable friends, he may share this secret.

Incidentally, he adds, another Penhew Foundation expedition is in Egypt. The Clive party is excavating at Giza, and they recently unearthed the mummy of an unknown female from a secret chamber in the smallest of the three Great Pyramids. Several authorities have speculated that it is Queen Nitocris, a mysterious figure of the Sixth Dynasty. Before tests could be carried out or the mummy unwrapped, the sarcophagus and contents disappeared, to the bewilderment of all concerned. Considerable efforts by the police have turned up no leads. The site was well guarded, and only one entrance to the secret chamber existed.

Wassif might help respectable investigators in several ways. He could find a reliable guide for them. He or the guide might help them find Najir or Besart. Wassif will pay a few piastres per news story that the investigators furnish—hardly enough to use to support themselves—but he'll refuse anything too controversial. If asked about research libraries, etc., he will direct them to the excellent Egyptian Museum, and commend to them an acquaintance there, Dr. Ali Kafour, who may be able to clear up bureaucratic snags holding back permits, or might ease small problems with the police.

NIGEL WASSIF, Proprietor of the Cairo Bulletin and Agent for the King of England

STR 11	CON 13	SIZ 13	INT 15	POW 15
DEX 11	APP 13	EDU 12	SAN 75	HP 13

Damage Bonus: +0.

Weapon: Polo Mallet 40%, damage 1D6

Skills: Accounting 20%, Arabic 70%, Archaeology 05%, Bargain 50%, Credit Rating 95%, Drive Automobile 30%, English 80%, French 65%, Gossip 79%, History 20%, Law 15%, Library Use 35%, Persuade 20%, Polo 40%, Psychology 25%, Ride 50%, Spot Hidden 35%, Tennis 35%.

Dr. Ali Kafour

Even if the investigators somehow ignore the *Cairo Bulletin*, the Egyptian Museum is the most likely and most systematic Mythos source in Egypt. The investigators can be referred to Dr. Kafour by chance, or the keeper might make them work their way through a bureaucratic maze in order to reach him. The museum, a staggering storehouse of Egyptian antiquities, is not far from the Nile and the Great Nile Bridge. The museum's large ochre dome is a prominent landmark in the city. This former palace houses an ever-growing collection of everything precious to the Egyptian past. It is open to visitors from 9 a.m. to 4:30 p.m.

Dr. Kafour is a short, thin man, alert and intelligent, who has never lost his love for the occult. When this older man grows excited in conversation, he characteristically jumps up and down with impatience. He is kindly and able. He may well be able to help investigators protect themselves from certain Mythos spells and creatures: he is an Egyptian ritual magician of some capacity, though he wants no one to know that he dabbles in sorcery.

DR. ALI KAFOUR

The museum has a large collection of Egyptian occult material; much of it is in hieroglyphics on papyrus scrolls. There also is a complete copy of *Al Azif* (the *Necronomicon*) in Abd al-Azrad's Arabic. Dr. Kafour, the resident expert in occult matters, oversees this portion of the museum. His interest will be piqued if the investigators ask about the Carlyle Expedition or about the Black Pharaoh. If the investigators hide their intentions with irrelevant researches, the good doctor will dismiss them: he is a busy man.

The core of the occult collection of the Egyptian Museum rests within several adjacent underground vaults of thick steel (to guard against damage from the nearby Nile). Vault walls are uniformly STR 100; the vault doors are STR 130 and sealed by excellent combination locks designed and built in Munich. Dr. Kafour has memorized the combinations; another set of the combinations rests in the ultra-secure and efficient offices of Munchen Geldschrankenwerk; a third and final set is in a sealed envelope in the personal safe (door is STR 50) of the Director of Antiquities, located on the second floor of the museum. Additionally, and unknown to anyone but Kafour, he has cast Egyptian ritual magic as STR 16 warding for the entire collection: for that spell, see the Seal of Isis in the rulesbook Lesser Grimoire.

Even if Kafour cooperates and grants the investigators permission to examine the occult holdings, the investigators need to be able to read hieroglyphic and hieratic Egyptian of various dynasties and conventions, Demotic Egyptian, Coptic, Arabic, Classical Greek, Latin, Aramaic, and Hebrew to comb these materials. If the investigators manage to intrigue him, Dr. Kafour will do some of the research.

Information from Dr. Kafour

THE CARLYLE EXPEDITION: Dr. Kafour believes that the Carlyle Expedition uncovered a secret pertaining to the Black Pharaoh, and that the discovery somehow led to their slaughter in Kenya. Sir Aubrey Penhew had long studied the Black Pharaoh, and Kafour and Penhew had several times discussed the topic and traded information about that subtle presence.

When last he came to Egypt, Sir Aubrey did not seek out Kafour. When Kafour visited the expedition dig near Dhashur, Sir Aubrey rudely rebuffed the doctor. Kafour vividly recalls marked changes in Sir Aubrey—physically the man seemed younger, and emotionally he was withdrawn, aloof, and curiously malicious.

THE BLACK PHARAOH IN HISTORY: at the end of the Third Dynasty a man known as Nephren-Ka came to Egypt. Nephren-Ka was a powerful sorcerer; he brought madness and death to his enemies at the flick of a finger. The stories say that he came from an ancient city in the deserts of Arabia, whose name was Irem, the City of Pillars. This place is mentioned in *Al Azif*. All who knew of it held it in dread.

Nephren-Ka revived the worship of an old, foul god—the Black Pharaoh. Soon Nephren-Ka and that god were interchangeable in the minds of the people, and the sorcerer became known as the Black Pharaoh. Now no one can distinguish their deeds and legends.

For many years the Black Pharaoh fought with Zoser's successors of the Third Dynasty for control of the land. So great was the power of the Black Pharaoh that no record of them now remains. For a time, Nephren-Ka ruled the Nile and its peoples. At last Sneferu arose, and founded the Fourth Dynasty, and with the aid of the goddess Isis thwarted the evil magic and slew Nephren-Ka.

Remarkably, however, a pyramid was built to contain the sorcerer's body—Kafour speculates that this perhaps insulated Egypt from still-potent magic within the corpse—but this structure collapsed even while Sneferu was building a second. The Collapsed Pyramid is at Meidum; the second pyramid is the Bent Pyramid at Dhashur. Records imply that Nephren-Ka's corpse was removed from Meidum and placed within the Bent Pyramid, but exploration of the site has discovered no trace. Another pyramid at Dhashur, the Red Pyramid, is also attributed to Sneferu; this pyramid is said to guard Dhashur, lest Nephren-Ka rise from the dead.

Upon his triumph, Sneferu ordered all traces of the Black Pharaoh stricken from the land. Nevertheless, worshipers of the Black Pharaoh remained, and schemed for the evil one's return. In time, the worshipers were driven south, out of Egypt and into the hideous swamps beyond the Sudan.

In the Sixth Dynasty, the cruel Queen Nitocris was thought in league with a new cult of the Black Pharaoh; though the proof of this is subjective, Dr. Kafour believes it to be true. In an aside, Dr. Kafour casually mentions that the Black Pharaoh is sometimes called by the name Nyarlathotep. Depending on what the investigators already know, this information might require a Sanity roll for 0/1D3 SAN, for the shock.

LEGENDS OF THE BLACK PHARAOH: some say he was one of a pantheon of abominable deities more ancient than the gods of Egypt. These old gods were utterly inhuman, and were dedicated to chaos and madness.

■ Nephren-Ka was said to possess a huge beast, of which the Sphinx at Giza is a small, inaccurate representation.

■ The voice of Nephren-Ka is said to have been carried throughout the land within a black wind, a wind which destroyed at his whim.

■ A prophecy implies that the Black Pharaoh will arise "fingers and toes after the Great Good One", a reference which many have taken to mean twenty centuries after Jesus. A new age then begins, destined to end the dominance of mankind upon the earth, and to bring freedom and stark truth to the Black Pharaoh's followers.

■ Man-like but inhuman worshipers of the Black Pharaoh were said to lurk underground in the deserts, occasionally waylaying innocent passersby.

■ The Great Sphinx at Giza is said to have had an important function in hideous rituals held by Nitocris.

WHAT DR. KAFOUR BELIEVES: he holds that the Black Pharaoh and Nephren-Ka existed, as yet do the pantheon of gods of which the Black Pharaoh was a part. He calls these entities the Elder Gods, and says they are led by the demon sultan Azathoth. Dr. Kafour has seen servitors of these gods in the desert, and knows for a fact that the Brotherhood of the Black Pharaoh exists in present-day Egypt, though he knows nothing of its organization, leadership, or activities. He also suspects that worship of the Black Pharaoh is growing in other parts of Africa. For example, he has heard of a cult called the Bloody Tongue in Britain's Kenya Colony. The cult worships a monstrous god which is another aspect of the Black Pharaoh.

QUEEN NITOCRIS: the unidentified mummy recently stolen from the Clive Expedition at Giza undoubtedly was the remains of that beautiful and evil ruler. She had been buried alive, but no trace was found until the Clive Expedition uncovered the secret room in the smallest of the

Great Pyramids. How or why she was stolen he does not know, but he thinks that the theft relates to the prophesied return of the Black Pharaoh.

THE PENHEW FOUNDATION: he has always respected Sir Aubrey, director Edward Gavigan, and the efforts of the Penhew Foundation. However, since Sir Aubrey died, there have been ten Foundation expeditions to Egypt, and among them there have been at least twenty deaths, numerous disappearances, several suicides, and one certified case of madness. Most have followed the same pattern of paranoid secrecy, erratic excavation, and bizarre incident that was set by the Carlyle Expedition.

AL AZIF: the Arabic *Necronomicon* in the museum's collection contains most of the Black Pharaoh information which Kafour relates to the investigators. It contains much more, and is definitely dangerous to life and Sanity to read. Kafour will not quickly let anyone examine such a tome.

DR. ALI KAFOUR, Ph.D., age 63, Curator of Occult Materials and Ritual Magician

STR 07	CON 14	SIZ 12	INT 18	POW 16
DEX 13	APP 15	EDU 18	SAN 70	HP 13

Damage Bonus: +0.

Weapons: none.

Spells: Chant of Thoth, Seal of Isis, Voice of Ra. These are Egyptian ritual magic requiring long rituals and a number of components for successful casting. All are in the rulesbook Lesser Grimoire. The keeper may supply more spells as he or she sees fit.

Skills: Anthropology 35%, Arabic 90%, Archaeology 95%, Astronomy 40%, Bargain 65%, Coptic 25%, Credit Rating 75%, Cthulhu Mythos 15%, Drive Automobile 30%, Demotic Egyptian 65%, Egyptian Greek 40%, Hieroglyphs 90%, Egyptian History 95%, English 65%, French 80%, Geology 25%, Hebrew 60%, Latin 40%, Law Concerning Antiquities 90%, Library Use 95%, Occult 80%, Persuade 60%, Psychology 50%, Sneak 40%, Spot Hidden 50%.

THE BLACK CAT

Wherein inquiries about the Clive Expedition lead the investigators to discover another power at large, and cause them to deduce that kindness and respect are always the best policies.

Inquiring about the Clive Expedition, the investigators soon learn that one member of the dig was dismissed a month or so after the group's arrival. Dr. Ali Kafour or Cairo journalist Nigel Wassif relate that a Dutch archaeologist named Janwillem Vanheuvelen was fired by Dr. Henry Clive, allegedly for incompetence and alcoholism. Wassif knows that Vanheuvelen couldn't afford a return ticket to Europe, and is still somewhere in Cairo.

Vanheuvelen is an insider from the Clive Expedition who may very well carry a grudge against them. Who could be a better source of information?

Keeper's Information

Unfortunately, Vanheuvelen is more troubled than informative. Fired from the expedition and left to fend for himself in Cairo, the ambitious but incompetent Vanheuvelen has tried for months to attach himself to another expedition or start one of his own, to no avail. A couple of weeks ago he tried to reconcile with the Clive Expedition. A surprisingly helpful Martin Winfield pointed the hapless Dutchman in the direction of a little-known back-alley temple in the Old City. There, said Winfield, Vanheuvelen might find a subject worthy of study, one that would not only get him back in Clive's good graces, but might also make Vanheuvelen famous in his own right. Winfield himself would have looked into it, but his time was taken up at the Memphis dig, or so he said.

Vanheuvelen ventured into the narrow, twisting streets and dingy passages of the Old City. After a circuitous journey he came to a small dark chamber beneath the city. A fire burned in a small brazier before an ancient obsidian statue of a sleek cat. Several live cats watched from the shadows. Vanheuvelen examined the statue, and was about to count the experience as an interesting footnote in his catalog of failures when he discovered a secret compartment in the base of the statue. Inside were several impossibly ancient papyrus scrolls covered with hieroglyphs, the *Black Rites*. There was no one to see him take the scrolls. Perhaps no one would miss them.

The little temple honored the cat goddess Bast, and was visited primarily by the feline population of the city. While humans do not worship Bast in any organized sense, they do still make offerings to her in time of need. A very select priesthood has managed to maintain itself through the centuries, perhaps only one or two during any given generation. In Cairo that position is filled by a creature of unearthly beauty and power. She can wear the form of a young woman or of a black panther. This woman, Neris, now seeks the return of the scrolls at any price.

For the past week Vanheuvelen has been deciphering the scrolls. In between drinking bouts he has learned that they are the work of Luveh-Keraph, a priest of Bast during the Thirteenth Dynasty. Vanheuvelen has also been the victim of a curious plague: everywhere he goes he is followed by cats. They watch him, follow him, and, when he approaches, they hiss at him. He has even drawn a fearful scratch or two from his feline pursuers.

In the coming days, Bast's priestess Neris approaches Vanheuvelen directly, requesting the return of the scrolls. Unwilling to give up his meal-ticket back to respectability, the archaeologist refuses, unwittingly provoking increasingly violent encounters with the priestess and the feline populations of Cairo. Into this confusion come the investigators.

Janwillen Vanheuvelen

The investigators have some difficulty tracking down the Dutch archaeologist. Wassif or Kafour may be able to discover his whereabouts within a day or two. Searching on their own, the investigators need several days to a week to find him. The members of the Clive Expedition either do not know where Vanheuvelen is, or claim not to know.

Vanheuvelen is living in the Street of the Moths, one of the poorest sections of the Old City, in a dingy room behind a tailor's shop. He has stooped to running errands for his tailor/landlord to pay for his room and board. When the investigators arrive at the shop, the grizzled old tailor is shooing several cats out of his shop with a broom, cursing in Arabic all the while.

The Dutchman's tiny room contains only a cot, a crude table and chair, a few innocuous books on Egyptian archaeology, an oil lamp, and a couple of wine-bottle candles. Vanheuvelen keeps the scrolls of the *Black Ritess* wrapped in canvas, in a shallow hole in the dirt floor beneath his cot.

The archaeologist is of average height, a little plump, slightly bloated from his bouts with alcohol. He is perpetually unshaven, and wears a tiny pair of spectacles perched on his nose. His clothes are rarely laundered, and he and his room smell of perspiration and body odor. Vanheuvelen is a nervous, excitable man with a lot of ambition but lacking in common sense. His drinking problem is intermittent: when he has money, he drinks, and when he drinks, he drinks to excess, drinking until his money is gone. He has a slight Dutch accent, but speaks fluent English and a smattering of Arabic.

Vanheuvelen is at best a middling archaeologist. He has no formal degrees, acquiring his knowledge as a practical matter, in the course of several field expeditions to Egypt. He now has a fair knowledge of Egyptian hieroglyphs, being a quick-minded man.

He is happy to see fellow Europeans, especially if they furnish drinks or spare a few coins. If the investigators ask about the Clive Expedition, he'll tell them what he knows, so long as they're buying drinks and dinner.

WHAT VANHEUVELEN KNOWS

He attached himself to the Clive Expedition when they arrived in Cairo. He stayed with them during their work at Giza, and was there when the tomb with the "unidentified" female mummy (Nitocris) was discovered. He relates the story of the mysterious nocturnal disappearance of the mummy and its guards (see above, "The Story Which Clive Peddles"). Vanheuvelen says that the scrolls found in the tomb were in good shape and quite legible, contradicting what Henry Clive claims. The Dutchman believes that the mummy was indeed Nitocris, about whom he knows next to nothing. He was fired abruptly just before the company packed up and left for Memphis. He claims his dismissal was based on a need to cut expenses.

Of the members of the Clive Expedition, Vanheuvelen expresses little but praise. He holds a slight grudge against Dr. Clive for firing him, but he acknowledges that his own drunkenness led to his dismissal. The Dutchman is grateful to Martin Winfield for his aid in locating the *Black Ritess* scrolls. Vanheuvelen is quite fond of Johannes Sprech, whose knowledge of Egyptian hieroglyphs has earned the Dutchman's respect. Vanheuvelen is also on good terms with

J. VANHEUVELEN

Agatha Broadmoor and James Gardner, though he feels that their theories about Egypt and the occult are far-fetched.

As the conversation with Vanheuvelen continues, a cat slinks into the room. The Dutch archaeologist interrupts his speech to toss a spoon at it, scaring it. It bounds out of the room.

Fortified with alcohol, Vanheuvelen tells of the find that will make him rich and famous. In a tiny lost temple he has found a set of scrolls containing an unknown tract setting forth ancient Egyptian rituals. He states that the scrolls must be at least Thirteenth Dynasty, if not earlier. He's translating them now. A few more days, maybe a week, and he'll have it finished. If pressed, or plied with more alcohol, Vanheuvelen may show the investigators his work, a Dutch version of the *Black Rites of Luveh-Keraph*.

THE BLACK RITES

If he trusts them, Vanheuvelen shows the investigators his translation of the ancient treatise. Though different in many ways, Dutch is a dialect of High German, and the German skill can be applied to it. He does not show the investigators the original scrolls, saying only that they are in a safe place. He says he discovered the scrolls in a lost temple beneath the streets of Cairo itself. He doesn't want to show the investigators the temple, however, until he's finished his translation and has studied more of the site.

Vanheuvelen's translation is often faulty. He has translated roughly half of the scrolls, mostly dealing with the worship of Bast. Vanheuvelen has also delved into the sections on Sebek, though he has wrongly identified the entity involved as Apep, one of the evil serpents of Egyptian myth who sought to stop the boat of the sun-god Ra from rising every morning.

Vanheuvelen's present version of the scrolls adds 1D4 Cthulhu Mythos and costs 1D4 Sanity points. The spell multiplier is only x1. Spells translated include Contact Bast, Summon/Bind Cat, and Summon/Bind Crocodile.

He needs about a week to translate it into written English, though he can with difficulty skim it in spoken English in about four hours, giving the investigators a good idea of some of its contents. Vanheuvelen's Dutch translation requires another month or so to complete. Then another 1D4 points of Cthulhu Mythos and another 1D4 Sanity loss will accrue, and all the spells will be available—if he lives to complete the work.

A Plague of Cats

Since he found the scrolls, Vanheuvelen has been the victim of a strange "curse": he has been constantly watched and followed by cats of all shapes and sizes. No matter where he goes, the cats are there. And in the past couple of days he has noticed another follower, a beautiful young Arab woman—this is Neris, the priestess of Bast. He has not yet associated the theft of the scrolls with the presence of the cats. Perhaps the investigators will help him with this easy deduction.

The cats seek to avenge his theft from the temple of Bast. Neris seeks the return of the scrolls.

In the hours after the investigators befriend and question Vanheuvelen, the plague of cats clearly intensifies. Each time they meet with the Dutch archaeologist thereafter, Spot Hidden rolls note an increased number of lurking observant felines. Each time the investigators notice these cats, charge them 0/1D3-1 Sanity points. Try to stage several encounters with Vanheuvelen, the investigators, and the cats. Once the investigators have noticed the cats, they may find cats in their hotel rooms, be followed by mysterious scurries in alleys which turn out to be caused by "harmless" cats, meet cats in taxicabs, toilets, and so on. Keep Sanity losses at 0/1D3-1. Use the cats as implacable, eerily intelligent pursuers, sure to set the investigators' nerves on edge with their unblinking all-seeing eyes.

If Vanheuvelen or the investigators kill or seriously injure any of these creatures, the cats begin to gather in force. As drama calls for, stage furtive attacks by them. Even if the cats are treated with care, Vanheuvelen is at least once scratched by a wrathful specimen.

Soon after Vanheuvelen's blooding, the beautiful priestess of Bast approaches him. The investigators may or may not witness this meeting, but they need to learn of it. Neris is a lithe, soft-spoken woman, sensual but aloof. At first her intentions seem friendly toward the unkempt foreigner, even vaguely seductive. Soon enough, however, Neris urges Vanheuvelen to return what he has stolen. Now the dark-eyed beauty's aloofness seems menacing. His theft has brought the curse of the cats upon him, she warns, and the wrath of the goddess approaches. Vanheuvelen refuses, and she departs angrily. If followed or threatened, she escapes her pursuers with cat-like ease and grace, bounding across perilous rooftops. A successful Jump roll each round is needed to stay up with her; missing the roll puts the investigator out of the chase and costs 1D6 hit points for injuries. If attacked, Neris later returns in panther form to take revenge upon her attacker.

PRIESTESS NERIS

Beginning a night or two after the meeting with Neris, Vanheuvelen and/or the investigators are visited by Neris, taking form of a large black panther. She might crouch on a nearby rooftop, growl from an alley, perhaps roll on and claw their beds. The first sighting of this creature costs the viewers 0/1D4 Sanity points. The creature fights only in self-defense, unless Neris herself was harmed earlier by an investigator. If so, she takes a warning swipe or two at her previous foe before loping away into the night.

If attacked, the panther lashes out until she loses half her hit points, then flees. If fleeing because of injury, Neris appears at her next encounter fully healed, by the graces of her patron, Bast.

On subsequent nights the panther repeats her visits, especially to the increasingly terrified Dutchman. As the panther, Neris' later visits also may increase in violence as she strains to force the return of the scrolls. The cat priestess' behavior

The Black Rites of Luveh-Keraph

Egyptian hieroglyphs, +9 Cthulhu Mythos, x3 spell multiplier, 1D6/2D6 SAN to read. Seven spells can be learned from the scrolls: Contact "The Goddess of Cats" (Bast), Summon/Bind Cat, "Bring Forth the Faceless Master of the Sands" (Contact Nyarlathotep, faceless sphinx form), "Call the Black Pharaoh" (Contact Nyarlathotep), "Summon the Carrion-Feasters of the Desert" (Contact Ghoul), "Call Forth the Terrible Lord of the Riverbanks" (Contact Sebek), "Summon and Abjure the Children of the Riverbanks" (Summon/Bind Crocodile).

This version of the *Black Ritess* consists of ten fragile papyrus scrolls dating to the Thirteenth Dynasty (1786-1633 BC). Almost every inch of each scroll is covered with tiny, crabbed Egyptian hieroglyphs. The first scroll in the sequence identifies its author as Luveh-Keraph, high priest of the cat goddess Bast. The first few scrolls discuss the worship of Bast in great detail, including means for summoning Bast and her feline kindred.

Later scrolls outline the worship of other Egyptian deities. Particular mention is made of "The Terrible Lord of the Riverbanks", crocodile-headed Sebek. His riverside temples are described, along with the rituals for sacrifices made in his name.

Cautionary chapters are devoted to darker members of the Egyptian pantheon. Nyarlathotep is discussed in the forms of the faceless sphinx and the Black Pharaoh, each presented as entirely separate beings. This information is identical to Dr. Ali Kafour's knowledge of the history and legends of the Black Pharaoh.

toward the investigators also depends on how much they interfere with her mission, and how much they seem to side with Vanheuvelen. Neris pursues the *Black Rites* while they are in Egypt. She attempts to murder anyone trying to leave the country with the scrolls.

See the end of this section for further events, including possible resolutions involving Vanheuvelen, Neris, and the scrolls.

THE TEMPLE OF BAST

If frightened enough by the plague of cats, the mysterious woman, and the black panther, Vanheuvelen agrees to lead the investigators to the temple where he found the scrolls. Whether he decides to surrender the scrolls is left for the keeper.

The temple is hidden in the Old City. The easiest access to it is via a narrow passage leading off of a dingy back-alley, a route that twists and turns and forks, crosses the corridor of a large building, climbs up across a rooftop, and finally plunges down a narrow and steep stairway into the earth. With Vanheuvelen along to guide, one Luck roll by a random player is required for the investigators to reach the temple.

Without the Dutchman's presence, his verbal directions yield only a POW x1 chance to find the temple. With a successful Idea roll, a clever investigator may double the chances of finding the temple to POW x2 by following a pious cat on its leisurely travels.

Whether or not Vanheuvelen guides them, during their search the party sees few people, none of whom admit knowing about such an unholy place. But they see cats everywhere.

The underground temple turns out to be a large dome-like space about 40 feet across, its walls dotted with many nooks and crannies within which its feline worshipers may perch and lurk, their wise and alien eyes glinting in the soft glowing light. One entrance exists. Against the wall opposite the entrance sits a seven-foot-tall statue of a beautiful cat-headed woman seated on a throne. If needed, a successful Archaeology or Anthropology roll identifies this as the ancient Egyptian goddess Bast, sometimes called Pasht or Bubastis. The statue is carved from a single block of obsidian. A Spot Hidden roll reveals the seams of a drawer between the feet, where Vanheuvelen found the scrolls. At the statue's feet a small brazier burns dimly, casting steady shadows across the whitewashed walls.

When the investigators enter, 2D10 cats already are present. If any of these creatures is attacked or molested, the rest of the cats swarm forth and attack without quarter whoever has come. Each round of the fight brings another 1D6 animals scurrying into the fray, seemingly out of the very walls.

If a cat is actually killed in their sacred sanctuary, all hell breaks loose as the vengeance of Bast is made known. She transforms 1D6 of the felines present into bloodthirsty big cats. These lions and panthers then attempt to kill the remaining transgressors, pursuing them to the streets if necessary.

If the investigators visit peacefully, they note the comings and goings of dozens, perhaps hundreds of cats. Every hour spent here there is a 10% chance a humble human pilgrim enters. Though surprised to see others here, the person is merely here to seek the beneficence of the cat goddess. If questioned (in Arabic), the pilgrim says that she is here to pray for her cat, who has been missing for several days. She hopes that Bast can return her companion to her or else see the creature's soul to its rest. She knows nothing about an organized Bast cult, only that her grandmother long, long ago told her of this place and its purpose.

Resolutions

How do the investigators handle their feline pursuers? How does the keeper play Vanheuvelen and Neris? Vanheuvelen needs to finish his translation and exhibit the scrolls in order to make his name. Neris wants the scrolls returned immediately, to re-establish the holy order of the sanctuary. These two goals directly conflict.

Vanheuvelen won't return the scrolls unless he is seriously injured or seriously frightened. The investigators may have to help convince him of his peril.

Neris first appears a day or two after the investigators' first meeting with the Dutchman. She spends two or three days trying to frighten Vanheuvelen into returning the stolen *Black Ritess*. After that, her tactics become more violent, even murderous toward Vanheuvelen.

If the archaeologist is killed Neris still won't know where the scrolls are. She may keep tabs on the investigators to see if they turn up the scrolls, at which time the discoverers find themselves experiencing a second plague of cats. If Neris kills Vanheuvelen, the investigators lose 1D4 Sanity points for their inability to help him escape his fate, but nothing for finding his corpse.

If Neris dies in either form, her killer incurs the wrath of Bast, who moves implacably to avenge her faithful priestesses.

The cat goddess can dispatch all the cats of the city if she wishes. Like a cat, she enjoys playing with her victims. At first the felines merely follow, then they threaten, and eventually they attack. This build-up costs the killer 0/1 Sanity points per day. If any of the harassing cats are killed, future sendings include big cats: lions and panthers. This curse ends only with the death of Neris' killer, regardless of whether or not the scrolls are returned, and follows its sufferer wherever he goes in the waking world, and even into the Dreamlands.

Leaving the country with the scrolls blocks Neris, though she will use lethal force to prevent such an escape. If she fails and the scrolls of the *Black Rites* leave Egypt, relentless Bast takes charge, as described above. Bast will ultimately succeed, but Vanheuvelen and/or the investigators will have enough time to make a full translation of the *Black Rites of Luveh-Keraph*.

For all concerned, the best outcome is for the investigators to convince Vanheuvelen to return the scrolls. This takes persuasion on their part, for the archaeologist has nothing without the scrolls, and he will be stubborn and desperate about them. But his life is secure if he hands over the scrolls to Neris, or returns them to the temple. With a little fleshing out, he might make a good replacement character for an investigator who dies in Egypt. Vanheuvelen's survival nets the investigators 1D3 points of Sanity, not to mention access to a significant part of the Cthulhu Mythos.

If Vanheuvelen survives this scenario he may assist and/or accompany the investigators during their stay in Egypt, and perhaps beyond. The investigators will have to pay the hapless Dutchman's expenses.

Vanheuvelen remains loyal to the Clive Expedition: he won't do anything to offend or oppose Clive and company. Unfortunately, he is also foolish enough to betray the investigators to these secret foes, in hopes of regaining his position with Clive.

Statistics

JANWILLEM VANHEUVELEN, age 39, Hapless Archaeologist and Alcoholic

STR 11	CON 11	SIZ 14	INT 14	POW 12
DEX 12	APP 12	EDU 17	SAN 51	HP 13

Damage Bonus: +1D4.

Weapons: none carried; all at base percentages only.

Skills: Anthropology 30%, Arabic 35%, Archaeology 45%, Credit Rating 01%, Dutch 85%, Egyptian Hieroglyphs 40%, Egyptology 40%, English 45%, Fast Talk for Free Drinks 65%, German 70%, History 25%, Listen 35%, Ride Camel 25%.

MISCELLANEOUS CATS

STR 02	CON 07	SIZ 01	INT 12	POW 13
DEX 31	MOV 12			HP 04

Damage Bonus: -1D6.

Weapons: Rip* 80%, damage 1D6-1D4
Claws (x2) 40%, damage 1D3-1D4
Bite 30%, damage 1D3-1D4

* *If both claws hit in a single round, the cat continues to hang on, biting and raking in that and each subsequent round.*

Skills: Hide 90%, Sneak 95%, Spot Hidden 80%, Track 65%.

NERIS, appears age 22, Were-Panther Priestess of Bast (human form)

STR 12	CON 14	SIZ 11	INT 16	POW 19
DEX 19	APP 18	EDU 18	SAN 46	HP 13

Damage Bonus: +0.

Weapons: Nails (x2) 85%, damage 1D4-2
Kick 70%, damage 1D6.

Spells: Contact Bast, Implant Fear, Summon/Bind Cat.

Skills: Arabic 90%, English 35%, Hide 85%, Listen 95%, Persuade 35%, Spot Hidden 90%, Track 40%.

NERIS, Black Panther Form

STR 18	CON 15	SIZ 18	INT 16	POW 19
DEX 24	MOV 10	EDU 18		HP 17

Damage Bonus: +1D6.

Weapons: Rake* 80%, damage 2D6+1D6
Claws (x2) 65%, damage 1D6+1D6
Bite 50%, damage 1D10

* *If both claws hit in a single round, the panther continues to hang on, biting and raking in that and each subsequent round.*

Armor: 1-point skin.

Spells: Contact Bast, Implant Fear, Summon/Bind Cat.

Skills: Hide 100%, Listen 95%, Sneak 100%, Spot Hidden 95%, Track 100%.

The Clive Expedition

With Vanheuvelen's help, it should be an easy matter to locate the Clive Expedition. It is possible that Vanheuvelen even may be able to arrange a meeting with the members of the Dig.

Financed by the Penhew Foundation, Dr. Henry Clive and his party have been excavating at Memphis for five months. The other principal members are Martin Winfield, Agatha Broadmoor, James Gardner, and Johannes Sprech. The rest of the expedition consist of overseers, diggers, water boys, guides, cooks, etc. All the Egyptian staff are Brotherhood cultists supplied by Omar Shakti. As they approach the camp, the investigators may notice (successful Psychology roll) the same sullen stares and silences as greeted them at Shakti's plantation.

The site at Memphis is impressively guarded. It lacks only minefields and machine guns to be up to WWI standards. Winfield greets the investigators and tries to discourage any inspection. Only if the investigators can think of a good excuse will they even be able to talk to anyone at the site. A good excuse might be a forged letter of introduction from Edward Gavigan, the sudden illness of an investigator, the presence of an important Egyptian or British bureaucrat or policeman, and so on. The investigators will not be allowed to wander about peeping, snooping, or idly asking questions without good reason.

THE THEFT OF THE REMAINS

The truth of the matter is that scrolls in a secret room in the smallest of the pyramids told the full story of the reign of the evil Queen Nitocris, and identified her remains as present in the chamber. The scrolls admonished that eternal vigilance was necessary lest Nitocris rise from the dead. Clive gave the real scrolls to Omar Shakti, and substituted fragments of useless junk from the 12th Dynasty to confuse the find.

Nyarlathotep intends that Nitocris return to life. The Brotherhood already possesses the Necklace of Nitocris and the Crown of Nitocris; when they steal the Girdle of Nitocris from the Mosque of Ibn-Tulun, they will possess all the artifacts required to bring her back to life.

Meanwhile, the sarcophagus of the queen has been moved to the Grand Chamber of Nyarlathotep, located far beneath the Giza Sphinx. As Gardner supposes, there is another secret passage in the third pyramid; it leads down and east to connect with a maze of tunnels deep in the rock. The entrance to the hidden passage is nearly a hundred feet from the hidden chamber of Queen Nitocris. The entire sarcophagus was raised and moved by powerful magic.

The Story Which Clive Peddles

If they manage to stay for a few hours, the investigators assemble a consistent story from the expedition members. The party discovered a secret chamber in Menhaura's pyramid, the smallest one of the three at Giza, which contained the unprepared but preserved remains of an unknown Egyptian queen. No hieroglyphs identified the body, but the marvelous funerary trappings convinced Clive that here rested a great ruler. Preparations for removal of the casket and the mummy were made in conjunction with the Egyptian authorities. Only an ornate gold coffer containing papyrus scrolls was actually taken from the chamber. "Alas," Dr. Clive says coolly, "all the scrolls were totally illegible, the result of improper sealing when the coffer was originally placed in the chamber."

DR. CLIVE

Three nights later, terrible screams echoed from inside the pyramid. When the archaeologists investigated, they found that the mummy, the sarcophagus, and the two Egyptian police guards were missing without a trace. The guards have not been found, and are presumed dead. No one knows how the thieves so quickly removed an alabaster sarcophagus weighing several tons; it would have taken the Clive Expedition several days, yet from the time of the hideous cry to the time that the party entered the pyramid no more than twenty minutes elapsed. The dust in the corridors was undisturbed except by the identifiable footprints of expedition members and antiquities authorities, nor were there signs of roller marks or of wear at inclines and elevations along the corridors where winches would have needed bracing. Everyone expresses bafflement at this turn of events, and worries that this inexplicable loss will discredit the great work of the expedition.

Everyone says that they never have heard of the Brotherhood of the Black Pharaoh or of the Cult of the Bloody Tongue. They know nothing about the Carlyle Expedition's work. Clive and the other principals have heard of the Black Pharaoh, but admit to no special knowledge. Clive explicitly denies that the sarcophagus contained Nitocris, saying that the possibility exists but that as a scientist he must be able to prove his conjectures before announcing them. The literal resurrection of Nitocris is condemned by Clive, Winfield, and Gardner as "mumbo-jumbo of the worst kind"; Sprech says nothing; Broadmoor hints it is possible.

AN OUTSIDE OPINION

If the investigators already have met Dr. Ali Kafour, he confirms that magical resurrection is possible. He has never heard of the Girdle, the Necklace, or the Crown of Nitocris. Both Broadmoor and Kafour say that the likeliest time for the resurrection of Nitocris is the night of, or the night before, the dark of the moon.

Kafour speculates that while a resurrected Nitocris might be a deadly foe, her true significance may be that efforts toward the return and empowerment of the Black Pharaoh are underway—a vast activation of long-dormant forces, of which Nitocris is but an important element.

SOME PRIVATE OPINIONS

Broadmoor and Gardner are watched constantly, and rarely leave the dig site, but if these two can be talked to alone, they tell a different story. According to them, the mummy was identified as Queen Nitocris from texts which Clive exhibited before they left London. Broadmoor and Gardner think that Clive has been overly discreet in not identifying the mummy. Both believe that the sarcophagus and its contents were not dragged from the pyramid. Agatha Broadmoor says that some supernatural entity was involved, "something ancient and unfathomable." Gardner, a skeptic in many ways, thinks that an undetected passage leads from the secret chamber to somewhere else—perhaps to one of the other pyramids in the area.

The district police agree with this theory, and have spent fruitless days trying to discover such a passage.

Broadmoor knows that the resurrection of the Queen requires the Crown of Nitocris, the Necklace of Nitocris, and the Girdle of Nitocris. By placing these three items on the mummy of the evil queen while conducting the proper ritual, Nitocris will rise from the dead.

Of incidental importance to the investigators is Gardner's belief that the riddle of the Sphinx involves an unnamed ruler of ancient Egypt. Gardner thinks that the reign was long before the advent of the Black Pharaoh (he is mistaken, of course). Gardner does theorize that an underground labyrinth, perhaps an entire city, exists or existed beneath the Sphinx and beyond, and agreed to join the Clive Expedition in order to investigate this. He was quite upset when Clive used the theft of the mummy as an excuse to shift operations upriver to Memphis, making it nearly impossible for Gardner to fulfill his responsibilities to the expedition and to work on the Sphinx. Clive has claimed that the Egyptian authorities refused permission to excavate near the Sphinx, but Gardner doesn't believe this.

Expedition Personalities

DR. HENRY CLIVE

Gray-haired with a small mustache, he affects an aristocratic casualness. He is actually a commoner, the youngest of three sons born to an impoverished Yorkshire schoolmaster. Clive is 58, and an excellent archaeologist. Clive seems kindly, but he has been a cultist for 35 years, and is long insane. He is not a priest of the cult, though he has considerable magic, and outside of Cairo he carries his revolver all the time.

Dr. HENRY CLIVE, age 58, Archaeologist and Member of the Brotherhood of the Black Pharaoh

STR 10	CON 15	SIZ 09	INT 16	POW 19
DEX 12	APP 13	EDU 18	SAN 0	HP 12

Damage Bonus: +0.

Weapons: Cult Club 35%, damage 1D8 with chance to impale
.38 Revolver 25%, damage 1D10

Spells: Call Azathoth, Call Cthugha, Contact Ghoul, Contact Nyarlathotep, Contact Sand Dweller, Contact Yig, Enchant Flute, Mindblast, Shrivelling, Summon/Bind Hunting Horror, Summon Servitor of Elder Gods.

Skills: Anthropology 40%, Arabic 50%, Archaeology 80%, Astronomy 35%, Bargain 35%, Credit Rating 65%, Cthulhu Mythos 20%, Demotic Egyptian 45%, Egyptian Hieroglyphs 85%, Egyptology 90%, English 90%, Fast Talk 30%, First Aid 65%, French 45%, History 40%, Law 15%, Library Use 65%, Occult 40%, Persuade 40%, Psychology 20%, Spot Hidden 75%.

MARTIN WINFIELD

He is tall, lean, blond, smug, malicious, and vindictive. Every investigator who receives a failing Psychology roll immediately hates him, while those who receive a successful Psychology roll know that they hate him because the man is a sadistic brute. He is also an archaeologist and member of the Brotherhood; comparatively young, he ranks low in the British branch of the cult. He is the well connected second son of a minister of Parliament. He enjoys inflicting pain, and relishes extracting information from victims. Winfield always carries a riding crop, and always wears a revolver while outside of Cairo. He believes that Clive's methods are unduly conservative and inhibited, though he fears Clive's magical powers.

MARTIN WINFIELD, age 24, Archaeologist, Sadist, and Member of the Brotherhood

STR 13	CON 12	SIZ 13	INT 15	POW 12
DEX 15	APP 14	EDU 16	SAN 0	HP 13

Damage Bonus: +1D4.

Weapon: Riding Crop 80%, damage 1D2+1D4 per 5 minutes of application to flesh.
Cult Club 60%, damage 1D8+1D4 with a chance to impale
20-Gauge Shotgun 55%, damage 2D6/1D6/1D3
.38 Revolver 45%, damage 1D10

Spells: Contact Ghoul, Dominate, Dread Clutch of Nyogtha, Enchant Whistle, Summon Byakhee

Skills: Arabic 70%, Archaeology 40%, Bargain 30%, Credit Rating 50%, Cthulhu Mythos 16%, Drive Automobile 80%, Egyptian Hieroglyphs 30%, Egyptology 55%, English 80%, Fast Talk 40%, French 65%, German 29%, Persuade 50%, Occult 10%, Ride 45%.

AGATHA BROADMOOR

She is elderly and a bit dotty; she knows nothing of the Mythos or the Brotherhood. She was paid to accompany the expedition because she is a medium, capable of contacting the spirits of the dead by trance. Her true motive in agreeing to accompany the expedition was to exorcise the great evil of Nitocris. With the disappearance of the mummy, she fears the queen may rise again. Her trances last 1D3 hours and drain her of five magic points an hour. One of her seances (she calls them sittings) has a 75% chance to foretell events accurately (but in a vague manner), and the same chance to contact the soul of a specific dead person.

While in the trance she does not recall what is asked of her, hence her usefulness to the Brotherhood. She is serious about her gift, and does a sitting only for good reasons.

AGATHA BROADMOOR, age 67, Psychic

STR 04	CON 08	SIZ 09	INT 13	POW 16
DEX 09	APP 09	EDU 12	SAN 35	HP 09

Damage Bonus: -1D4.

Weapons: none.

Skills: Arabic 25%, Archaeology 10%, Astronomy 40%, Credit Rating 45%, Egyptian Hieroglyphs 05%, Egyptology 35%, English 70%, French 20%, Occult 25%, Psychic Arts 75%.

JAMES GARDNER

Shorter and stouter than Winfield, he is a good archaeologist strongly influenced by Carl Jung. Gardner has written three books concerning ancient Egypt, none of which were well written or well received, but a theory he has sponsored concerning an underground maze beneath the Giza Sphinx is essentially correct. Since the theft of the Nitocris mummy, he routinely wears a .32 automatic. He is not a member of the Brotherhood, though his dream research and his other arcane studies of the human collective unconscious have given him some inkling of the awful threat of the Mythos. Clive brought Gardner along because Nyarlathotep commanded that he do so. The god has not yet revealed the purpose behind his command.

Of the Clive Expedition members, Gardner is the most likely to be a useful investigator ally. If he could extricate himself from Egypt and the expedition, he would probably return to England.

JAMES GARDNER, age 40, Archaeologist

STR 12	CON 13	SIZ 12	INT 15	POW 07
DEX 10	APP 11	EDU 16	SAN 40	HP 13

Damage Bonus: +0.

Weapons: .32 Automatic 25%, damage 1D8.

Skills: Anthropology 70%, Arabic 45%, Aramaic 45%, Archaeology 35%, Assyrian 15%, Bargain 25%, Credit Rating 30%, Cthulhu Mythos 05%, Egyptian Hieroglyphs 15%, Egyptology 40%, English 90%, History 35%, Library Use 60%, Persuade 25%, Occult 10%, Psychology 20%.

JOHANNES SPRECH

The fourth archaeologist, Sprech has a formidable ability to sight-read hieroglyphics, and is uncannily good with codes and ciphers of many kinds—this last is a talent which the German army happily employed in WWI. Sprech is an occultist of some repute who seeks magical artifacts with which he can rescue his beloved Germany from its present agony, granting to his homeland its rightful place on the throne of nations. His occult studies indicate that a champion of der volk soon will arise, but he is unsure who that will be. Since the minions of Nyarlathotep have plans for the National Socialists, they'll keep Sprech alive if at all possible, and there is a 05% chance that Nyarlathotep might resurrect him once. Sprech is an enthusiast of physical culture, and rises early most mornings for rigorous exercises and a cold shower.

JOHANNES SPRECH, age 39, Archaeologist and German Mystic

STR 13	CON 16	SIZ 12	INT 16	POW 17
DEX 16	APP 10	EDU 17	SAN 50	HP 14

Damage Bonus: +1D4.

Weapons: 9mm Automatic Pistol* 65%, damage 1D10
Fist 65%, damage 1D3+1D4
Kick 45%, damage 1D6+1D4
Fighting Knife* 25%, damage
    1D4+2+1D4

* Sprech always carries his Luger in a holster, and always has his fighting knife strapped to his right leg.

Skills: Arabic 70%, Archaeology 60%, Astronomy 20%, Bargain 30%, Codes and Ciphers 50%, Credit Rating 25%, Cthulhu Mythos 04%, Drive Automobile 40%, Egyptian Hieroglyphs 85%, English 55%, French 35%, German 85%, Hide 20%, History 20%, Jump 40%, Linguist 45%, Listen 30%, Occult 70%, Persuade 40%, Pilot Aircraft 20%, Psychology 15%, Ride 25%, Sneak 50%, Spot Hidden 50%, Swim 50%, Throw 45%, Track 10%.

Cultist Guards

A number of cultists from the Brotherhood of the Black Pharoah are used as guards by the Clive Expedition.

SIX CULTIST GUARDS

	1	2	3	4	5	6
STR	12	13	14	13	13	15
CON	10	11	10	09	07	09
SIZ	13	13	11	12	13	10
APP	08	06	09	07	08	09
INT	13	13	13	10	12	11
EDU	01	02	05	02	01	01
DEX	13	13	12	12	10	10
POW	08	10	11	04	07	07
HP	12	12	11	11	10	10

Damage Bonus: +1D4.

Weapons: Cult Club 55%, damage 1D8+1D4 plus chance to
    impale
Fighting Knife 50%, damage 1D4+2+1D4
Short Sword 35%, damage 1D6+1+1D4
Garrote 20%, damage 1D3 asphyxiation per round; match STR
    vs. STR to break free

Skills: Arabic 55%, Be Tempted 45%, Cthulhu Mythos 08%, English 10%, Hide 75%, Listen 55%, Sneak 60%, Spot Hidden 45%.

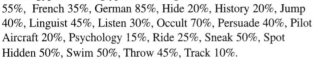

THE HORRORS BELOW

*The cultists openly parade to their foul ceremonies;
to follow their clear trail, one must also dare that which lurks
in the dark and loathsome passages far underground.*

"It was then that the smile of the Sphinx vaguely displeased us, and made us wonder about the legends of subterranean passages beneath the monstrous creature, leading down, down, down to depths none might dare hint at—depths connected with mysteries older than the dynastic Egypt we excavate, and having a sinister relation to the persistence of abnormal, animal-headed gods in the ancient Nilotic pantheon."
— H.P. Lovecraft, "Under the Pyramids"

Entrances to Horror

As indicated on the nearby plan, near the Sphinx are four entrances to the underground labyrinth the existence of which James Gardner has so brilliantly hypothesized. The two burial shafts (Entrances B and C) are two of many which surround the Giza pyramids. The investigators must be looking for some sort of entrance before the keeper should request a Luck roll to find one of the burial shaft entrances or the hidden entrance (D) near the Menkaura pyramid. If the roll succeeds, tell the investigators merely

that the shaft likely leads to "something". Choose randomly whether they find entrance B, C, or D—they find A only by impersonating cultists on a ritual night.

ENTRANCE A: this entrance is magical, a stele erected by Thutmosis IV. It stands before the Sphinx. Its four sides exhibit the lengthy tale of how Thutmosis found the Sphinx buried in the Egyptian sands, and how he unearthed it. Scattered in a subtle pattern through the front side of the stele are thirteen glyphs which, if taken together, form a statement:

Mighty Is the God Whose Breath Brings Death and Whose Form Brings Madness!

At night, by reciting aloud this passage in ancient Egyptian (demotic pronunciation will serve), and by sacrificing twelve magic points to the stele, the stele becomes intangible and translucent though still visible. This effect lasts for two minutes. An investigator with Egyptian Hieroglyphs of ten percent or more might guess the pronunciation of the ritual statement, but also would need a successful Idea roll to locate the sentence and a successful Cthulhu Mythos roll to

ENCOUNTERS BENEATH THE SPHINX

D20	Result
01-04	No encounter; investigators proceed without incident
05	A random investigator stumbles and falls; slimy luminous moss coats hands, elbows, and knees, and cannot be rubbed off.
06	Successful Listen roll hears snatches of Arabic conversation; two men are saying that intruders may be in the tunnels. The voices cannot be located.
07	Random investigator falls, tearing trousers or skirt.
08	Warm liquid drips from the tunnel ceiling; the stone beneath is slick and red; the blood has no apparent source.
09	A foul stench engulfs the investigators; failure to get a successful CON x3 roll forces an investigator to vomit, so that he or she cannot move in that round.
10	Some shapeless thing is glimpsed, but it leaves neither trace nor track of its passage.
11	Macabre chuckles, growls, or groans are heard in the blackness—maybe a single sound, maybe a hideous cacophony of noise erupts without reason.
12	A violent blast of wind extinguishes all unshielded candles and carries off any loose paper.
13	A small rock falls from the ceiling and strikes that investigator whose Luck roll was highest: the luck is that the stone does only 1D2 damage, no damage if wearing a hat.
14	With a successful Spot Hidden, jet-black roses are seen to be bordering the tunnel floor. The investigator who picks one loses 1D3 hit points from poisonous thorns.
15	Branch tunnel only; ignore for main tunnel. The passage abruptly slopes steeply up; receive successful Climb roll or fall. Lose 1D4 hit points damage from sharp rocks, but ignore with successful Dodge roll.
16	Branch tunnel only; ignore for main tunnel. Cave-in rains rocks on the investigators: call for Dodge rolls. Investigators with failed rolls take 2D6 damage. A result of 12 for the damage roll also indicates that the passage is permanently blocked.
17	Narrow, deep pit looms at your feet. Successful Spot Hidden avoids the slippery edge. If the roll fails, roll 1D4 to determine depth of the pit and damage to the investigator.

1D4	depth in ft	damage
1	10	1D6
2	20	2D6
3	30	3D6
4	40	4D6

D20	Result
18	Branch tunnel only; ignore for main tunnel. A chasm sprawls across the tunnel; it is at least 100 feet deep, with sheer, slippery sides. Roll 1D4 to discover width: 1=5 feet; 2=10 feet; etc. Investigators who did not bring rope will have to turn back.
19	1D6+4 Children of the Sphinx attempt to seize one investigator (in a branch tunnel) or two investigators (in the main tunnel). Roll any die: odd indicates the Children come from the rear, even indicates they come from the front. There is room for two Children to grab at one time in a branch tunnel, and room for four to grab at once in the main tunnel. As the keeper wishes, captives are taken to the cells, or to the Great Chamber of Nyarlathotep for more immediate sacrifice. See the description of and statistics for the Children at the end of this section.
20	Ask a Sanity roll for a random investigator. If the roll fails, the investigator perceives that the walls of the tunnel are rhythmically moving in and out, like bronchial tubes in the lungs. Sanity loss is 2/1D6+3.

determine the right sequence of words. Among the cultists, only the high priest knows the ritual phrase which opens the way. Upon sacrificing his magic points, the high priest enters, followed by the eager crush of his insane flock.

Once within the stele, entrants instantaneously find themselves in a chamber (the circled A on the map nearby) which exits into a tunnel. There is no trace of the surface world, now more than 200 feet above. By standing in the center of the chamber and invoking the name of Nyarlathotep, the speaker of the name is transported back to the surface.

Investigators disguised as cultists can pass freely through the stele (or enter without disguise) while the spell keeps the stele open.

ENTRANCE B: a second entrance, the circled B on the nearby plan, is a hole in the ground located about 300 yards south of the stele entrance. The shaft falls fifty feet straight down without a break, then bends to the left and becomes a ramp declining at nearly twenty degrees for another 200 feet. Cultists occasionally throw or lower a victim down here, and occasionally chuck garbage here as well. The hole is fenced off; it is wide enough to admit only one climber at a time. The walls of this shaft are nearly impossible to climb up or down without rope and other equipment (subtract 60 percentiles from any Climb roll made that way). The walls have few handholds, and most of the surfaces are slimy—who knows from what!

ENTRANCE C: the third entrance, the circled C on the nearby map, is another burial shaft—this one 300 yards north. In most respects it is identical to Entrance B, except that the shaft bends slightly several times before concluding fifty feet down. There it turns into a steep ramp. The walls are equally slick and difficult to climb—subtract 60 percentiles from any Climb roll made without proper equipment.

ENTRANCE D: this entrance, the circled D on the nearby map, is found beneath an ancient-looking stone slab in the rock tombs some fifty yards southeast of the Menkaura pyramid. It connects with the long, winding main tunnel which ends at the secret chamber of Queen Nitocris within the Menkaura pyramid. Its sloping stone floor is easily negotiated.

The Main Tunnel

Far below the earth the silence is ceaseless and oppressive. Above is a terrible weight of suspended stone and earth. Occasional drafts pass down the main tunnel, causing candles or torches to gutter momentarily.

The main tunnel winds from the secret chamber of Queen Nitocris all the way to the entrance chamber below the stele of Thutmosis (Entrance A). It is about a mile in length, though the straight-line distance is little more than half that. Approximately mid-way between those points is the Grand Chamber of Nyarlathotep, where horrible rites occur. The main tunnel is of hewn stone, obviously man-made. The floor of the main tunnel is generally level, and always at least eight feet wide and eight feet high.

There is no light, except for an occasional glow from livid purple or putrid green fungi—slimy stuff disgusting to touch. Side tunnels and tiny votary alcoves frequently open to either side. Along the main tunnel, loathsome images panel the walls, depicting men with the heads of animals, animals with human limbs, and alien entities performing cruel, disgusting, and obscene activities. If the investigators use lights and thereby comprehend the pictures, they risk a cumulative loss of 1D3 SAN points while negotiating their passage.

The Branch Tunnels

Some parts of these black passages are obviously cut from the stone; other parts look like old water courses, or rock fractures, or as if acids had eaten through the stone. Still other parts have obviously been hacked clear by alien tooth and claw. On the plan of the tunnels, the branches are shown as straight lines, and it is true that their direction is consistent, but the angles of the walls, floor, and ceiling constantly change, and the passages themselves may narrow to as little as two feet across, or be as much as fifteen feet wide by fifteen feet high. More strikingly, the ways constantly rise or fall, so that it is impossible to see far ahead or behind. Thus blocked, the beams of lamps or strong flashlights reveal little. These tunnels have an organic feel, suggesting that some great alien beast had been imprisoned within the stone, had then somehow gotten free, and that the investigators now creep along the spaces left by its bones and sinews.

Because the lines of sight vary, if the investigators include those with ranged magical or physical attacks, keepers may want to monitor the march order of the investigators, to see if those guns or spells can be brought to bear.

Encounters and the Tunnel Map

Two tunnel types, main and branch, are shown on the nearby map. The main tunnel is indicated by the heavy double lines which wind across the length of the map; the branch tunnels are the light double lines leading in all directions. Single short lines cross both tunnel types at regular intervals. When the investigators arrive at such a mark, roll once on the encounter table. The marks are approximately two hundred feet apart in the main tunnel, and approximately one hundred feet apart in the branch tunnels. The interval between the encounter marks in either tunnel represents approximately one minute of quiet, cautious movement by the investigators.

At his option, the keeper may add to or ignore the encounters table. If the keeper wants to rely heavily on the table, he should prepare additional encounters. They are optional devices intended to trim party sizes, test the nerve of players, and emphasize the fearful forces arrayed against mere investigators. Since they are necessarily random, they usually have little or no connection with the plot. Always have some purpose in mind if you choose an encounter. If play is proceeding satisfactorily without an encounter, don't bother.

Great Chamber of Nyarlathotep

This great hall is the center of ritual for the Brotherhood of the Black Pharaoh. Guarding their holiest site are 2D10 Children of the Sphinx. From the main tunnel, wide steps lead another hundred feet down into the hall. As befits the Black Pharaoh, only a few torches light the way or illumine the vast courts within, reflecting everywhere from the gleaming black marble walls. Special locations indicated on the plan are discussed below.

The floor is of black marble flecked with white. Cultists boast that each fleck is a soul snared by their lord. The floor is exceptionally shiny and slick. The hall is approximately 400 x 500 feet, with ceilings (if they could be seen in all this darkness) soaring more than 100 feet high. The hall is so vast that only loud noises echo—ordinary voices are damped by the huge space, and die.

THE PILLARS: numerous ebon pillars support the enormous vaulted ceiling. With proper light—a flashlight will do—the pillar tops are seen to be splaying out into the tops of black trees, the branches which visibly sway and wave in extra-dimensional winds. All viewers lose 1D2 SAN when seeing this.

STAIRS TO THE UNDERWORLD: entirely different from those leading into the Great Chamber, these stairs lead to a floor or places lower than the chamber. A hideous ruby light pours up from below; the stairs disappear down into the red-glowing mist. Occasional hideous shrieks or moans can be heard. These stairs lead out of this scenario and into adventures of the keeper's devising. If the keeper wishes to refuse the investigators entrance to the underworld, put an invisible shield across the steps or devise a horrible death for the investigator who leads the way down.

THE LEECH PIT: this open pit is seventy-five feet square and averages twenty feet deep. Water fills it to within eight feet of the top. At first this water looks totally black and featureless, but a successful Spot Hidden roll notes the ceaseless play of tiny ripples across its surface. The unfortunate who slips or is thrown into the water is attacked by hungry leeches. He or she is drained of blood, losing 1D3-1 hit points per melee round until dead. Pulled out of the water before death, three successful DEX x1 rolls pull off all the unsated leeches and thereby stop the blood loss. These need not be consecutive and more than one person can try at the same time. The be-leeched survivor's Sanity loss is 2/2D10+1 SAN.

With a second successful Spot Hidden, a set of narrow, slippery, black marble steps without railings can be detected leading down into the leech pit. Tethered beside the steps is a jet-black ceremonial raft which can be poled around the pit, ensuring that the sacrifices feed all the leeches, and not just the swarms lurking near the walls of the pit. The raft and its two attendants can tow four unconscious victims at a time.

Sometimes a random conscious victim is hurled screaming onto one of the shoals in the pit. These shoals are built up entirely of human bones and skulls, and rise to within about eighteen inches of the water's surface. A victim thrown on to such a place may survive from several minutes up to half an hour.

Once weekly, the cult unceremoniously dumps a dozen or so people into the pit. There is a 15% chance that the investigators come upon one of these routine feedings. On ritual nights, however, fifty or more drugged or screaming humans are flung to their doom. Great booms are mounted at the corners of the pit for these high rituals, so that victims can be lowered in, become coated with leeches, and then be raised again, forestalling death and allowing the cultists to savor the situation. Witnessing this horrible prolongation costs 1/1D8 SAN.

THE ALTAR: the altar is about twenty-five feet square at the top. From three sides, steps lead fifteen feet up to where the sarcophagus of Queen Nitocris rests on a white sacrificial block. Stone braziers are built into the four corners of this altar. They burn with a sickly yellow light.

THE THRONE: beyond the altar is another structure, a hideous throne of vile green, sweating stone, carved with violent and cruel acts performed by humans, sand dwellers, deep ones, and other species and entities. The two seats of the throne are designed for human-sized figures. Hieroglyphics above proclaim this the throne of Nitocris. The throne block stands thirty feet above the floor. To the front only, facing the hall, a set of narrow and precarious steps leads steeply down to the floor of the hall.

THE PROCESSIONAL BRIDGE: as one faces the hall from the throne, a long bridge leads horizontally to the left wall of the hall. Its supports are also carved with disgusting figures and writhing tentacles. The bridge is of the same bilious green, weeping stone as the throne block, and has no railings. Its surface is thirty feet above the floor. In ancient times Nitocris and her priests and priestesses strode across this bridge, awing the gibbering faithful squealing below.

THE STELE: where the bridge leads to the wall, a stele stands a few feet out from the wall. This stele is the same size as the one before the Sphinx, though the glyphs are different. The functions of the two steles are identical, and only the priests of the Brotherhood know the special invocation which allows them to transport individually from the entrance chamber and to emerge from this stele. Made intangible, both steles lead to the entrance chamber at the circled-A on the nearby plan.

Hidden behind the stele at the end of the processional bridge is an unlocked door which opens into a branch tunnel. Investigators could enter by this door and remain unnoticed while they peeped around the sides of the stele.

THE ENORMOUS HOLE: in the wall of the Great Hall, behind the throne, is an enormous irregular hole, about 90 by 125 feet, evidently torn open by vast force. The hole is always pitch black, no matter how much light is aimed within it. Entering it, a scout sees, hears, and feels nothing. The scout spends 1D6 minutes within the hole, is convinced that he has been everywhere within it, and yet has nothing to report. It is a hole to nowhere.

This is literally true. The hole is an inter-dimensional

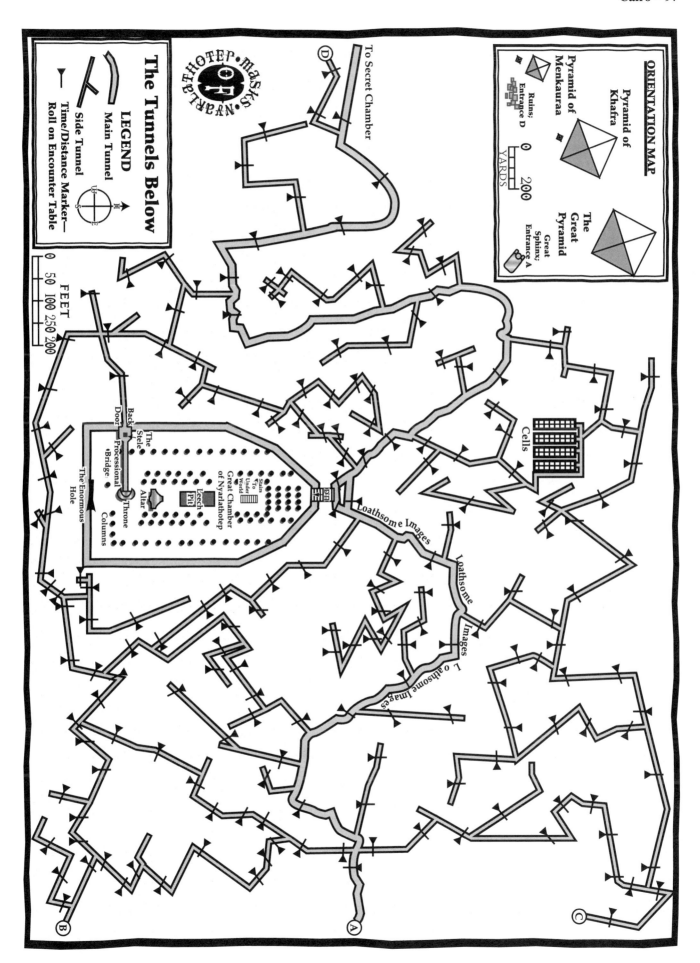

ORIENTATION MAP

Pyramid of Khafra

Pyramid of Menkauraa

Ruins; Entrance D

The Great Pyramid

Great Sphinx; Entrance A

0   200
YARDS

NYARLATHOTEP·MASKS·OF

The Tunnels Below

LEGEND

Main Tunnel

Side Tunnel

Time/Distance Marker—

Roll on Encounter Table

0 50 100 250 200
FEET

To Secret Chamber

Back Door

The Stele

Processional Bridge

Throne

The Enormous Hole

The Altar

Great Chamber of Nyarlathotep

Stairs To Under World

Leech Pit

Columns

Loathsome Images

Loathsome Images

Loathsome Images

Cells

gate between Earth and a plane of particular comfort to Nyarlathotep. By expending twenty magic points in the proper ritual, the hole will Gate anyone inside it to Nyarlathotep. The proper ritual appears in Olaus Wormius' Latin translation of the *Necronomicon*, an apparent interpolation by an unknown author.

Less obviously, the hole also allows the Black Sphinx, a monstrous spawn of Nyarlathotep, easy access to the Great Hall. Seeing it costs 1D10/1D100. But the Black Sphinx occupies the hole only after the Summon Black Sphinx spell has been cast as part of ritual night. Anyone inside the hole when the Black Sphinx is summoned is in deep trouble. See that entity's description and statistics a little further below, at the end of this underground section.

It is because of the Black Sphinx's enormity that this sacred temple is so large.

The Mass Ritual

Once a month, as many cultists as possible gather in the Great Chamber of Nyarlathotep. The monthly ritual night may be death-based or sex-based, as depicted as occurring at Edward Gavigan's estate in England. Or it could be an initiation ceremony for new cultists or priests (the Egyptian branch of the Brotherhood has twenty priests in addition to Omar Shakti). During the ceremonies, initiates perform sacrifices. For cult faithful, the victims are slowly beaten to death with cult clubs. For new priests, magical murders are performed. Both initiations conclude with the calling forth of Nyarlathotep's regent, the Black Sphinx.

Watching an initiation rite costs 0/1D6 SAN per physical death, and 1D6/2D6 SAN per magical death. This assessment is in addition to any cost in witnessing death in the leech pit.

Investigators discovered violating a ritual night are put to death immediately. The dimness and gargantuan proportions of the chamber make it a place easy in which to hide, however—add 40 percentiles to all Hide rolls. Since cultists here wear the same full robes as in England, investigators disguised as cultists should be able to pass scrutiny if they can stay sane.

SPECIAL RITES FOR QUEEN NITOCRIS

If the Brotherhood steals the Girdle of Nitocris from the Mosque of Ibn Tulun, they will attempt to raise Nitocris from the dead. That is the next great rite to be performed in the Great Chamber, and the keeper should take pains to lead the investigators into it.

Present at this ritual will be twelve priests, including Omar Shakti and Martin Winfield, nearly 800 cultists, including Dr. Henry Clive, and 100 Children of the Sphinx. The rest of the Clive Expedition will also be there—as sacrifices. The din and screams will be loud and sustained.

The ritual has several ghastly components.

First they force Agatha Broadmoor to use her powers to contact the spirit of Nitocris, while the cultists hurl a hundred victims to the leeches. Drained corpses are heaped like empty bags before the throne block, and Shakti shoves the

now-empty sarcophagus of Nitocris down from the altar onto dismayed cultists.

Then the priests link hands and slice open the throats of Gardner and Broadmoor. As their blood drains into the withered mummy on the sacrificial block, its dried flesh begins to swell and glow with life, until at last the Ghoul Queen Nitocris rises in all her deadly beauty. The braziers beside the throne are then lit, and Nitocris steps lightly over the corpses to take her place. A Child of the Sphinx brings her a goblet of fresh blood to enjoy while she gives the command to bring forth the Black Sphinx. Using magic points from Shakti, Clive, and Winfield in addition to her own, the Contact Nyarlathotep spell is cast, and the Black Sphinx emerges to place a gigantic paw upon the throne seat beside her.

Witnessing this horrible ritual up to the appearance of the ghastly Black Sphinx costs 1D6/1D20 SAN. The Enormous Hole and the Black Sphinx sections provide the investigator-breaking cost to witness the Black Sphinx. If anyone stays sane to see the rest of the show, the Sphinx becomes so compelling that they drunkenly mime its hideous gluttony. Satiated, the Sphinx withdraws into the enormous hole, the ritual ends, and the cultists stagger into the placid Egyptian night.

FOILING THE RESURRECTION OF NITOCRIS

Her mummy must be destroyed before the resurrection ritual begins. This is not easy. Fire, acid, explosives, spells, or dissection will not affect the mummy, nor is it even possible to unwrap the corpse. There are three ways to foil the resurrection, though none are obvious.

First, one of the three items of power necessary to the resurrection—the Crown, the Girdle, or the Necklace—could be destroyed. All three are impervious to normal destruction in the same way that is her mummy, but each is susceptible to specific magic. The Crown may be destroyed by a Shrivelling spell doing at least 10 points of damage, the Necklace can be dissolved in water containing several doses of Space Mead, and the Girdle can be severed by an enchanted knife such as is used in the spell Summon Dimensional Shambler. Actually destroying an item of power while the ceremony is in progress will be difficult. Foiling the ritual gains each participating investigator 1D20 SAN.

The second way is to use the spell Contact Nodens. If successful, Nodens appears and gives the caster a dagger and instructions to plunge the knife into the left eye of the mummy. The mummy will disintegrate to dust, but the dust must be scattered or it becomes a usable component in a Resurrection spell. The stab of the dagger is also instant death to anyone already resurrected, and also will disintegrate many other corpses protected by magic. It appears to be an ornate dagger of unusual design, and it otherwise does normal fighting knife damage. If the knife-wielder succeeds, he regains 1D20 SAN. He'll need it that night, when Nodens sends 1D3 nightgaunts to retrieve the dagger. Investigators accompanying a successful dagger-bearer also regain 1D20 SAN. The Mask of Hayama, discussed in the New York chapter, also may promote contact with Nodens.

The third way is the easiest, but the least honorable: if Agatha Broadmoor dies, the ritual cannot occur, for the cultists know of no other with her powers. The keeper should not suggest this method, even through his or her characters. It is possible, however, that an investigator may deduce Broadmoor's function—and a successful Spot Hidden the night of the ritual discloses her bonds.

Broadmoor begins her trance to contact the shade of Nitocris about thirty minutes after the ritual starts, and it will take her another 1D10+10 minutes to establish contact. Exactly twelve minutes elapse between the time she contacts Nitocris and the time when her throat is cut, after guiding Nitocris to her mummified self. If Broadmoor dies during those twelve minutes, the spirit of Nitocris is lost forever among the planes. If Broadmoor dies before those twelve minutes, the resurrection is only delayed, though the delay may be of some years. Because of intervening figures and the pervading darkness of the Great Chamber, lower the effectiveness of all ranged weapons by 20 percentiles or as the keeper sees fit. The investigator who kills Agatha Broadmoor loses 1D10 SAN for the murder of this innocent. Allow him or her a 1D20 SAN gain because the resurrection of Nitocris has been prevented.

Statistics

The Black Sphinx

"It was something quite ponderous, even as seen from my height, something yellowish and hairy, and endowed with a sort of nervous motion. It was as large, perhaps, as a good-size hippopotamus, but very curiously shaped. It seemed to have no neck, but five separate heads springing in a row from a roughly cylindrical trunk; the first very small, the second good-sized, the third and fourth equal and largest of all, and the fifth rather small, though not so much as the first. Out of these heads darted curious rigid tentacles which seized ravenously on the excessively great *quantities of unmentionable food placed before the aperture. Once in a while the thing would leap up, and occasionally it would retreat into its den in a very odd manner. Its locomotion was so inexplicable that I stared in fascination, wishing it would emerge farther from the cavernous lair beneath me.*

"Then it did emerge...The Great Sphinx!... What huge and loathsome abnormality was the Sphinx originally carven to represent? *...That five-headed monster as large as a hippopotamus... the five-headed monster—and that of which it is the merest forepaw...."*

—H.P. Lovecraft, "Under the Pyramids"

As the hapless hero discovered, the Sphinx is indeed a representative carving. But he did not know that the thing it represented was a relative of Nyarlathotep. The Black Sphinx is huge, and its face has a wrinkled, eyeless forehead and myriad maws placed asymmetrically in its oval face. It otherwise looks like a living Sphinx. With two great animated forepaws it alternately scoops up sacrifices into floor-level maws—drooling blood and bones—or lifts sacrifices high into other fang-rimmed mouths, or highest of all sets terrified humans into the mouth of a mocking, leering, infinitely evil rubbery face seventy feet across.

THE BLACK SPHINX

STR 800	CON 410	SIZ 350	INT 26	POW 75
DEX 09	MOV 06			HP 380

Damage Bonus: enormous.

Weapons: Forepaw Smash* 80%, damage 16D6
Forepaw Munch 60% x3 per round, damage is death
* *the Black Sphinx can attack thrice per round.*

Armor: 38-point unearthly hide.

Spell: Contact Nyarlathotep.

Skills: Sense Prey 35%.

Sanity Loss: 1D10/D100 SAN.

Cultists

See the Brotherhood of the Black Pharaoh box at the start of this chapter for additional information on Cultists.

RANDOM CULTISTS OF THE BROTHERHOOD

	1	2	3	4	5	6	7	8
STR	09	15	08	12	09	10	11	14
CON	07	07	05	10	11	10	18	10
SIZ	08	12	09	10	11	08	11	10
APP	15	08	09	08	06	09	06	04
INT	14	09	08	11	10	10	08	09
EDU	02	01	01	01	02	05	01	01
DEX	16	10	10	13	13	12	11	12
POW	14	07	07	08	10	11	09	10
HP	08	10	07	10	11	09	15	10

Damage Bonus: +0.

Weapons: Cult Club 40%, damage 1D8 plus chance to impale
Fighting Knife 40%, damage 1D4+2
Short Sword 35%, damage 1D6+1

Skills: Arabic 45%, Cthulhu Mythos 10%, English 01%, Fast Talk 29%, Hide 35%, Listen 45%, Sneak 40%, Spot Hidden 35%.

Children of the Sphinx

"I would not look *at the marching things. That I desperately resolved as I heard their creaking joints and nitrous wheezing above the dead music and the dead tramping. It was merciful that they did not speak ... but God! their crazy torches began ...to cast shadows on the surface of those stupendous columns. Hippopotami should not have human hands and carry torches ... men should not have the heads of crocodiles...."*

—H.P. Lovecraft, "Under the Pyramids"

These Sphinx-spawn come in great variety. Lovecraft speaks of men with the heads of bulls, ibises, falcons, and cats, of objects walking with nothing above the waist. Children of the Sphinx may come as any human-animal composite, as long as the grouping has some basis in Egyptian religion or mythology. Except for "objects walking with nothing above the waist," all Children of the Sphinx can attack in some form or another. These creatures should be found only beneath the Great Sphinx in this campaign, but could certainly be found anywhere that dynastic Egypt left traces.

RANDOM CHILDREN OF THE SPHINX

characteristic	roll	Average
STR	4D6	14
CON	2D6+6	13
SIZ	3D6	11-12
INT	3D6	3-4
POW	3D6	11-12
DEX	2D6	7
Hit Points	varies	

MOV 7

Damage Bonus: varies

Sanity Loss: 0/1D8 SAN.

weapon	%	damage
Fist (all)	50%	1D3
Cheetah's Bite	40%	1D6
Bull's Gore	35%	2D4
Crocodile Bite	35%	1D10
Hippo Bite	35%	2D6
Falcon Beak-Stab	30%	1D4
Ibis Beak-Stab	25%	1D3
Kick (all)	25%	1D6

All are able to strike with hands and feet; most lack melee weapons. They charge in groups, knock down their victims, and do their damage.

SAMPLE HEADED ONES

type	Bull	Ibis	Hipp	Chee	Hipp
#1-5	1	2	3	4	5
STR	12	15	16	08	13
CON	15	12	15	15	12
SIZ	14	07	13	14	13
INT	01	06	01	06	03
POW	11	11	12	11	13
DEX	08	05	06	10	10
HP	15	10	14	15	13
Attack %	45%	35%	45%	30%	45%
Mode	gore	beak	butt	bite	butt
Damage B.	+2D4	+1D3	+2D6	+1D6	+2D6

type	Falc	Bull	Chee	Ibis	Hipp
# 6-10	6	7	8	9	10
STR	21	14	15	12	23
CON	18	15	17	11	16
SIZ	07	11	10	12	18
INT	04	03	03	03	03
POW	11	11	08	09	03
DEX	10	12	03	09	02
HP	13	13	14	12	17
Attack %	35%	45%	40%	35%	45%
Mode	beak	gore	bite	beak	butt
Damage B.	+1D4	+1D10	+1D6	+1D3	+2D6

Nitocris in Cairo

Once Nitocris is raised, Shakti continues to rule the Egyptian Brotherhood, but now must allot considerable resources to her as she establishes new branches of the Brotherhood throughout the Middle East and Europe. She assumes the identity of Shefira Roash, a wealthy woman of mysterious origin who lives lavishly in the Old City. As Shefira, she furthers the will of Nyarlathotep. The keeper may freely use her in other scenarios to generate adventures as she sends out agents and begins to link the cults of the Mythos to attempt world domination. Investigators knowing of her resurrection carry a secret dangerous to their existence; if she learns of their knowledge, she will not hesitate to exterminate them.

SHEFIRA ROASH

Shefira's international organization corresponds to nation-states as they exist at the time. As a general tactic, agents whom she has bound to her shall infiltrate or otherwise be accepted by the powerful and the important of a country or region. For at least several years the agents gather intelligence. Eventually, they learn enough to be able to protect limited cult activity, perhaps through blackmail or by using non-cultists who yet enjoy some of the proclivities of cultists. Gaining such influence constitutes the second policy goal of the organization.

In a small nation, agents might need to influence only a few portions of the ruling family, bend a few oligarchs, or polish the epaulets of a handful of generals. In an extensive nation such as the United States, regional organizations would need building, requiring more time. The third goal would be to inflame portions of the existing society in order to create racial, religious, or economic class differences, so that the cult could safely acquire sacrificial victims.

The fourth goal, which might take generations, requires creation of a global atmosphere of tension and fear, in which control of society is everywhere concentrated in fewer and fewer hands. The final policy goal, of course, would be to control that power-elite which in turn controls humanity.

The statistics below represent Nitocris/Shefira after about six months of life in the twentieth century.

CIRCLET OF THE NAJA HAJI: on her left arm Shefira wears a magical circlet wrought like an Egyptian cobra. It is made of gold, alabaster, and onyx. Once per combat round, a wearer can transmit one or more magic points into the circlet and cause a living Egyptian cobra to drop to the floor or other surface beneath the circlet.

The generated cobras are entirely normal Egyptian cobras, except that they will never bite the wearer of the circlet. The smallest cobra so-produced is one foot long and injects POT 2 venom; for each additional magic point sacrificed to the circlet, the cobra produced is approximately another foot longer and two points more potent. For example, ten magic points creates a cobra about ten feet long, whose venom is POT 20. The circlet does not accept more than twelve magic points per combat round, and cannot create more than one cobra per round.

However dangerous they are to the servants, Shefira enjoys keeping several little chums slithering around.

SHEFIRA ROASH, apparent age 29, the Revivified Nitocris, once Queen of Egypt, and now leader of the international Brotherhood of the Black Pharaoh

STR 12	CON 15	SIZ 12	INT 16	POW 16
DEX 13	APP 18	EDU 12	SAN 0	HP 14

Damage Bonus: +0.

Weapons: Fingernail Rip* 60%, no damage but nails are poisoned
Dagger* 50%, damage 1D6 damage and usually poisoned as well
Circlet of the Naja Haji—special; see in text.

* Shefira brews a POT 16 poison that takes effect in ten combat rounds.

Armor: crown, necklace, and girdle provide her with 15 hit points of magical protection over her entire body. Thus, with an attack doing 16 hit points of damage, she would take only one hit point of damage.

Spells: as many as the keeper desires.

Skills: Arabic 60%, Archaeology 30%, Bargain 50%, Cthulhu Mythos 35%, Egyptian History 30%, Egyptology 50%, English 20%, Fast Talk 75%, French 10%, Hide 30%, Occult 60%, Persuade 55%, Pharmacy 45%, Propaganda 60%, Psychology 50%, Sixth Dynasty Egyptian 95%, Sneak 75%, Spot Hidden 80%.

Egyptian Cobra (Naja Haji)

A smaller, less beautiful serpent than the king cobra of India, the Egyptian cobra is darker with a narrower hood. Its appearance is adequate to make the bravest investigator sweat.

The cobra's strike is not amazingly fast or accurate. If the investigator can see the strike coming, allow a normal Dodge roll to evade the attack (after all, a cobra may aim for a pants cuff rather than a leg, or even forget to inject venom). The bite of a cobra does not do significant damage in itself, but the sharp fangs can penetrate two points of armor. The poison is relatively slow-acting. Approximately fifteen game minutes should pass before swelling or sweating and temperature rise from a bite occur.

EGYPTIAN COBRA

characteristics	roll	average
STR	1D3	2
CON	1D6+3	6-7
SIZ	1D2	1-2
POW	1D6	3-4
DEX	2D6+6	13
Hit Points	4	
MOV	3/3 swimming	

Weapon: Venomous Bite 40%, damage is POT of poison, equal to CON+POW of the serpent.

MACHINATIONS OF THE BROTHERHOOD

*Wherein for a few hours the investigators bid adieu
to busy bureaucrats and cutthroat cultists,
and encounter instead true heroes of the struggle against evil.*

The Mosque of Ibn Tulun

Faraz Najir had heard that the Brotherhood wanted an item located in the Mosque of Ibn Tulun. The investigators should follow up on this lead.

The mosque is about half a mile due west of the Citadel of Saladin, very nearly due south of the Ezbekia Gardens. The easiest way to get there is by hired car: go out Sharia Mehemet, and then turn right, toward the Nile. The windswept wilderness of the City of the Dead begins less than a kilometer south of this mosque.

Ibn Tulun is the oldest complete mosque in the city of Cairo, and is less ornate than many of the later Cairene holy places. As in any place of worship, quiet is the order of the day. Visitors should remove shoes when entering. Women may not be allowed. During times of prayer, non-worshippers are unwelcome.

Traditional mosque design imitates the courtyard of Mohammed's Medina house, where the great prophet first taught. It is an walled court, open to the sky, with shade along several sides.

If the investigators ask an attendant for an audience with one of the ulama, the learned scholars of Islam, the chance that they randomly get the right man is very low—more than thirty teachers discourse daily here on subjects ranging from geometry to the Koran to the *hadith*, and of them only a few know of the Girdle of Nitocris. If several investigators receive successful Credit Rating rolls, or if one speaks Arabic and receives a successful Persuade roll, or if the attendant that day happens to be a venal man who delicately suggests a bribe, then the investigators may learn that they should speak with the nazir of the mosque, who acts as civil administrator as well as having profound religious duties.

That man, Achmed Zehavi, is busy and uninterested in foreign Christian tourists. He will not see the investigators unless they straightforwardly mention the Girdle of Nitocris or the Black Pharaoh. In that case, they will be received in a building adjacent to the mosque.

Zehavi is a patient, gentle, devout man, upset about recent attempts to break in and steal the Girdle. Zehavi wants to learn what the investigators know about it, though he will not reveal that the Girdle of Nitocris is at the mosque.

If asked directly, Zehavi delicately deflects all questions about the Girdle unless he thinks the investigators have sufficient information or skills to be of help. A successful Persuade roll convinces him. Once convinced, he reassures them that the Girdle is well guarded. "The evil ones shall not have it. In'shallah." A demonstration of magic can convince him to show the artifact to the investigators. Zehavi perceives Mythos gods and minions as instances of the demonic menaces mentioned in the Koran. He has zealously arranged the defense of the Girdle, but in the purity of his faith he does not understand the danger to the world to be as pervasive and all-threatening as it is.

ACHMED ZEHAVI

THE GIRDLE OF NITOCRIS

The Girdle rests beneath Zehavi's office in a guarded cellar. One enters the cellar only through an iron door (STR 50) at the back of the office. The door is kept locked. Behind the door, stairs lead down twenty-five feet. Here it is cool and dry, the very conditions which have preserved so much of Egypt's heritage. The stairs end at another locked iron door (STR 50). Behind this door is a bare room, 20 x15 x10 feet high, with walls of thick stone.

A small chest in the center of the room holds the Girdle. The Girdle proves to be a narrow band of intricately-linked gold chain, with what appears to be a large, uncut ruby marking the clasp. Studied, the polished stone appears to shift unpredictably its shape and color.

Six ulama, all old and all armed with scimitars, guard the Girdle. Each spends a few hours daily on the surface, walking and conversing; there is a 50% chance that five rather than six are in the room, but Nessim Efti, chief of the guards, always should be present during an attack. Ninety years old, Efti stands guard with the Sword of Akmallah, a marvelous scimitar made many centuries ago which does normal scimitar damage to any entity from any plane of existence. The lives of these men have concluded except in their zeal for

God: here they testify, expound, and contemplate, waiting for death or a final chance to prove the temper of their faith.

Twice daily, two boys bring food to the guardians, using the only key to the door (Achmed Zehavi carries keys for both doors). The boys work promptly, never entering the room but knocking on the heavy door and waiting for one or more of the guards to receive the food. They then immediately return the key to Zehavi.

If Zehavi sufficiently trusts the investigators, he'll call up Nessim Efti for the meeting as well. Yes, they know there was a Black Pharaoh, a scourge destroyed by the power of Allah. The Black Pharaoh's name, Nyarlathotep, is known to them, but they do not pronounce it aloud and do not appreciate hearing it. Prophecies agree that Nitocris, another legendary evil power, rises again by means of the Girdle, and they guard the Girdle to prevent her ascension. These holy men have tried to destroy the Girdle, but so far it has defeated their efforts. The Brotherhood tried to steal the Girdle, a clumsy attempt easily foiled. The ulama do not know of Omar Shakti,

NESSIM EFTI

who moves in much more worldly company. Zehavi and Efti believe that the Carlyle Expedition stirred an ancient evil which now threatens the spirits of many men.

If the investigators find a way to steal the Girdle, the Brotherhood learns about the theft, and gladly dispatches hordes of fanatics to recover the priceless artifact. If the investigators manage to destroy the Girdle, the same waves of cultists can be sent to avenge the loss.

Should the investigators come into possession of the Girdle, they forestall a powerful assault upon the mosque, and if they can conceal the artifact, they make the resurrection of Nitocris impossible. Zehavi can quickly confirm their success. The grateful ulama may even award the Sword of Akmallah to these Westerners, upon the condition that they dedicate their lives to the struggle against evil. Many doors in the Muslim world are then open to them.

"TRAGEDY AT THE MOSQUE OF TULUN"

If the investigators do not take or destroy the Girdle, several days later they read in any Middle Eastern venue the news clipping *Nyarlathotep Papers #32*.

ITEM. Story in the *Cairo Bulletin (Nyarlathotep Papers #32)*.

Relevance of the Information: implies the theft of the girdle of Nitocris and the triumph of the Brotherhood, bringing the resurrection of Nitocris measurably closer.

Zehavi's state of shock (referred to in the story) is his catatonia induced by the sight of a chthonian burrowing up through the floor of the room in which the Girdle was kept. With the Sword of Akmallah, Nessim wounded the great beast before it carried off both him and the enchanted blade.

Players of investigators who contact the police should make Luck rolls. One successful roll reveals that Emil

Nyarlathotep Papers #32

Tragedy at the Mosque of Tulun

Six of Ibn Tulun's most respected scholars died last night in the collapse of the ceiling of their study room.

The cause of these tragic deaths is being investigated.

Still missing, but presumed dead, is Nessim Efti. The nazir of Ibn Tulun, Achmed Zehavi, survived, but was taken to hospital in shock.

The collapse occurred in a building adjacent to Ibn Tulun itself; the historic structure is undamaged.

Vabreaux, the Cairo police's forensics expert, found an odd substance at the scene, samples of which have been sent by military courier to labs in both Paris and Geneva for further testing.

A second successful Luck roll or a successful Persuade or Fast Talk roll gains the investigators an interview with Vabreaux, a subtle and imperturbable scientist. From the wreckage of the cellar, Vabreaux collected nearly three kilos of a body tissue with which he is completely unacquainted. One surface seems to be natural integument of some sort; the other surfaces exhibit a series of layers. The tissue samples apparently were cut away by an exceedingly sharp instrument. The majority of the samples are in cold storage at his Cairo laboratory, but kept even at below-freezing temperatures those samples are beginning to deteriorate.

Vabreaux's mystery tissue is chthonian flesh, hacked away as Nessim Efti furiously attacked the thing. If the investigators have the chthonian-skin-bound copy of *People of the Monolith* and they show it to this expert, Vabreaux recognizes the surface texture as identical to his samples. The keeper should privately determine whether or not Vabreaux becomes an important ally for the investigators. It is likely that he has some acquaintance with Nigel Wassif, though the temperaments of the two men are very different.

Once the Girdle of Nitocris is in the hands of the Brotherhood, the investigators have no further chance at it until the night Nitocris is resurrected.

ACHMED ZEHAVI, age 73, Nazir of Ibn Tulun

STR 05 CON 07 SIZ 10 INT 16 POW 10
DEX 10 APP 14 EDU 18 SAN 70 HP 09

Damage Bonus: -1D4.

Weapon: none.

Skills: Arabic 99%, Archaeology 35%, Astronomy 25%, Bargain 50%, Cthulhu Mythos 10%, Egyptian Hieroglyphs 15%, English 40%, First Aid 75%, French 75%, History 55%, Koran 99%, Muslim Law 90%, Occult 25%, Spot Hidden 68%.

NESSIM EFTI, age 90, Bearer of the Sword of Akmallah

STR 10 CON 10 SIZ 10 INT 18 POW 12
DEX 08 APP 06 EDU 18 SAN 75 HP 10

Damage Bonus: +0.

Weapon: Scimitar* 45%, damage 1D6+2

* *Efti's scimitar, the Sword of Akmallah, is a magical weapon which inflicts normal sword damage on any creature from any plane of existence.*

Skills: Arabic 95%, Archaeology 10%, Astronomy 15%, Bargain 50%, Cthulhu Mythos 10%, History 80%, Koran 95%, Medicine 25%, Muslim Law 95%, Persuade 70%, Spot Hidden 70%.

FIVE GUARDIAN ULAMA

	1	2	3	4	5
DEX	14	13	11	11	09
POW	12	13	17	10	11
SAN	70	64	80	55	60
HP	10	11	09	10	09

Damage Bonus: +0.

Weapon: Scimitar* 25%, damage 1D6+2

* *these scimitars are not magical.*

Nyiti of El Wasta

Having spoken to Warren Besart, the investigators may wish to question Nyiti and her son Unba. El Wasta is a few hours up the Nile. Knowledge of Arabic is essential here. A few merchants and functionaries have some very limited English and French, but they also have duties to perform and deals to strike. There are too many Nyitis in town for that name to be significant. The right Nyiti is impossible to find without adequate Arabic and a systematic search. Careful questioning in Arabic throughout town for 1D6+2 hours at last leads to a tiny hovel.

The first person the investigators see is Unba, Nyiti's son. His right arm and shoulder and the right side of his face have been gouged away. If any of the investigators know the effect of a Hunting Horror attack, then that investigator correctly supposes that a Hunting Horror maimed Unba. This large man's speech is slow and halting. If the investigators patiently persist, Unba at last agrees to bring them to his mother.

Nyiti looks extremely old. Her jaw and both of her hands have been burned away. Normally she is quite insane but, seeing the investigators, her eyes light. She makes awful gurgling noises, and she points with her stumps to a corner of the hut. This disturbs her son, who rushes to her. If the investigators are too stupid to look in the indicated corner, Unba can eventually bring an artifact to their attention.

NYITI OF EL WASTA

In the corner, amidst blankets, pots, etc., is a rush basket painted with a red symbol. A successful Occult or Archaeology roll identifies the glyph as an ancient Egyptian symbol of protection. Within the basket is a 7x9-inch slab of white stone several inches thick. Its irregular edges make apparent that it was broken from a larger piece of worked stone. A second successful Archaeology roll or a successful Geology roll suggests that the incisions are many centuries old and that such limestone was used as facing on many pyramids. With a successful Spot Hidden roll, an investigator carries the artifact into the sun and perceives that the stone fragment is not white, or creamy white, but actually has a pinkish cast—a facing color used only on the Red Pyramid at Dhashur.

Nyiti pleads for the investigators to take the stone. When they accept it, she lapses into dullness, her last goal accomplished. She is of no further help.

ITEM. The fragment of Nyiti, a broken piece of rock bearing part of a simple image (*Nyarlathotep Papers #33*).

Relevance of the Information: there is at least one other part to this apparently magical image.

Though the investigators cannot know it, the fragment is half of a warding symbol which was worked into the capstone of the Red Pyramid. The ward is known as the Eye of Light and Darkness. The investigators see only the right-hand portion of the symbol, showing half an eye and the inverted ankh. Nyiti recovered the stone after Roger Carlyle broke the ward's power. Jack Brady has the other half of the ward.

The fragment can be of use if the investigators learn the ritual of activation, which is in one of the *Seven Cryptical Books of Hsan*. Dr. Kafour may recognize the symbol and be able to recreate it, surmising that it is a protective sign of some power, but he does not know how to activate it. With a successful Occult roll, an investigator can understand the symbol's importance.

INTO THE SANCTUM

The dogged investigators, having survived monsters, cultists, and magic-laden priests,
decide to tour some of the monuments of Egypt's past glory.
Among them is an unusual asymmetric pyramid.

In Dhashur are two pyramids, the Red Pyramid and the Bent Pyramid, which Sneferu, first pharaoh of the Fourth Dynasty, caused to be created. In Meidum, Sneferu had built a third great structure—the Collapsed Pyramid.

The Collapsed Pyramid, where Warren Besart saw the Black Sphinx rise, yields few clues. Locals say that strange things happen here occasionally, but that the desert is always strange. Like the Giza locals who see cultists heading toward the Sphinx, Meidum residents know better than to tell things to strangers. If investigators poke around in the dark at the Collapsed Pyramid, they have a 50% chance of being attacked by 2D4 cultists each hour that they are there. All entrances to that pyramid are completely blocked by fallen stone and rubble which would take months to remove.

The Red Pyramid, originally faced with pinkish limestone, bore a protective ward for the Dhashur area, but Roger Carlyle destroyed its power by breaking its ward, a fact known by Omar Shakti. The pyramid is otherwise unremarkable.

The Bent Pyramid

The Bent Pyramid is so called because it is asymmetric. The northern face is steeper than the other three faces, so that the pointed capstone of the pyramid does not occur at the precise center of the pile, but is removed some seventy feet northward.

Entrances to the Bent Pyramid exist on its west and north faces. The north entrance leads to a funerary chamber reputedly for Sneferu. (Archaeologists found no mummy or furnishings, however.) Four Egyptian soldiers always guard the north entrance. Though the west door is unguarded, a wooden barricade blocks passage.

The guards are friendly and chatter to investigators about local happenings. They are on watch here to prevent more of the mysterious accidents which happen in the Bent Pyramid,

but they know nothing about those events except that strange movements supposedly occur within the pyramid and in the area immediate to it.

Investigators can give a gift to the guards and be allowed inside, though one guard will go along to make sure the foreigners cause no damage. The north entrance leads to a bare, poorly painted chamber of no interest.

The investigators should save their money or cigarettes, and break through the western door. Anyone knocking on or otherwise touching the wood notices several loose boards which can be shoved aside to allow entrance. A passage leads to a false funerary chamber roughly in the center of this great pile of stone. The chamber is devoid of artifacts, though two remarkably thick alabaster columns stand at the rear of the room. They are nearly indestructible. The one to the right contains a secret door, at this moment noticeable by any investigator whose player even attempts a Luck roll. The opening discovered, twenty steps lead up to where a series of ramps ascend. The ramps climb nearly to the interior of the pyramid's capstone. There a secret room exists, the earthly throne room of Nyarlathotep.

Nyarlathotep's Sanctum

An asymmetrical arch signals the entrance to the throne room of Nyarlathotep. If an investigator has read *Life as a God*, a successful Idea roll lets him recognize the room from Crompton's description.

The six lights which Crompton reported are from six five-foot-high pillars topped with alien gems. If flame is put to these gemstones, they burn like torches, but with a cold, unceasing fire. Lighting all six gems summons the Black Pharaoh to his throne.

THE THRONE: the indestructible throne chair is carved of black obsidian, and encrusted with precious stones which a successful Geology roll proves to be of unknown origin. The great chair rests above the floor, on a stepped dais. If a mortal sits on the throne while Nyarlathotep is summoned, then the god possesses the trespasser and takes on his appearance. For practical purposes, Nyarlathotep is in the chair speaking and acting, though his appearance is that of a friend. When the god chooses to depart, only the mortal's twitching corpse remains, his or her foolish bravado summarily punished by the god. If no one sits in the chair, then the god appears in the guise of the Black Pharaoh.

THE BAS-RELIEF: raised inscriptions cover the wall behind the throne, glyphs partly of the Cthulhu Mythos and partly Egyptian in origin. If any investigator can read Egyptian hieroglyphs, double the chance to translate the signs. They foretell the impending birth of the child of Nyarlathotep within the Mountain of the Black Wind. The date for this event is vague. Choose it in accord with the general progress of the investigators, who may wish to attend such a special function. The prophecy further foresees that vast destruction heralds the great birth, though the nature of the destruction is unstated.

Because of the poor light, quietly decrease any Photography skill application by 20 percentiles, and inform the players of this only after the investigators have fled the chamber. A failed skill roll produces useless photos—perhaps the alien gems gave off alien light which reacted poorly with film or plates designed for Earthly sunlight. If Dr. Kafour is along, he can easily translate the glyphs. A pencil rubbing of the symbols produces a perfect transcription.

THE ASTRONOMY WALL: the wall to the left of the throne

Nyarlathotep Papers #33

holds two bas-reliefs, a large star chart and a smaller depiction of specific planetary positions in this solar system. Formidable-looking astrological symbols ring the latter relief. All the points on the star chart are within our galaxy, but even with successful Astronomy rolls only Fomalhaut, Aldebaran, Deneb, and a few other visible stars can be recognized. The rest of the hundreds of points have Mythos or astronomical significance incomprehensible to sane human astronomers.

THE PYRAMIDS AT GIZA AS MONTGOMERY CROMPTON SAW THEM

The planetary positions chart can be understood by successful Astronomy and Occult rolls. Study and calculations indicate that the next matching planetary configuration occurs on January 14, 1926. A successful Idea roll sends an investigator to current ephemeris or almanac: on that day a total solar eclipse races across the Indian Ocean.

THE HEMISPHERIC MAP: on the wall to the right of the throne is a distorted map of Eurasia, Africa, Australia, and the western Pacific. Mountains, rivers, and continental outlines are easily recognized; no cities or nations are shown. An elongated triangle is formed by three uncut rubies respectively marking points in the East China Sea, central Kenya, and western Australia. Because the decorative map is inaccurate, precise locations cannot be determined. An inlaid ebony band marks an arc crossing the Indian Ocean, an arc identical to the arc of totality for the solar eclipse of January 14, 1926.

Arcane symbols border the map, which a successful Cthulhu Mythos roll infers as meaning: *The Old Ones Shall Come Hence. All Shall Tremble Before Their Awful Might.*

NYARLATHOTEP ARRIVES

The god comes when all of the alien gems are set burning, when someone sits on his throne, or when the investigators have examined the room. If not before, then the gemstones automatically catch fire. When Nyarlathotep arrives, the entrance to the throne room solidifies into solid rock, pushing out anyone standing in the archway. Those left outside the throne room then will be dismayed to see 1D6 Ghouls (Sanity loss 0/1D6 SAN) push up through solid stone and attack them. These creatures will not pursue victims beyond the entrance to the pyramid—they disappear when they die or when they have cleared the passage to the west entrance.

The Carlyle Expedition and the Pyarmids

The day Roger Carlyle, Hypatia Masters, Robert Huston, and Sir Aubrey Penhew disappeared within the Bent Pyramid, they stumbled into Nyarlathotep's sanctum in the same way as did the investigators. Via the hemispheric map, they were transported to ancient Egypt, a feat especially pleasing to Sir Aubrey. They spent weeks in that time. Many potent spells were taught to the three men while they were being indoctrinated into the worship of Nyarlathotep—in particular, they were taught how to break the warding spells guarding the three defining angles of the triangular gate. In his human aspect, Nyarlathotep meanwhile seduced Hypatia, implanting in her the seed of a child which could be born when convenient. Jack Brady (strong-willed, faithful, and magically defended) was excluded from this great adventure as being unsuitable for Nyarlathotep's purposes.

Inside the throne room, Nyarlathotep appears in full Black Pharaoh aspect, cruel and glittering, full-voiced and magnificently evil. If the investigators saw his bust in the secret basement room at the Penhew Foundation, they'll recognize him now and lose 1/1D6 SAN each for the privilege.

THE BLACK PHARAOH

To his left and right, the air boils and bends—two hunting horrors hover in the air, invisible until their god bids them attack. Foul, unearthly music toys with the minds of the investigators, taunting and disappointing them. The smell of death is everywhere.

If the investigators attack the god, the hunting horrors become visible (Sanity loss 0/1D10) and counterattack. If these entities are unable to handle the job, Nyarlathotep takes a hand, using the rod and ring of his office as foci through which he casts energy blasts. Each blast does an automatic 20 points of damage to a random member of the party. Nyarlathotep inflicts the damage every other combat round by means of a casual gesture with one of the foci. The god is diverted by this amusing activity, chuckling as his victims (horribly withered and seared) scream, writhe, and die. After one or two die, he ceases his attacks unless the investigators continue to attack. The keeper may decide if any defense exists against such an awesome god.

If powerful investigators manage to do fifteen or more hit points of damage to Nyarlathotep's human aspect, he changes into an indescribably monstrous, mind-wrenching form and departs (SAN cost 1D10/D100). The Hunting Horrors also leave. The archway to the throne room remains solid stone, and the survivors are left trapped within. Two men with picks can break through the stone in 1D3+1 12-hour days—either through the archway or through the capstone from outside—but strong explosives cannot be used without risking the death of those inside, from the shock of the explosion.

NYARLATHOTEP'S MESSAGE

If the investigators do not attack, or cease attacking when they see their situation is hopeless, Nyarlathotep deigns to speak to them. He says they are foolish to continue their present efforts. The gods they defy are too powerful to be discomfited by mortal efforts. The investigators should meekly and gratefully return to their homes to await the inevitable. "Look you," he says, "at the fate of those who came before you." He waves a hand, and images form of the Carlyle Expedition camp in Africa. Kenyan bearers come and go; the principal members of the Carlyle Expedition can be seen. All is peaceful until terrible screams are heard, and scores of hunting horrors descend from the sky, while out of the earth lurch ghouls, formless spawn of Tsathoggua, and other frightful beings. The carnage is unspeakable. As mere witnesses, Sanity cost to the investigators is 1D10/D100. All of the white members of the expedition can be identified as being ripped to shreds and their African employees die in droves.

The god sneers. "Even the brave know their lot. All doors

are closed to you; all your dreams are doomed; all your struggles are futile." If the investigators already have met Jack Brady or other members of the expedition, they will be confused by the contradicting vision. If so, let them stew. Were the members of the expedition killed? If they met a member, was that an illusion? Did Nyarlathotep or other gods resurrect the Carlyle Expedition to use as slaves in some unfathomable scheme?

In truth, Nyarlathotep lies, though the investigators cannot be certain of it—Psychology rolls against a god are useless.

Nyarlathotep offers more proof of his potency. At another wave of a hand, the hemispheric map shimmers and dissolves. In its place is an archway: beyond stretches ancient Egypt. The archway opens onto ground-level; it is simple to step through. The locale is the same area as that surrounding the pyramid, but the Red Pyramid does not exist. The dimensional gate seems to have opened into a marketplace. Craftsmen work busily. Everything is real. Sanity cost for this daunting event is 0/1D3 SAN.

If at least half of the investigators incautiously walk through the new archway, they hear Nyarlathotep roar with laughter, and a moment later the archway shimmers. Each investigator has one chance to Jump successfully back through the archway; if the roll fails, that investigator is trapped in ancient Egypt.

Whether or not any investigators fall for the archway trap, Nyarlathotep slowly disappears, as does the archway. The stone slab filling and blocking the asymmetrical entrance to the throne room now dissolves, and the shaken party may stumble back to the secret door in the pillar. Once they have all gone through, that doorway also dissolves and no longer exists. They never get another chance to enter the sanctum of Nyarlathotep. They may correctly conclude that their meeting with the god was either arranged or fated.

The throne room can be destroyed with sufficient high explosive. The immediate cost for the explosive is 1400 Egyptian pounds; the delayed cost for blowing up a pyramid is thirty years in an Egyptian prison.

If the resurrection of Nitocris already has been foiled, Nyarlathotep may be harder on these pesky mortals, killing more of them and driving insane the rest. Gods have short tempers when they don't win.

Addenda

Strive to present this episode. The throne room contains important information, and the appearance of Nyarlathotep is an effective climax to many sessions of leg work and deduction. If the investigators neglect the Bent Pyramid, give them more clues. After all, Nyarlathotep himself baits the hook—can a god fail to attract the attention of such fish?

Once met in the Bent Pyramid, cause images of Nyarlathotep to dog the investigators while they remain in

THE GREAT SPHINX

Egypt: a quick glimpse in a crowd, a lurking vendor in a bazaar, a reflection in a window. As wished, keepers may or may not require Sanity rolls. It will be fun if investigators come to believe that every other person in Egypt is Nyarlathotep or his cultist double.

Nyarlathotep's cultists are less likely to be interested in grand designs and amusing traps, and more interested in using their clubs to slaughter investigators. Balance the apparent tolerance of the god with pressure by murderous cultists.

Conclusion

If the investigators have the attention of the Brotherhood, repeated assassination attempts shortly should make clear that it's time to move on. Keepers may find useful a concluding adventure of escape and pursuit. The scenario can be short—an hour or less, perhaps filling up the end of a session. The easiest one to run postulates cultists swarming across Cairo, blocking railways, roads, and Delta-bound steamers. This situation forces the team up the Nile, then overland by caravan to some fictitious port of Egypt's eastern coast, from where the investigators take passage either north or south along the Red Sea, as their cash and their strategic itinerary dictate.

No serious attacks need be mounted during this episode, if the investigators are grateful to escape with their skins. Needless to add, however, foolhardy investigators always should receive realistic chastisements. ■

KENYA

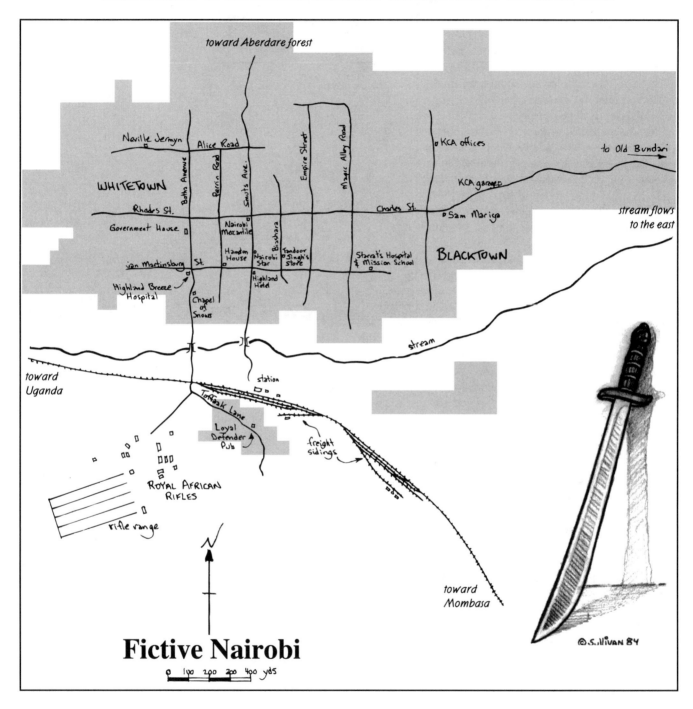

toward Aberdare forest

Neville Jermyn

Alice Road

to Old Bundari

WHITETOWN

KCA offices

Botha Avenue

Perrin Road

Smuts Ave.

Empire Street

Magee Alley Road

KCA garage

stream flows
to the east

Rhodes St.

Charles St.

Government House

Sam Mariga

Nairobi
Mercantile

Bashara

BLACKTOWN

van Martinsburg St.

Hamdon
House

Nairobi
Star

Tandoor
Singh's
Store

Starat's Hospital
& Mission School

Highland Breeze
Hospital

Highland
Hotel

Chapel
of
Snows

stream

toward
Uganda

station

Toftaak Lane

Loyal
Defender
Pub

freight
sidings

ROYAL AFRICAN
RIFLES

rifle range

toward
Mombasa

© S.llivan 84

N

Fictive Nairobi

0   100   200   300   400 yds

"[It was] a kind of force that acts and grows and shapes itself by other laws than those
of our sort of Nature. We have no business calling in such things from outside, and only
very wicked people and very wicked cults ever try to."
  –H.P. Lovecraft, "The Dunwich Horror"

Lacking a dirigible, the investigators probably reach Kenya by steamship. Many lines call at Mombasa, the seaport; a reliable British line is Baffrey's. Ships from Port Said travel through the Suez Canal, and lay over several days at Aden. Ships from Shanghai stop at Hong Kong, Singapore, Ceylon, Bombay, and perhaps Aden before reaching Mombasa. Ships from London or New York touch Freetown, rest most of a week at Cape Town, and overnight at Durban.

The investigators could, of course, go up to the White Nile through the Sudan, a distance of about 3000 actual miles, crossing sullen deserts and trackless, disease-ridden swamps. Survivors would have trekked for about six months, and reach Nairobi before finding Mombasa.

Arriving at Mombasa, they may take the Uganda railway some 300 miles inland to Nairobi. From there, if they dare, the investigators can safari to the Mountain of the Black Wind, and learn what that fearsome place has to do with the fate of the Carlyle Expedition. (What worthy investigator could fail to be interested in the appearance of the son of Nyarlathotep?)

The primary question to be solved in Nairobi is the location of the Mountain of the Black Wind. If the investigators talked with Jonah Kensington in New York City, they have leads to Johnstone Kenyatta, Lt. Mark Selkirk, and Nails Nelson. If they questioned Arthur Emerson (Emerson Imports, New York City), they know that a Mombasan exporter named Ahja Singh made regular shipments to Ju-Ju house. They may know the priestess's name, M'Weru. If they already have met Jack Brady, then they have a detailed map showing the way to the Mountain of the Black Wind. (If they have none of these leads, it's hard to understand why they sailed to Kenya! If they did anyway, use the *Nairobi Star* to direct them to one or more key contacts in Nairobi.)

No white man in Kenya Colony knows the location of the Mountain of the Black Wind—the English term is just a translated one, from several Bantu dialects. Similarly, Mt. Kenya is called that only by the English and Boers; black Africans call it Kere-Nyaga.

Investigators have a chance to acquire some useful items and to learn valuable information while at work in Kenya. Smart investigators will examine every lead before jumping off toward Aberdare Forest and the perils of the Mountain of the Black Wind. They are not in much danger while in Mombasa or Nairobi, despite the harassment of Tandoor Singh. If she hears of them at all, M'Weru will wait until they are isolated targets in the countryside.

Help may come from friendly tribes, and especially from African magicians in the area. Little or no help is likely from the colonial administration and police; the scattered contingents of the King's African Rifles are unlikely to take action without direct orders or without clear and present need. Those few high-level representatives of the Crown are ignorant of organized Bloody Tongue activity.

Expect massive Sanity loss in this chapter. Do not be squeamish in applying it. Unless the investigators are foolish or unlucky, they will live through these events without much difficulty—although it certainly won't seem that way to them!

Mombasa

If the investigators came from Cairo, Mombasa is an excellent transition for them. This city is Arabic, with those famous narrow and redolent alleys, elaborately decorated balconies, mosques and minarets, muezzins and veils. This famous merchant city and former slave-trading center is only a few centuries newer than Cairo itself. About 30,000 live here on the edge of the Indian Ocean, combining bits and slabs of Arabic, African, Indian, Portuguese, and British ways of life.

Pre-colonial traders built Mombasa on a coral island just offshore, for purposes of defense. A railway causeway and foot-traffic ferries now connect island and continent.

If a player suggests and successfully rolls a Spot Hidden for his investigator, that worthy notices that the same Indian (Tandoor Singh, actually) has been watching the party at several different times, and at several different locations. It is a logical deduction that he is following them. If they attempt to approach him, he always melts into the crowd and disappears. Singh has been alerted by telegraph, and his plans are long formed: he wants to eliminate these defilers well before they can approach the holy birth site deep in Kenya.

AHJA SINGH

Before or after their trip to the Mountain of the Black Wind, the investigators may decide to pay Ahja Singh a visit. Singh, you recall, was the chief African exporter to Ju-Ju

Selected Connections for this Chapter

NP#	clue or lead	obtained from	leads to
31	interview	Warren Besart	Kenya, Messenger of Black Wind
—	interview	Nigel Wassif	Kenya
—	Ahja Singh (Mombasa)	Arthur Emerson	Ho Fong, Ju-Ju House, Randolph Shipping, Tandoor Singh (Nairobi)
20	Carlyle Exp. alive?	letter from Elias	Kenya
21	"Sam Mariga rr-sta"	Elias' Kenya notes	Johnstone Kenyatta
21	Johnstone Kenyatta	Elias' Kenya notes	Okomu, Old Bundari
21	people to question	Elias' Kenya notes	Carlyle Exped., Neville Jermyn, Dr. Starret, Reggie Baines, Sam Mariga, Lt. Selkirk, Col. Endicott
21	Cult of Bloody Tongue	Elias' Kenya notes	the cult does exist
21	Nails Nelson	Elias' Kenya notes	Jack Brady, China
—	interview	Nat. Smythe-Forbes	Tandoor Singh and Sir Aubrey
—	back files information	*Nairobi Star*	local perspective on expedition
—	interview	Okomu	Mountain of the Black Wind
—	cultist paraphernalia	T. Singh's house	Cult of Bloody Tongue, *Cthaat Aquadingen*
—	Mountain of Black Wind	various sources	Hypatia Master, M'Weru

House of New York City. His Mombasa warehouse and office are at the Kilindini harbor, not 200 yards from where the investigators' steamer docked. Anyone in the area can point out the ordinary-looking building. Singh himself is in India, to return in three to six weeks. His factotum humbly asks if he may serve such notable customers.

Singh exports African art all over the world. There is nothing in his building or in his home linking him with Mythos cults. He is no cultist. He is a stocky, greedy businessman with few morals who keeps a multi-national crew of thugs on hand. At least four of them sleep nightly in the warehouse, and they'll be happy to break the heads of anyone breaking in.

If they make it inside, the investigators find nothing of interest except a locked iron safe (STR 65). A safecracker can hear its tumblers and work out its combination. Men with sledgehammers and cold chisels could quickly open it, as could a stick of dynamite. The safe weighs about 300 pounds; it could be moved to the countryside if need be. Alternately, a successful Locksmith roll could do the trick.

Though it's bulky, it's really not much of a safe. Determined investigators will make quick work of it

Inside the safe is the equivalent of about $300 U.S. in British and Egyptian pounds and Indian rupees, as well as miscellaneous invoices, some granulated sugar, a desiccant against the humidity, and a ledger. The ledger is kept mostly in Hindustani. A successful Accounting roll deciphers enough of the crabbed non-Hindustani addresses to show shipments to Ho Fong Imports (Shanghai), the Penhew Foundation (London), Omar Shakti (Egypt), Silas N'Kwane (c/o Emerson Imports, New York), Randolph Shipping Co. (two Australia addresses, Port Hedland and Darwin), and so on. There are many entries for Tandoor Singh in Nairobi. Most of the international shipments are entered as objets d'art; those sent to Tandoor are entered as casks or bricks of tea.

FOUR EQUAL-OPPORTUNITY THUGS, Hirelings of Ahja Singh

	Indian	African	Irishman	Arab
STR	14	16	15	15
CON	13	12	14	18
SIZ	14	14	13	11
APP	09	12	10	13
INT	10	11	11	14
EDU	01	01	06	01
DEX	14	13	12	11
POW	12	11	11	10
SAN	25	38	36	40
HP	14	13	14	15

Damage Bonus: +1D4.

Weapons: Blackjack 60%, damage 1D6+1D4
Knife 55%, damage 1D6+1D4
Fist 45%, damage 1D3+1D4
Head Butt 40%, damage 1D4+1D4
Kick 40%, damage 1D6+1D4

Skills: Arabic 35%, Bargain 25%, English 35%, Hide 45%, Hindustani 35%, Listen 45%, Sneak 50%, Spot Hidden 55%, Swahili 35%, and such other skills as the keeper may desire.

CULT OF THE BLOODY TONGUE (KENYA)

In East Africa, the investigators face the parent cult of the Bloody Tongue, beside which the New York branch is an insignificant tendril. Here the cult flourishes mainly in the bush, not in Nairobi or Mombasa. It is mostly black African, and has existed for thousands of years. Its holiest rites are held at the Mountain of the Black Wind, beyond the Aberdare Forest, some 120 air miles north of Nairobi. There lives the priestess M'Weru, more beautiful and more savage than ever. The cult uses all African tribal weapons, but always performs ritual murders and mutilations with the pranga. Tandoor Singh, an Indian tea-seller, leads the cult's Nairobi agents. Though the colonial administration denies the existence of the cult, most Kenyans of long residency vaguely know of it. Tribes in the Aberdare Forest region, particularly the Masai and the Kikuyu, detest the Bloody Tongue, and their members may aid the investigators. But those people also fear the cult and distrust non-tribesmen: aid must be carefully negotiated and the investigators will somehow have to prove themselves reliable.

AVERAGE BLOODY TONGUE MEMBER (Kenya)

STR 14	CON 16	SIZ 14	INT 08	POW 12
DEX 16	APP 02	SAN 0	EDU 01	HP 15

Damage Bonus: +1D4.

Weapons: Pranga 50%, damage 1D6+2+1D4
Spear 50%, damage 1D8+1+1D4
War Club 45%, damage 1D10+1D4
Bow 40%, damage 1D6+1

Skills: Cthulhu Mythos 11%, Hide 75%, Jump 65%, Kikuyu 40%, Listen 60%, Masai 40%, Nandi 40%, Sing 25%, Sneak 45%, Spot Hidden 60%, Swahili 30%, Track 85%, Tribal Dance 55%.

On the Ugandan Railway

The investigators' train to Nairobi is arranged in the following order:

wood burning locomotive
* * *
wood tender
* *
flatcar (blacks and freight) without protection from sun or rain
* * *
mail, baggage, and freight car
* * *
third-class (brown) car with row seating
* * *
dining car
* * *
first-class car (white) with compartment seating

There is no Pullman-style sleeping car. If the keeper prefers, the engine can burn poor-quality coal instead of wood—that produces more smoke and makes a dirtier and slower ride. This track concludes at Lake Victoria, in Uganda. It reached Kampala in 1931.

On this line seating is by class and by color. The flatcar, directly behind the locomotive and its tender, is left for baggage, light freight, and poor blacks; the third-class car is mostly left for brown peoples—Indians, Arabs, and better-off blacks. Poor whites of no status can ride more cheaply there. The last car, the one furthest from the smoky, smelly engine, is reserved for whites (and occasionally wealthy Arabs and Hindus, at the discretion of the conductor). The dining car serves brown peoples once between Nairobi and Mombasa (the tablecloths are removed and the nice china and silver jealously hidden). Blacks on the flatcar have to stay there; there is no way for them to get to the dining car. In these days it is perfectly normal to encounter deliberate, almost innocent racism. Rare protests against it are understood by authorities to indicate tendencies toward idiocy, bomb-throwing, and criminal madness.

The journey takes 15 to 18 hours. After climbing out of a narrow coastal belt of open forest and dense brush, the investigators see the wide plains of Africa. It is still hot, but less humid. Though farms can be found, exotic animal life is much in evidence—elephants, rhinos, giraffes, lions, hyenas, herds of various herbivores, and so on—are all seen at one time or another from the train. The land is gentle and rolling, broken occasionally by precipitous ravines and canyons. Dry grass spreads everywhere, interrupted by thorn and baobab trees. (Baobabs look something like hoofless dark young of Shub-Niggurath; their bulbous trunks are grayish and shiny.) Rainy seasons center on April and November; travelers during those seasons probably see verdant green plains, and may imagine that they are in Eden.

The line climbs steadily. Halfway along, a great snow-capped peak can be seen to the west: Mt. Kilimanjaro looms high in the sky, though it is fifty miles distant. If the train winds away to the west or east for a few minutes, glints of more great white mountains may be seen far off to the north—before them is Nairobi, beside them lies Aberdare Forest, and beyond them rests the Mountain of the Black Wind.

THE FIRST ATTACK

Tandoor Singh took the same train as the investigators. Unless they rode third class, they cannot see him because of the way the train is organized. (If they do ride third class, Singh will continuously read his two-month-old *London Times*.) Long after sunset, less than an hour from Nairobi, he judges that the time is right. From the safety of the third-class car toilet he summons and binds two fire vampires. Like living stars, the entities hover in the night just outside the window, then drift down the length of the train; occasional screams and shouts of astonishment mark the progress of these glowing, swirling, flaming apparitions as they go. Beside their targets, the walls of the coach begin to buckle, discolor, and smoke as the merciless things burn their way in: bound to Tandoor Singh, they

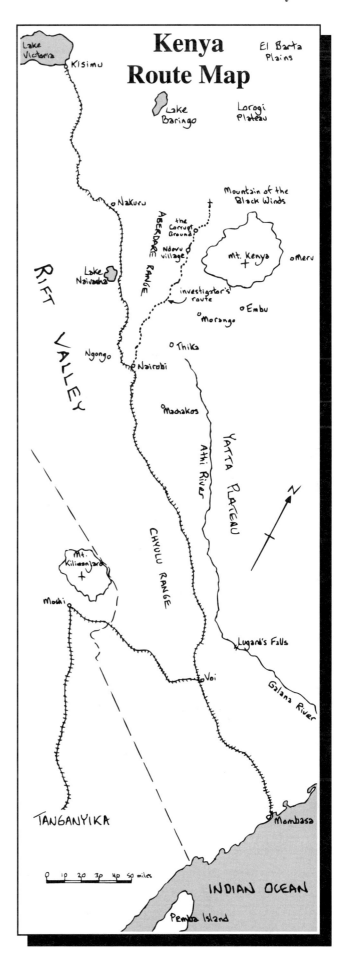

FIRE VAMPIRE ATTACK

attack until the investigators die or until the fire vampires are destroyed.

If the investigators know about fire vampires, the train has decent resources with which to fight them. If the players can successfully make Idea rolls or Spot Hiddens, their investigators remember or notice the fire buckets and ashtrays in the passageway which are filled with sand. The large metal pitchers in the toilets each contain about a gallon of water. There are nearly forty gallons of water available in the dining car (bottles of port and sherry will work in a pinch, but whiskey and brandy only encourage fire vampires), and the locomotive's tender has hundreds of gallons of water which could be drained out and used. The burns which the fire vampires inflict on the first victim should convince the investigators as to the course of action to be taken.

Singh wants to kill the investigators. The one certain consequence of the attack is that a major portion of the car in which the investigators are traveling will be gutted and left a smoking ruin. As the alarm spreads, the train halts. Everyone turns out to fight the fire. The fire vampires attack only the investigators. To the fifty other passengers and crew the behavior of those big sparks is uncanny, but not supernatural. The conductor sternly chastises surviving investigators for carelessness with their cigars, and threatens them with damages. So long as the investigators stay within reach of the Kenyan courts, keepers may want to harass them with the passenger-car suit.

THE FIRE VAMPIRES

THE REDDISH FIRE VAMPIRE

CON 06	SIZ 01	INT 12	POW 15
DEX 12	MOV 11		HP 06

Weapon: Touch 85%, damage 2D6 fire plus magic point drain

THE BLUISH FIRE VAMPIRE

CON 08	SIZ 01	INT 15	POW 10
DEX 16	MOV 11		HP 08

Weapon: Touch 85%, damage 2D6 fire plus magic point drain

Material weapons cannot hurt fire vampires, but materials useful in fighting fires will be effective against them: water does 1 hit point of damage per two quarts poured over a fire vampire, a typical hand-held fire extinguisher does 1D6 hit points per successful application, a bucket of sand does 1D3 points damage. Other substances also can have effect; let the investigators be ingenious.

Because of the fire vampire attack, the train is delayed and arrives late at night in Nairobi. Let the investigators check in at the Highlands Hotel and sleep. This allows Tandoor Singh to replenish his magic points.

All of the investigators wake late the next day, and have a leisurely breakfast; any who were badly hurt are in the Highlands Breeze Hospital not two blocks away from the hotel. If investigators died, services can be held today or tomorrow, or other arrangements made at the Chapel of the Snows. Local officials want statements and depositions concerning deaths, damages, etc. It is sunset before the investigators can track down leads.

NAIROBI

*Vengeance for the Carlyle massacre was swift and stern,
but fell on the innocent. If investigators can't fan up consciences
in Nairobi, they literally may perish in fire.*

At the time of the adventure, Nairobi is a new colonial town of about 8,000 people. Just beyond it rise Mt. Kinangop and the beautiful Aberdare range; Mt. Kenya soars a little further north and east. The town was founded in 1900 as a railway siding before the mountains, the last spot where locomotives could shunt. At an elevation of more than 6,000 feet, the region is relatively cool and dry, the views superb, the water adequate, and the soil excellent for farming. Europeans sweltering in Mombasa quickly noticed these advantages, and settlement began.

Until 1920, Kenya is known as the British East African Protectorate. At the time of the investigators' visit, it is Kenya Colony, mostly self-administered, though it owes grateful allegiance to the Crown, which oversees most foreign and Commonwealth matters. Two under-strength battalions of British regulars garrison Kenya. There also exist over one thousand paramilitary police, usually blacks and Indians led by white officers.

The fictive Nairobi presented in this scenario bears no resemblance to the modern Nairobi of more than 500,000 residents.

At the time of the adventure, Nairobi was divided into districts, the normal situation in European colonies—and in former colonies such as the United States. Nairobi had three districts, one each for white-, brown-, and black-skinned inhabitants. In this adventure they are referred to as whitetown, browntown, and blacktown, respectively. These divisions are policed and forcibly maintained. Offices, hotels, clubs, etc., may be marked as Whites Only. There may be separate entrances to administrative facilities such as courts. Jails are segregated. Toilets at the railway station are emphatically separated. Whites who enjoy slumming may penetrate colored areas with impunity, but black men and women in white areas without reason may be arrested, physically ejected, or escorted out.

OUTSIDE NAIROBI

Beyond the towns and white-owned plantations, the life of African blacks continues much as it has for centuries. The tribal cultures are stable and well adapted to the land. Though sometimes deadly enemies of other tribes, most of the people are friendly and curious about strangers. They show emotion openly and without reservation. They are not savage. European explorers seeking the source of the Nile strolled from village to village as though on weekend tours. The locals threw lots of parties for them, and most of those journalist-explorers found themselves in no hurry to leave.

In Nairobi, English is generally spoken. Outside of Nairobi and a few other towns, most blacks speak little or no English. The common language of East Africa is Swahili, a Bantu-structured trading language with a predominantly Arabic vocabulary (Arabs controlled East Africa's coastal and oceanic trade for a millennium, including the once-profitable slave trade). Swahili is a well developed language, resembling Middle English in flexibility, subtlety, and the impact of diverse foreign vocabularies on it. It is not a trade speech, such as is Pidgin at this time in the western Pacific. Though every major tribal grouping has its own language, including Kikuyu, Nandi, and Masai, a speaker of Swahili has little difficulty being understood anywhere in Kenya. If the investigators speak no Swahili, and hire no interpreter, it is unlikely that they can get any but the most rudimentary information from country-dwellers.

The largest bloc of the black population is the Kikuyu tribe, which is Bantu-speaking. Second in number are the Luos, representatives of the Nilotic peoples. The Kikuyus and the Luos are rivals. A third major ethnographic grouping is that of the Somalis, but they are a Hamitic people whose traditional territories lay to the east of the uplands and the locations of this chapter. The Nilo-Hamite nomads, a fourth grouping, includes the Masai and the Kipsigi. The warlike Nandis, a Nilotic people, fought the push of the Ugandan railroad and were decimated in return. Many of the cultists in the area are Nandi-related, who have turned to the Outer Gods for succor in a difficult time.

The Nairobi Star

As the investigators sit at dinner on the screened verandah of the hotel, it happens that a newsboy (black, 53 years old) passes by, peddling copies of the *Nairobi Star*, a large-paged, single-sheet daily newspaper. Though he can't read, the vendor swears that the *Star* is the best newspaper in the world; this he knows because Mrs. Smythe-Forbes is a fine lady, and a hard worker whom he has enjoyed serving for these past ten years. The office is right down the street, he says; see how all the windows are lit? The story of the coach fire seems accurately presented, and the writer can't be blamed for not knowing that fire vampires caused the conflagration. The only paper in Nairobi, the *Star's* back issues are a likely resource.

Someone else thinks so, too. Through binoculars, Tandoor Singh watches the hotel from the second story of his browntown house. If the investigators take an evening stroll over to the offices of the *Star*, he launches another attack—it has occurred to him that he can discredit these meddling strangers even if he fails to kill them. Another fire or two linked to the investigators, and the authorities will incarcerate them as menaces to public safety, and hustle them out of Kenya on the first ship. Extensive property damage or loss of life might even mean imprisonment or a murder trial.

There are too many diners on the verandah (and too many handy water pitchers) for his scheme to work there. The *Star's* offices, on the other hand, are semi-private, and paper burns well. The *Star* has always strongly backed measures incidentally repressing Singh's demonic secret religion. He would be very pleased to send fire vampires into the *Star* to do their worst. If he can, about eleven minutes after they enter the *Star*, the whole building is blazing and the investigators are writhing under multiple fire vampire attacks.

If the investigators do go to the *Star* that night, Natalie Smythe-Forbes, a typographer, and several printers are at work in the moderately sized building. Mrs. Smythe-Forbes is a brisk woman in her late forties. She's concerned about politics in Kenya. She's rather blind about black African affairs, and uninterested in the fate of those peoples, though she is personally kind.

She's a secret spiritualist, of no psychic talent. If the investigators approach matters in a genteel and delicate fashion, she reveals that she too

N. SMYTHE-FORBES

believes in the unseen forces of the supernatural planes. She could be romantically attracted to the most handsome male investigator, and strive to take him on buggy rides to waterfalls, elephant matings, etc., etc. If her newspaper burns down and her intuition reveals to her that the investigators are suspiciously connected, she'll be their implacable opponent and powerful enemy. However, the rest of the chapter is written as though she and the investigators become friends.

NATALIE SMYTHE-FORBES (white), age 48, Publisher of the Nairobi Star

STR 6	CON 8	SIZ 7	INT 14	POW 13
DEX 11	APP 12	SAN 65	EDU 12	HP 8

Damage Bonus: -1D4.

Weapons: none.

Skills: Accounting 50%, Credit Rating 85%, Drive Automobile 30%, English 80%, Fast Talk 55%, History 45%, Law 25%, Persuade 40%, Printing 30%, Psychology 25%, Ride 50%, Spot Hidden 45%, Swahili 50%.

Aftermath of the Fire

Though the *Star* would be his favorite target, Tandoor Singh could strike on any day after dusk. If he does start a second or even a third fire, the local authorities accuse one or more of the investigators of arson ("Those blokes have started

every fire! I'll stake my pension on it!") If a trial follows, so does acquittal, after some delay. Trial or not, formal expulsion from Kenya is the result. Informal ostracism from Nairobi hotels, restaurants, and other services begins immediately. Long before any trial, white society in Nairobi has isolated the investigators.

The investigators will be able to avoid most of this by pushing on toward the Mountain of the Black Wind, but it means that their preparations and investigations would be very incomplete.

What the Nairobi Star's Files Show

If the *Star's* back files burn, anyone in town could have a set for 1919. The most promising candidate would be Neville Jermyn, but that may make him entirely too fecund a source. Keeper's discretion here—perhaps Mrs. Smythe-Forbes simply recalls everything (she wrote it, after all).

THE ARRIVAL OF THE CARLYLE EXPEDITION: initially pretending to be making a relaxed big-game safari into the Great Rift Valley, the members of the expedition soon began to chat up another cover story—a trek to confirm data gathered in Egypt concerning the followers of a religious leader who migrated southward into Kenya. While in Nairobi, the Carlyle principals stayed at Hampton House, a hotel owned and managed by Reggie Baines since before WWI.

The expedition also dealt with Dr. Horace Starret and Mr. Neville Jermyn. A departure photo shows Sir Aubrey looking exceptionally young, and Hypatia Masters looking exceptionally dumpy. Any female investigator or male doctor instantly perceives that Hypatia is pregnant.

THE DISCOVERY OF THE BODIES: the report which led the patrol to the massacre site came from Sam Mariga, a gardener at the railway station. He lives on Charles Street in blacktown. Visiting a cousin in the village of Ndovu in the Aberdare Forest, he heard how many lay slain and unburied, and of how it was unwise to go near. That region is due north of Nairobi. Many miles separate it from the Great Rift Valley. Lt. Mark Selkirk and a squad of men found the remains. A photograph shows five Nandi corpses swinging from five ropes.

FROM MRS. SMYTHE-FORBES: "The Carlyle people were a strange, rather unhealthy lot. Hypatia, poor dear, was sick some of the time. Indisposed in the mornings, I think. Yes. Carlyle himself I scarcely saw—quite a nervous young man who liked his whiskey. And Sir Aubrey, though attractive and virile, had dealings with people not at all of his station. I especially recall that Tandoor Singh, a slimy little man, was at Hampton House a lot. A mere tea-peddler. He's still in Nairobi. Perhaps he would tell you what they talked about. I'm sure I don't want to know. The doctor, Huston, was very aloof."

She remembers Jackson Elias as a strong-willed, rather rude man of genius. She suggests talking to Roger Corydon at Government House and to Captain Montgomery of the African Rifles.

A Red Herring

If you wish to introduce a red herring into Kenya, the characters can encounter Colonel Endicott as they leave the Star. See "The Game Lodge" for this encounter.

Other Nairobi Contacts

From the Nairobi Notes of Jackson Elias and discussions with Mrs. Smythe-Forbes, investigators should have a long list of people to talk to in Nairobi. A number of minor encounters are mentioned in this section.

Hampton House

The best hotel in Nairobi, this white, rambling, two-story establishment is well-appointed, and has carefully tended plantings and lawns.

The proprietor, Reggie Baines, a port-swilling old fellow, remembers the Carlyle episode. It was thrilling to host them, despite their devastating deaths. It's been a long time now to remember very much. He does recall a lot of contact with brownish individuals, and blacks, too. When one goes into the back country, those sorts are useful, of course. Baines helped Sir Aubrey arrange some shipments to London—quite a bit of stuff. The fellow was a real collector.

Sam Mariga (black)

For a while, the new peoples of the British Empire endured personal discrimination at the hands of whites but were of

SAM MARIGA

two minds about it, for racial conflicts, hierarchies, and hereditary castes were normal in many places before the Empire arrived, just as later they were re-established after the Empire departed. The oddly democratic promise which the Empire proffered, that of many peoples made one prosperous and equal whole through the undeniable power, stability, and achievement of the Crown, was greatly appealing. During the Great War, British spokesmen persistently suggested that the wartime services of Indians, Africans, and Asians would not go unrewarded.

But the hopes which propaganda raised were afterward dashed as England preoccupied itself with internal questions. In the Commonwealth, especially in India and Africa, true nationalist movements began forming when the promises went unkept. Meanwhile the European settlers attempted to strengthen their own positions.

If the investigators go to Charles Street in the evening or to the rail station during the day, they easily find one such African nationalist, a Mr. Mariga. The plantings at his house and at the depot are lush and brilliant, better than anything in whitetown, which prides itself on floral display. Though the house is a humble shack, the Mariga residence plantings are the pride of Charles Street. Mariga is a large, strong man. He finds himself now too old and too familied to be an organizer for an independent Kenya, yet he occasionally speaks toward that end and frequently uses his rail pass to visit up and down the line, especially searching out intelligent, energetic youngsters and putting them in contact with one another.

Part of Mariga's nationalism comes from his knowledge of minor portions of the Cthulhu Mythos. Having witnessed events of which the West is ignorant and incapable of assimilating, he does not imagine that Europeans are omnipotent.

Mariga knows nothing of the Carlyle Expedition. If the investigators ask questions pertaining to the supernatural, Mariga directs them to Johnstone Kenyatta. Sam is well liked by the rail agent at Nairobi, who allows him to set his own schedule so long as the plantings remain immaculate: Mariga can guide the investigators all the way to the Mountain of the Black Wind, if they like.

SAM MARIGA (black), age 53, Kikuyu Father, Gardener, and Nationalist

STR 16	CON 15	SIZ 18	INT 13	POW 17
DEX 13	APP 13	EDU 03	SAN 50	HP 17

Damage Bonus: +1D6.

Weapons: Head Butt 70%, damage 1D4+1D6
Fist 65%, damage 1D3+1D6
Kick 55%, damage 1D6+1D6
Large Club 50%, damage 1D8+1D6
Fighting Knife 50%, damage 1D4+2+1D6
Short Spear 45%, damage 1D8+1+1D6

Skills: Bargain 50%, Climb 70%, Cthulhu Mythos 10%, Dodge 75%, English 35%, First Aid 60%, Hide 20%, Kikuyu 65%, Listen 65%, Luo 35%, Occult 25%, Psychology 65%, Sing 50%, Sneak 40%, Swahili 50%, Swim 50%, Track 80%, Throw 70%.

Neville Jermyn (white)

He is a descendant of the African explorer Sir Wade Jermyn, who wrote *Observations on the Several Parts of Africa*, and who went mad in 1765. See H.P. Lovecraft's short story "Facts Concerning the Late Arthur Jermyn and His Family" for details.

NEVILLE JERMYN

When speaking to Mr. Jermyn, a successful Psychology roll suggests that this man is as odd as his mad ancestor. Jermyn is a barrister at Government House, and will see visitors there. He never answers a knock on the door of his home.

Neville Jermyn firmly believes that the massacre of the Carlyle Expedition was a cult matter achieved with supernatural aid. Unfortunately, he has entirely the wrong cult—that of the White Gorilla—in mind, and twists all evidence to fit his preconception. He says that Sir Aubrey knew of this cult and its stronghold, and that Sir Aubrey hoped to learn the location of the ruined Congo Basin city which Sir Wade Jermyn found in the eighteenth century, and which one theory proposes to be the foundation from which sprang all human civilization. If the investigators mention the Black Pharaoh, Neville says that of course he must have come from there. A successful Psychology roll indicates that Neville Jermyn firmly believes this. Everything traces from the ruined city in the Congo.

There is in fact such a city, deep in the jungles of the Congo Basin, and Neville has maps leading to it which were obtained by Arthur Jermyn while that ancestor was in what became the Belgian Congo. An expedition to the city could be slightly shortened by taking the Uganda railway. Neville has always wanted to go to the city of the White Gorilla, but lacked the nerve. (It is not true that Sir Aubrey wanted to go there; that was another cover story.) If the investigators use Persuade or Fast Talk on Jermyn to learn more about the White Gorilla cult, they might get him to lead them on this complete red herring. If the keeper wants to build a scenario out of this, it should have nothing to do with the plot of *Masks of Nyarlathotep* or with the Cthulhu Mythos.

Neville Jermyn can help the investigators with suggestions about trekking into the back country, hiring bearers, and so on. He declares that he hired all the men for the Carlyle Expedition—a lot more men than they needed, though Sir Aubrey insisted that it be so. The logical conclusion is that they meant to bring back more than they took, but actually Sir Aubrey required an adequate human sacrifice to the god of the Bloody Tongue. Names like Bloody Tongue, the Black Pharaoh, or M'Weru mean nothing to Jermyn.

Investigators can get into Neville Jermyn's home by breaking and entering. Inside are many African artifacts, some of an occult nature as a successful Occult roll shows. Incidentally, Neville also owns one Mythos piece, an ebony carving of a hunting horror. Possession of it allows the holder to cast a Bind Hunting Horror spell without knowing the spell. Neville obtained the carving from a Luo tribesman in Nakura.

In the top drawer of Jermyn's writing desk are the old maps showing the location of the city of the White Gorilla.

NEVILLE JERMYN (white), age 38, Barrister and Oddball

STR 08	CON 06	SIZ 10	INT 13	POW 10
DEX 08	APP 10	SAN 15	EDU 16	HP 08

Damage Bonus: +0.

Weapons: none.

Skills: Anthropology 25%, Archaeology 35%, Cthulhu Mythos 03%, English 80%, History 20%, Law 35%, Library Use 45%, Occult 15%, Persuade 40%, Ride 50%, Swahili 70%.

Dr. Horace Starret (white)

A medical doctor and an Anglican rector for Nairobi, Dr. Starret is today at the hospital and mission school in blacktown which he helped to start. If the investigators mention that they're heading into the back country, he'll lecture them on African diseases, poisonous snakes, spiders, and frogs,

and suitable precautions, and adds that the Aberdare Forest area is cool and quite healthful.

The Carlyle expedition came to Dr. Starret to purchase a small quantity of medical supplies—petroleum jelly, opium, and so on—which happened to be otherwise unavailable in local chemist shops for a few weeks. In return, Miss Masters very generously donated to the work of the church, for which Dr. Starret was most grateful.

DR. HORACE STARRET

He was therefore particularly upset at the subsequent news of the massacre. He participated in the medical examination of certain bodies returned to Nairobi for burial. Those corpses were torn to pieces. The pieces should have been devoured by animals, or should have thoroughly rotted. They were in astonishingly fresh condition after having lain on the ground for weeks. The examiners apparently found many other reasons to confirm that the length of time since death had indeed been several weeks. "An eerie conclusion, you'll agree. But it confirmed me in my faith, gentlemen: those poor men were doomed by a brush of the Devil's hand! Supernatural evil is the only conclusion!"

Dr. HORACE STARRET (white), age 61, Anglican Rector and Medical Doctor

STR 06	CON 12	SIZ 10	INT 13	POW 05
DEX 12	APP 09	EDU 18	SAN 70	HP 11

Damage Bonus: -1D4.

Weapon: blind faith

Skills: Anthropology 10%, Bargain 25%, Chemistry 30%, Doctrine and Life 60%, Drive Automobile 15%, English 75%, First Aid 95%, History 50%, Law 25%, Medicine 55%, Persuade 60%, Psychology 20%, Spot Hidden 40%, Swahili 50%.

Roger Corydon (white)

Mr. Corydon is colonial undersecretary for internal affairs, and a genial and useful contact. He oversaw the investigation into the Carlyle massacre, though the governor of Kenya Colony got the credit. The affair long has been closed. He shrugs. Some Nandis were punished, though doubtless many more rotters escaped who deserved punishment. Corydon is intrigued that the matter is still of interest. "Your Mr. Elias also spoke to me, in fact. Quite a romantic, excitable fellow. I'm afraid I disappointed him." The bearer corpses were preserved by unseasonable cold in the region. The Nandis undoubtedly murdered and mutilated the whites as part of some ghastly secret ceremonies. Perhaps one day the remains of Carlyle and his friends will be found, and the curtain drawn upon this dreadful incident.

ROGER CORYDON

Investigators may examine the public records in order to track down witnesses. Some of them are now dead, including

Lt. Selkirk (a tragic accidental fire). Most have moved on to other stations, nations, or continents. The army keeps its own personnel records. Perhaps they can help the investigators.

Montgomery and Bumption (white)

CPT. MONTGOMERY

At the Nairobi headquarters of the African Rifles, Captain Montgomery smoothes his mustaches in pleasure at the greeting from Mrs. Smythe-Forbes, and offers his full cooperation to the investigators. A lengthy search through the records reveals that only one man who saw the site now remains in Kenya: Sergeant Leonard Bumption, who was then a boyish message-rider. Sergeant Bumption is at the local barracks. Captain Montgomery has him brought to his office.

Bumption says that there were several search parties in the area. His party searched for nearly two weeks before finding the ghastly clearing. According to him, there was solid evidence that Carlyle, Sir Aubrey, etc., were present and indubitably dead. He even claims to have seen the cloven head of Hypatia Masters. He does believe that a mysterious cult was responsible for the deaths. In this Lenny is being a good soldier, not wanting to renew matters which his superiors told him should remain settled. Bumption is a practiced liar. Successful Psychology rolls cannot reveal whether or not he tells the truth. *Nyarlathotep Papers #34* is the most important part of his statement.

If the investigators think to ask, Bumption does know Nails Nelson, in a casual drunkard's way. He says that he saw Nelson last night at the Loyal Defender, a pub near the barracks. He will gladly volunteer to lead the gentlemen to the pub, but Captain Montgomery's patience ends, and he dismisses this valiant warrior who has done little more than waste everyone's time.

Bertram "Nails" Nelson (white)

As Lenny predicted, Nails Nelson is or soon will be hard at work in the Loyal Defender pub: 65% chance per hour after the investigators arrive that he appears. Nelson is scruffy and ill-shaven, of medium height and with powerful hands. He whines and begs contemptibly. He's fallen on hard times, and now must hang out in an enlisted men's watering hole.

NAILS NELSON

Nelson has little solid information. He doesn't remember anything until the investigators buy him a drink. If they refuse, there is a 75% chance that he becomes belligerent. If they accede, he reports that he saw Brass Brady in Hong Kong, sometime or other (three drinks are necessary to get much further). Once his throat is oiled, he recalls that the

Sgt. Bumption's Statement

SGT. BUMPTION

"It were right 'orrible. I seen nothin' to match it. Bodies everywhere—not bodies, mind, but bits o' bodies. An 'ead 'ere, an arm there, torn to shreds like you would a newspaper. Something grabbed those poor blokes and chewed the 'ell out of them, beggin' your pardon, ma'm. You woulda thought the jackals and buzzards woulda et 'em down to the bone by the time we arrived, but the niggers said the animals shied off and wouldn't touch the free meal. Even animals get bad feelin's, I'm thinking. Well, I never want sight o' such a thing again."

Nyarlathotep Papers #34

year was 1923. Brady was in the Yellow Lily Bar, on Wan Shing Street, near Causeway Bay. That's all he remembers. He's sure there was nothing more. There wasn't, of course. Brady would never trust this sort of man with a secret.

Nelson was still His Majesty's prisoner for dereliction of duty when the Carlyle Expedition came to Africa. He has heard hundreds of stories about all kinds of cultists, and will gladly make up some more stories if the investigators buy the drinks. He would love to work for them and claims to know Africa like the back of his hand. He has a smattering of many languages, mainly nouns he learned from bartenders and verbs he learned from prostitutes. As long as the investigators exercise stern discipline over him and keep alcohol and narcotics from him, Nelson could be useful. If ever they must depend on him, he will run, first stealing what he can. He doesn't know the location of the Mountain of the Black Wind, but has been to the Aberdare Forest.

NAILS NELSON (white), age 36, Feckless Solider of Fortune

STR 15	CON 13	SIZ 15	INT 11	POW 06
DEX 13	APP 07	EDU 04	SAN 30	HP 14

Damage Bonus: +1D4.

Weapons: Kick 70%, damage 1D6+1D4
.303 Lee-Enfield Rifle 55%, damage 2D6+4
20-Gauge Shotgun 50%, damage 2D6/1D6/1D3
Small Club 50%, damage 1D6+1D4
Fighting Knife 45%, damage 1D4+2+1D4
Head Butt 35%, damage 1D4+1D4
Fist 30%, damage 1D3+1D4

Skills: Act Before Thinking 55%, Bargain 15%, Climb 55%, Demolition 25%, Dodge 65%, Electrical Repair 15%, English 45%, Hide 75%, Jump 40%, Kikuyu 18%, Listen 25%, Luo 19%, Masai 15%, Mechanical Repair 40%, Nandi 10%, Sneak 60%, Spot Hidden 50%, Swahili 25%, Swim 35%, Throw 35%.

Johnstone Kenyatta (black)

This man is mentioned in the notes of Jackson Elias. Sam Mariga knows him. Mrs. Smythe-Forbes, Roger Corydon,

Captain Montgomery, and many Nairobi whites know of him, but their references are uncomplimentary. Sometimes they claim he is a revolutionary; at other times they call him a charlatan and a witch doctor (actually a slur against his grandfather, who was the latter). They repeatedly mention Kenyatta's connection to magic. He lives in blacktown, on Marianna Street, though most of the time he can be found in the office of the Kikuyu Central Association, a black African organization devoted to gaining black representation in the colonial government. Anyone in blacktown, Kikuyu tribesman or not, can direct the questioners to the KCA offices and to this charismatic, knowledgeable man.

JOHNSTONE KENYATTA

White or brown men do not often enter the KCA storefront. Kenyatta is there and immediately notices the investigators. When they mention Jackson Elias, the Bloody Tongue, or any Mythos-related event, Kenyatta studies them intently and then invites them into an adjacent room, "Where it is more private, gentlemen." His English is excellent.

He listens carefully, deferring their questions until he understands their mission in some detail. "These old ways are cruel," he says, "and my knowledge of them imperfect. More than twenty years ago I fled my home where I heard many such stories, for my grandfather was a great *murogi*, a diviner. I have tried to leave that world behind, and to enter yours, gentlemen. How ironic that, as I strain toward your heritage, you reach toward mine."

He thinks for a while. "Much of what you say I do not understand, and even more of it I find hard to believe. But I perceive something about your party. Perhaps traces of my grandfather cling to me. If you are willing, there is a man you should meet. I did not send Jackson Elias to him, for Elias seemed doomed to me, and I could not burden my friend with such a difficult gift. But your destinies are unfinished: perhaps you have great victories to live for—or perhaps you will undergo tragedies as terrible as can befall mortal men."

If the investigators agree to the meeting, Kenyatta disappears for a few minutes. "A friend waits for you beside the door. You must follow him at a distance. He will make sure you are not left behind. If he stops and waits, then you also must stop and wait. The door he enters will have yellow paint; that door you will enter also, swiftly and without hesitation. I am glad to have met you." He holds out his hand to each investigator.

A remarkably tall black man in white shirt and pants but without shoes waits for them, smiles, then goes out the door. Kenyatta motions the investigators to follow the tall man, and calls, "Good day, gentlemen."

Johnstone Kenyatta (until the late 'teens Johnstone Kamau, and by the late 1930s Jomo Kenyatta) is not only of great help to the investigators, he is also one of those delights of *Call of Cthulhu* roleplaying, a famous person whom players can meet before he becomes famous. Keepers interested in the folklore of Kenya are directed to his book, *Facing Mount Kenya*. The several biographies of Kenyatta offer good Nairobi background for the time. He will at last lead Kenya to independence and become its first president. In 1952, the British charged him with leading the Mau Mau terror campaign, but actually the Bloody Tongue was responsible—another horror perpetrated by Nyarlathotep and the Outer Gods.

If the investigators continue into Blacktown, they will likely meeet Okomu and Old Bundari (see p. 125).

Tandoor Singh

Browntown's best tea-seller lives behind his Biashara Street shop, a small clapboard frame building topped by a tin cupola. Though not a priest, Tandoor Singh is an important agent for the Bloody Tongue. They have given him informal rule over the foreigners (Indians, British, and so on) in Kenya Colony, a right earned by his perfect cover-up of the conditions surrounding the Carlyle massacre. As foreigners, the investigators are within his province. He has not sent word of their presence to M'Weru, because they are his. He will ask for aid, however, if the investigators visit him, fearing that his identity has been compromised.

TANDOOR SINGH

Singh's shop is well known in Nairobi. If no other way occurs to the keeper, an investigator notices Singh's advertisement when reading the *Nairobi Star*.

By watching the shop at night, the investigators have a 25% chance per night to see a few Africans wearing red headbands quietly enter the shop, then leave a little while later. They bear messages from M'Weru concerning various cult matters. If the investigators have seen other Bloody Tongue cultists, they'll recognize the men for what they are. Unless the investigators take care to conceal themselves, Singh has a 75% chance to notice the stake-out—and to mount another attack. For extended watching, the investigators' best chance is to rent space near the shop and look on from concealment.

If the investigators talk to Singh, he denies all knowledge of the Bloody Tongue. Yes, he did speak several times with Sir Aubrey Penhew and other members of the expedition: it was to sell them tea; Sir Aubrey enjoyed a particularly-fragrant oolong, and only humble Tandoor Singh stocked it. He will brew some. Shall we talk of poetry?

Snooping at Singh's

At about 2 p.m. and again at about 7 p.m., Singh goes to a nearby cafe for food and talk with other merchants. Every Wednesday night, Singh plays chess with a countryman from about 7 p.m. to nearly midnight. Nairobi has laws prohibiting most Sunday commercial activity; Singh often goes to the countryside on Sunday afternoons.

The tea shop has a front and a side door. Both are padlocked (STR 10). Since Biashara Street is often busy the side entrance is more discreet and is the one used by cultists.

There is nothing unusual in the shop. It is a storefront with a counter, a curtained-off bedroom, and a storeroom. The door to the storeroom is padlocked at STR 10. The bedroom reflects Singh's ostensible religion, with several pious lithographs, and a fine carving in fragrant wood. He keeps a ledger beneath his pillow, but it shows only that Tandoor Singh mostly ships to and receives from his relative Ahja Singh of Mombasa, as one might expect.

The storeroom is piled with small chests and cakes of tea. Beneath an empty barrel is a trapdoor, plainly visible once the barrel is moved aside. A short flight of stairs leads downward.

The Cellar of Tandoor Singh

The single room is about 15 feet square with an 11-foot-high ceiling. There is a center support pillar, and the walls are shored up with boards and timbers. Surreptitiously, Tandoor excavated the room by hand over a period of many months. It smells death-like, probably because he buries his human sacrifices in the dirt floor. (A successful Spot Hidden reveals a number of overlapping but regular depressions in the floor, each about three feet wide and six feet long.). Three niches each on the north and south walls hold candles.

Against the east wall (the facing wall as you descend the stairs) is a four-foot-high statue of crudely carved black stone, a deformed dwarf-like figure with four eyes. Its four arms each bear a tulwar. Three large tentacle-like appendages take the place of feet. The statue represents another of the thousand aspects of Nyarlathotep, a form known in India as the Small Crawler. Occasionally, Tandoor lures in a street child or prostitute and makes sacrifice before this statue, but Nairobi is a small town, and he cannot do this nearly as often as he would prefer.

The central pillar has a set of handcuffs attached to it.

In the northwest corner of the cellar is a large stone cabinet, padlocked at STR 15. In it are significant items.

MEAT CLEAVER: this tool has a handle of twisted wood. On the one-edged blade is etched a symbol for the Small Crawler (successful Cthulhu Mythos roll to identify). Tandoor uses this cleaver to kill his sacrifices. A successful Anthropology roll identifies the workmanship of the cleaver as North Indian.

INCENSE CONES: a packet of 1D10+5 cones. This is the Incense of Other Planes. When burned and inhaled, the inhaler sees the planes upon which the Outer Gods dwell. These terrible visions test the Sanity of the inhaler (lose 1D3/1D10 SAN). If the essence from more than one cone is absorbed at one time, make the Sanity loss cumulative per cone, but do not change the power of the visions. Inhaling the vapor adds 1 percentile to the investigator's Cthulhu Mythos skill. A major deity from the Mythos is never seen in such visions, but lesser sorts of troubling and horrifying things will be. Up to fifty people can be affected by a single

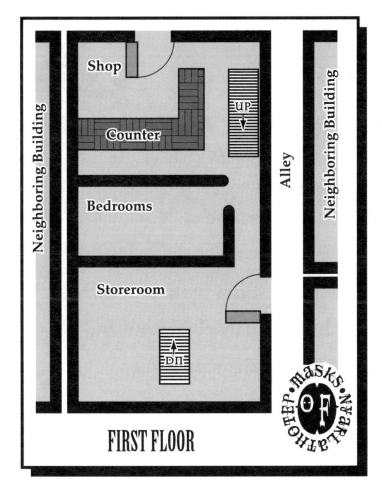

FIRST FLOOR

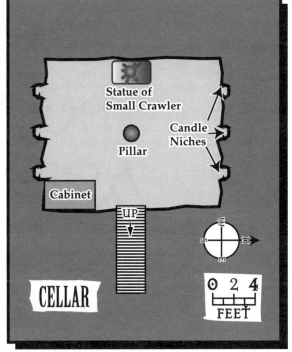

Tandoor Singh's

STRIKE BLIND, a spell

The caster's magic points are matched against the target's magic points on the resistance table. If the target is overcome, he or she loses 1D10 SAN points and 1D4 hit points—the eyes suddenly melt and flow from their sockets as the target is horribly blinded. The target is unable to do anything other than react to the overwhelming pain. The target must be visible and be within thirty yards of the caster. The spell requires 20 magic points and 1D8 SAN to cast. Only ten seconds are needed to intone this spell.

incense cone. With a successful Spot Hidden, unburned fragments of these cones can be found in the candle niches.

THE **CTHAAT AQUADINGEN**: though written in a Hindi dialect, this tome otherwise is very similar to the Latin version summarized given in the *Call of Cthulhu* rules. This version contains an interesting annotation (*see Nyarlathotep Papers #35*).

A date in the Hindu calendar is given for the eclipse, corresponding to January 14, 1926. The leopard spoken of could be the man-eater who actually appeared in India in 1926, and who was credited with 125 deaths before being slain in May of that same year. An interesting scenario might be created concerning this beast.

A YELLOW ROBE: embroidered with the same symbol that appears on the cleaver; obviously a ceremonial robe.

Nothing in the cellar immediately links Tandoor Singh to the Bloody Tongue, but there is more than enough imagery here to raise investigator suspicions. Singh will do his utmost to destroy interlopers, for they threaten his standing in the world and with his cult. Investigators who run to the police without firm evidence (finding one of the fifteen skeletons buried in the dirt floor would be adequate) will not gain satisfaction. "No crime in having a bizarre room in your basement—plenty of the best people do, you know—and besides, this sort of thing is to be expected from those unchristian chappies. Now then, no more of this breaking and entering, if you please."

Once he has come to the attention of the police, Singh contacts M'Weru and requests her help. If she responds, the investigators are in big trouble.

TANDOOR SINGH (brown), age 45, Tea-Seller and Agent of the Bloody Tongue

STR 08	CON 10	SIZ 09	INT 15	POW 19
DEX 15	APP 12	EDU 06	SAN 0	HP 10

Damage Bonus: +0.

Weapons: Meat Cleaver 50%, damage 1D4+2

Dagger* 35%, damage 1D4

* Singh hides a small dagger on his person; he does not know how to throw the dagger.

Spells: Strike Blind, Summon/Bind Fire Vampires, Voorish Sign.

Skills: Accounting 35%, Bargain 75%, Chess 50%, Credit Rating 25%, Cthulhu Mythos 19%, English 35%, Fast Talk 35%, Hide 65%, Hindi 35%, Kikuyu 15%, Listen 55%, Persuade 45%, Pharmacy 35%, Psychology 20%, Punjabi 65%, Sneak 35%, Spot Hidden 35%, Swahili 35%, Urdu 20%.

Nyarlathotep Papers #35

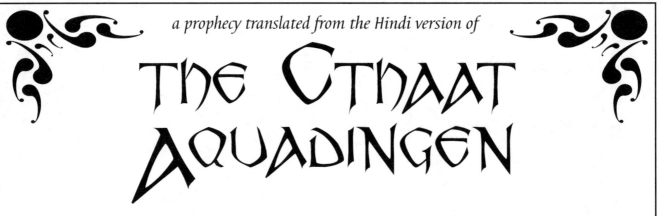

a prophecy translated from the Hindi version of

THE CTHAAT AQUADINGEN

And then shall the gate be opened, as the sun is blotted out. Thus the Small Crawler will awaken those who dwell beyond and bring them. The sea shall swallow them and spit them up and the leopard shall eat of the flesh in Rudraprayag in the Spring.

THE GAME LODGE

*Wherein the investigators meet Colonel Endicott,
a Great White Hunter, and learn of the juvenile horrors
infesting the lands near his Lodge.*

A red-herring episode, this adventure concerns the misfortunes of Colonel Endicott, self-styled Great White Hunter and purveyor of the Real Africa to wealthy and gullible tourists. The Colonel's business has currently fallen off, due to a series of bizarre murders near his lodge.

A tiny band of ghouls reside near the Colonel's night platform, a small hut on stilts miles from the main compound. It offers shelter from rain and roaming predators, yet provides fine views of the wild animals. The Colonel was unfortunate enough to build his night platform near a tribal burial ground that had long attracted ghouls.

Oddly enough, this site provides the ghouls with recruits as well as with sustenance. For more about the ghouls and their behavior, see the notes accompanying the statistics for the Small Ghouls, at the end of this section.

Encountering the Colonel

The investigators do not so much discover this adventure as have it thrust upon them in the person of Colonel Endicott.

IF THE *NAIROBI STAR* NEWSPAPER EXISTS

Whenever they choose to visit the *Nairobi Star*, their exit coincides with the dramatic entrance of Colonel Endicott.

Bearing an elephant gun, which he will discharge at the ceiling if he believes he is being ignored, the Colonel rants that his livelihood is being destroyed by meddlesome journalists who claim something "unnatural" is going on at his lodge in the bush, when everyone knows there is nothing so natural in the bush as violent and bloody death. He makes no concessions for the sensibilities of Natalie Smythe-Forbes, whom he now considers an implacable foe out to ruin him. The Colonel

COLONEL ENDICOTT

has invented several reasons why this could be so, though none of them make any sense. Indeed, the Star is reporting the deaths near his lodge for the self-interested reason that they are news, and with the altruistic hope that such reports may help stop others being killed.

Expressions of interest in or sympathy with the Colonel get him talking and soon he will invite the investigators to his lodge, especially if they seem to know about investigations or murders. If one or more investigators are English, that earns more respect from the Colonel. If the investigators

are rich, he smells an opportunity for profit as well. Before long he has collared them to help him uncover the mysterious deaths plaguing his business.

IF THE *STAR* IS DESTROYED

For some reason, if the investigators do not visit the *Star* and if Singh still should attack it, then the Colonel seeks the investigators at their hotel, believing they are reliable sorts who may accept his commission. He has been accused of the attack on the *Star* himself because of his previous threats. He is being ostracized in whitetown. Can the investigators clear his name? He offers whatever standard rate the investigators choose to set. First, though, he insists they see that he had no reason to attack the *Star*. The claims his lodge is dangerous are poppycock and he aims to prove it. The deaths are the result of wild animals meeting careless tourists, nothing more.

THE COLONEL

Colonel Endicott is a loud, large, florid man, reeking of desperation and malt whiskey, and impossible to ignore. Choleric and pugnacious, the Colonel never takes no for an answer and protects his lodge and its reputation like a lioness protects her cubs. He stands more than six foot three. His brick-red face, aggressive mustache, and slouch hat make him a sight to behold. Ever present is his massive elephant gun ("Mrs. Carruthers", memorializing a boarding-house keeper he seduced in the Great War).

The locals regard him affectionately, or apprehensively loathe him if they have felt his wrath. Die rolls can determine who is friendly to him and who is not: an odd result with a die means that a particular local citizen dislikes him, and an even result means the opposite. Because of his isolation at the lodge and obvious disdain for Nairobi society, he is no source of information regarding the investigators' real quest. He may seem a desperate madman, trying to lure them to their doom. He is only a crude, anxious ex-officer, denied his generalship by the untimely (to him) end of the war.

He is quite alone. His only staff member who has not fled is Silent Joe, a taciturn local who does not speak because he has nothing to say to the Colonel or his guests. Silent Joe remains at the lodge compound.

Tales of the Lodge

Here is the information the investigators can glean about the lodge and the mysterious deaths connected with it. Each report is true. Put some items in newspaper reports and others in the mouths of Nairobi residents—all in the latter, if the *Star* is in ashes. Keepers should feel free to add untruths if they desire to lead the investigators astray. Cannibal tribes and crazed, wandering, murderous white men are good, especially the latter, which offers good bait for the investigators if the incidents themselves do not entice them.

Five deaths have occurred. Three were tourists, one English man and two Americans, all guests of the Colonel's. Two were servants from the Colonel's lodge. All were on safari around the vicinity of the Colonel's lodge when they were killed. None were found in the same place, but examination of the positions and a successful Idea or Navigate roll notices that the deaths cluster around the night platform.

Remains of the corpses had been partially eaten. Local hunters say the bite radius of some wounds were tiny, like those of monkeys. Owing to the isolation and condition of the remains, no autopsies have been performed.

The Boyoyva tribe, in whose territory the lodge and night platform are found, have long said that travelers should avoid the area, because of the many jackals and big cats found there.

An evil tribe in the Boyoyva area is said to have been wiped out by neighboring tribes centuries ago.

The *Star* has decided that the five deaths are due to a rogue lion who should be tracked down and killed by the authorities. Natalie Smythe-Forbes of the *Nairobi Star* does not deny that local stories are told of strange small creatures in the area of the murders. Nor does she think it unreasonable that grazing animals might shun an area where large numbers of predators are found, nor even that some tribal religion or cult might exist in connection with such a phenomena. Mystery boosts newspaper sales. The newspaper will not accuse the Colonel of wrong-doing, whom Smythe-Forbes believes to be entirely innocent. But her duty is to warn of the danger in the area, and this bad publicity does not sit well with the Colonel.

The official police and military story is likewise one of lions or packs of jackals happening on unfortunate tourists. They dismiss other evidence and stories as native gossip. Lengthy questioning among the police and colonial government might get someone to suggest that the Colonel was probably neglectful by reason of drink, but without witnesses or evidence the suspicion is baseless.

The Drive to the Lodge

If the adventurers are at all sympathetic to the Colonel, he eagerly whisks them off to his lodge, situated due southwest from Nairobi, in what will be the Nairobi National Park.

Since Nairobi itself is that rarity, a city on the fringe of wilderness, the Colonel has taken advantage of this by building his lodge where wealthy, indolent tourists can view wild animals and feel as though they are roughing it after a mere four hours' drive from the city. The drive is rough on vehicles and passengers, but the vast vistas, distant mountains, and exotic wildlife keep everyone interested The Colonel has his own truck, which seats three in the front and two more, with rather less comfort, in the back. The Colonel will never allow a white woman to ride in the back.

The Lodge

It is close to a water-hole and game trails, so that visiting tourists can watch animals not far from the comfort of permanent lodgings. This is especially necessary for night viewing, which can be dangerous. The night platform has been built for safety, a few miles distant.

As his guests the Colonel encourages the investigators to safari. The investigators can see the death sites, which are all near the night platform (see the comment under Tales of the Lodge). For those investigators so inclined, game in the area includes zebra, wildebeest, impala, giraffe, black rhinoceros, lion, cheetah, leopard, warthog, and ostrich. Elephants are rare but occasionally appear. Crocodiles and hippos bask in the pools of the Mbagathi-Athi River, not far distant.

Use or adapt statistics given in the "Beasts and Monsters" section of the rulesbook. Let their game be gazelles or impala. Treat these as having Dodge 75%, Scent 60%, Move 15, and 18 hit points.

The Main House

The main house is the classic safari lodge, with animal heads mounted on the walls, zebra and lion rugs, and lots of guns gleaming on gun racks (eight in fact, of size up to an elephant gun). The house is composed of a long sitting room and study in its front half, kitchen, bathrooms, and servants' quarters at the back, and six bedrooms upstairs. The level of comfort is high, with water available out of a pump and food cooked by Silent Joe. There are also outbuildings—a shop, garage, a water tank, and whatever else the keeper finds useful—all surrounded by a thick thorn bush fence and gate.

(The small ghouls may attack the main house after following the investigators back from the night platform. Some steal in through the upper windows, while more lurk in the tall grasses to grab those who flee the building.)

SILENT JOE

He is Endicott's only servant, the rest having fled or been laid off by the Colonel owing to the lack of business. Silent Joe can speak but pretends to being dumb to relieve himself of the need for conversation with a man like Endicott, who admits to no view except his own. Barring catastrophe, Silent Joe remains in the main house once night falls. He has a good idea that small demons lurk in the area, and that they have caused the deaths. If treated with kindness and respect, he might secretly warn the investigators, but he does not communicate while Endicott is present. If the

SILENT JOE

small ghouls attack, he proves to be energetic, intelligent, and more capable than Endicott. If lives are at stake, he does not hesitate to communicate, make plans, or give orders.

The Night Platform

After admiring the main house and compound, perhaps while touring the death sites, investigators may wish to investigate the night platform, a small three-room hut built on stilts close to the banks of the Mbagathi-Athi River. It contains dried food and water for three days, two pairs of binoculars, and a case of Glenlivet (this is the Colonel's own private stash). Seven cot beds are here. Two Lee-Enfield bolt-action rifles (damage 2D6+4), a Webley pistol (damage 1D10), and 100 rounds each of ammunition for the three weapons are in an inconspicuous locker—successful Spot Hidden roll to notice the seam of the small door in the wall.

The platform is reached by a ladder that creaks with age and is badly secured to the platform stilt on which it rests, an accident waiting to happen. Climbing this requires a successful Climb roll, despite the ladder. A fumble dislodges the thing. Falling from it costs 2D6 damage. Two hours, a hammer and nails, and a successful Mechanical Repair fixes the ladder. It is the only way up or down: no rope can be found in the night platform.

BY DAY

By day the place seems harmless enough. It's a strikingly beautiful spot. The Boyoyvas think so too, finding solace in the beauty in times of loss. Close scrutiny and successful Track rolls reveal a child's footprints dotting the sand a few hundred yards from the river. Entrances to the ghoul tunnels from this side have been closed in by the adult ghouls, who know there is heavy human traffic about. If uncovered, the entrance mouths still only resemble large rabbit holes, far too small to admit any investigator. Require a successful Cthulhu Mythos roll to reveal them as anything unusual.

BY NIGHT

The best way to uncover what is happening is to stake out the area at the night platform for a full night. It is also the most dangerous idea to take up, since the platform's occupants have so far accounted for all the white victims. Their bodies were dragged off and away from the platform. The Colonel presumes they wandered away and got attacked, and does not imagine that the bodies were deliberately moved.

Any night an investigator remains at the night platform he or she is subject to attack by the small ghouls. Emerging from the tunnels near the platform, 1D10 small silently creep to the ladder and climb it. Allow each investigator a Listen roll to notice the stealthy creaks from the ladder when the small ghouls sneak up.

When they attack, they shout and squeal, gibbering in ghoul talk. A successful Cthulhu Mythos roll can identify them as ghouls from their speech, but there is no way to communicate or negotiate with their sullen, degenerating minds.

They fall on the investigators with gusto, going for faces and bellies first, their strength and speed belying their small size. If these are destroyed, more can come. If more than twenty are lost, they regroup and return in mass, bashing and chewing the stilts of the platform, all thought of secrecy lost in a frenzy of bloodlust.

Falling with the platform costs each person in the night platform 2D6 hit points. Check for incapacitating wounds or injuries: those investigators cannot flee to safety. Each incapacitated person is attacked by 1D6 small ghouls.

Run the ghoul attacks with all the lurid nightmare frenzy you can muster. Doll-like creatures of terrifying strength and abominable appetites attacking in organized fashion are something the survivors of this adventure are quite unlikely to forget.

Failure to defeat the investigators here brings the ghouls to the main house. The remaining number will try to destroy whoever knows of their existence, since they are intelligent enough to know they face destruction if discovered.

The Burial Ground

Less than half a mile from the night platform is the burial ground of the Boyoyvas. Exploring the area uncovers the remains of 1D3+1 new corpses, all of whom died of natural causes, but who have since been gnawed at by ghouls from underneath, or dug up and eaten by other scavengers.

Tunnels lead from here to near the night platform and to the small ghoul burrows along the river. They were burrowed by the small ghouls. Only an adult of SIZ 8 or less could crawl into them; anyone else occasionally must receive successful Climb rolls or become wedged tightly in the tunnel until the first ghoul discovers him or her, or until other investigators can extricate their unfortunate friend. The burrows themselves teem with a number of tiny ghouls. Meeting this seething mass of predators in the confined dark costs 1D3/1D10 Sanity. The ghouls will protect this area carefully.

Survival Rewards

Freeing the area of ghouls results in a gain of 1D6 Sanity points after the adventure is completed. If the Colonel is still alive it also results in his undying gratitude, for whatever that is worth.

Statistics

COLONEL SIR HENRY ENDICOTT (white), age 62, KCGB, DSO, etc. Modesty forbids more.

STR 14	CON 12	SIZ 16	INT 11	POW 10
DEX 09	APP 10	EDU 13	SAN 50	HP 14

Damage Bonus: +1D4.

Weapons: Mrs. Carruthers 75%, damage 3D6+4
Hunting Knife 85%, damage 1D6+1D4

Skills: Bluster 90%, Credit Rating 25%, Leer 90%, Sneak 66%, Track 78%, Trap 88%.

SILENT JOE (black), age 53, Taciturn Servant of Colonel Sir Harry Endicott

STR 10	CON 11	SIZ 11	INT 15	POW 14
DEX 13	APP 12	EDU 10	SAN 70	HP 11

Damage Bonus: none.

Weapons*: .303 Lee-Enfield Rifle 55%, damage 2D6+4
Kitchen Knife 55%, damage 1D4+2
Hammer 35%, damage 1D8

Although usually quiet and peacable, Silent Joe will not hestitate to use his weapons if lives are in danger

Skills: Chemistry 15%, Cook and Clean 70%, Credit Rating 10%, Drive Truck 30%, English 40%, Hide 65%, Kikuyu 85%, Listen 90%, Mechanical Repair 55%, Nandi 35%, Natural World 85%, Operate Heavy Machinery 60%, Persuade 55%, Swahili 30%, Track 90%.

SAMPLE SMALL GHOULS

	1	2	3	4	5	6	7	8
STR	15	16	17	18	19	20	21	22
CON	14	12	11	14	09	13	17	14
SIZ	06	04	05	05	04	06	06	04
INT	11	10	10	09	11	12	14	12
POW	12	11	12	09	10	14	15	09
DEX	21	20	18	18	17	16	15	15
HP	10	08	08	10	07	10	12	09
DB:	+0	+0	+0	+0	+0	+1D4	+1D4	+1D4

Damage Bonus: none.

Weapons: Claws 30%, damage 1D4
Bite 30%, damage 1D3 + automatic worry, 1D4 until STR vs STR succeeds.

The Small Ghouls: An Ecology

"... Can you fancy a squatting circle of nameless dog-like things in a churchyard teaching a small child how to feed like themselves? The price of a changeling, I suppose—you know the old myth about how the weird people leave their spawn in cradles in exchange for the human babes they steal. Pickman was shewing what happens to those stolen babes—how they grow up—and then I began to see a hideous relationship in the faces of the human and non-human figures."
–H. P. Lovecraft, "Pickman's Model."

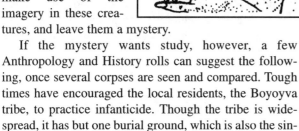

Dozens of these darting, voracious creatures inhabit warrens near the night platform. If the players allow, make use of the imagery in these creatures, and leave them a mystery.

If the mystery wants study, however, a few Anthropology and History rolls can suggest the following, once several corpses are seen and compared. Tough times have encouraged the local residents, the Boyoyva tribe, to practice infanticide. Though the tribe is widespread, it has but one burial ground, which is also the single customary and permissible site at which to abandon infants. Endicott chose to build his night platform there because of the game attracted to the area, never bothering to ask why more predators and scavengers were found there than elsewhere.

The Boyoyvas visit this place of horror only in the greatest need. Why Endicott wanted to build there they do not understand, but the burial place was the least desirable spot in all of their traditional territory, so they politely ignore his disgusting choice. His shooting of predators does make the burial ground safer to visit.

For years, the infants (mostly girls) abandoned at the burial ground have been rescued by a tiny band of meeping ghouls. They have gleefully shared their disgusting food and obscene ways with these abandoned children. Conversion to a ghoul is complete at an early age. By age eight or nine the once small ghouls are adults, true ghouls, and are then cast out of the pack to make their way to other parts of the region. Though initially human, these ghouls are as casually vicious as their teachers and benefactors, and are indistinguishable from those born as ghouls. Given several specimens to study, anyone can observe the increasing degeneration of the specimens, and correlate this against their increasing ages.

For adult ghouls, see the rulesbook.

SMALL GHOUL, age 3-6

characteristics	rolls	averages
STR	3D6+6	16-17
CON	2D6+6	13
SIZ	1D6	03-04
INT	2D6+6	13
POW	2D6+6	09
DEX	4D6	14
MOV 8		HP 8

Damage Bonus: none.

Weapons: Claws 30%, damage 1D4
Bite 30%, damage 1D3 + automatic worry, 1D4 until STR vs STR succeeds.

Armor: as for their larger siblings, halve firearm or missile damage done to these brutes.

Spells: none; too young to learn magic.

Skills: Burrow 75%, Climb 85%, Hide 60%, Jump 75%, Listen 70%, Scent Decay 65%, Sneak 80%, Track 50%.

Sanity Loss: 1/1D6 SAN to see a small ghoul and recognize its human origin.

OLD BUNDARI

*Hard to meet and harder to know, his office hours are
far from normal. Investigators may come to respect
his powers, but be baffled by his motives.*

Progress through blacktown goes smoothly. If any of the players succeeds in an Idea roll, his investigator realizes that their guide is as much watching for people following them as he is leading the investigators to ... who knows whom?

This part of Nairobi is poor, but its people are cheerful and have not given up hope. Most of the houses are one-room, mud-wall buildings, roofed by bundled grasses and broad leaves. Occasionally the larger home of some entrepreneur makes a striking contrast. Prosperity is mostly judged by how well one's roof sheds water—roofs made of shingles, tile, or amalgams of packing crates and hammered-out metal sheets have higher status than moldy straw bundles.

When the investigators step through the yellow door, they find themselves in a small shed, beside a high-wheeled yellow Rolls-Royce roadster of indifferent condition. Their guide holds open the door and motions them to sit in the car. In a few minutes they are bouncing along a dirt track several miles outside of Nairobi, scattering bicycles and animal-drawn carts as they go, and leaving behind a long cloud of dust. Their destination is Boyovu, a small village. There lives Old Bundari, one of the most powerful and respected tribal magicians of East Africa.

Without introduction, it is unlikely that the investigators ever would learn of Bundari's existence. Introduced, the investigators still must pass the scrutiny of Bundari's assistant, Okomu. If they happen to have magical artifacts with them that they can show Okomu, they will be taken seriously more quickly.

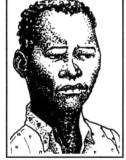

OKOMU

They stop just beyond a circle of huts. Their guide gets out, but motions them to stay in the car.

He talks at length and in persuasive tones to Okomu, a young, delicate-looking man. It's hot in the car. Rather soon the village children gather around and peer in, their bright round eyes polite and curious. When the investigators wave or speak, the children giggle and whisper.

At length the guide haltingly introduces them to Okomu. Despite his excellent English, Okomu is irritatingly rude, constantly pressing the investigators for details, reasons, and rationales behind their statements, and sneering at their answers. One of the investigators must receive a successful Fast Talk or Persuade roll in order to convince Okomu that they are worthy to speak with the great Bundari. If the rolls fail, the investigators must return and try again tomorrow.

Once convinced of the urgency of their mission, Okomu becomes gentler. He knows of the Bloody Tongue, and acknowledges that the cult was responsible for the Carlyle massacre. The deaths were the result of evil magic by which unnatural beasts were summoned from the Other Sides to kill and carry off victims.

Those carried away were brought to the Mountain of the Black Wind, a terrible place shunned by everyone. Even the greatest spells cast against that place have no effect. It is so called because a terrible god inhabits it. Once per year he unleashes the Black Wind, which brings plague, famine, and disaster.

To satisfy the god, the cult abducts villagers and sacrifices them. Then the god appears in all his terrible glory. He is nearly as tall as the mountain itself. He has no face; only a blood-red tongue hangs down from where the top of his head would be. Monsters of all descriptions attend him. The mere sight of this hideous god can drive men mad.

The god's priestess is M'Weru. She lives in the Mountain. It was she who prophesied the coming of the god's child, part human and part monster, who is soon to soak the land with blood.

Okomu can draw a map leading to the Mountain of the Black Wind, though he advises against going there. No protection is possible, he says. Ancient tales speak of a great sign, the Eye of Light and Darkness, which could forever chain the cruel god within his mountain, but no one knows what the sign might be. Some magicians who are far-seeing say that the sign existed until a few years ago, when the god tricked men into destroying it. If the investigators received the half of the ward that Nyiti had at El Wasta in Egypt, or that Jack Brady had in Shanghai, and if they show it to Okomu, he becomes excited. He and Bundari must study it for a month to try to discover the means to use it. There is a 5% chance that they succeed, to be rolled again each month that the investigators wait for results. (See p. 196 for information on the Eye of Light and Darkness.)

Though Bundari is powerful in his magic, Okomu says that as Bundari worked to strengthen himself, the magician had to become more conjoined with the Other Sides. The presence of the great magician is now in flux between this reality and many others. It is Okomu's job to guard this reality for Bundari, and to protect his shell—his body. Bundari has other (unimaginable) assistants who perform similar functions at the loci of his presences on the Other Sides. The investigators must wait patiently for the attention of Bundari to flow to and to collect in this reality. The process may take hours, yet they must sit beside Bundari's shell, or the great one may not be drawn to it for days.

From the outside, Bundari's hut has the smooth curves of a Masai hut. It is larger and differently constructed than the conical mud dwellings of the rest of the village. A gated fence surrounds it, as do similar fences surround the other houses. Passing the door curtain, the investigators realize that Bundari's house is formed like a snail's shell—the entrance passage winds all the way around the outside of the single center room before opening into it. The way is unlit, but everyone sees fetishes, signs, masks, and so forth arranged on both the inside and outside whitewashed walls of the passage. In the central room, more such symbols can be seen, arranged in arcane patterns. A successful Occult roll identifies warding symbols worked into the roof and the dirt floor. A successful Mythos roll identifies some of them as having to do with the Outer Gods. Across from the interior door is a small old man, sitting so still that he seems to be dead. Occasionally Okomu unfolds a leg and rubs it to restore the circulation, then folds back the leg to its original position.

OLD BUNDARI

The investigators must sit across from him for 1D6+6 hours before Bundari begins to stir. Okomu offers them unshelled peanuts, baked plantain, and milk, but the investigators must not converse, for that would "too rapidly" draw out Bundari from his interdimensional voyages.

At last the body of the old man stiffens and swells, and the investigators perceive an intangible liveliness to the figure which was not present before. Bundari's eyes open. He studies each of the investigators. Perhaps he mentions something from each one's past to establish his own credentials.

Using Okomu as translator, he says: "Your mission is perilous, and the time is desperate. Shall I tell you pleasant things, or the truth? The Bloody Tongue grows arrogant. People across the land disappear into the Mountain, stolen by the cult for a horrible sacrifice to come. Leaders are brought low by corrupt thoughts and deeds. Many of us must pray continuously to Ngai, the lord of the Kere-Nyaga"—Mt. Kenya—"to stave off this evil."

"If you seekers have courage, you may achieve much. You must hurry. Okomu can help make the arrangements you need. But he cannot do what I can: I have gifts for you."

As the keeper wishes, the destinies of Bundari and Okomu may or may not cause them to accompany the investigators to the Mountain of the Black Wind. Okomu recommends Sam Mariga as a steady man for the trip; Kenyatta would agree, if asked. Okomu (11 hit points) will never fight, using his body only to shield Bundari. Old Bundari can cast magic, if he is on this plane. For the most part, his body would have to be carried, since his mind mostly would be on the Other Sides.

If the investigators know how to use the warding symbol of the Eye of Light and Darkness, Bundari volunteers to go with them to find an appropriate site for activation.

OLD BUNDARI (black), age 80, Great Tribal Magician

STR 03	CON 18	SIZ 07	INT 13	POW 25
DEX 12	APP 14	EDU 03	SAN 50	HP 13

Damage Bonus: -1D6.

Weapons: none.

Spells: Call Power of Nyambe, Cast Out Devil, Earthly Serenity, Heal, Journey to the Other Side, Seek the Lost, Speak With Bird/Speak With Snake, and other spells as the keeper sees fit. All of Bundari's spells are African tribal magic, secretly handed down through many generations. Investigators never will be taught them. But the investigators could be helped by Bundari if they gained his trust. Tribal magic spells cost no Sanity points to cast.

Skills: Bargain 50%, Cthulhu Mythos 15%, Dodge 60%, English 24%, Foretell 90%, Hide 65%, Kikuyu 85%, Listen 75%, Medicine 40%, Occult 80%, Persuade 65%, See Past as Though Still Present 80%, Sneak 35%, Spot Hidden 75%, Swahili 55%, Track 50%.

Bundari's Gifts

THE FLY WHISK

It has an ebony handle carved with Kikuyu symbols. In many African cultures, the fly whisk is thought a defense against evil spirits, for such spirits often take the form of flies. Magicians there universally have whisks among their paraphernalia, as any percentiles in Occult or Anthropology will reveal. This fly whisk has two special powers, though Bundari explains only that it can find and resist evil.

(1) It adds 6 magic points to the holder's ability to defend against magic. It cannot be used to help cast spells or to help overcome another entity's POW. Augmentation of defensive magic points occurs only at the moment required. If the holder is overcome, the whisk still augments with 6 magic points for a later defense.

Three Tribal Magic Spells

EARTHLY SERENITY

This spell deadens the recipient to even the most intense pain for a period of one hour. It can also be used to bring an insane person to calm sanity for the same hour only. It costs 3 magic points to cast.

SEEK THE LOST

Each magic point expended increases by 10 percentiles the chances of finding a lost object. The object to be found must be known to the caster, and the range of the spell may not be further than 300 feet. The spell takes one minute to cast, and it lasts for ten minutes.

SPEAK WITH BIRD/SPEAK WITH SNAKE

Though two separate spells, they are cast in the same manner. Each costs 2 magic points and empowers the caster to speak with whatever bird or with whatever snake he or she comes across. This spell lasts for 1D6+6 minutes.

(2) The whisk can be used to find hidden evil. To that end, it adds 25 percentiles to the holder's chance for success with any skill so used. For example, searching for the hidden entrance to a Mythos temple, it could add to the holder's Spot Hidden percentage, or examining a Mythos tome, it could improve the holder's chance for a successful translation. The fly whisk would not add to the chance to learn or use a spell.

THE CHAMELEON

In a small wooden cage is a strange-looking reptile, a warty gray-brown thing with three horns sticking forward from its forehead. "This is my friend, Who-Is-Not-What-She-Seems. You may call her Who for short. Take her with you, and feed her well and daily with flies. She will protect you once, but not against magic. You need but open her cage and free her."

It is wonderful how insects of every sort completely avoid Who's vicinity, giving the investigators complete protection from bug-bites. But this means that someone must spend a lot of time out alone in the brush, trapping flies.

In her normal form, the three-horned chameleon weighs a few pounds and has two hit points. If mortal cultists attack the investigators and if Who is then freed, she transforms to SIZ 64, and tries to eat up all the aggressors as if they were flies. Then she disappears. If the investigators neglected to feed her, when she is released, Who is so hungry that she tries to eat the investigators, too. Once she has gulped down any three of these big investigator-flies, however, Who disappears, returning to Old Bundari.

Freed or not, Who is plainly uneasy once brought upon the Mountain of the Black Wind. The longer the investigators stay there, the more listless Who becomes. The power of Nyarlathotep saps the magic surrounding Who. At some presumably crucial point, especially if the investigators have wasted time or have decided to depend on her, Who will be snapped back to her ground state at Boyovu, and simply disappear from the Mountain.

WHO-IS-NOT-WHAT-SHE-SEEMS, Hungry Chameleon (Large Form)

STR 70	CON 85	SIZ 64	INT 03	POW 14
DEX 12	MOV 9			HP 75

Damage Bonus: +7D6.

Weapons: Sticky Tongue Lash* 75%, damage 1D6, range 40 feet, stickiness of tongue STR 7D6
Incidental Foot Smash, damage 7D6, Luck or Dodge roll to avoid

Who's long, prehensile, sticky tongue is her main weapon. Being stuck and rolled up in it causes an incidental 1D6 damage, and takes one combat round. The target has one chance to work free of the STR 7D6 hold. On the next round, the victim goes into Who's stomach and automatically dies. Thus each Tongue Lash attack actually takes two rounds to complete.

Armor: 8-point hide; 2-point tongue

Skill: Spot Two-Legged Flies 80%.

MOUNTAIN OF THE BLACK WIND

The deadly mountain towers above the stark plain.
Within it horrble secrets will test the strength of the investigators.
A terrible ritual unfolds on its slopes.

Careful, systematic investigators now have a fair number of both allies and resources. M'Weru probably does not know of their presence, so they still have some small chance to foil the birth of the god's child. Nonetheless, they must be discreet during this leg of the adventure or face awesome wrath.

Ndovu Village

Ndovu village is Kikuyu, about a day south of the Carlyle Expedition massacre site. From the massacre site it is a second day to the Mountain of the Black Wind. Using the slopes and trees of the Aberdare as cover, it takes four to seven days to pack in from Nairobi. The plains route through Thika takes little more than half that time, but is much more easily watched by cultists. By either route there are no roads, rail lines, or rivers leading to Ndovu, only footpaths.

The village is small, and much like those which the investigators have already seen, except that the roofs are uniformly of better quality, and that ditches and bridges are frequently seen. Higher yet than Nairobi, and close to high mountains, it often rains here.

If the investigators hired Sam Mariga or someone like him, he'll represent them, cautioning the investigators to say nothing of their true mission. The people of Ndovu greatly fear the Bloody Tongue, and will have nothing to do with anyone seeking it out. If the investigators keep their goal to themselves, they can use Ndovu as a base, and perhaps learn some of the local gossip (see p. 128 for a listing of relevent gossip). Knowledge of Kikuyu or Swahili (or use of a translator) is necessary.

No one in this area voluntarily goes near the Mountain of the Black Wind, nor will they seek out the site of the Carlyle massacre—in the green luxurance of the Aberdare Forest that dark, desolate field is known locally as the Corrupt Ground. Villagers give directions to both places, but earnestly warn against going to either.

The Local Gossip

■ In the region, more than a dozen men, women, and children have disappeared in the last few weeks. Little search has been made; their fate at the hands of the cult is presumed sealed.

■ The freshly killed carcasses of two elephants were found yesterday, a few hours east of the village (ndovu is Swahili for elephant). The investigators may see the carcasses, if they wish. The deaths were highly unnatural: no natural beast could tear an elephant to shreds. The bodies, shunned even by vultures and jackals, have swollen enormously, and purple-green matter oozes out of them.

■ The great magician of Swara village was cursed by the sorceress M'Weru because he dared mock her powers. Now his hair has fallen out, he is blind, and he babbles like a child. Swara village is a half-day's travel toward Mt. Kenya; there is nothing of interest but the drooling wreckage of the once-mighty man.

The Corrupt Ground

Of the world's tropical forests, Aberdare is uniquely temperate. Giant cedars, olives, camphors, and figs thrive here, gradually giving way to montane bamboo as the altitude rises. Undergrowth often is very thick, making for slow travel off the trails. Frequently the mountain slopes are cool and wet from mist, fog, or rain. Many rapid streams must be crossed. Forest antelopes, giant hogs, duikers, elands, leopards, and lammergeiers (a bird of prey as large as an eagle)

are seen. At lower elevations, the lethal green mamba, an incredibly quick and dexterous tree-snake, can be found, as can be cobras and puff adders. (The black mamba, whose bite nearly always is fatal, prefers a drier climate.)

Snow-capped mountains rise to either side. The air is clear and exhilarating. A wide saddle-shaped pass—the Neri-Nanyuki corridor—separates Mt. Kenya from the Aberdare range. As the investigators stroll down the north side of the pass, they come upon the Corrupt Ground.

The place was originally a mountain meadow of considerable beauty, perhaps a half-mile broad. Now it is blackened, as though someone had seared the ground with a gigantic branding iron. All animal trails now skirt the area, and investigators have to hack their way through disturbing, deformed underbrush to reach the Corrupt Ground. Once there, the soil feels squishy: nothing grows in it. A foul odor hangs over the place. Successful Biology, Geology, or Natural History rolls establish that nothing natural could affect the area in such a way. Criss-crossing the spongy soil uncovers no information or clues, but should unnerve the investigators.

The Mountain of the Black Wind

A day north of the Corrupt Ground, a dank conical mountain rises abruptly from the broadening plain. Everywhere else the forest has thinned and the grass taken hold, but on the slopes of the Mountain of the Black Wind a dark and lurid green forest persists—here the god of the mountain has sway over nature.

This episode culminates the Kenyan investigations. Preferably the visit to the mountain comes at or just before the birth of the Spawn of Nyarlathotep. Attempt to fix the date of this event so that investigators can be present, but don't be annoyed if smart investigators try to avoid attending such a mind-blowing event. They can follow up matters at a later date.

If the investigators received Who-Is-Not-What-She-Seems from Old Bundari, be sure to set up one or two scrapes with poorly armed cultist patrols in order to tempt them to waste Who's great hunger before a clash with M'Weru's guards.

Just above the plain, the ash and cinders of the mountain have washed away and exposed a sheer rock face. A narrow, steep trail leads part way up. At the end of the trail, a hidden entrance to a cavern exists, requiring a successful Spot Hidden roll to find. M'Weru lives in the cavern, and occasionally addresses cultists from its entry ledge.

The Cavern of M'Weru

This cavern (a natural lava tube) has been enlarged to suit the cult. As stone goes, the creamy-red walls are fairly soft until exposed to air for a while. An investigator with a pick

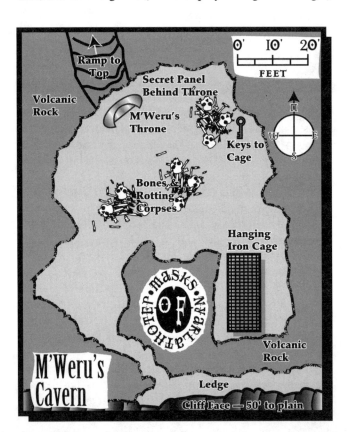

Ramp to Top

Volcanic Rock

Secret Panel Behind Throne

M'Weru's Throne

Keys to Cage

Bones & Rotting Corpses

Hanging Iron Cage

Volcanic Rock

M'Weru's Cavern

Ledge

Cliff Face — 50' to plain

0' 10' 20'
FEET

could hack out a man-sized tunnel of about ten yards a day.

The cavern contains several points of interest.

STATUE OF NYARLATHOTEP: some 15 feet high, this is Nyarlathotep in the aspect of the Bloody Tongue, in its fully obscene form. An investigator loses 0/1D4 SAN just for looking at the statue.

Chiseled from the front of the statue's base is the throne from which M'Weru holds court. There is a 25% chance that M'Weru is present in the cavern. If she is, an elite bodyguard of ten cultists attends her. If she is not, only prisoners are in the cavern.

MARINE CHRONOMETER: a successful Spot Hidden directed toward the throne reveals a small, hardwood box on the floor beneath the throne. Inside is an ordinary ship's timepiece, set to exact Greenwich Meridian Time, three hours behind Kenya time. This precision clock will tell the Spawn when to begin the Great Gate ritual and when it must be ended.

SECRET PANEL: directly behind the statue is a door-sized secret panel which opens to reveal a 20-foot-wide ramp leading on up to the peak of the mountain, where the Great Temple of Nyarlathotep is secreted. A successful Spot Hidden while surveying this area discloses some suspiciously regular patterns. A successful Luck or Archaeology roll finds the mechanism which opens the panel.

THREE MOUNDS: each is a pile of bones and rotting corpses, the most recent sacrifices. Their odor pervades M'Weru's cavern. Housekeeping is not her strong point.

THE CELL: if the investigators come here before the birth of the Spawn of Nyarlathotep, some fifty prisoners languish in this sturdy cell—men, women, and children from district tribes, and probably a missionary or two as well. If the investigators come here after the birth, only 1D10 prisoners are left in the cell. The cell is an iron cage (STR 70), closed with excellent padlocks. The keys hang on a wall forty feet away.

The Great Temple of Nyarlathotep

The mile-long tunnel curves constantly upward. Here and there a torch flickers. No pictures or inscriptions decorate the walls. Occasionally the stone of the tunnel has pulled apart, leaving narrow and deep fissures—or has slumped, forcing the investigators to climb or descend sheer clefts and embankments. (M'Weru's divan is of course lifted up over such obstacles.) Half an hour of steady climbing reaches the Great Temple. Entrance into the Great Temple is through a secret panel similar to the one in M'Weru's cavern.

There is a second entrance to the Great Temple, open only during the most important rites and rituals. During such ceremonies an enormous staircase magically appears, deployed by Nyarlathotep himself, leading up the mountain to the second entrance. From the proper angle, the vast flight of steps resembles a stepped pyramid thousands of feet high.

The Great Temple has an irregular, cancerous form. Jagged tentacular and bulbous intrusions shape the stone, to no apparent purpose. The walls are of a darker, more ominous stone than M'Weru's cavern. Because of the dim light,

investigators can easily hide behind the columns or in side tunnels. When rituals are in full frenzy, the cultists never notice the investigators. Except for Hypatia and the pets in the pits, the Great Temple is empty half the time. If not empty, M'Weru and her guards are here. If she is not in the Great Temple when the investigators enter, there is a 25% chance each succeeding hour that she and her guards enter with little warning.

THE CEILING: a dim brownish glow comes from the fungus-coated ceiling.

THE COLUMNS: six enormous columns support the roof of the temple. Their shapes are those of swollen, suckered tentacles. Carved from stone, each column writhes in a grotesque fashion, though at so slow a rate that the movement is invisible until the investigator receives a successful Idea roll; the recognition automatically costs the investigator 1D3 SAN. Iron loops are embedded in these columns; ritual sacrifices are tied there during ceremonies, slowly lifted and moved in time to maniacal rhythms unknown to man.

THE WALLS AND FLOOR: these surfaces, cut from the same primeval stone, carry barbaric symbols and images referring to no recorded culture.

THE ALTAR STONE: a large, bluish, irregular stone about 3x3x7 feet long. A successful Geology roll establishes that it is not earthly stone. The altar absorbs the magic points of the victims sacrificed on it, to a maximum of 400 magic points. It contains about 300 magic points at the moment. By touching the stone, its magic points can be used to cast spells. The stone feels unpleasantly alive when touched: Sanity cost per touch or use is 0/1D2.

If investigators broke off a fragment, the fragment could be used to store a proportional amount of magic points—each cubic foot retains six magic points when full. The stone is STR 200; breaking it up is a lot of work. New magic point storage is possible only by slaying fresh victims on the stone. Each cubic foot weighs 120 pounds.

When a hapless victim is sacrificed on the stone, he or she partially dissolves while dying. The stone glows as this occurs. Watching the flesh melt from the bones costs 0/1D6 SAN per victim.

THE SACRIFICIAL PITS: there are three, each about ten feet square and ten feet deep. In cult ritual they symbolize the melding of the natural and the supernatural, an impure blending which only the greatest god may make, thereby celebrating Nyarlathotep's omnipotence. Landing in any pit means death. Seeing anyone die in these pits costs 1/1D8 SAN.

The snake pit contains thirteen each cobras, mambas, and puff adders, coiled singly or in glistening balls. Occasionally a snake rises part way up a pit wall before falling back. When a human approaches, all the snakes turn to him or her, and begin to bob in unison upon their coils.

Within the rat pit are 169 large black rats, with glowing red eyes and gleaming incisors. They set up a hideous squeaking if anyone approaches the edge of the pit. If an investigator does, and if his or her player misses the Luck roll, one rat scrambles out and attacks the leg of that investigator: the rat has a 45% Bite, and does 1D2-1 damage.

The ant pit contains 666 giant driver ants, each up to six inches long. When someone nears the edge of the pit, a rustle of tiny mandibles can be heard, and the ants begin to form murky, hideous shapes as they climb onto each other in a vain effort to reach such tempting prey.

THE BONE PILE: M'Weru's crew hasn't got around to cleaning up after the last sacrifices. A successful Biology or Natural History roll identifies portions of the skeletons as 1D20+10 human sacrifices.

THE THRONE OF THE MOTHER: upon a dais sprawls what used to be Hypatia Masters. Semi-circular steps lead up to her; her beautiful face is still recognizable, but instead of her lithe body her face now sits atop an amorphous, pulsating mass of sallow flesh—little more than a swollen container encasing the Spawn of Nyarlathotep. Two baleful eyes can be seen glaring through the translucent yellow membrane of her belly. Hypatia's head babbles constantly in sing-song schoolgirl English about college friends and photography, and her metamorphosis to the bride of a god. Seeing Hypatia in this horrible state costs 1D3/2D10 SAN for each investigator.

Her state is determined by when the investigators penetrate the Great Temple; before birth, attacks on her are the same as attacks on the Spawn of Nyarlathotep; see that monstrosity for details.

ORDINARY RITES OF THE CULT

Cult rituals take place at the dark of the moon, on the plain in front of the cavern of M'Weru. These are death rites—artistic mutilations followed by the summoning of Nyarlathotep bless the sacrifices. Viewing the rites forces a possibly disastrous Sanity roll, but there are plenty of bushes and gullies around the surrounding plain from which investigators may watch without fear of discovery

Nyarlathotep always appears in the aspect of the Bloody Tongue, ghastly and mind-shaking (Sanity loss is 1D10/D100 SAN). The sound from drums, whistles, and flutes comes in numbing cacophony and volume. Usually an honor guard of hunting horrors, shantaks, and fire vampires hover and churn the air like a nimbus around the god. Hundreds of cultists make the daunting journey to worship their god and to participate in the exhausting frenzy.

These ordinary rites occur monthly. Keepers should dramatize such an event only if the Ritual of the Birth is badly timed, or if it is for some other reason not desirable.

THE RITUAL OF THE BIRTH

This is the ritual that the investigators should witness—an extraordinary rite, perhaps the greatest earthly ritual for Nyarlathotep since the beginning of humanity. This is a big deal for all the bad guys; in presenting it, make it surprising, and force the investigators to participate in it by making them shift positions as new events happen. Many opportunities for dummy die rolls exist—passing swarms of cultists, swooping shantaks seeking out more sacrifices, nearby bushes offering better cover, ants crawling up investigator legs, and so on. None of these rolls actually represent threats: there is almost no chance that investigators could be noticed.

Shortly after darkness falls, M'Weru emerges from her cavern to address the throng—estimate 10,000, but suggest that's a low number. Those assembled before her come from East Africa, Europe, the Middle East, and Asia. Most wear their best regalia in honor of the approaching marvel. Sudanese, Arabs, Bushmen, Indians, and Europeans can be seen, as can many Malays. The faithful have trekked from many lands for many weeks. If they want, the investigators could pretend to be cultists and approach with impunity, unless M'Weru has been warned by Tandoor Singh.

In Swahili she declares "Tonight is the time of greatness, when our lord sends us his chosen seed! Tonight comes the dread child and its terror to confirm us! Nyar shthan, Nyar gashanna! Nyar shthan, Nyar gashanna!" The echo rolls back from the mountainside and fills the plain.

M'Weru repeats this chant over and over, and the vast throng before her picks up the chant. Drums pound the rhythm of the words again and again, and the thousands of cultists begin to sway. "Nyar shthan, Nyar gashanna! Nyar shthan, Nyar gashanna!" The echo rolls back from the mountainside and fills the plain.

Clothes come off as the frenzy builds. If investigators are impersonating cultists, they'd better follow suit. The starlit sky grows darker as clouds build up. Lightning flashes, closer and closer, heading directly for the peak. The peal of thunder grows louder. A wind rises—chill, thin, and sharp. A plume forms above the mountain.

"Nyar shthan, Nyar gashanna!" The naked cultists grab random prisoners, and hack at them in the most cruel and despicable fashion; the blood of dozens of men, women, and children washes the plain. After an hour of frenzy and blood-letting, beneath the storm-wracked sky, an enormous bolt of lightning strikes the mountain-top with a hideous roar. Every investigator must lose 1 SAN from its mind-blotting power.

Where the bolt struck, the vapor solidifies, and gradually the god of the Bloody Tongue takes form—seeing this costs each investigator 1D10/D100 SAN. "He bestrides the mountain as he bestrides the world," M'Weru shrieks. "Nyar shthan, Nyar gashanna!"

With a wave of his vast, hideous arms, Nyarlathotep causes to form long stairs from the plain to the Great Temple. M'Weru leads the thousands up the stairs, directly between Nyarlathotep's gigantic legs. As they pass, the insatiable god scoops up random clusters of cultists; if they please him, he crushes them; if they fail his scrutiny, he smashes them to earth. If the investigators push up the stairs with the other cultists, each individual stands a 5% chance to be picked up by the god. Those crushed are doomed; those he rejects and tosses to earth take 3D6 damage.

Smart investigators wait. Once all cultists pass him, Nyarlathotep shimmers and disappears, becoming the Black Wind which soon races across the countryside. The investigators have no way to see this, but that night death and destruction range across the region.

At this stage, the investigators may ascend the great stairs to the temple without being noticed or stopped. The hour is too electric, the great event too near. No one will question the investigators even if they are clothed—and if they're stripped, they unquestionably belong at this party.

Up, up to the temple mouth makes an exhausting climb, either by the physical tunnel or by the magical stairs. An hour goes by before the cultists have filled the temple or have pushed and shoved as closely as they can. Now and then an incautious cultist gets nudged off one side or the other of the unprotected stairs and wheels away through the air like a child's toy, tumbling smaller and smaller, screaming to his death, unnoticed and unmourned. Wails and nebulous magical visions of what is within hold the attention of those outside, as Hypatia gives birth to the child of the dark god.

In the next hour, nearly two hundred captives are beheaded, mutilated, chopped to pieces on the altar stone, thrown into the three ghastly sacrificial pits, or eaten alive by hordes of insane cultists. Men, women, children, and babies are destroyed indifferently. Call for whatever Sanity rolls are needed for the intensity of your story development, and shorten or extend the scene as you need.

M'Weru, aloof, waiting at the altar stone, at last raises her hands, and her guards enforce the command to silence. A cold stillness blows across the crowd. M'Weru one last time calls, "Nyar shthan! Nyar gashanna!" As onlookers gaze expectantly, the baleful yellow eyes within Hypatia's distended belly begin to glow. Hypatia's head screams once in mortal agony, and then explodes.

The bloody fragments and pulp fly through the air, spraying the wide-eyed cultists, who eagerly grab for these holy relics. As they watch, the membrane forms a seam, then ruptures. Slime cascades down the steps of the dais. Atop the dais in all its awfulness stands the Spawn of Nyarlathotep. Slithering toward M'Weru, its tentacles strain for the nearest

unimportant cultist: it will feed itself for the first time. Investigators lose 1D6/1D20 SAN to see this.

The cultists cheer at the tender sight, spontaneously singing brazen hymns promising death and destruction to all that lives. Once the Spawn is born, the cultists dance and disport themselves in obscenities until all are exhausted and fall asleep. The drums pound, and the Black Wind howls across the land. For hundreds of miles around, cyclones flatten villages, earthquakes collapse bridges and buildings, firestorms erupt in forests, and evil devours innocence.

(The colonial government does not make much of this. News of these disasters takes weeks to reach the capital, and by then the events seem so unconnected as to be unfortunate, nothing more. Charity balls are held to relieve the villagers.)

If the investigators continue to observe the Spawn, they see it begin to shimmer after a bit, then grow smaller and coalesce into an exact duplicate of Hypatia Masters. This isn't her. M'Weru embraces and kisses this aspect of the Spawn, then both go to M'Weru's cavern. The mountain rumbles, the ordinary cultists are chased away, the great stairs disappear, and the mouth of the temple closes. From this time forward, the Spawn is present either in the temple or in M'Weru's cavern. Its task now is to learn and perform properly the gate-opening ceremony on January 14, 1926.

Aftermath

Allow the investigators who are still alive to retreat peacefully to Nairobi. They may try to make the authorities believe their tale, but who would listen? Those chaps obviously went through hell, but just as obviously they've been delirious. Perhaps they'll feel better after a few days in the hospital. Johnstone Kenyatta and Old Bundari believe the investigators, but they are unable to convince colonial society. They can take some precautions and, if necessary, aid the investigators to flee Kenya if the cult closes in.

Agents of Evil at the Mountain

M'Weru

Unlike most wizards in this campaign, M'Weru has a ready source of hundreds of magic points, and would very gladly use her spells to butcher the investigators. She is beautiful and bloodthirsty. All who know her power fear her, and this makes her imperiously proud.

M'WERU

During her work in New York, she evaluated the ways of the modern world, and found them to be childish, stupid, and weak. She will not waste time negotiating with intruders, but if caught alone she may try to befriend the investigators, or even pretend to be a victim of the cult. Her power is obviously greatest in the Great Temple of Nyarlathotep, where she can draw upon the altar stone for large sums of magic points. Would she and Nitocris peacefully divide Africa, or fight it out? Only the most daring investigator would become involved in such a power struggle.

M'WERU (black), age 26, High Priestess of the Bloody Tongue

STR 10	CON 20	SIZ 10	INT 17	POW 19
DEX 16	APP 18	EDU 15	SAN 0	HP 15

Damage Bonus: +0.

Weapons: Dagger 50%, damage 1D4
Pranga 30%, damage 1D6+2

Mythos Spells: Call Cthuga, Contact Chthonian, Contact Nyarlathotep, Contact Sand-Dweller, Contact Yig, Create Zombie, Dominate, Dread Clutch of Nyogtha, Dread Curse of Azathoth, Enchant Whistle, Fist of Yog-Sothoth, Hands of Colubra, Mindblast, Power Drain, Send Dreams, Shriveling, Summon/Bind Byakhee, Summon Dark Young of Shub-Niggurath, Summon/Bind Hunting Horror, Voorish Sign.

African Tribal Spells: Bind Driver Ant Column, Bind Green Mamba, Bind Leopard, Bind Monkey Spider, Bind Rat, and other spells the keeper desires.

Skills: Bargain 80%, Bluff 90%, Cthulhu Mythos 35%, English 55%, Fast Talk 60%, Hide 70%, Incite Frenzy 95%, Kikuyu 90%, Luo 58%, Masai 54%, Nandi 58%, Occult 50%, Persuade 70%, Sneak 95%, Swahili 95%, Spot Hidden 50%.

Bind Animal Spells

M'Weru knows the African tribal magic spells of Bind Driver Ant Column, Bind Green Mamba, Bind Leopard, Bind Monkey Spider, and Bind Rat. These spells work just like the Binding spells described in *Call of Cthulhu*; however, there are no corresponding Summon spells. The Bind Driver Ant Column spell works on an entire ant swarm. The other spells work on only a single creature at a time. Bind spells working on other native animals might exist for African witch doctors. Amerind medicine men and other magicians of long established cultures may possess corresponding spells.

The commanded creature must be able to comprehend and perform the command. To instruct it to "fly to Mexico" has no meaning to a raccoon, and the instruction "kill Jonathan Kingsley" only baffles tarantulas—they have no way to identify any Mr. Kingsley. On the other hand, a command such as "bite all nearby humans" could be attempted by any creature.

There is plenty of room for confusion and error in applying Bind spells.

M'Weru's Bodyguards

This fascinating lady is always accompanied by ten muscular cultists armed to the teeth. They are a matched set, and so are their stats. She likes it that way.

TEN BODYGUARDS (black), age 22, True Believers All

STR 18	CON 18	SIZ 16	INT 08	POW 13
DEX 17	APP 10	EDU 01	SAN 0	HP 17

Damage Bonus: +1D6

Weapons*: Pranga 90%, damage 1D6+2+1D6
War Club 85%, damage 1D10+1D6
Thrown Spear 75%, damage 1D10+1D3

Each bodyguard carries a pranga and a war club. About 60 spears are stacked both in M'Weru's cavern and in the Great Temple.

Skills: Climb 85%, English 01%, Hide 65%, Jump 60%, Listen 50%, Sneak 55%, Spot Hidden 60%, Swim 50%, Swahili 30%, Track 75%.

The Spawn of Nyarlathotep (Three Aspects)

The Spawn might be referred to as it, him, or her. After birth, it can change sexes at need.

THE SPAWN UNBORN: before it breaks from the womb-sac it made from poor Hypatia Masters, the Spawn is not defenseless. It can summon Nyarlathotep to fight off attackers, which the god does as brutally as possible. If necessary, Nyarlathotep carries off mother and child into another dimension, returning with them at the time of birth.

HYPATIA MASTERS

While unborn, the Spawn has 25 hit points; it must lose them all in an initial attack or else Nyarlathotep is summoned, who incidentally heals any damage done to the Spawn. If Hypatia is killed but the Spawn is not, there is a 50% chance that the Spawn dies anyway.

THE SPAWN TAKING AFTER FATHER: after birth, the Spawn has two aspects, the monstrous form described in this section, and as an exact double of Hypatia Masters. The monster-style chip off the old block has a huge, roughly-triangular, bottom-heavy body with two yellow oval eyes at the apex of its slithery form. Just below the baleful eyes droops down a long, writhing, crimson tentacle. Five fanged and drooling maws randomly decorate the ventral side of this thing. The hide is a lurid, blotchy orange. Many nine-inch-long appendages sprout from this form—there is a claw at the end of each. As it slides along, it leaves behind a trail of orange vomit. The Spawn is slightly radioactive as well.

If killed in this form, the Spawn dies permanently.

The Spawn can make as many attacks as it can bring to bear. It does not shape-shift. If using Bulk Smash, that is its only attack that round—but several investigators can be knocked down and run over at the same time. To resist being knocked down, roll STR vs. STR on the Resistance Table; if more than one investigator is being smashed, they may combine STRs in resisting the Spawn. After a Bulk Smash, the Spawn grabs with claws and tentacle.

To break free from the tentacle requires the investigator roll STR vs. STR on the Resistance Table. If the Spawn makes any other attack in that round, rate the tentacle at STR 20.

The Spawn's eye-ray emerges only from its left eye, as seen from the front. The ray gives the appearance of jetting liquid, for the obscene energy drips and evaporates as it gushes out. The energy has a pinkish cast.

SPAWN OF NYARLATHOTEP (orange), Monstrous Aspect

STR 40	CON 25	SIZ 44	INT 43	POW 50
DEX 10	MOV 7			HP 35

Damage Bonus: +4D6.

Weapons: Crimson Tentacle 80%, damage 1D10 while being clutched and transferred to a maw.
Seven Claws 85% each, damage each 4D6, 1D4 claws can attack a single target in a combat round.
Five Maws 100%, touch attack each, damage 1D20 each maw per combat round
Bulk Smash 90%, damage 4D6 includes radiation burns
Eye-Ray 50%, damage 1D10, range 30 feet

Spells: Contact Nyarlathotep (special cost 1 magic point).

Skills: Listen 30%, Spot Hidden 35%.

Sanity Loss: 1D6/1D20 SAN.

THE SPAWN TAKING AFTER MOTHER: after birth, the Spawn can switch forms between that of Hypatia Masters and the hideous form described just above. This process takes a few minutes, during which the Spawn twitches and writhes, but cannot move. In taking Hypatia's form, the Spawn has some of her previous skills but none of her memories. In the form of Hypatia only, M'Weru trains the Spawn in magic. On January 14, 1926, the Spawn must perform the gate-opening ceremony. Then it emerges into the world, much to the world's detriment. If killed in human form, it reverts to monster form. But if killed in monster form, it stays dead. Nyarlathotep will be angered by the death of his child, and his wrath surely finds those responsible.

SPAWN OF NYARLATHOTEP (white), age 30, Resembles Hypatia Masters but More Beautiful and Never Ages

STR 09	CON 19	SIZ 10	INT 43	POW 50
DEX 15	APP 20	SAN 0		HP 15

Damage Bonus: +0.

Weapon: Sharpened Fencing Foil 65%, damage 1D6

Spells: The Spawn's spells can be chosen by the keeper. They should be varied by the length of time since the birth of the Spawn, at the rate of one new spell per month after the first month.

Skills: Bargain 35%, Drive Automobile 65%, Egyptian Hieroglyphs 15%, English 70%, French 55%, History 30%, Italian 30%, Latin 35%, Law 35%, Library Use 50%, Photography 65%, Ride 60%, Swahili 30%, Swim 70%, Tennis 55%. ∎

AUSTRALIA

CHAPTER FIVE, WHEREIN THE INVESTIGATORS JOURNEY TOWARD STRANGE RUINS DEEP IN THE AUSTRALIAN DESERT. THEIR EXPEDITION IS FRAUGHT WITH PERILS, NOT LEAST OF ALL FROM THEIR OWN CHOICES.

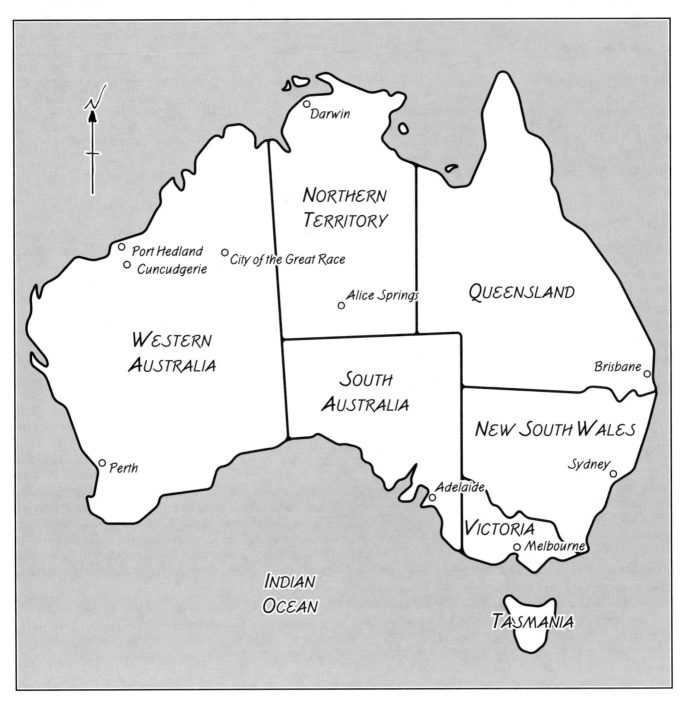

"The incalculable age and brooding horror of this monstrous waste began to oppress me as never before, and I could not keep from thinking of my maddening dreams, of the frightful legends which lay behind them, and of the present fears of natives and miners concerning the desert and its carven stones."

—H.P. Lovecraft, "The Shadow Out of Time"

If the investigators have done their jobs, a variety of clues lead them to Port Hedland, Cuncudgerie, and the parched interior of Western Australia. The plot does not require that they go to Australia—Nyarlathotep's scheme can be foiled in Kenya or on Gray Dragon Island, near Shanghai. But the investigators cannot complete their knowledge of the Carlyle Expedition nor be free of the threat posed by Huston unless they quell the cult activity in the Great Sandy Desert.

If investigators have chosen to head to Australia after finishing the New York chapter, or with only the Shanghai chapter intervening, then they must have interviewed Prof. Cowles, and therefore must have seen the four photographic plates sent by the executor of the MacWhirr estate. This man, Robert B.F. Mackenzie, appears as a local helping hand in Lovecraft's "The Shadow Out of Time." Then he lives in Pilbarra and is about fifty years old. At the time of this campaign he is about age forty and living in Port Hedland, where he was known and trusted by Arthur and Emma MacWhirr.

Do not let Mackenzie die. Regardless of the outcome of the investigators' efforts in the year 1925, he writes to Nathaniel Wingate Peaslee in 1934 after being shown Peaslee's articles in the *Journal of the American Psychological Society*. (Peaslee had described stones similar to those in the photographic plates.) Mackenzie finally journeyed to the region in 1932, where he found similar dressed stones and made photos of them. All of this and more is told in "The Shadow Out of Time."

Even if they never see the photographic plates made by Arthur MacWhirr, they still may reach the City of the Great Race by following other lines of inquiry.

A FEW SUGGESTIONS

Before presenting this adventure to the players, keepers are strongly urged to read or review H.P. Lovecraft's story, "The Shadow Out of Time", upon which this scenario is based.

One or two non-player characters may accompany the investigators for part or all of this adventure. These characters also may be assigned to players, perhaps becoming true investigators in their own right by replacing retired or deceased investigators. Statistics for Anthony and Ewa Cowles appear in the New York chapter. Statistics for David Dodge, the best possibility, appear further below.

About Australia

Australia in the 1920s is a modern country built upon immemorial roots. Distances and travel times here are continental in scope.

At this time, Australia is an independent dominion within the British Commonwealth. Internally, it is a federation. There is no meaningful central taxation until 1942. There is no one standard rail gauge, reflecting days not long past when only ships connected the separate colonies.

The Australian continent—especially the western two-thirds—is an ancient and stable tableland, notable for strikingly-eroded terrain, including single rocks the size of small mountains.

Though the Australian continent is vast, nearly all of the people live in the narrow, fertile bands along the east, southeast, and southwest coasts. The greater part of the continent is semi-arid or desert where scattered native clans wander traditional ranges. Along the north coast, monsoon rains occur and the land becomes tropical. Across the vast majority of the continent, daytime temperatures can climb to well over 100°, and nighttime temperatures can fall to freezing.

In the past 30 years, major gold strikes in the west (the Pilbarra, Kimberly, and Coolgardie fields) have opened portions of the interior, and stockmen searching for new pasturage and markets have traversed much more. Still, large areas of western and central Australia above the Tropic of Capricorn are little known until after World War II.

Where the whites settled along the coasts, the Koori clans were exterminated, and little is known of them. Since the European voyage of discovery by Cook, the native population has been halved to about 170,000. Though some Asian laborers were imported, the rigid exclusionary laws of 1901 have since limited non-white entry to negligible numbers.

Australia in the 1920s is a rugged land. Scholars and the like are rare. Australian tall tales may hold good clues for investigators, as may the more mundane stories told in pubs where the countrymen drink astonishing amounts of excellent lagers and stouts.

Keepers should be guided by English common law and

Selected Connections for this Chapter

NP#	clue or lead	obtained from	leads to
—	photos of ancient ruins	Cowles at M.U.	Robert B.F. Mackenzie, Hedland.
23	summary of lecture	Cowles at M.U.	Sand Bat cult, ruins, Western Australia, etc.
—	interview	Cowles at M.U.	David Dodge and MacWhirr
36	MacWhirr's diary	Cowles or Dodge	warns of hostile action near City
—	map in sanctum	Bent Pyramid	Western Australian desert
—	interview	Brady, Shanghai	Dr. Huston & W. Australian desert
—	account book for 1925	Randolph Shipping	Mortimer Wycroft, Penhew Foundation, Ho Fong
—	wooden idol	Randolph Shipping	Penhew Foundation
—	artifact invoices	Ho Fong, Shanghai	Randolph Shipping
—	strange device	Randolph Shipping	exchanging minds with a Yithian
—	rumors	pub in Cuncudgerie	Huston, the City of the Great Race
—	packing crate	Penhew Foundation	Randolph Shipping Co.
—	invoices	Singh (Mombasa)	Randolph Shipping Co. and Mortimer Wycroft
30	Shakti's log book	home in Gezira M.	Randolph Shipping Co
—	*Wondrous Intelligences*	Wycroft's apartment	discusses City of the Great Race
—	info from ambushers	desert Koori	intelligence about Huston
—	*Gods of Reality*	Huston's manuscript	Gray Dragon Island, Mountain of the Black Wind, etc

CULT OF THE SAND BAT

Dr. Huston has reorganized and racially integrated the cult of the Sand Bat, an aspect of Nyarlathotep long feared by the Kooris of Australia, though the cult of the Sand Bat had all but died out among them. Huston brought energy and new knowledge to the cult, prompting its resurrection.

Sand Bat is a horror out of Dreamtime, a foe of the nature god Rainbow Snake. The Bat is said to erupt like a sandstorm from a great cave in the sky. Among the Gadudjara, in whose original cave the City of the Great Ones exists, the black shape is known as Hungry Wing. Further east, the Bindubi know the entity as Face Eater.

Huston tends to recruit cultists from the slums of Sydney and Melbourne. Drawing upon the academic psychologist Thorndike's early work, Huston has created a subtle personality test which, administered by trusted aides, every recruit must pass. Huston also rules one small Koori clan which patrols and sometimes attacks interlopers nearing the City of the Great Ones, or seizes for sacrifices innocent Kooris chased from the Pilbarra gold fields far to the west. Several hundred Sand Bat cultists now infest Australia.

Cult murders in the cities are performed with the cult club, a polished length of eucalyptus studded with sharpened nails. The Koori members in the Great Sandy Desert carry clubs embedded with thorns, bat teeth, and the claws of bats.

Huston, a megalomaniac, is the only priest of the cult. He has created acolytes who each have a few magic spells. They also administer the psychological screenings of recruits. To create an acolyte, add 1D6 POW and 1D6 INT to the average cultist, and an extra 20 percentiles each in Cult Club and Psychology. Give the acolyte 1D6 spells from the following: Contact Nyarlathotep (Sand Bat aspect), Enchant Item, Power Drain, Shrivelling, Summon Hunting Horror, or Voorish Sign. At any particular time, there are 1D3 acolytes each in Sydney and Melbourne, and one each in Perth, Port Hedland, and Darwin.

The average cultists statistic below represents a recruited slum-dweller. The members of the Koori clan are given in "The Great Sandy Desert", below.

AVERAGE CULTIST OF SAND BAT (white)

STR 14	CON 12	SIZ 10	INT 08	POW 10
DEX 13	APP 08	EDU 01	SAN 0	HP 11

Damage Bonus: +0.

Weapons: Fist/Punch 55%, damage 1D3
.45 Revolver 50%, damage 1D10+2
Grapple 40%, damage special
Cult Club 25%, damage 1D10

Skills: Climb 40%, Cthulhu Mythos 11%, Hide 50%, Jump 45%, Listen 60%, Sneak 50%, Spot Hidden 40%.

general common sense while in Australia. Rifles, shotguns, and pistols should not be carried or discharged in settled areas without good reason. Australian authorities have no notion that a cult practicing human sacrifice exists in Australia. Within reason, authorities will act promptly upon evidence supplied to them.

ABOS, ABORIGINES, KOORIS: In the 1990s, Australia's native peoples have come to prefer the word "Koori" over "Aborigine", a term which they find burdened with too many racist connotations. Aborigine also denies ethnicity while stressing primitivism. As a term, Koori is used in the same way that Maori is for New Zealand's native peoples.

Koori is something of a misnomer, for the Koori peoples are a specific tribe of Australia's eastern region. Notwithstanding, the term is finding increasing acceptance as a convenient neutral label.

The term "Abo", a truncation of "Aborigine", is now felt by most Australians to be contemptuous and impolite, and in effect resembling the word "nigger" as used in the English-speaking world.

But 1920s Australia, of course, was be different. Then words like nigger, wog, or worse might be heard informally among the white population. "The Natives" might encountered. "Aborigine" or "Abo" might be used by a few people who are academically inclined.

In *Masks of Nyarlathotep*, when the narrator writes, native Australians are called Kooris. When an Australian of the period is quoted in speech or writing, the word "Abo" is the usual reference.

THE LAND: Australia is the driest, flattest, and smallest continent. It is as big (2,966,200 square miles) as the continental United States, but has a fraction of the inhabitants—six million people in 1925, about twice that of Britain's American colonies in 1776.

Three quarters of the land is outback, beyond the settled areas, scrub plains and grasslands that seem to sweep on forever. A wild mountainous backbone in the east, the Great Dividing Range, stretches from northern Queensland to the island of Tasmania. In the north, dripping rain forest covers the eastern slopes of these mountains. Further south, west of Sydney, where the climate is more temperate, the forests are eucalyptus. Yet further south are the Australian Alps, where snow is common in winter. Many rivers run off to the east of the divide, nourishing the fertile coastal strip.

To the west, streams flow out to the endless plains, eventually vanishing into desert or salt lakes. Immediately west of the mountains the land is arable. West of these farms, the inland is drier yet, and less settled. Here exist huge cattle and sheep stations (ranches). The stock is watered by windmill-driven wells with bore holes from fifty to five thousand feet deep.

Beyond the stations shimmers the arid heart (known as the Center) of Australia, where many of the surviving Kooris roam. This outback is a colorful and forbidding landscape of red sand, plains of gibber stones, rock ranges, and tracts of spinifex and mulga scrub.

CLIMATE: The north of Australia resembles India or the Sudan in climate, and the rain comes principally in a single monsoon season. The southern states of Victoria and New South Wales are more like California or Southern France. Seasons are in opposite phase to the Northern Hemisphere: summer lasts from December to February, autumn (not referred to as fall) from March to May, winter from June to August, and spring from September to November.

REACHING AUSTRALIA: No air service exists to or from Australia in the 1920s. Aircraft first cross the Pacific Ocean in 1928. The first direct Australia-to-United-Kingdom flight is in 1936. Ships are the way to reach the continent.

Regular airmail between Australia and England begins in 1934, and with the U.S. in 1937. From Europe or America, sea mail involves a transit of six weeks to three months. From the 1870s, cable telegraph has connected Australia with the world.

INTERNAL COMMUNICATION: Mail is land-carried. Regular airmail service between principal cities does not appear till the 1930s. Telephones are uncommon in rural areas. The telegraph system, on the other hand, spans the land, and a picture-graph system between Sydney and Melbourne opens in 1929. Wireless arrives during the 1920s, with establishment of many radio stations from 1923 onward. The new inland wireless system is a boon to remote settlements.

In the outback, word spreads at the speed it is carried. The Overland Telegraph runs down the middle of Northern Australia, forming a communications backbone. But messages relayed to a station along the line, as with letter and package mail, must wait for the addressees to pick them up.

TRAINS: The railways are the common form of interstate travel in the 1920s. Rail lines creep around the country's fringes, mainly serving the populated southeast. The last major rail route opened in 1917, linking Perth with the eastern states. Not all the lesser lines were completed, however. It was not possible to take a through trip from Brisbane to Cairns till 1924, and the Northern Territory was not reachable by track from South Australia until 1929. Melbourne to Sydney takes 17 1/2 hours, and Brisbane to Sydney 23 hours. The big problem with the railways are the breaks in the gauges. The tracks, originally constructed independently by different state governments, were built to different widths, and so were the cars and engines that ran on them. Hence, the traveler must transfer to a new train at the border of each new state.

STEAMSHIPS: The alternative to rail travel is steamship. Protectionist laws prohibit non-Australian steamers from carrying passengers between the state capitals, so a variety of native companies flourish. Journeys rarely take more than a few days. At smaller coastal towns, the steamer anchors, and light craft take passengers on and off board. Darwin and Port Hedland rely on the sea to reach the rest of Australia.

AUTOMOBILES: Australians love automobiles. By the end of the 1920s, half a million cars are registered.

Roads are bad. In particular, country roads are rough, potholed, and unpaved. Punctures and breakdowns are common, and service stations almost non-existent. This situation improves as the decade progresses and the Road Boards gradually upgrade the byways, but Mechanical Repair is a must for anyone considering a trip of more than a few miles.

Gasoline is two shillings a gallon. A new car costs at least £200, and averages about £300. Motor coaches operate beyond the reach of the rail network. These powerful touring vehicles can cover 150 miles a day, pulling a two-wheeled trailer loaded with mail-bags and luggage.

Roads for automobiles are few outside of urban areas. The route from Darwin to Alice Springs (the closest the Northern Territory has for a highway) is little more than a miserable track. Choosing to travel by automobile, investigators need to take plenty of water, food, camping gear, spare parts, winches, cable, rope, jacks, saws, axes, spare tires and many spare tubes, poles (for levering out autos stuck in sand or mud), tire patches and adhesive, and lots of gasoline in small drums.

AIR TRAVEL: Australia is air-minded in the 1920s, enthusiastically following the record-setters. In 1922, thirty companies have charter aircraft available. Regular air services exist in central Queensland and in the thinly-populated northwest. Regular flights between Adelaide and Sydney start in 1925, and other routes slowly open (Perth-Adelaide in 1929, for example). Investigators in a hurry can charter a plane to almost anywhere, however.

TRAVELERS' NOTES: Each state capital has a public transport system. All major towns have a tram system, mostly electric though a few cable trams exist. All have taxis. Ferries are in use, especially in Sydney, where they link the sides of the harbor. Horse carts are a common sight: baker's vans, beer wagons, milk carts, ice carts, etc., stay in use through the Depression. Among other advantages, horses are easier to move door to door, and they can learn a route, sparing driver energies.

In the wilderness, horses are useful, but they require steady supplies of grass and water. Camels (and Afghan handlers) were imported as an alternative (a camel covers a little less than three miles an hour).

Visiting Five Cities

Perth

If the investigators come here, let them run around the town for a while. There are simply no clues here, though the keeper eventually can offer them a trip to Darwin, Sydney, or Port Hedland. Perhaps Cowles can introduce them to Dr. E.M. Boyle of Perth, who has some knowledge of Koori artifacts and ways. Lovecraft mentions Boyle in passing, in "The Shadow Out of Time."

Sydney

The investigators may stop at Sydney on their way to Western Australia. In Sydney is the Cowles home, and in that bungalow, in the professor's study, is the diary of Arthur MacWhirr, who discovered the City of the Great Race in 1921 (see *Nyarlathotep Papers #36*).

Nyarlathotep Papers #36

Mar. 7—Jock Kuburaga says that abos are following us. Most unusual if true. Primitives have every reason to fear guns—and our bush ranger predilection for using them. In the past, I have always known them to head the other way as soon as they sight white men.

Mar. 21—We are about equally distant from Joanna Spring and Separation Well, east of an awful line of dry lakes. The heat is terrible. Our hopes are low—there is nothing here, certainly not quartz reefs! L.'s notations are in systematic error. He is a complete duffer as a surveyor.

Today we sighted several enormous birds flying lazily far above us. How did they get here, and where can they be going?

Mar. 22—At about noon today we found Jock, partly buried in a gully. His body was scoured and covered with hundreds of small punctures, as though somebody had sandblasted him, We buried him, of course. I shall miss his counsel, and he was an excellent hand with the camels.

Mar. 23—We have discovered what appears to be remnants of an ancient city, rising from the shifting sands! I believe I have secured several good photographs of this amazing find, though the heat has ruined all but six of my photographic plates. By the pitting of the stone, the blocks and pillars appear to be more than 10,000 years old! Incredible!

Mar. 24—Four camels killed in the attack last night. I saw at least two abos, and more must have been skulking out there. I'm sure I hit one. That ends this trip—we'll have to head back to Cuncudgerie and report this incident.

More than men were out there last night. I saw shapes much bigger than men during the attack. My evidence is the body of Old Sam the camel, punctured and scraped is the best way I can described the remains, just like poor Jock. Since the attack lasted only a couple of minutes, it's hard for me to believe that anything human could have done so much damage so quickly. But then what was it?

Cowles has left his home in the care of Professor David Dodge, also of the University of Sydney. Dodge is a bachelor, just finishing his current term, and looking forward to some vacation time. A letter from Cowles silences any suspicions that may occur to him. Dodge's eyes open wide if he hears of the Great Sandy Desert find, for Cowles has told him nothing as yet (Cowles feared the impetuous Dodge would mount his own one-man expedition, before Cowles could get funding for a proper group effort). Dodge will try to go along with the investigators if they give him the chance (keepers, note that the party needs someone with the Navigate skill to find the buried city). He doesn't care if participating makes him late for next term—a find like this could establish his name and get him tenure and a full professorship at any of a hundred universities.

DAVID DODGE

Dodge might be recruited as a player character. He grew up in Western Australia, and knows the land and the people. Dodge is 5'11", 175 pounds, and blond. He's outgoing and optimistic. Dodge's forearms are quite freckled.

DR. DAVID DODGE, age 34, Assoc. Professor of Archaeology

STR 16	CON 17	SIZ 17	INT 17	POW 11
DEX 13	APP 12	EDU 18	SAN 70	HP 17

Damage Bonus: +1D6.

Weapons: Fist 65%, damage 1D3+1D6
.45 Revolver 60%, damage 1D10+2
Grapple 60%, damage special
War Boomerang 40%, damage 1D8+1D3

Skills: Anthropology 40%, Arabic 30%, Archaeology 65%, Australian Outback Lore 70%, Bargain 40%, Climb 35%, Credit Rating 20%, Dodge 55%, Drive Automobile 40%, English 90%, Fast Talk 45%, First Aid 40%, Greek 20%, History 25%, Jump 40%, Koori Lore 50%, Listen 60%, Library Use 50%, Navigate 45%, Pidgin English 10%, Psychology 20%, Sneak 30%, Spot Hidden 40%, Throw 25%.

ITEM. A 4" x6" pocket diary of brown cloth stamped with the year 1921. Each page bears space for two days. Ruled lines guide the writer. The little book is crammed with smudgy penciled observations in MacWhirr's neat printing. (*Nyarlathotep Papers #36*)

Relevance of the Information: suggests that the Sand Bat cult was behind several attacks on MacWhirr's party, and that the attackers had supernatural aid.

OTHER STOPS IN SYDNEY

A bustling modern metropolis, Sydney offers many opportunities for research, if the investigators have need. Here the keeper may also create almost any facility—sanitarium, hospital, gunsmith, scientist, etc., useful to the story. Four actual institutions follow.

THE AUSTRALIA MUSEUM: at College and Williams Streets. Among its Koori holdings are depictions of a great entity with bat-like wings and a three-lobed red eye. An investigator recalls, with a successful Cthulhu Mythos roll, that Nyarlathotep has just such a form, called either the Haunter of the Dark or the Fly-the-Light, and used (in our solar system) primarily on Yuggoth.

Secondly, in the Polynesian collections are three ancient stone blocks with odd carvings. If the investigators have seen other artifacts from R'lyeh or a deep one city, a successful Idea roll connects them. Officials say that the blocks supposedly come from a sunken city in which a god sleeps—a notion common throughout Polynesia.

THE STATE LIBRARY: At Shakespeare Place. A successful Fast Talk roll, or a letter of reference from Profs. Dodge or Cowles gives the investigators the right to search through the older books in the library. A successful Library Use roll yields the information that throughout the earliest legends of Australia are songs about a city beneath the Great Sandy Desert of Western Australia, a city built by gods who were vanquished by the wind.

THE NATIONAL ART GALLERY: at Shakespeare Place. Among the gallery's Koori collection is a bark painting depicting a dying man, his body bloated and black. Figures holding small jagged clubs surround him. The curator says that the piece represents a ritual sacrifice by a cult of bat-worshipers. He believes that the piece is very old, but there is no way to know just how ancient.

THE UNIVERSITY OF SYDNEY: on George Street. Once they understand the investigators' area of interest, administrators unanimously refer the investigators to Professors Anthony Cowles or David Dodge. If the investigators do not already have Dodge's name and address, they learn it now. Dodge may or may not know about the MacWhirr diary.

Darwin

The investigators are likely to visit Darwin only if they already have been to Shanghai. Darwin is nearly three times further from Huston's desert hideout as that hideout is from Cuncudgerie and Port Hedland. If the investigators visit Port Hedland first, keepers should reset most of the Darwin information in Port Hedland, especially Toddy Randolph and his shipping company.

Located on a narrow peninsula, Darwin is a town of a few thousand. So empty is the Northern Territory of Australia that Darwin is the biggest city for more than a thousand miles. Proximity to East Asia and a gold rush fifty years before gives Darwin a racial diversity rare in Australia. Keepers may have fun treating this respectable town as a sweltering tropical shantytown, full of brawls, shady adventurers, and fast money.

As befits the latter sort of place, rumors abound. It does not much matter whether the following data comes from constables, shopkeepers, bartenders, stockmen, sailors, etc. Since pubs are easy to find, center the investigation in Bertram's Outback Inn. By partaking of Bert's beery wel-

Randolph Shipping Co.

KEY: 1: MIND MACHINE. 1D3 HOURS TO FIND CRATE. 1/2 MECH REPAIR TO ACTIVATE
2: CTHULHU IDOL. POW OR DEX X3
3: LOCKED DESK (LEDGER) STR5

come, for every rumor the investigators get, charge them an Australian pound (almost identical to the value of a British pound), for drinks for the house. If the investigators don't have the cash, require a successful Credit Rating, Fast Talk, Listen, or Persuade roll for each of the following.

■ A few Kooris in the Great Sandy Desert are worshipping a bat-god, apparently a quite nasty one. Corpses have been found by caravans and drovers. The victims were diseased and covered with hundreds of tiny puncture wounds.

■ A master of a regular camel caravan is said to have actually seen the bat-god, which sight he proclaimed to be the worst thing he'd ever seen. Unfortunately, the camelmaster is making his swingaround, and won't be back for months.

■ A white madman is said to lead the bat cult, though scoffers say that "white" just means "half-breed".

■ A new Koori tale says that in the Great Sandy Desert there is a wonderful city. Buddai, a great old man who sleeps with his head in his arm, snores beneath it. One day Buddai will rise and devour the world. This tale is attributed to a Koori, Johnny Bigbush, who works in Darwin at the Randolph Shipping Co.

THE RANDOLPH SHIPPING COMPANY

The little building is dockside, not far away. The owner, Toddy Randolph, is a fat, brutal man who is surly unless talking to other drunkards. The warehouse holds a variety of goods, a fraction of it smuggled in, contraband, or otherwise illegal. Exposure to customs would cost Randolph a fine and perhaps a prison sentence, depending on how valuable are the goods. Randolph sleeps in the warehouse, on a moldy cot in one corner. Next to the cot is his roll-top desk.

If questioned about Johnny Bigbush, Randolph says that he was a troublemaker, and so Randolph fired him weeks ago. He thinks that Johnny went back to his clan somewhere near the Daly River, a hundred miles south. Randolph knows nothing about Koori legends, and has no other information.

TODDY RANDOLPH

As the investigators talk to Randolph, a successful Spot Hidden shows that a crate addressed to the Penhew Foundation, London, and marked with the symbol of the Cult of the Sand Bat rests unsteadily on other crates at the edge of the warehouse loading dock. If the investigators know the meaning of the Penhew Foundation, a successful DEX x3 roll lets an investigator surreptitiously knock the crate down into the mud. If the investigators do not know about the Penhew Foundation, a successful POW x3 roll causes an investigator to clumsily knock into the stack, with the same result.

Looking down, everyone sees that the weak softwood crate has splintered, revealing the contents, a grotesque wooden idol about three feet high. It is Koori-made, covered with white painted geometric lines. The idol is humanoid, without hair, and with strange, round, thick whiskers like tentacles. The creature's hands and feet end in flipper-like appendages. The eyes are round, with jagged facets, and have a cruel expression. For someone who could never have seen that visage, this is an excellent representation of Cthulhu.

Randolph of course curses at the clumsy investigators and orders them off his property.

If they decide to return later to search for clues, the investigators find that Toddy Randolph and his remaining helper, Billy Burraglong, are down the street at a pub, and will be there for hours. A successful Mechanical Repair roll picks the lock, or the investigators can quickly force open the STR 10 door.

The only item of interest in the warehouse is in Randolph's locked (STR 5) roll-top desk. His account book for 1925, the sole ledger in the warehouse, shows that several shipments to a Mortimer Wycroft in Cuncudgerie are marked with the symbol of the Cult of the Sand Bat. Those shipments went by coastal packet to Port Hedland, then inland by rail to Cuncudgerie. Also so marked are shipments to Fong Imports in Shanghai, and the scheduled shipment of the Cthulhu idol to the Penhew Foundation in London. In the latter entry two crates are marked as to be shipped, though the investigators noticed only one.

The symbols in the account book indicate cult shipments, for which the Sand Bat cult pays Randolph double the normal cost. No wonder he was upset when the statue fell to the ground.

It takes 6D10 minutes to find the second crate, during which time several drunks wander noisily by the warehouse. Unless keepers think it's time for a little action, none are Randolph. If it is Randolph, try to avoid a gunfight. There's too much to be done to lose half the party in Darwin.

BILLY BURRAGLONG

In the second crate is an odd device composed of machined rods, wheels, mirrors, and an eye tube. The thing is about two feet high and one foot wide and deep. It is one of the devices used by the Great Race of Yith to contact minds. Huston recovered the artifact from the City of the Great Race. In an enclosed letter, he describes it as a "short-term survey device employed by the Yithians".

The Device of Rods, Wheels, and Mirrors

A successful halved Mechanical Repair roll enables an investigator to activate the self-powered instrument. Before then, while inspecting the device, a successful Idea roll suggests that experiments are better performed in laboratories than in warehouses, and that the investigators should wait to find out what the device does. However, if anyone powers up the instrument and then insists on looking down the eye tube, he or she falls into a coma, his or her mind transferred far up the stream of time to the antediluvian epoch when the City of the Great Race throve. The mind of a Yithian from that time transfers into the investigator's body. The investigator's mind is trapped within a Yithian body for 1D4 weeks. and while trapped loses 1D4 SAN each week.

The Great Race inhabitant settling into the victim's body is unable to cause it to speak or otherwise to communicate. Astonishing grimaces and distortions pass across the investigator's face. After 1D3+1 days the new inhabitant of the investigator's body has learned what is necessary to make its way, and begins practicing with the new body. He inspects the entire building, avidly reading newspapers, books, and magazines, then returns to bed and shams unconsciousness, attempting to learn as much as possible before interacting with other creatures. The Great Race transferee is scouting the epoch, to decide if a full-term (five year) transfer promises an adequate return of knowledge. In this case, the Yithian decides that Darwin (or Port Hedland) is not the cultural center he needs, and departs after 1D4 weeks.

When the Great Race observer transfers back to its original body, the investigator awakes in his or her own body. He or she is subject to the same flashes of recall noticed by the victim in "The Shadow Out Of Time" and, like him, quickly recovers previous memories if taken to the Australian ruins of the City of the Great Race. These memories, returning to the victim whenever a POW x1 roll succeeds, could be useful to keepers as narrative hooks and ploys with which to keep the action moving, or to help the investigator guide his companions once they enter the vast and mysterious city of the Yithians.

TODDY RANDOLPH (white), age 46, Alcoholic Businessman

STR 13	CON 12	SIZ 14	INT 12	POW 10
DEX 11	APP 11	EDU 06	SAN 24	HP 13

Damage Bonus: +1D4.

Weapons: Fist 65%, damage 1D3+1D4
.38 Revolver 50%, damage 1D10
Grapple 50%, damage special

Skills: Accounting 35%, Bargain 50%, Credit Rating 20%, Dodge 30%, Fast Talk 40%, Fill Out Documents 55%, Hide 15%, Listen 09%, Persuade 20%.

BILLY BURRAGLONG (Koori), age 29, Secret Sand Bat Acolyte

STR 15	CON 16	SIZ 10	INT 09	POW 10
DEX 17	APP 09	EDU 01	SAN 0	HP 13

Damage Bonus: +1D4.

Weapons: Dagger* 70%, damage 1D4+2+1D4
Cult Club 40%, damage 1D10+1D4
Grapple 20%, damage special
* Carries 3 daggers; prefers to throw them.

Spells: Contact Nyarlathotep (Sand Bat aspect), Power Drain, and keeper's choice of Shrivelling or Voorish Sign.

Skills: Climb 40%, Drive Automobile 10%, Hide 50%, Jump 45%. Koori Lore 30%, Listen 60%, Psychology 20%, Sneak 50%, Spot Hidden 40%, Throw 70%, Track 40%.

Port Hedland

The village of Port Hedland is the terminus and port facility for a small railroad which winds back into the Pilbarra country. Rich deposits of gold have been found among the low, flat-topped hills. The richest mines are found at the present railhead, Cuncudgerie, 150 miles southeast of the port and terminus. It is likely that the investigators will be travelling through Hedland on their way to Cuncudgerie and then the City of the Great Race.

ROBERT MACKENZIE

If the investigators are accompanied by David Dodge, or have an introduction from Prof. Cowles, they can stay at the home of Robert B.F. Mackenzie. Mackenzie says that Arthur was absolutely convinced of his desert discovery, and that Arthur was a respectable and upright citizen. A successful Psychology roll shows that Mackenzie has no doubt about what he says.

Curiously, Mackenzie continues, an American came to see him several years ago, also asking about Arthur's photographs, notes, etc. He did not say how he had learned that the material existed. After he lent "Mr. Howston" nearly all of Arthur's material, the fellow disappeared. Damned inconsiderate! If the investigators have a photo of Robert Huston, MacWhirr exclaims in recognition. Huston or Howston is the thief! The four plates and the diary are all that Huston did not steal.

If they tell him they are going into the outback, Mackenzie can telegraph for their vehicles and supplies at Cuncudgerie, or David Dodge can handle matters if he is

along. Their precise destination Mackenzie has long memorized: 22°3'14" South by 125°0'39" East, deep in the Great Sandy Desert of Western Australia.

Mackenzie has too many professional responsibilities to accompany such a journey. Arthur MacWhirr planned to return to the site with a survey expedition, but he died of influenza late in 1921. Without him, talk of an expedition languished, and life moved on.

Cuncudgerie

The narrow-gauge railway to Cuncudgerie has one train daily, a freight train. If the investigators ride on the flat car, a few Kooris sit at the other end and look curiously at them. The trip takes eight hours. The day is scorching. The land is dry, the watercourses empty. Low trees trace some of the ravines, but nothing like forests or even copses exist. There are no farms. During the journey nothing moves except three very large birds, winging lazily far in the distance. Given the rocking of the train, use of a telescope or binoculars for better identification is impossible. If the investigators have read MacWhirr's diary, those large birds might give them pause.

A mining town, Cuncudgerie bustles even in the heat of the day. Besides the established mines and miners, the place caters to many prospectors, thousands of horses, camels, and mules, hundreds of trucks, and a few ladies of easy virtue who define the difference between lust and fantasy.

Wandering around the small town, the investigators pick up rumors and tall tales without much effort. As usual, each item costs an Australian pound in drinks, or a successful Credit Rating, Fast Talk, Listen, or Persuade roll.

- Gold-bearing reefs (exposed lines of mineral deposits) occur eastward for hundreds, maybe thousands of miles. But the fellow declaring this is clearly trying to impress his mate.

- Deadly snakes exist in the deep desert. (True enough, there are deadly snakes all over Australia.)

- There was a big mining disaster far to the east, but the company responsible paid off the politicians and the whole thing was hushed up. Some twenty-five men were killed, among them Derby Dave the Welshman, who did some work for Mortimer Wycroft. This was a while ago.

- A crazy American bloke took a crew of two dozen men into the bush, had them dig a shaft thirty feet deep, then told them to stop, gave them a big bonus, and sent every man jack to Darwin to collect his pay. This was a while ago. (This is a distortion of the time when Huston hired miners in Cuncudgerie. Unfortunately, the miners' actual end was much less happy.)

- Some drovers who brought in beef over the Canning stock route swore that things the size of bears stole some of their cattle. That was "about a year ago". The attacks were alleged to have taken place somewhere east of the Percival Lakes.

- The Slatterys, who live out by Dingo Falls, are quite unfriendly, and should definitely be avoided.

- An American gentleman named John Carver (who bears a strong resemblance to Dr. Robert Huston, if the investigators have a photo) conducted surveys and exploratory diggings along the Canning stock route, which flanks the eastern side of the Great Sandy Desert.

- There's been a ghost, seen up North recently (near Dingo Falls). It could pass its hand straight through someone's body. (This particular tale is told by an old man named Mad Ginger Muldoon. If investigators show interest in the tale, it is elaborated on below, in "Researching Bill Buckley")

- Three huge birds were seen in the area about two weeks ago. The teller swears they must have been twenty feet at the wing. He took several shots at them, to try to bag one, but they were well out of range.

- The American fellow who dug the mine shaft in the sand and the American John Carver are one and the same. His outfitting was done by Mortimer Wycroft, right here in town.

- A weird, sinister tribe of incredibly tall and emaciated Kooris has been encountered far to the east of here.

- Five or six years ago a bloke claimed that he found big squared-off blocks of stone out in the desert. Wasn't Abo work, he said. And he bought drinks for the whole pub to prove he was telling the truth. If the questioner gets a successful Luck roll, the storyteller remembers that the fellow's name was MacWhirr.

- There is an underground city somewhere in the desert. Ways exist in and out of it, but the sand shifts constantly, burying and exposing the entrances. Evil things live there.

RESEARCHING BILL BUCKLEY

While listening for rumors in Cuncudgerie, investigators may come across tales of a strange ghost seen near Dingo Falls. This is the ghost of Bill Buckley, who was slain by the Slatterys years ago. His full story is told in "Buckley's Ghost". Following are the leads investigators may discover regarding him in Cuncudgerie.

If investigators do not look into the strange case of Bill Buckley now, they may later, after encountering his apparation at Dingo Falls.

MAD GINGER MULDOON: Mad Ginger is the source of the stories about the terrible apparition. He now sits in the Cuncudgerie Grand (its pub), trying to drown the memory of the frightful thing that came at him in the night. He is fairly stupefied with drink, but conviviality, sympathy, and patience reap his story.

Four nights ago he camped at a place called Dingo Falls. Why it is so named he cannot say, since he found neither dingo nor falls, just a water-hole from which he drank. He then settled down nearby for the night. It was a lonely place

to build a fire, but preferable to the company of the only locals, a mad drunkard and his two mad sons.

No sooner had Ginger dropped off to sleep than a light awoke him. He thought it was the Slatterys, come to drive him off, rob him, or worse. But the thing that confronted him was immeasurably more horrible, and not remotely human. An effigy of a man, glowing white and red, its flesh running off its bones, its staring eyes cooking in its skull, its mouth wide open for a scream that was all the more terrible for being silent. It advanced on Mad Ginger Muldoon.

He tells of bravely fighting off the thing with a stick. This is a lie. He fled, actually, but will never admit it. When the hot sun was high overhead, he crept back, reclaimed his gear, and quickly tiptoed away. That is all that Muldoon knows.

If the investigators provoke or inadvertently cause a fight (doubting Muldoon's word is enough provocation), use the statistics for Frank Slattery, pg. 147.

NEWSPAPERS: Cuncudgerie doesn't have a newspaper or a morgue, but it does have a telegraph at the Mining Office. A telegram (Australians never call them wires—wire is something you build a fence with) to a reliable researcher or contact in Perth or Sydney uncovers the fact that a Bill Buckley vanished ten years ago this month. He was last seen in Cuncudgerie.

Vern Slattery, Buckley's murderer, has no idea that Buckley was known to outsiders. If he did, he would get drunk immediately, for the deep hole called Dingo Falls has Buckley's bones in it, at its bottom.

OTHER GOSSIP: A few Cuncudgerie locals might remember Bill Buckley as the only man who ever deliberately went to Dingo Falls. He had talked himself into believing that a drift of gold must be there. They remember him as a harmonica player and good drinker (meaning he would pay for a round of drinks now and then, an instant if expensive way of endearing oneself). Buckley never came back to Cuncudgerie—maybe he died in the desert, no way to tell. Most locals know Vern Slattery but have no reason to connect Slattery with Buckley. They might mention Slattery's as a possible way-station, but most fear the drunkard and his sons, and give them a wide berth wherever they encounter them.

A few local Koori have seen Buckley's ghost and know it as a tortured white man. (They never brought fire near the thing, so have not encountered its angry shape.) They have heard of Muldoon's wild tale, but imagine the silly bugger was probably drunk at the time and didn't know what he saw—or else he encountered a yowie, a mythological Australian creature.

MORTIMER WYCROFT

The Kooris call Wycroft the Deadfella Man, because his skin is as white as a lizard's belly. His eyes are sunken, and his frame skeletal. His outfitting business is slow, but Wycroft doesn't seem to mind. Three Kooris help him. They pretend not to speak English. Wycroft speaks their tongue (Kariera) as well. He often closes shop and heads east with a truckload of equipment. Sometimes he's gone for weeks. Day by day, he and his men stay in the store building. He sleeps upstairs;

his men sleep in the shop. The shop fills the lower story of a dilapidated building on the outskirts of Cuncudgerie.

The dingy shelves behind the U-shaped counter are stuffed with coveralls, cookware, boots, rope, chain, heavy rope, miners' lamps and hats, underwear, arc lights, flashlights, batteries, truck parts, blocks and tackles, engines, engine parts, tinned food, picks, assay kits, and much more. In a shed alongside are shoring timbers, bags of cement, iron rails, mining carts, etc. In a shed a little removed from the main building are cases of dynamite, blasting caps, and fuses. A small gasoline pump at the front of the building connects to a large buried tank of 600-gallon capacity.

The three Kooris lounging beside the store understand enough English to pump gas. Gestures and the words "Mortimer Wycroft" also get action, soon fetching that gentleman from the back. A successful Spot Hidden roll reveals that the tallest one bears tattoos of a spiral and of a bat on his left bicep.

Mortimer Wycroft has no interest in answering questions. If asked about Derby Dave the Welshman, he knows nothing except that the man was a bad mechanic, and got what he deserved. If asked about John Carver, he'll claim never to have heard of him, though a successful Psychology roll shows him to be lying. If he chances to remember (50% chance), he'll mention being questioned about Mr. Carver the next time he visits Robert Huston.

He is more cult agent than cultist. He supports Sand Bat because of his unhealthy love for the City of the Great Ones. An initiate of the cult but not tattooed, he uses the greasepaint under his bed to draw the bat symbol on his body.

It's hardly necessary to ask a Psychology roll to check Wycroft's sanity. His mind is thoroughly blown. He hardly knows he exists. He would sooner hide from a fight than participate, unless his precious book is threatened. His whole life centers on his trips to the city where the Great Race once lived. His fondest dream involves changing minds with a member of the Great Race, but Wycroft is too sorry a specimen to interest them.

Wycroft's "boys" are cultists. They carry small knives, and usually their boomerangs are in reach. They prefer to use their cult clubs, but they have none of the disease potion. When traveling to the buried city, all of their listed weapons are in reach. They may decide to attack the investigators without telling Wycroft. These attacks could take place in Cuncudgerie. If Wycroft notices that the investigators follow his two trucks to the buried city, he'll direct the trio to attack the investigators, perhaps with boomerangs and spears. The three protect Wycroft at the command of the cult, but they would just as quickly kill him should the cult demand.

There is nothing concerning the Mythos in the store or shed. Upstairs, Wycroft's home is little more than a bed, a stove, a dresser, a wardrobe, an icebox (there is a small ice plant in Cuncudgerie), and a hat rack. Wycroft keeps only invoices and records of payment. He hides his money in a cookie jar—currently it holds 1D6 x 10 Australian pounds in it. He keeps a shotgun behind the counter of his store and takes it to his room at night, propping it nearby.

Under his bed rests a jar of black greasepaint and a book in English, *Wondrous Intelligences*, by a 17th century Englishman, James Woodville (+3 percentiles to the reader's Cthulhu Mythos skill, no spells, -1D4 SAN). Well thumbed by Wycroft, the book is a first edition worth five hundred Australian pounds. Along with the author's tedious self-congratulations and dogged explications of his singular sexual practices (penile corsets are the least of it), Woodville describes the Great Race of Yith. The keeper's data in the Cthulhu rules is a fair summary of the contents. This Mythos tome also contains a chilling evocation of a war with deadly beings who whistle down dark caverns and dwell within windowless basalt towers. Wycroft obsessively pursues and attempts to kill anyone who steals this precious book.

Whether or not the investigators learn about Wycroft,

have him depart soon for the buried city, so that his small force can be on hand if fighting breaks out. He can be a mobile reserve, useful or not depending on how well the investigators do, or offer an easy preliminary victory for the investigators.

MORTIMER WYCROFT (white), age 48, Grim as a Ghost

STR 10	CON 10	SIZ 12	INT 09	POW 05
DEX 11	APP 09	EDU 10	SAN 02	HP 11

Damage Bonus: +0.

Weapons: 12-Gauge Shotgun 45%, damage 2D6/1D6/1D3

Skills: Accounting 25%, Climb 20%, Credit Rating 15%, Cthulhu Mythos 06%, Drive Automobile 30%, Electrical Repair 15%, English 50%, Hide 20%, Jump 25%, Kariera 15%, Listen 40%, Operate Heavy Machine 20%, Pidgin English 30%, Spot Hidden 40%.

LYNN (Koori), Number 1

STR 13	CON 12	SIZ 10	INT 06	POW 12
DEX 16	APP 07	EDU 01	SAN 0	HP 11

Damage Bonus: +0.

Weapons: War Boomerang 65%, damage 1D8
Grapple 40%, special damage
Cult Club 70%, damage 1D10
Dagger 35%, damage 1D4+2

Skills: Climb 40%, Cthulhu Mythos 05%, Dodge 55%, Drive Automobile 20%, English 20%, Hide 50%, Jump 45%, Kariera 40%, Listen 60%, Pidgin English 35%, Sneak 50%, Spot Hidden 40%, Throw 65%, Track 65%.

SHANNON (Koori), Number 2

STR 15	CON 12	SIZ 10	INT 08	POW 10
DEX 10	APP 07	EDU 01	SAN 0	HP 11

Damage Bonus: +1D4.

Weapons: War Boomerang 45%, damage 1D8+1D4
Grapple 45%, damage special
Cult Club 65%, damage 1D10+1D4
Dagger 55%, damage 1D4+2+1D4

Skills: Climb 40%, Cthulhu Mythos 04%, Dodge 40%, English 10%, Hide 70%, Jump 45%, Kariera 45%, Listen 60%, Pidgin English 45%, Sneak 90%, Spot Hidden 40%, Throw 45%, Track 35%.

JANICE (Koori), Number 3

STR 11	CON 10	SIZ 09	INT 09	POW 09
DEX 07	APP 05	EDU 01	SAN 0	HP 10

Damage Bonus: +0.

Weapons: War Boomerang 45%, damage 1D8
Grapple 20%, damage special
Cult Club 50%, damage 1D10
Dagger 55%, damage 1D4+2

Skills: Climb 80%, Cthulhu Mythos 05%, Dodge 50%, English 15%, Hide 50%, Jump 65%, Kariera 50%, Listen 60%, Sneak 50%, Pidgin English 35%, Spot Hidden 40%, Throw 45%, Track 20%.

BUCKLEY'S GHOST

*"Buckley's Chance" is Australian slang for having less than no chance at all.
The investigators are not in quite so desperate a state as poor Buckley,
but Dingo Falls waits for them as well.*

Australian folklore tells of many ghosts, usually those of white settlers lost or murdered under strange circumstances. This adventure is no exception. (Koori spirits are very different. of course—see the Mimi in this adventure as an example.) It takes place between Cuncudgerie and the investigators' ultimate desert destination. It may be encountered accidently, or due to investigations in Cuncudgerie. Bill Buckley and the murderous Slatterys have nothing to do with Dr. Huston and his mad schemes, but nonetheless they may be dismayingly deadly.

Keeper's Background

Ten years ago Bill Buckley, an old tramp (a swaggie or swagman, Australians would say) took to the outback beyond Cuncudgerie in search of gold. Instead he met his death at the hands of an insane and jealous miner, Vern Slattery, who himself believed he had discovered gold and that Buckley had come to rob him.

A brutal coward, Vern Slattery killed poor old Buckley by stealing upon him in the night, bludgeoning him, then burning him alive in his own campfire.

Buckley had made the fatal mistake of passing the Slattery hovel the day before and asking after food. Then as now, Slattery lived with his two sons, Frank (a brute) and Jacko (a moron). Neither youth knew of his father's crime. These days Frank suspects the truth, due to some drunken ravings of his father's. But he does not know for sure. Only Slattery and Buckley know. Remarkably, the dead man is more likely to reveal the truth.

Many have vanished in the outback, never to return. One more missing swagman was hardly noticed. No inquiry was made into Buckley's disappearance, and no court bothered to declare the penniless man dead. Only Bill Buckley's ghost craves to bring his murderer to justice, and the ghost prefers his own brand of justice.

Recently local Koori (as well as one white traveler, Mad Ginger Muldoon), have seen the apparition. Muldoon saw it in its hideous "angry" form, and barely managed to escape it. He is trying to drink away the memory in Cuncudgerie.

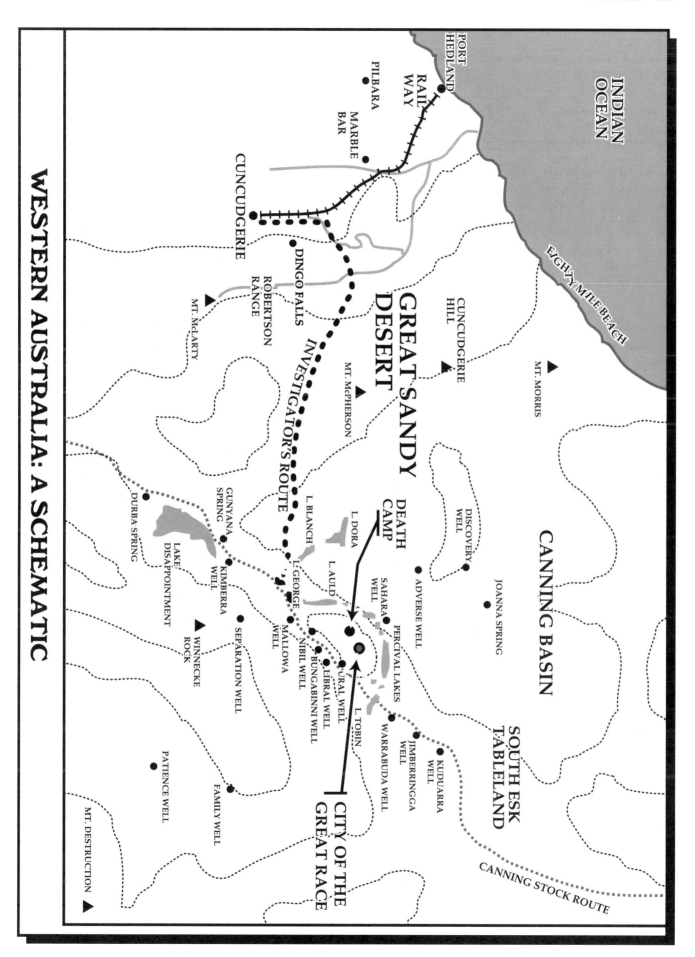

WESTERN AUSTRALIA: A SCHEMATIC

INDIAN OCEAN

PORT HEDLAND

RAILWAY

PILBARA

MARBLE BAR

CUNCUDGERIE

DINGO FALLS

ROBERTSON RANGE

MT. McLARTY

INVESTIGATOR'S ROUTE

GREAT SANDY DESERT

CUNCUDGERIE HILL

MT. McPHERSON

MT. MORRIS

EIGHTY MILE BEACH

CANNING BASIN

DISCOVERY WELL

JOANNA SPRING

GUNYANA SPRING

DURBA SPRING

LAKE DISAPPOINTMENT

KIMBERRA WELL

WINNECKE ROCK

SEPARATION WELL

L. BLANCH

L. DORA

DEATH CAMP

L. AULD

L. GEORGE

SAHARA WELL

PERCIVAL LAKES

ADVERSE WELL

MALLOWA WELL

NIBIL WELL

BUNGABINNI WELL

LIBRAL WELL

RURAL WELL

L. TOBIN

WARRABUDA WELL

JIMBERRINGGA WELL

KUDUARRA WELL

SOUTH ESK TABLELAND

PATIENCE WELL

FAMILY WELL

MT. DESTRUCTION

CITY OF THE GREAT RACE

CANNING STOCK ROUTE

Involving the Investigators

It is quite likely that investigators will already be looking into Dingo Falls due to rumors that they picked up in Cuncudgerie. If this is not the case, the keeper can arrange to have them accidently encounter Buckley's ghost.

Slattery's place is en route between Cuncudgerie and the location of the ruins, deep in the desert. A pool is nearby, with water in it for most of the year. Since Buckley's death site is unremarkable except after scrutiny, investigators might accidentally camp at it on their first night out of Cuncudgerie.

Dingo Falls

Great red rocks jet up from a rocky, scalloped ridge. The rock formation in part resembles a wave of surf about to crash down, frozen forever in stone. This is Dingo Falls. The formation makes a catchment pool shielded from quick evaporation by the sun. Above the pool are three deep caves.

The pool is about fifteen feet across. Animals come here in the night, including snakes. Any Koori the investigators have wisely brought along drink out of the pool only by straining the water through a straw mat placed under the chin, a device like the head of a straw broom. No ritual significance lies in this: they do it to strain out animal dung. Though a rare source of water in the wilderness, the pool is otherwise unremarkable.

THE CAVES

A little higher up the wall than the pond are three steep, deep stone caves, extending back sixty feet and down into the rock. A successful Climb roll reaches any of their bottoms. A torch or other light is needed to explore them. Given the downward curve of the rock openings, their bottoms cannot be seen from their mouths, no matter how powerful the light. The floor of the first (the left) cave is empty, the second and middle has a nest of 1D4+2 poisonous snakes (POT 14, Dodge 80%, 3 HP each), and the third and right cave holds the white bones of Bill Buckley, clearly identifiable as human. In this arid place, scraps of Buckley's clothes remain as well. A successful Idea roll notices that no shoes or boots are here. Buckley's boots and his harmonica were stolen by the Slatterys.

MEETING BUCKLEY'S GHOST

See description below. Unless antagonized by fire, the ghost of Bill Buckley appears as he did in life, a worn swagman with a big beard and eyes always looking over the next horizon. The ghost does not terrify but beckons visitors to the cave of its remains. Following the ghost can avoid dangerous trial and error in the caves. The ghost wants a just revenge dealt to its murderer. This can be accomplished one of two ways, by the investigators finding the evidence in Slattery's hovel and alerting the law

BUCKLEY'S GHOST

or, preferably as far as Buckley's ghost is concerned, by bringing Vern up to Dingo Falls to confront his victim.

If Vern Slattery can be forced or tricked into coming to Dingo Falls at night, Buckley's ghost attempts to possess him and jump down the nearest of the three caves, killing Slattery, so that Vern must remain with his victim forever. Failing this the ghost tries to possess the nearest investigator and use him or her to push Vern down the hole or otherwise murder him. (See the description below to resolve conflict with the ghost.) Once the ghost has accomplished its desire, it quits the possessed person and Dingo Falls forever.

Slattery's Hovel

Slattery's hovel is two miles east of Dingo Falls. Evidence of Bill Buckley's murder waits in this tin shack, and associated shed and outhouse. They are shared by Vern Slattery and his sons, Frank and Jacko. The shack has four rooms—three bedrooms and a central living area. These rooms are strewn with filth, the detritus of squalor and aimlessness. The shack is unbearably hot most of the day.

The outhouse is a large block, tin walls around a floor of concrete. It contains one toilet section and another wider area which has an ancient bathtub with claw feet. Water has to be brought from the corrugated iron tank near the main building.

The Slatterys are mining for gold at a rudimentary dig about a mile east from their home. It is a long, low set of tunnels, badly maintained but safe enough, week to week.

THE FATHER, VERN

Vern Slattery is uncouth and mean, a thin hard leathery man with sparse hair, a dog's growl for a voice, and a gift for cruel invective. He is also a drunk and a murderer. He has killed before in his youth, but only Buckley in the vicinity of his home. He will kill again to protect himself. His mine at first paid a small amount which, though it quickly played out, allows his sons and himself to eke out a living in the state of degradation they have come to like. He passes his days

VERN SLATTERY

drinking or pretending to dig in the mine. Vern Slattery never goes to Dingo Falls.

THE OLDER SON, FRANK

Frank Slattery is a vicious larrikin. A larrikin is an Australian term which originally meant a specific sort of thief, which has come to encompass any thug or hoodlum. Sometimes it is used with affection but not when applied to Frank, who inspires as much affection as a shoe full of funnel-web spiders. Tall, blond, and athletic, Frank would be handsome without his permanent sneer and abrasive and hostile demeanor. If cornered he turns to violence, unless faced with clearly superior odds.

THE YOUNGER SON, JACKO

Jacko is a semi-moron who enjoys catching and torturing small animals. Physically he is quite like Frank, except for a vacant, clear-eyed stare that masks his instinctive malice. Unobservant investigators may sentimentalize Jacko's idiocy, but a successful Psychology roll shows they do so at their peril. Jacko's constant companion is Bill Buckley's harmonica, on which he habitually blows one long, eerie, wailing note.

CLUES

Two clues here lead to Vern Slattery as the murderer of Bill Buckley. Unfortunately for the investigators, neither clue is

FRANK SLATTERY

specific. Investigators might use trial or error with the ghost, since it will not respond to Frank or Jacko, though Jacko was not old enough at Slattery's death to represent a real candidate.

Frank will put forward his suspicions about his father should he feel endangered. Investigators who presume by his revelation that they have an ally in Frank are dangerously mistaken. He is likely to conspire with his father to kill them as soon as he can safely do so, and will only help them while they outnumber or otherwise overpower him. If all else fails, Vern and Frank will try to put the blame on the hapless Jacko.

BILL BUCKLEY'S BOOTS: the boots were taken by Vern Slattery because they were almost new. They proved to be too small for any of the Slatterys. Those boots now molder, forgotten, behind the bathtub in the outhouse. They can be found after a half hour's search of the area and a successful Spot Hidden. *B.Buckley* has been burned into each boot tongue, on the outside.

BILL BUCKLEY'S HARMONICA: this is the property of Jacko, who won't relinquish it except in a momentary exchange for some other item of interest. But then he wants the harmonica back, and becomes violent if not appeased. The harmonica has the name *Buckley* scratched into its casing.

JACKO SLATTERY

OTHER EVIDENCE: the keeper can supply more evidence of Slattery family complicity in Buckley's death if there is special reason to involve the law. The following "Just Rewards" conclusion is the preferred one.

Just Rewards

Finding Buckley's boots behind the bathtub, or his harmonica in Jacko's possession is enough to convince the local authorities, who hold long-standing grudges against the Slatterys. Frank turns witness against Vern, and Vern is tried and hung for Buckley's murder. This outcome earns 1D3 Sanity points for each investigator.

Should the investigators conspire to lure Vern Slattery to the ghost site and subsequently acquiesce in his murder, the outcome is more disturbing. Though justice is served, the investigators earn no Sanity points. Further, if they remain at the site another night they find that Bill Buckley's ghost has vanished, but that another miserable phantom (Vern) has taken its place.

Should they push on immediately, rumors reach the investigators of this new phantom before they leave Australia's shores. Either way, the investigators lose 1/1D6 Sanity for their share in Vern Slattery's supernatural fate.

Statistics

VERN SLATTERY (white), age 61, Patriarchal Murderer

STR 12	CON 15	SIZ 13	INT 13	POW 11
DEX 13	APP 10	EDU 10	SAN 09	HP 14

Damage Bonus: +1D4.

Weapons: Fist/Punch 65%, damage 1D3+1D4
.30-06 Bolt Action Rifle 60%, damage 2D6+4
Kitchen Knife 50%, damage 1D4+2+1D4

Skills*: Dodge 50%, Psychology 25%, Sneak 60%, Spot Hidden 75%, Swear Like A Trooper 90%.

*Vern is drunk half the time. Halve most skills until he has a chance to sleep it off, but in the meantime increase Swear to 99%.

FRANK SLATTERY (white), age 29, Vicious Larrikin

STR 14	CON 12	SIZ 14	INT 12	POW 15
DEX 13	APP 13	EDU 08	SAN 20	HP 13

Damage Bonus: +1D4.

Weapons: Fist/Punch 55%, damage 1D3+1D4
.30-06 Bolt Action Rifle 45%, damage 2D6+4

Skills: Dodge 60%, Mechanical Repair 50%, Sneak 50%, Spot Hidden 45%, Sneer 89%, Track 55%.

JACKO SLATTERY (white), age 23, Dim-Witted Accomplice Thug

STR 16	CON 12	SIZ 14	INT 03	POW 10
DEX 11	APP 11	EDU 06	SAN 20	HP 13

Damage Bonus: +1D4.

Weapons: Fist/Punch 55%, damage 1D3+1D4
Switchblade Knife 40%, damage 1D4+1D4

Skills: Art (Harmonica) 10%, Dodge 30%.

BUCKLEY'S GHOST, Vengeful Haunter

INT 10   POW 12

Sanity Loss: 0/1D3 SAN for Ordinary Form, 2/1D8+1 SAN for Angry Form

Bill Buckley's ghost haunts the site of his death. It has two forms. The first is of a bushman in wide-brimmed felt hat, big bushy beard, baggy pants, worn shirt, and cloth vest. Incongruously his feet are bare: Buckley was surprised asleep on the night of his murder and his ghostly remains include his clothes, but not his boots. The keeper can ask for a Spot Hidden to notice this detail, or state it baldly, as seems useful. Sanity loss to see this form is 0/1D3 SAN.

The second form is the angry form, the burning man. It capers with blistering flesh, eyeballs simmering in their sockets and hair streaming alight from the glittering phosphorescent fire that tortures its soul. As with the first form, observe the detail of the missing boots. Sanity loss for seeing this form is 2/1D8+1 SAN.

The angry form appears to those who bring fire to Bill's

resting place at night, since it was by fire he was killed. The ghost harasses anyone holding any form of fire. Electric lights and torches are not a threat. If the fire is not extinguished within 1D6 rounds, the ghost attempts to possess someone and douse the fire using that person. It will try the one nearest the fire first, working its way out. Match POW vs. POW on the Resistance Table. Its horror at the fire is such that it will even hurl the whole possessed body onto a fire to extinguish it. Once the fire is extinguished, the possession ends. If the ghost is not angered, it acts according to the sub-section, "Meeting Buckley's Ghost."

Both forms are transparent, and obviously phantoms.

THE GREAT SANDY DESERT

In the desert, even surviving is an adventure in itself.
As the investigators make their treks towards the City of the Great Race,
occur many encounters, some of them quite deadly.

Regardless of who handled the outfitting, the investigators have two excellent Daimler light trucks, and enough supplies for six weeks. Their water must be replenished by visits to the wells along the Canning stock route—a way through the desert used for long Kimberly-origin cattle drives to Wiluna and Kalgoorlie in the south.

The trip to the coordinates Mackenzie supplies takes a minimum of four days. If the keeper wishes, he or she can make four rolls on the encounter table in this section, or simply choose the encounters that seem appropriate.

For hundreds of miles, the landscape slowly increases in desolation. The daily heat and dust are constant, but at night the temperature drops precipitously. In their none-too-thick bedrolls, the investigators stare up at unfamiliar skies, dominated by a brilliant constellation, the Southern Cross. When the heat vanishes, the air is very clear, and the mornings and evenings are poignantly beautiful.

There is little to see but scrub, dust, and rock. A rise a few hundred feet high is tall enough to be noted on large-scale survey maps, and perhaps even be given a name. No running stream exists. Every few miles the party crosses burro or camel tracks, or perhaps the ruts of a car or truck. David Dodge says that there is no telling when vehicle tracks were made—the desert is so dry that tracks may stay visible for years.

Surprisingly, they see smoke from distant fires two or three times a day. Dodge explains that Kooris use fire to trap game as well as to cook, and that smoke plumes can be navigation aids when traveling at distance across the flat, nearly featureless land.

Once they top a rise and find the long rear slope eroded into strange cone shapes capped by smooth flat rocks. Another time they find an enormous red sandstone boulder smoothed by the wind, with a billowy hole blasted through it. The piece stands part way down another slope, sighted beautifully against the rising sun.

Wycroft's Route

Though plagued by flat tires, split radiator hoses, and other minor automobile problems, Dodge leads the party expertly. On the third day they unexpectedly cross what appears to be a well traveled route. Many vehicles have passed up and down it—it is Wycroft's route to the City of the Great Ones. Wycroft takes various routes to and from Cuncudgerie, but this far out he has established a single way through the dunes and lake beds, and follows it each trip. Huston's Kooris patrol Wycroft's track and are prepared to ambush a small party.

If the party is unable to Navigate to the site of the buried city, or have lost their navigational instruments, some clue left on Wycroft's track could lead them to follow it. If the investigators do, they veer north directly into the Great Sandy Desert. If they continue to follow it, it then turns east for about seventy miles, to end at Huston's shaft to the buried city.

If David Dodge is the route master, he wants to turn south, to reach Nimberra Well before sunset. If Dodge prevails, read on. If the investigators follow the north-turning track, bring them quickly to "The Ambush" section, a little further below.

Nimberra Well is a brackish pond edged by green scum. Lots of wildlife, including extremely poisonous snakes, creep down to drink between dusk and dawn. Wise investigators camp some distance away. At this well, the investigators intersect the Canning stock route. Signs of the passage

Desert Survival

A human of SIZ 10 or 11 needs at least a gallon of water and extra salt daily to keep going under desert temperatures. Sunburn and sunstroke are the worst enemies. A foot-traveler travels more securely at night, in the early morning, and the later afternoon. By moving when it is coldest and resting when it is hottest, the traveler best conserves body heat and water. If he or she is only a few days from help, food can be foregone if water is present. For longer travels, the traveler must forage for food, greatly slowing his or her pace and thus requiring more water.

Desert Encounters

While traveling in the outback, the party has a 50% chance of an encounter each day. If an encounter occurs, roll 1D6. Do not repeat an encounter. For more control, ignore the rolls and select the encounters.

D6	Result
1	snakes: a death adder or tiger snake
2	a Mimi
3	a prospector
4	1D3 Koori hunters
5	a bush fire
6	a sandstorm

SNAKES: These snakes are common in the region. A Medicine roll may prove useful. A snakebite kit adds 10% to that skill's chance of successful use. For more horror, have several or many snakes be attracted by the warmth of the evening campfires, or of sleeping bodies, or of cozy boots.

A tiger snake is five to six feet in length, aggressive, with brown striping and deadly poison, POT 2D6+10. If the poison overwhelms the victim's CON, death follows in 1D4+2 hours. If the attack fails, reduce the target's hit points by half and leave him or her confined to bed for 1D4 days. Statistics: STR 2D6+6, CON 2D6, SIZ 1D6, POW 1D6, DEX 3D6, Bite attack 35%; Hide 90%, Sneak 85%.

A death adder is two to three feet long, gray-brown and dark-banded. It hides itself in sand and strikes backward like a steel spring. Its poison has 1D8+6 potency. If the poison overwhelms the victim's CON, death follows in 1D10+5 minutes; if the victim survives, he or she is too ill to travel for 1D6 days. Reduce the victim's hit points by three quarters. Statistics: STR 2D6, CON 1D6, SIZ 1D4, POW 1D3, DEX 3D6+4, Bite attack 45%; Hide 98%, Sneak 95%.

MIMI: The Mimi are spirit-creatures of the Australian Dreamtime. They are taller than humans, and as light as straw. They are old foes of the flying polyps, as is only natural for creatures so vulnerable to wind. They need not appear in this scenario at all, but if they do take action, they can take the investigators directly to the inside of the underground city, bypassing the guards without. Mimi are not altruistic and must have a reason before they will help.

Because of Huston's cult and the renewed activities in the City of the Great Ones, the Mimi have come through from the Dreamtime in force. The Mimis' main goal is to close the city, or at least eliminate some of the flying polyps, but they cannot do this themselves—a single polyp could devastate a whole squad of Mimi.

But perhaps humans could help. The Mimi watch the investigators traveling through their desert. If more than half the investigators are obviously armed (with a long gun or large-caliber pistol) and more than half the investigators are male (the Mimi are less confident of females' fighting ability), then at a convenient moment, a Mimi steps from behind a rock to confront the investigators, giving them a 0/1D6 SAN loss. He makes no hostile action.

Hostility of any sort causes the Mimi to flee. If the investigators bargain with the Mimi (a gift of yams or perhaps candy would be perfect), they are understood and responded to, but in a curious way; drawing incredibly fast, the Mimi paints his answers on nearby rocks. Via picture, the Mimi invites them home. If they accept, the Mimi splits open a boulder with its finger and steps through. Investigators who wish to go with the Mimi must enter by the third time that the keeper asks whether or not they want to go. The Mimi accepts only the complete party. If even one member of the party refuses to go, the Mimi refuses all of them.

If the investigators follow, they feel very, very odd, and see things as if they are moving high above the ground. Glowing colors are everywhere, and there is a moment of complete disorientation, costing 0/1D4 SAN. Then they suddenly find themselves in a cave filled with other Mimi. For further information, go to the section further below "The Cavern of the Mimi."

PROSPECTOR: This desert-weary fellow is astride his camel. He says he is leaving the area to the east because strange things are happening. Sometimes the ground shakes. There are bat swarms in the desert. Kooris are vanishing. He says he's going to go to Meekatharra, where it's civilized, and to hell with this place.

KOORIS: These men try to avoid meeting the party. They have been shot at in the past, and don't want it to happen again. If the party can reassure them, then sign-talk and Pidgin reveals that they have heard of the bat cult, and know that the area to which the investigators want to travel is dangerous, and to be avoided. The Kooris say that they have heard that the bat—Ngunung-Ngunnut—has returned in the form of a white man. Gifts of food and tobacco bring more information. The people draw sand-pictures of a strange track (of a flying polyp; see the illustration on p. 150 for the tracks) and the symbol of the Sand Bat cult which is tattooed on the bodies of all devout cultists.

BUSH FIRE: A bush fire threatens to overtake them. In the distance, everyone can see that the flames reach thirty feet into the air. The investigators can choose to try to outrun the flames and reach a nearby dry lake bed or decide to turn around and crash through the wall of flame.

If they try to outrun the flames, each player of a driver must succeed in a Drive roll. A failed roll means that the truck blows a tire. A failing roll of 96-00 bounces the truck over a huge rock and breaks an axle from the increased speed. In case of either disaster, the vehicle still reaches the lake bed before the flames can engulf it, but the party must change the tire. A broken axle cannot be repaired—they must travel on foot henceforth or find some other way to transport the party.

If the drivers try to crash through the flames, each driver's player must attempt a Drive roll and an Idea roll (to pick the thinnest section of the flames). If either roll fails, that truck catches on fire. The truck makes it through the flames, but then it catches fire. The riders must bail out quickly and lose any gear they can't carry in their hands.

SANDSTORM: A sandstorm or dust storm approaches. The storm forces a halt to movement and lasts for three hours. After it is gone, the carburetors of both trucks are clogged and must be disassembled and cleaned. The storm costs an entire day, and completely obliterates any tracks that the party followed.

of cattle are easy to find. Dodge points out that dried dung makes a fairly good fuel for fires. Several members of the party busily boil water into the evening, replenishing the supply of potables.

The Death Camp

In the morning, if the party drives northeast along the stock route, the plan will be to turn due north into the dunes to arrive at the position indicated by MacWhirr. Between Mallowa and Nibil Wells, everyone notices the tracks of many vehicles leading from the stock trail into the sandy hills to the north. This road, as good a road as one is likely to find in this part of Australia, apparently runs directly toward the location pinpointed by Arthur MacWhirr.

If the investigators agree with Dodge that this road is a stroke of luck too good to pass up, then the powerful Daimlers go bouncing off into desert even more trackless. (If not, then the party continues on to Bungabinni Well, and then turns north to make its own trail, avoiding the Death Camp episode starting in the next paragraph.)

The road has not been used in some time: drifting sand frequently obliterates the way. In a few places the investigators notice that scrubby grass has grown up into the wheel prints. Travel is steady, without detour. The party sees no sign of the

TRACKS OF A FLYING POLYP

cyclopean blocks shown in MacWhirr's photos, though the terrain resembles that shown in the prints. In two hours, the party travels forty miles due north. Then the road ends.

A Mining Camp

Huddled beside a twenty-foot-high rocky outcrop are a dozen or more tent shells, many head-high stacks of crates, various long tubes and bits, a tiny shack marked *Explosives*, and an undamaged small building with mechanical gear secured on top of it. An old Ford truck rests at the end of the row of tents, squashed and broken as though a giant had stepped on it. Any successful Geology, Idea, or Know roll tells the investigators that this has been a mining camp of some sort. There is still no sign of the strange curvilinear blocks.

When they get out of the vehicles, they see human bones amidst the sand and rubble. Several skeletons are more or less whole, but with broken bones.

A successful Spot Hidden roll near the wooden structure uncovers a club about thirty inches long, half-buried in the sand. Embedded in the striking end are many small, sharp white teeth. A successful Natural History roll identifies the teeth in the club as probably from large bats.

THE MINE SHAFT: the small wooden-frame building protects the top of a deep shaft, and acts as the engine mount and cable wind for the small open elevator poised at the top of the shaft. The light from a flashlight or the sound from an object thrown down the shaft merely reveals that the shaft is very deep. A successful Mechanical Repair roll turns on the gasoline engine which powers the elevator. A second successful Mechanical Repair says that the cables, winch, car, etc., are in good working order and perfectly safe. The car can be operated internally.

If the investigators turn on the winch engine and send the car down, then rubble in the shaft stops the car at the 200-foot level. A successful Geology roll establishes that a wall has collapsed, and argues that the upper shaft shoring may not be as safe as it appears. The only way out is up.

THE EXPLOSIVES SHACK: the lock on the door has been broken, and the inside of the tiny building is bare except for two stout, empty wooden boxes with dovetailed joints. Their outsides detail the specifications of the powerful mining dynamite which once filled them. Each box held 48 sticks. Inspection turns up several other empty dynamite boxes near the shack: these are weathered and half-filled with sand.

THE INTACT TENT: all the tents were torn savagely, but one was carefully sewn together again. Inside it are bits of clothing, fresh matches, tinned food (and empty cans of the same), several lanterns, kerosene, and other household items. Of all the camp, this one tent appears to be freshly lived-in.

THE SPRING: a successful Spot Hidden or Geology roll reveals one other point of interest about the camp. On the rocky red wall beyond the tents, a dark stain on can be seen. In the center of the dark spot is a tiny spring of fresh water, jetting out in a stream the width of a carpenter's nail, bubbling into a white enamel wash basin wedged in the rocks below. Overflow from the basin runs into a crevice in the rocks and disappears. The water is cool, sweet, and clear.

AROUND CAMP: wandering about, any investigator receiving a successful Spot Hidden roll notices a strange set of tracks which start and end abruptly, as though the maker had flown down, walked a while, then flown away. A successful Track roll establishes that the signs are fresh. Each track seems to have five toes, but the tracks themselves are enormous, about six feet long. A successful Cthulhu Mythos roll suggests that the marks are traces of a flying polyp.

HEADING TOWARD THE CITY: if the party tries to go from the camp toward the location indicated by MacWhirr's diary, they find that soft sand and a long scarp block vehicle movement. If, however, they go either north or south for about two hours, and then turn east, they find fairly smooth going. Going in either direction, they eventually cross old vehicle tracks which lead exactly toward 22°3'14" S, by 125°0'39" E. On either route, the same danger of an ambush exists. See "The Ambush", further below.

Jeremy Grogan

After the party has explored the site, they hear animal yelps from the other side of camp. Shortly thereafter they make out a half-dozen dog-like shapes, who study the party from the lip of a nearby dune. Then a human whistles, and the animals retreat down the dune and out of sight.

If the investigators pursue, they must ascend the low, sandy hillock. There they find dog prints. A short way down the other side, the dog prints join human shoe prints. The makers of so many tracks are not hard to follow. In a few minutes the investigators come upon a swarm of reddish-brown dogs surrounding a man naked but for oxford-style shoes. The man stands within a five-foot-wide circle of stones gathered from the outcrop.

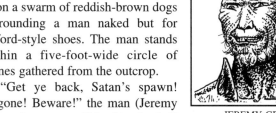
JEREMY GROGAN

"Get ye back, Satan's spawn! Begone! Beware!" the man (Jeremy Grogan) screams. "My friends shall rend you!" Sure enough, the dingoes spread out, and begin to creep to either side of the party, preparatory to the attack.

A successful Credit Rating, Fast Talk, Persuade, or Psychology roll convinces the man that the party poses no immediate threat. With a little patience on the part of the investigators, he tells his story.

If he is unconvinced, the dingoes sense that too, and move to the attack, their sharp teeth glinting. If one investigator is seriously mauled or killed, Grogan calls back his canines, waiting for the investigators to leave. If the investigators stay, he sics the animals on them again and again, each time killing another investigator.

The circle of stones has no significance except in Grogan's insane mind. But if the investigators shoot him, the dingoes attack without hesitation, aiming to kill the person who fired.

JEREMY GROGAN, age 36, Insane Miner and Dreamer of Great Potential

STR 12	CON 13	SIZ 11	INT 12	POW 12
DEX 12	APP 11	EDU 09	SAN 0	HP 12

Weapons: .30-06 Rifle 45%, damage 2D6+3
Grapple 30%, damage special

Skills: Cthulhu Mythos 03%, Dreaming 15%, Explosives 30%, Fast Talk 35%, First Aid 50%, Geology 30%, Hard Rock Mining Lore 45%, Hide 75%, Listen 60%, Mechanical Repair 45%, Operate Heavy Machinery 50%, Sneak 45%, Spot Hidden 60%, Track 20%.

MAGICAL DINGOES

	1	2	3	4	5	6	7
STR	08	09	11	10	08	11	10
CON	13	14	17	15	13	17	14
SIZ	06	05	07	04	05	06	04
DEX	15	17	12	14	13	17	11
POW	12	12	12	12	12	12	12
HP	n/a	n/a	n/a	n/a	n/a	n/a	n/a
Dam. Bon.:	+ 1D4	-1D4	+0	-1D4	-1D4	-1D4	-1D4
MOV 12							

Weapon: Bite 90%, damage 1D8

Armor: Physical damage has no effect on these magical creatures. At the keeper's desire, appropriate magic could dispel them.

Skills: Do What Grogan Wants 100%, Frolic with Grogan 100%, Spot Hidden 85%, Track by Scent 95%.

JEREMY GROGAN'S STATEMENT

Read this section aloud, or hand out a photocopy of it.

"I don't know how long it's been. Years, I think. I was down on my luck in Cuncudgerie when I met a Yank who claimed he had a map to a wonderful gold strike a long way east. Well, he seemed a shifty sort, like all bosses, but he was willing to pay a sign-up bonus on the spot, so I took the work, mining work it was.

"He hired a lot of men, twenty and more, and all of us agreed that the fellow was daft, and that we'd work until the loony's cash ran out, and then come back to town. That's what a workin' man does, you see—one job, and then another.

"The bloke's name was John Carver. He led us out here where it's impossible for gold to be, leastwise gold-bearing quartz, and set us a-digging at an exact spot. 'My researches are infallible,' he said again and again, and Lord how we used to laugh about that! We made sure we got paid right to the day, because this fellow was going to take a tumble. So we worked through the sand, and then sediments, and then rock. And then the man's money ran out. No work, no pay, we agreed, and like we promised sat down to wait for the supply trucks from Cuncudgerie the following week. They would take us back.

"Meanwhile the Yank began to act strange, walking into the desert, pretending to talk with invisible beings, making gestures, and the like. Then he disappeared for an entire day and part of another, and when he came back, his eyes were wild and evil-like. 'There is a way,' he said, 'there is another way, and God has shown it. Leave if you wish; you are of no use to me now.'

"One of the men said something about wanting wages for

the days spent waiting for the trucks, and several more used very rude language to the Yank's face, for this camp wasn't exactly no hotel. Carver jumped a foot at this, and he swore foully at us. He got a most cruel look on his face. 'If that is how you feel,' he said, 'then I shall endeavor to speed you on your way—all of you.' Well, that didn't sound too good, but what could he do with one of him and two dozen of us?

"He walked away, into the desert. That night, a couple of the fellows caught me cheatin' at cards, and they run me way into the bush before I lost them. When I was sneakin' back to camp I saw Carver appear on the wall of rock, gesture and point, and then a great winged thing with talons like ropes descended from the sky, destroyed the camp, and killed every man-jack there.

"When the men knew that guns would not stop it, they squealed like trapped animals. Lord!

"Goin' into the desert seemed a better way to die, so I wandered off. Anything would be better than meeting such a devil-man or his demon. I found some shade the next day and lay down to die. For some reason that made my mind easy and clear. I slept for days.

"When I woke, the dingoes were with me. They are my friends," Grogan says. "But they are not real. They are magic, I think, because they stay slippery in my mind, and I forget which is which. And they never eat."

GROGAN'S ANSWERS

In answer to questions, he thinks that Carver took the other truck, the dynamite, and other supplies, but he does not know where he went. The dingoes have several times protected Grogan against a band of Kooris who seemed bent on murder. These cruel people carry clubs inset with tiny teeth.

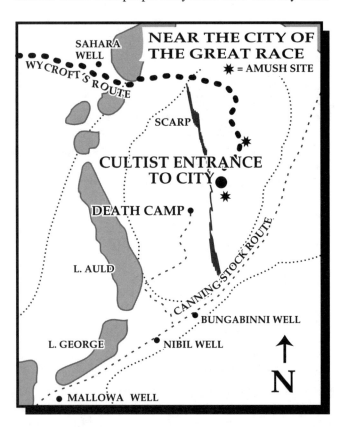

NEAR THE CITY OF THE GREAT RACE

✴ = AMUSH SITE

SAHARA WELL

WYCROFT'S ROUTE

SCARP

CULTIST ENTRANCE TO CITY

DEATH CAMP

L. AULD

CANNING STOCK ROUTE

BUNGABINNI WELL

L. GEORGE • NIBIL WELL

MALLOWA WELL

N

Since the dingoes ate two, the remaining Kooris take pains not to come near.

A SMALL SECRET

Grogan is right about the dingoes. In his madness and loneliness, he dreamed them into existence. He has no idea how he did this, nor is he likely ever to be able to do it again. The dingoes are out of the Dreamtime or perhaps the Dreamlands, and not of this world. They cannot be harmed by physical attack.

GROGAN'S CHARACTER

Grogan is insane. He talks in bursts, separated by seconds or minutes of silence. He is a sly man. A successful Psychology roll shows that ordinarily he could not be trusted, but that in important matters the truth struggles out of him, whether he invites it or not. Beyond the dingoes, which should remain inexplicable, the stream of water is the only evidence of his talent for Dreaming. Repeated questioning pressures him and makes him sullen and uncommunicative. Investigators willing to sit with him for a long time get the entire story.

If the investigators offer to take him along, he refuses vehemently and runs away and hides, or retreats within his circle of stones. Only when his dingoes disappear will he be ready to leave this place.

The Ambush

Approaching the entrance to the City of the Great Ones from the west or the south, the party must descend through a ravine where an ambush waits. The ambush is set by the Kooris whom Huston uses as scouts and roving guards. Sighting a motor vehicle, they roll several large boulders to block the road, then (after the vehicle has stopped or slowed) they'll roll more boulders to attempt to destroy it and its occupants or, failing that, at least to block its retreat.

Roll one boulder per vehicle. Each boulder has a 30% chance of striking a truck, demolishing it and dealing each rider in it 2D6 damage. If anyone in the vehicle receives a successful Spot Hidden, he or she shouts a warning. If then the player of the driver makes a successful Drive Automobile roll, he or she evades the boulder and passes safely through the ambush.

The boulders rolled, and if one or more trucks have been hit or stopped, the Kooris wait for investigators to get out of the trucks, then attack the survivors with war boomerangs and spears. Unless the players specifically state that their characters are preparing their weapons, allow all the Kooris a free shot at the investigators when the party dismounts. Investigators with prepared weapons may fire in the first combat round, in DEX order. The rest must wait till the second combat round, when all may attack in DEX order. Remember that each Koori can throw a spear or boomerang only every second round.

When three or more ambushers have been killed or seriously wounded, or when they have no more spears and boomerangs, they break off the fighting and disappear into the desert. Each investigator who has percentiles in a Track skill can follow one of the ambushers and continue to engage him. Additional investigators can go with a tracker, of course. Wounded or otherwise cornered ambushers choose to surrender. They will tell all they know. If more ambushers flee than there are investigator-trackers (including David Dodge), then some get away to alert Huston of the group's approach.

Captured ambushers try persistently to escape, making nuisances of themselves, but they are unguarded in speech and try to answer almost any question. If flattered and given gifts of tobacco, candy, or other food, they grow boastful and expansive, talk endlessly, and supply all of the information below. Read the following aloud to the players, or use selected individual sentences to answer investigator questions.

■ The road ends in the middle of fields of strange stones. There is a hole, into which many go and few return.

■ After the stairs end, there is a great cave which goes forever. In it live ferocious things which should not be disturbed. Men who make loud noises at the wrong times are eaten by those creatures, who are too horrible to describe.

■ In another part of the cave lives the white man who rules the desert and who gives us captives for flesh and sex. There are many captives in the cave. In another part of the cave lives a strange being who knows everything but nothing about us, and who is free and yet the captive of the white leader.

■ The white leader says that Father of All Bats may soon return to this world, though he does not know just when. To prepare for that time, the leader must touch certain stones when it is time.

The ambushers' conceptions are childlike in that they must depend on rumor, story, innuendo, and overheard conversation to define their own place. No one has done more than inflame their grossest desires. The investigators may persist in questioning. The more they attempt to reason out new information, the more the keeper should consider allowing the investigators to control unconsciously the replies of their captives.

For instance, the ambushers grow fearful of punishment, and finally refuse to answer except with "no" (in reply to questions that end in vowels), "yes" (in reply to questions that end in consonants), and "maybe" (in reply to questions ending in the letter Y). If done carefully, this manner of reply ensures that the investigators hear what they want to hear, or what they don't want to hear. Neither desire has much to do with truth.

KOORI AMBUSHERS

	1	2	3	4	5	6	7	8
STR	16	14	13	17	11	12	13	11
CON	14	16	12	13	11	14	16	13
SIZ	14	14	12	11	13	16	16	13
DEX	18	17	16	15	14	13	12	11
POW	19	09	11	13	16	09	11	14
HP	14	15	12	12	12	15	16	13
DB:	+1D4	+1D4	+1D4	+1D4	+0	+1D4	+1D4	+0

Weapons: 1H Spear 65%, damage 1D6+1+1D4
War Boomerang 70%, damage 1D8+1D2
Cult Club 55%, damage 1D10+1D4

Each ambusher carries one war boomerang, three 1H spears, and one cult club.

Skills: Climb 55%, Cthulhu Mythos 09%, Dodge 45%, Gadudjara 45%, Hide 40%, Listen 65%, Pidgin English 15%, Sneak 55%, Spot Hidden 70%, Track 65%.

CITY BENEATH THE SANDS

A final battle against Huston's cultists, in an ancient city buried beneath the Australian Sands. While exploring, investigators may meet an alien being older than the human race itself.

Whether or not the investigators have encountered Mortimer Wycroft, surviving ambushers may have alerted Huston that strangers (angry ones) approach the City of the Great Race.

The scene resembles MacWhirr's photos, except that the sand has been packed down by foot and tire, and that a good deal of early 20th century garbage has been strewn about. If Wycroft has arrived, and he probably will have been more prompt than the investigators, then in the center of the area are several light trucks, parked and mostly emptied. Some goods have been put under a tarpaulin beside a small shed.

The shed covers a low wall of sand bags. They surround an electrical generator and a set of wooden stairs within, descending into the silent earth. The generator runs constantly. Its *PUT!-put!-PUT!-put!* reaches far into the desert. As far as Huston or any of the cultists know, this entrance is the only way into the City of the Great Ones. A single guard is on watch here at all times. When Wycroft comes, though, the guard is pressed into service as a porter, leaving the entrance unguarded for some time.

If the Kooris have reported to Huston that the investigators are approaching, then the entrance is well guarded by a half-dozen cultists armed with rifles. The sandbags make excellent cover, though the parked trucks seriously block some angles of fire. To compensate, one cultist each would lay beneath the two trucks.

Enough stone blocks stick out of the sand to provide excellent concealment for investigators creeping up toward the entrance, but the last fifty yards or so are across bare sand. It would take six or seven seconds to cross that clear ground, enough for each cultist to get one very good shot at targets that get closer and closer, easier to hit.

If the investigators are stymied at the excavated entrance and unable easily to enter the buried city, a flaming truck or one loaded with dynamite cleans out the cultists and leaves a way into the city open for the investigators. The information given by the ambushers argues against this tactic. In any case, this approach requires that the truck be driven; the driver must have either Drive Automobile or Operate Heavy Machinery; and for success in the tactic the driver must receive either a successful Drive Automobile/Operate Heavy Machinery roll or a successful POW x2 roll.

The driver suffers 2D6 damage jumping out of the truck and from the subsequent blast, plus the damage from any bullets (quarter the riflemen's chances of hitting the driver) which hit the mark. If no one volunteers for the job, the investigators may wish to seek another entrance, for which see the next section.

The force of the explosion draws the attention of flying polyps, who are a few miles distant. If the investigators do not get underground in the next hour, a polyp flies overhead and randomly attacks any two investigators.

Underground

The stairs are nearly 300 feet long. Nyarlathotep revealed a quick way in to Huston, but a lot of work had to be done to make the way accessible. Electric lights, hung sparsely but regularly, illuminate the steps after the first fifty feet or so. At the bottom of the stairs is a back-up electrical generator matching the one at the top of the stairs. Several 50-gallon gasoline drums nearby argue that the way to the outside could be shut off without harm for a considerable time.

The first impression is of coolness. The earth at this depth maintains a constant temperature of 57°F. There is a silence and a stillness beyond life and death. No tomb has ever existed for so long as these passage have, nor had such treasures in it. Beyond are great halls and thick dust, and the gleam of increasingly tiny light bulbs leading off into unfathomable darkness. Here is eternal darkness.

As a by-product, the cavern has attracted bats from across the continent. The lower stairs drip with their excrement. They line the ceilings. A loud noise or an explosion sends millions of bats pouring out the entrance. At dusk, they all leave the city daily.

It is possible to go in any direction, but the lights are irresistible beacons. Everyone notices that a trail has been pounded through the thick dust along the line of electric lights, and that elsewhere the inches-thick dust is undisturbed. In the darkness, the investigators see almost nothing of the extent of the city.

Most of the cultists live not far from the bottom of the long stairs, in an area they have come to call the Bunkhouse. The place is far enough from the second generator that its noise does not keep them awake. The place is a series of four rooms, each about thirty feet square and each holding up to 1D10+2 cultists.

From the Bunkhouse a good draft carries away the smoke from the heating and cooking fires, up the stairway to the surface.

The rooms hold filthy bedding, obscene artifacts, bones, and lurid art. Cultists who own guns or knives always carry them, or return to find their guns, knives, coins, etc., stolen by their fellows. In one of the rooms, two typed and mimeographed orders from Huston lay crumpled on the floor. The investigators need Luck rolls to find them in the foul-smelling jumble. These orders are reprinted nearby as *Nyarlathotep Papers #37.* They can be read aloud or handed out.

ITEM. Memos to All Acolytes (*Nyarlathotep Papers #37*)

Relevance of the Information: indicates that several cultists here may have deadly magical powers, that it is possible to evade searching cultists in these vast passages, halls, and rooms, and that someone or something called "line-walkers" exist here. The initials R.H. could stand for Robert Huston. Keepers also notice that the investigators might come across the "two-legged deer" that Huston mentions, a human potential ally and gold mine of information.

Nyarlathotep Papers #37

```
TO: All Acolytes
SUBJECT: Learning Magic
DATE: - - 1925

MESSAGE: Acolytes are reminded that
their duty to their god includes the
prompt and persistent practice of
necromantic gestures and intonations
necessary to spell-casting. A test of
your Shrivelling abilities takes
place two weeks from today.

R.H.
```

```
TO: All Acolytes
SUBJECT: Our Recent Hunt
DATE: - - 1925

MESSAGE: We still have not found our
last "2-legged deer." There is
utterly no excuse for not being able
to find an unarmed human who has nei-
ther food, nor water, nor magic.

Remind the line-walkers to be alert.

R.H.
```

Lights and noise almost always come from the bunkhouse, and no one ever stands guard. Below are statistics for twenty of the inmates. Each set contains an acolyte who can cast spells. If Huston learns of the presence of the investigators, he'll send out such five-man groups as teams to hunt down the investigators.

CULTIST A-SQUAD

	One	Two	Three	Four	Five
STR	12	13	14	12	12
CON	14	11	10	10	12
SIZ	10	11	08	12	10
INT	13	09	11	10	09
POW	14	09	04	09	10
DEX	12	12	12	12	12
HP	12	11	09	11	11

Damage Bonus: +0.

Weapons: .45 Revolver 50%, damage 1D10+2
Lightning Gun* 50%, damage 8D6/4D6/1D6
Grapple 40%, damage special
Cult Club 25%, damage 1D10
* *Lightning gun for Number Three only.*

Spells: (magic for Number One only) Contact Nyarlathotep (Sand Bat Aspect), Enchant Item, Shrivelling, Voorish Sign.

Skills: Climb 40%, Cthulhu Mythos 09% or 20%, Hide 50%, Jump 45%, Listen 60%, Sneak 50%, Spot Hidden 40%. Number One also gets 20 points more of Cult Club, and of Psychology.

CULTIST B-SQUAD

	One	Two	Three	Four	Five
STR	11	13	11	13	12
CON	11	13	11	09	10
SIZ	15	13	17	15	14
INT	12	09	11	10	09
POW	12	12	09	08	11
DEX	11	11	11	11	11
HP	13	13	14	12	12

Damage Bonus: +1D4.

Weapons: .45 Revolver 50%, damage 1D10+2
Lightning Gun* 40%, damage 8D6/4D6/1D6
Grapple 40%, damage special
Cult Club 25%, damage 1D10+1D4
* *Lightning gun for Number Two only.*

Spells: (magic for Number One only) Contact Nyarlathotep (Sand Bat Aspect).

Skills: Climb 40%, Cthulhu Mythos 09% or 20%, Hide 50%, Jump 45%, Listen 60%, Sneak 50%, Spot Hidden 40%. Number One also gets 20 points more of Cult Club and Psychology.

CULTIST C-SQUAD

	One	Two	Three	Four	Five
STR	15	17	15	18	13
CON	15	15	15	16	17
SIZ	11	11	11	12	13
INT	11	09	10	11	08
POW	11	10	08	10	09
DEX	10	10	10	10	10
HP	13	13	13	14	15

Damage Bonus: +1D4.

Weapons: .45 Revolver 50%, damage 1D10+2
Lightning Gun* 40%, damage 8D6/4D6/1D6
Grapple 40%, damage special
Cult Club 25%, damage 1D10+1D4
* *Lightning gun for Number Five only.*

Spells: (magic for Number One only) Contact Nyarlathotep (Sand Bat Aspect), Enchant Item, Shrivelling.

Skills: Climb 40%, Cthulhu Mythos 09% or 20%, Hide 50%, Jump 45%, Listen 60%, Sneak 50%, Spot Hidden 40%. Number One also gets 20 points more of Cult Club and of Psychology.

CULTIST D-SQUAD

	One	Two	Three	Four	Five
STR	10	11	12	11	10
CON	10	11	10	11	10
SIZ	12	13	12	11	10
INT	11	11	10	10	10
POW	10	12	08	07	11
DEX	09	09	09	09	09
HP	11	12	11	11	10

Damage Bonus: +0.

Weapons: .45 Revolver 50%, damage 1D10+2
Lightning Gun* 40%, damage 8D6/4D6/1D6
Grapple 40%, damage special
Cult Club 25%, damage 1D10+1D4
* *Lightning gun for Number Two only.*

Skills: Climb 40%, Cthulhu Mythos 20%, Hide 50%, Jump 45%, Listen 60%, Sneak 50%, Spot Hidden 40%. Number One also gets 20 points more of Cult Club and Psychology.

Spells: (magic for Number One only) Contact Nyarlathotep (Sand Bat Aspect), Enchant Item, Power Drain, Shrivelling, Summon Hunting Horror, Voorish Sign.

Here are several other points to keep in mind about the city:

- The investigators cannot read any of the Great Race documents in the city; even the nominal instructions on some of the machines are too alien to decipher.

- Artifacts designed for Great Race use are awkward for humans to hold or employ.

- Geology rolls show the buried city to be extremely old. Some parts have been covered by hundreds of feet of wind- and water-born deposition that has since turned to sandstone. Where these deposits have later subsided or fallen has left the way open to deeper levels of the cyclopean city.

- The city is solidly built of massive stone. Explosives are the only way to destroy structures. Explosives, however, are sure to draw flying polyps.

- Warding the city with the Eye of Light and Darkness stymies the opening of the Gate at the time of the solar total eclipse.

- Keepers should add encounters as desired with the flying polyps. Their numbers can be a function of how many lightning guns the investigators find, and of just how often they are willing to trust themselves to such devices. But remember that polyps are tough customers. Even one might be enough to destroy a whole group of unready investigators.

The Second Entrance

The nearest shelter is about 700 yards from the entrance which Huston (alias Carver) has opened. Behind this hillock is a good spot from which to watch the cultists and make plans.

If the investigators have already seen a flying polyp track, a successful Ideal roll points out that the polyps must have a separate way out. A patrol of the area locates a second cave about four miles distant. This one has no tire tracks leading to it, but around the opening in the sand are large, fresh tracks, each about six feet long. The investigators may have seen such prints already, during the Death Camp episode. A successful Cthulhu Mythos roll identifies the marks as made by flying polyps. This entrance is no doubt from where the earlier polyp emerged.

The wide cave is a vertical hole nearly fifty feet across. The air which blows outward from the obviously new entrance has a stale antiquity that raises the hackles of everyone present.

Inside the City

Nearby is a schematic diagram of points in the city pertaining to this adventure: the city is a continuous structure for dozens of miles. Later sections of this adventure are mostly keyed to the items on this map. Because of its utterly alien quality and the threat of the flying polyps, assess each investigator one point of Sanity loss for each day spent wandering below the surface; if they're locked up in single rooms or otherwise detained, ignore the Sanity point.

The City of the Great Race was not built underground, though many of the important thoroughfares were internal and not exposed to the sky. Its upper levels were destroyed, perhaps by the flying polyps and certainly by the passing eons. Gradually the dust and sand of the ages covered all. But the lower levels remain intact, despite collapses and infiltrating. When Huston failed to tunnel down directly to the most useful portion of the city, Nyarlathotep led Huston to an easier entrance nearby. "Nearby" is a relative term: Huston's current excavations are miles from the entrance Nyarlathotep revealed.

Great ramps inlaid with octagonal stones connect the buildings and structures of the city. These ramps are very wide. Bordering them, walls and fallen earth create corridors where there were none before. The ramps incline strangely, but of those across which the lights lead only two incline drastically.

Inside the buildings, heavy doors (each requiring STR 25 to open) lead to mazes of rooms. The rooms are empty of life, though strange and gigantic furniture, artifacts, and art testify to the previous inhabitants, ten-foot-high and -wide cylinders with elongated, mobile heads, two arms, and elaborate floral-like feeding organs on a fourth, symmetrically placed appendage.

Distances and sizes are more gigantic than anything the investigators have seen, except perhaps for R'lyeh itself. Curvilinear symbols are carved into most of the structures. At certain points rubble blocks the way. The rubble (as marked on the city schematic map) must be climbed over carefully. Hurried motion requires a successful Luck roll or 1D3 points of damage from shifting stone is done to the climber.

In this pervasive alien darkness, the silence has no end. Who knows what once happened here? Who knows what might be lurking here?

A Flying Polyp

The investigators might safely roll or stumble down the steep sandy sides of the hole to reach a gently sloping area about a hundred feet down, but it is impossible to climb back up the steep slope with only crumbling sand sides for support. If the investigators want to return to the surface this way, they need to fix ropes to some of the nearby stone blocks and lower themselves down. Once in the primordial rooms and halls, they'll need a compass to find their way toward Huston's entrance.

Refer to the section above, "Inside the City," for a general description. This is also a good time to read aloud some of Lovecraft's descriptions from parts VI and VII of "The Shadow Out of Time". The second entrance opens a part of the city in which no cultist has traveled. For the most part the way is clear and free of rubble. The dust on the floors is very thick, except for points where those disturbing six-foot-long tracks suddenly begin. Footsteps are muffled. The fine dust of eons clings to the clothes, hands, and faces of the investigators.

It is miles underground to the nearest string of lights put up by the cultists. When they do near the lights, the investigators also hear engine noise from one of the gasoline-powered generators which the cultists have installed. Keeping to the compass heading is relatively simple. There is one obstacle—an open trap door to the domain of the flying polyps.

The keeper's material in *Call of Cthulhu* includes an entire page of material concerning polyps. Keepers should review that data. Polyps use tentacle and wind attacks, may possess spells, ignore most physical attacks, and cost 1D3/1D20 SAN when encountered. They are terrifying, smart, malevolent, and very tough.

The Shaft into Darkness

The investigators come to a deep shaft about fifteen feet square which completely blocks their path. Lights show no apparent bottom to the shaft. There is no way around it now, although broken ramps and collapsed corridors once offered many ways. This chasm is square and regular along its sides, plainly created for a purpose.

On the investigators' side of the shaft is a great shallow box, approximately the size of the shaft's mouth. A few min-

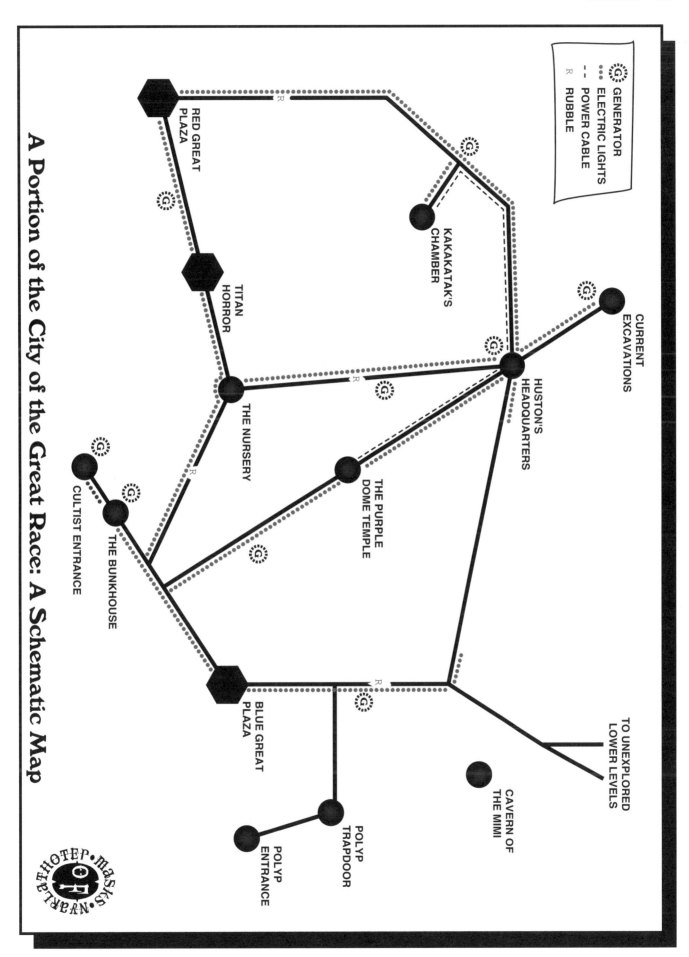

A Portion of the City of the Great Race: A Schematic Map

utes of inspection of the massive hinges along the shaft side and the elaborate alien latches along its far side make it plain that the thick box is actually a lockable lid to be swung over the chasm and latched, sealing the shaft and making a bridge. A combined STR of 60 is needed to push up and swing over the lid.

The thunder of dropping the lid into place has a 75% chance of drawing a flying polyp up from the fathomless depths. Unless the door is latched shut, the polyp blasts right through it, knocking the lid back to the open position, and launching an attack that will probably kill all the investigators. Latching the heavy lid takes 1D3 minutes, for the alien latches are heavy, bulky, and conceived for other than human hands and minds. The polyp arrives in 1D20 minutes. If the latches hold, the investigators hear hideous bashes and sucking noises emanating from under a scant few inches of metal.

Is there another shaft nearby. Wise investigators do not wait to find out.

AN OPTION

If the keeper wishes, when the investigators near the chasm and the hinged lid, there is a 15% chance that a polyp is already there. This chance raises 5 percentiles each time that the players make clear to the keeper that they haven't the slightest idea of what to do! Loud noises in the area up the initial chance, as does very bright light (such as from flashbulbs or flashlights used to illuminate the bottomless shaft).

Alternately the investigators may only hear the strange whistling sound that characterizes a polyp. They continue to hear it in the immediate area of the chasm. The sounds seem far in the distance, and far below them. As they move away, then it is closer.

FIVE AVERAGE FLYING POLYPS

	One	Two	Three	Four	Five
STR	48	51	47	47	43
CON	24	25	27	22	30
SIZ	52	51	55	48	56
INT	11	14	12	10	15
POW	15	17	16	12	19
DEX	13	14	12	14	13
HP	38	38	41	35	43

MOV 8/12 flying

Damage Bonus*: +2D6.

* use only in connection with the Windblast attack, which see.

Weapons: 2D6 Tentacles 85%, damage 1D10 each tentacle
Windblast** 70%, Special Damage, lower by 1D6 per 20 yards of distance.

** The polyp's wind attack is too complex to be summarized. See the flying polyp write-up in the creatures section of the rulesbook.

Armor: 4 points, plus invisibility, plus their alien nature allow polyps to always take only minimum damage from physical weapons. Enchanted weapons, and forces such as heat and electricity do normal damage.

Spells: these five have no spells. The keeper may generate spellcasters with reference to the rulesbook.

Skills: nothing that a human can understand.

Sanity Loss: 1D3/1D20 SAN.

BEYOND THE BOTTOMLESS SHAFT

Having passed over the yawning opening to the black basalt cities of these malevolent things, the investigators noticeably descend for most of a mile. A distant light glimmers—a single light bulb. As they get closer, they hear the distant sound of a gasoline engine. This is another electrical generator at work, sustaining part of the dozens of miles of electric lights which the cultists have installed.

When the investigators reach the line of electrical lights, they may ignore it to wander about in the Stygian darkness. Let them. If their movement becomes aimless, bring them up against the bottomless shaft and the hinged door intended to defend against the flying polyps. That experience should discourage further wanderings. Once the investigators follow the electrical light lines this maze of a city becomes understandable.

Lines of Light

Use this section as a guide and summary for all of the wired lines of communication between the important points of the buried city.

The electric power lines have grown so long that Huston assigns two cultists to their upkeep. A number of independent generators feed the lines. Those generators are marked on the city map by small circles containing the letter G.

Besides the vastness, the cool stone, and the unfathomable purposes of the city, the investigators notice that many human feet have passed to and fro where the lights are strung, and that rarely if ever do the prints stray from the islands of light to enter the unending blackness. Four types of encounters regularly occur on these routes. The investigators can almost always avoid an encounter by ducking into the blackness.

LINE WALKER: every twelve hours a cultist inspects the lighting in the city. He or she carries a flashlight and wears a miner's hat with a carbide lamp. Ordinarily the job is to replace burnt-out bulbs and refill the tanks of the electrical generators. Each day the next one of the seven generators is stopped for servicing and adjustment. These are otherwise kept running constantly. The line walker is not a trained fighter. He or she does have good knowledge of the portions of the city along the route.

The line walker also carries an unusual weapon, the lightning gun, an artifact of the Great Race. The cult's ready employment of this weapon, as well as discretion in their underground activities, has left them free of flying polyp interference.

WORK PARTY: a gang of ten zombified workers and two cultists passes daily between the headquarters site and the work site, where Huston has ordered excavations to attempt to locate certain Great Race devices. The workers plod along dully, and cannot be roused or made curious, though they respond to short, firmly voiced instructions. The unarmed cultists carry wire whips with which they mete out penalties.

RUBBLE: at four points on the routes, the map indicates major rubble. These areas are difficult and somewhat dangerous to pass over. Investigators who receive failed Climb

rolls sustain 1D3 points of damage from falls, sprains, bruises, etc. People falling and taking injury also may make noise: each fall has a 5% chance to attract one flying polyp.

ELECTRICAL GENERATORS: nearby each generator are a few boxes of parts and tools. Further away are stacks of five-gallon gasoline tins. Most of the tins are full. In the dead air, hints of gasoline fumes can be detected for up to half a mile.

Cavern of the Mimis

The investigators can get to this spot only if they have had a previous encounter with a Mimi.

The cavern is about fifty feet in diameter and is sealed. It has no exits. The walls and ceiling glow softly. The only way in or out is by the grace of a Mimi, or by pick, shovel, and dynamite. The fifteen Mimis in the cavern watch the investigators intently. They wait until the investigators speak, then a spokesman replies by writing on the floor or wall.

They wish the investigators to kill the Living Winds (by which they mean the flying polyps). Mimis are susceptible to wind. They are uninterested in cultists, members of the Great Race, or even Nyarlathotep. They offer no information or reward.

If the investigators agree, a Mimi walks to a wall, splits it with his finger, and leads them (with the same disorientation and coloring of objects as occurred when the Mimi took the investigators to this cavern) to the open shaft and hinged

---

The Lightning Gun: Model B

A successful Idea roll establishes that this device is a weapon. There is no way, other than experimentation, to determine which way the tubular construction fires. Guessing wrong and being careless, an investigator takes 8D6 damage.

As the Great Race material in the rulesbook notes, there are many versions of the lightning gun. The following version is used throughout this adventure.

About the size of a submachine gun, the weapon has a base range of 100 yards and has 1D20+3 charges in it. Charges are integral to the weapon, and not like ammunition for a human gun. There is no way to recharge this model of lightning gun, though there is no reason to tell the players that. Every cultist who carries one knows that his or her lightning gun may not work the next time it is fired.

It takes two hands to fire a lightning gun, though the procedure is simple once understand. It can fire one lightning bolt per round, and possesses 14 hit points. Base chance to use it is 35%. Like a shotgun, the damage it does depends upon range: damage 8D6/4D6/1D6 at 50/100/200 yards respectively. The lightning gun does not impale.

The keeper should individually number the lightning guns occurring in this adventure, and roll up the actual number of shots each contains.

---

hatch near the cultists' entrance. After arriving, a polyp floats up through the open door in 1D10+1 minutes. The investigators are on their own: they can try to close the enormous hinged cover but, unless they have lightning guns, fleeing is their best alternative. The Mimis make no effort to stop them if they do, but may decide on vengeance if the investigators stay very long below ground, stalking and murdering them at random.

If the investigators refuse the request, the Mimis offer food and drink. Those who accept turn into Mimis in 1D3 hours. The process is irreversible. Those who refuse food and drink are offered sex (in particular, Mimi females are less elongate than the males, and reputably have nice bosoms). Those who accept turn into Mimis in 1D3 hours; this process is also irreversible. Those who become Mimis acquire such different motivations that they are out of the campaign. Collect their investigator sheets. David Dodge can strongly warn against such cooperation, as does a successful Occult roll.

The Mimis abandon those who refuse both their inducements. They simply split open cracks in the walls with their fingers, step through, and close the cracks behind them, trapping the investigators in an sealed chamber of solid rock. But investigators who keep their heads find a section of wall which sounds hollow. It takes 3D20 man-hours to chip through the wall with other rocks as tools—1D20 man hours to break through with steel tools that the investigators may have been carrying.

After a day of stumbling around in the dark (a compass will at least lead them west), the group comes across the easternmost line of electric lights somewhere near the rubble area.

If the investigators challenge the Mimis, these magical creatures easily dodge physical attacks. The Mimis' high personal POWs deflect most spells. These Dreamtime horrors subdue the investigators, and then eat the outer flesh from the face of whoever instigated the investigator attack. The wounds are not life-threatening, but the gnawed investigator feels horrible pain, loses 1D20+4 Sanity points, and his or her APP drops to 01. Thereafter he or she is a figure of horror who must wear a full-face mask or bandages in polite company. Witnesses to this gruesome sight lose 1/1D8 SAN.

SAMPLE MIMI

STR 50	CON n/a	SIZ 19	POW 30
DEX 20	Move 20		HP n/a

Damage Bonus: +3D6.

Weapon: Enchanted Spear 100%, damage special

Armor: invulnerable to physical weapons

Mimis fear strong winds such as created by flying polyps, for strong winds snap their scrawny necks. When a Mimi spear hits, it makes a POW against POW attack on the Resistance Table (use the Mimi's POW for the attacking factor). If the attack succeeds, the target dies immediately. If it fails, the victim is comatose for 1D6 months. Male or female, all Mimis have identical statistics, though the females are in appearance much more human than the elongated males.

The Great Plazas

As shown on the schematic map, two great plazas exist. Two of four self-powered areas shown on the map, these plazas are enormous octagonal halls, with featureless walls and ceilings, but with floors that radiate light. The floor of the eastern plaza is a soft, glowing blue; the floor of the western plaza is a soft, glowing red. Their purposes are unknown. Each space is nearly half a mile across. Since these areas are self-illuminated, the cultists have not strung lights across the floors.

The Purple Dome Temple

This marvel is 2000 feet across and is mostly intact even after a hundred million years. It is a perfect hemisphere, entered by archways equally spaced around it. Within, at the bottom of the hemisphere is a gray stone floor. In the center of the floor is a second hemisphere, pulsating and glowing with a strong purple light, five hundred feet in diameter. Occasionally, it seems to move in a way which makes it seem alive.

The function of the purple hemisphere is obscure. Huston believes it to be a profound energy source tapping alien dimensions, and plans to install a stepped transformer to try to tap its energies.

At the archway through which the investigators first enter, sand has entered the dome. Sticking out of the sand is a gnawed-on human femur and a portion of a human skull.

On one side of the smaller hemisphere is a three-foot-high stone block which plainly has been dragged in recently from outside the building. Dark stains mar its surface and cover the floor nearby. Ashes and charcoal mark the site of a fire which was lit on the floor.

Behind the sacrificial stone is a 25-foot-high statue of Nyarlathotep in his black, bat-winged aspect. Flanking him are lesser statues of other gods, including Cthulhu, Azathoth, Yog-Sothoth the Gate, Zoth-Ommog, Cthugha, and Shub-Niggurath. As a whole, the assemblage is sufficiently horrible to demand a loss of 1/1D10 Sanity points.

Each statue is a conductor and storehouse of life-force. When a living being touches one of the statues, he or she loses 1D3-1 POW, and then half of his or her current magic points. Second and later touches drain only magic points. A Resistance Table roll of POW vs. POW is possible; each statue has a nominal POW of 1D20+10. The POW drained is stored in the statue. As the Messenger, protocol demands that Nyarlathotep be touched first. That statue alone now contains nearly 500 magic points.

All the statues are made of stone. Each weighs well over a ton. Huston cannot use the magic points stored in them when he wants, unlike M'Weru's stores. These points are dedicated to opening the Gate. Huston must conduct his ritual here, and offer up the magic points at the proper moment during the total solar eclipse.

If Huston is killed or captured some time before the Gate ritual occur, an acolyte is trained in his stead. Only if the cult is all or mostly destroyed here, and its entrances obliterated, perhaps with the aid of the Mimis by stirring up the flying

THE MIMI BECKONS

polyps, can the Australian location be silenced when the sky begins to open.

THE THREE GUARDIANS

Behind the statue of Nyarlathotep are three large bat-things. They are black in color, shaped like toad-bats, and equipped with loose, curiously rumpled wings and eyeless and mouth-less heads. These are the large bird-like things that the investigators noticed while riding the railroad to Cuncudgerie, and that were mentioned in MacWhirr's diary.

They are living things, not statues. During ceremonies, they ensure that Nyarlathotep receives the greatest share of the sacrifices.

When not involved in rituals, they guard the temple. They begin to stir when anyone enters. As a successful Cthulhu Mythos, Occult, or Psychology roll suggests, their increasing malevolence can be placated by any servile praise of Nyarlathotep, such as Hail Nyarlathotep! or Nyarlathotep Rules! and so on. A successful Cthulhu Mythos roll tells the investigators what to say, but the player has to come up with the idea of saying something. If intruders leave the temple quickly, the guardians gradually return to sleep and do not pursue.

GUARDIANS OF SAND BAT

	One	Two	Three
STR	33	35	38
CON	44	36	40
SIZ	24	24	24
INT	3	4	2
POW	10	12	14
DEX	12	8	10
HP	34	30	32

MOV 6/12 flying (can carry a person with a SIZ of 1/4 or less the monsters STR).

Damage Bonus: +3D6.

Weapons: Grapple 40%, damage special
Drain 100%, damage 1D3 + attribute drain

These agents of evil are stupid, but persistent. Once they've succeeded in grappling a victim, they'll either press their target against the Nyarlathotep statue to diminish his magic points or wrap him in their huge, shaggy wings and drain him themselves.

In the Drain attack, the wings extrude countless small needle-like projections, which enter the body of the victim and systematically drain him or her of body fluid, costing 1D3 hit points per round plus lowering the victim's currently highest characteristic (STR, CON, etc.) by 1 point per round.

If the investigators do not praise Nyarlathotep, but stay long enough that the guardians wake and move, then the guardians attempt to capture one investigator each, and press him or her against Nyarlathotep's statue until each victim dies. If other investigators linger, then the guardians grab new victims. There is room for three guardians with three victims around the statue. The guardians will not pursue the investigators beyond the walls of the temple.

The guardians are gifts from Nyarlathotep to a prized worshiper. They have been useful in raiding Koori camps for sacrifices. For some time Huston has tried using them for aerial surveillance, with indifferent results—the things are too stupid to be able to understand the significance of much of what they see. Huston, always tinkering, has decided to see if they could carry small cultists aloft. If the keeper likes, the investigators could witness that test while at Jeremy Grogan's camp.

CULT RITUALS

The purple dome temple is the hot-spot for cult activities. These rituals feature weekly and quarterly celebrations of the dark powers.

In the weekly rituals, the cultists build a small fire on the floor of the temple near the altar (the sacrificial stone). As they chant and circle around the fire, thousands of bats wheel overhead. No more than 1D3 victims will be sacrificed, each by being run through a gauntlet of naked cultists, each of whom is armed with the cult club and a flail. Each flail drips with a sticky brown goo which has been fresh brewed.

The goo is POT 17, matched against the CON of the target on the Resistance Table. Its topical application through cuts and welts causes the victim to begin to bloat and black-en almost immediately. Death occurs in 1D4 days. Anti-rabies serum has a 50% chance to save the victim. The victim usually survives the gauntlet of flails, and is then bound to the statue of Nyarlathotep. There he or she waits, being drained of magic points while writhing in increasing torment from the rabies-like potion.

The weekly ceremony usually is presided over by an acolyte, though occasionally Huston attends the show. Attendance is 1D10+20 cultists. Sanity cost for viewing the ceremony is 0/1D3 SAN.

QUARTERLY RITUALS

In the quarterly rituals, Sand Bat is invoked and appears. Huston conducts this ceremony in utter darkness, to honor this aspect of Nyarlathotep. However, the Bat's psychic force, stimulated by the ritual torments and chanting cultists, causes all those viewing the ritual to be able to see clearly, despite the total darkness. This weird sensation, of vision which is not sight, costs each investigator 1/1D6 SAN.

Up to 1D10+9 men are sacrificed to the statues, and at least one victim is bound to each statue. The gauntlet must be run, as per the weekly ceremony. In addition, a matching number of female victims are despicably assaulted first by the Guardians and then by the cultists. Children born of such unions prove to be monstrous hybrids, dangerous even to Huston. Those still alive have been locked away in the Nursery, a point on the schematic map. Such horrific experiences drive mad most of the female victims. In many cases, the mother does not survive the difficult birth. Sanity cost for viewing this ceremony is 1D3/2D6 SAN.

The Nursery

In a wide level area, the electric lights encircle a dark pit perhaps sixty feet deep and two hundred feet wide. There is no railing at the edge. From the hole come nauseating and mind-numbing smells and terrible moans, cries, and growls. One cry is a human baby's. Without using additional light, though, nothing but ripples and vague movements can be seen at the bottom of the hole. Sanity cost to come near this pit is 0/1D2.

The price goes up if an investigator shines a flashlight. He or she then sees aberrant, appendaged, blasphemous, bulbous, depraved, festering, hideous, and Sanity-shaking forms sprawl, hop, and ooze across the floor, far below. Most often the shapes resemble the purple temple's guardians, who are themselves simulacra of Nyarlathotep. Many of the god's foul forms are present in miniature.

The keeper should go into as much detail as the investigators wish, but make a Sanity-point charge for each new monstrosity they choose to study. The price of the pit as a whole is 1D4/1D10+1 SAN; the price for individual study of each new monster is 1/1D4 SAN. Sixty-six monsters are in the pit, so the pit-as-a-whole represents a bargain.

If a flashlight or other additional light source is used, the noise in the pit becomes deafening. The detainees think they are about to be fed.

Huston protects the failed results of his breeding program by stashing them here. These horrors are the sacred progeny of beings from beyond space and time.

A Titan Horror

At first the investigators may think that this is another great plaza, less well-lit than the others. But as they approach it, they can see that it is only a huge stone ring atop a gigantic organism, impressing the center of it into a very slight dome. The rest of the creature's body must be under the city—it is impossible to tell its vast extent. Everyone looking at the vastness of this creature, with its throbbing veins and flaccid swellings, loses 1/1D20 SAN. The creature is inert. The investigators cannot discommode it, nor does it react to them.

Huston's HQ

As marked on the map, the lines of lights intersect. Near that intersection is a new wood-frame building. This is Huston's headquarters. From the outside, lights are visible on each of the three floors.

THE GROUND LEVEL

Here is stocked mining equipment, including arc lights, shovels, picks, ropes, lumber, block and tackle gear, pumps,

Father of All Bats

In this form Nyarlathotep somewhat resembles a gigantic bat. Its only facial feature is a single three-lobed burning eye. Thin, writhing tentacles trail beneath its tattered wings as it soars through the sky, also trailing out a smoky vapor of frothing protoplasmic bubbles. This writhing, living spoor dissipates as the horror flies on, but lasts for at least a minute. The Father of All Bats aspect of Nyarlathotep is only semi-material, and can fly through solid objects at need, though it can also manipulate material objects.

This version of Nyarlathotep is also called the Fly-the-Light or Haunter of the Dark and is well-known to the Fungi from Yuggoth. It can endure extremely dim light, such as starshine, but not stronger light. Clearly it is better suited to deep space than to the surface of the Earth. Brightness from arc lights or welding torches damage the horror— a strong flashlight beam kept trained on the beast does 1D6 points of damage, if it would stand still for the treatment. Even a large candle held aloft does a point of damage for each round the Bat is within fifty feet of the flame. A torch costs it 1D6 hit points, car headlights or street lamps 3D6 hit points, and so forth, based on the keeper's perception of the intensity of the light source. Full daylight costs it 10D6 hit points per round (the light of the full moon does 2D6). Steady light for the appropriate number of rounds can dissolve the horror, causing it to disintegrate into nothingness until the next summoning. Brief, powerful flashes of light such as lightning or flashbulbs do it no harm, though it will growl its displeasure.

Its psychic force is such that ordinary humans who come near it receive a monstrous ability to see in the dark—the cursed sight-which-is-not-sight. This ability, though sometimes useful, costs all sane humans 1/1D6 SAN, as it forces them into alien perceptions of the universe. Even blind humans have vision in this way, for the ability is unrelated to the optic nerves.

In an attack, Father of All Bats might swoop low and make a grab with one or more of its tendrils. Each target within its 50-foot wingspan can be attacked by one tendril. Anyone hit receives a fearful electrical shock and burn, taking 4D6 damage (ignore potential armor or electrical grounding).

If the victim survives, he loses 1D3 points from his highest characteristic (STR, CON, and so on) from each shock, as well as losing hit points. Anyone caught in the semi-living trail of alien froth Sand Bat leaves behind while flying loses 1D4-1 hit points for each round of exposure (without other reason, charge for only one round).

SAND BAT, Father of All Bats, Avatar of Nyarlathotep

STR 70	CON 45	SIZ 60	INT 86	POW 100
DEX 19	MOV 30 (fly)			HP 53

Damage Bonus: +7D6.

Weapons: Tendrils 60%, damage 4D6 electrical shock and burn
Protoplasmic Trail 100%, damage 1D4-1

Armor: 5-point skin. Impaling attacks do no extra damage. Attacks using heat, solids, electricity, or atomic radiation do no damage, unless a stream of light accompanies them; a lightning gun would affect Sand Bat.

Sanity Loss: 1D10/D100 SAN.

gasoline drums (empty and left unstopped, to dissipate the fumes), spare electrical generators, wheelbarrows, drills, and several heavy carts for carrying equipment.

If a systematic search is made, the investigators find three lightning guns in a crate. As per earlier comments, the keeper should individually number each gun and roll 1D20+3 for each to learn the number of charges that it contains, then mark off the charges as the gun is used. Remember, when the lightning gun has no charges, it is useless thereafter except as a 14-hit-point club. Lightning guns were discussed in the "Lines of Light" section, above.

There is a 50% chance that ten zombified miners are sleeping in this area. Kidnapped long ago for another of Huston's endless schemes, they are victims of a mind-control device he has learned to operate, and now live as zombies. They are the underlings in the work party mentioned in "Lines of Light."

Statistics for the two cultist overseers occur nearby. The miners respond to whomever gives an order, and they do as the order instructs them. In case of a logical conflict, the miners respond to that order given by the person with the higher personal Power. The miners are ineffective with ranged weapons but their hand-to-hand capabilities are considerable.

The miners make no reaction to the investigators. If they have adequately spied out the situation, the investigators can attack the two cultists and casily control the entire squad.

DYNAMITE AND GASOLINE: In a small locker not far away, a successful Locksmith roll undoes the padlock, and the investigators find 48 sticks of dynamite, with fuses, blasting caps, and a manufacturer's manual. Beside the locker are piled full drums of gasoline, as many as the keeper wishes.

ALAN (white), Cultist Thug

STR 12	CON 10	SIZ 10	INT 08	POW 10
DEX 13	APP 08	EDU 01	SAN 0	HP 10

Damage Bonus: +0.

Weapons: Fist/Punch 55%, damage 1D3
Grapple 40%, damage special
Cult Club 20%, damage 1D10

Skills: Climb 40%, Cthulhu Mythos 14%, Hide 50%, Jump 45%, Listen 60%, Sneak 50%, Spot Hidden 40%.

ZOMBIFIED MINERS

	One	Two	Three	Four	Five
STR	12	15	14	14	17
CON	14	12	13	14	15
SIZ	13	10	11	12	13
INT	05	04	05	06	04
POW	03	03	03	03	03
DEX	07	07	07	07	07
HP	14	11	12	13	14

Damage Bonus: +1D4.
Fist/Punch 60%, damage 1D3+1D4
Grapple 40%, damage special
The miners grapple only to get a purchase in order to choke. Their grip causes 1D3+1D4 damage per round. The grip may be broken by STR vs. STR on the Resistance Table in any round.

Armor: the miners do not feel pain or shock.

Skills: Follow Orders 95%.

THOMAS (white), Cultist Thug

STR 14	CON 12	SIZ 10	INT 08	POW 13
DEX 12	APP 09	EDU 04	SAN 0	HP 11

Damage Bonus: +0.

Weapons: Fist/Punch 65%, damage 1D3
Grapple 50%, damage special
Whip 65%, damage 1D3
Cult Club 25%, damage 1D10

Skills: Climb 40%, Cthulhu Mythos 14%, Hide 50%, Jump 45%, Listen 60%, Sneak 50%, Spot Hidden 40%.

MORE ZOMBIFIED MINERS

	Six	Seven	Eight	Nine	Ten
STR	16	17	17	18	18
CON	16	18	17	16	18
SIZ	18	16	17	16	18
INT	05	04	05	06	04
POW	03	03	03	03	03
DEX	07	07	07	07	07
HP	17	17	17	16	18

Damage Bonus: +1D6.
Fist/Punch 65%, damage 1D3+1D6
Grapple 60%, damage special
The miners grapple only to get a purchase to choke. Their grip causes 1D3+1D6 damage per round. The grip may be broken by STR vs. STR on the Resistance Table in any round.

Armor: the miners do not feel pain or shock.

Skills: Follow Orders 95%.

THE MIDDLE FLOOR

The large ascending ramp leads to the two floors above. The middle floor of the three holds nothing but seven large cubical cages made of dirty, scaled steel rails that have been carefully welded together. The locks of these latticework cages are magnetic, opened by a small rectangular device which Huston keeps in his pocket. The resistance factor of the locks is 75, 85 for the bars. Strong electric charges can bollix the locks, but may also be conducted to the people locked inside.

The cages hold many prisoners, many of them Kooris. They set up a great moaning when the investigators enter. If he is upstairs, this uproar has a 25% chance of drawing Huston's attention. Re-roll the chance every fifteen minutes, or if the investigators are unable to decide how to quiet these people. All captured investigators are in this room.

One cage contains only pregnant women, victims of the quarterly breeding ceremonies. A 10% chance exists that one is giving birth: assuming that the investigators stay around, the sight of the green, wart-covered reptilian thing which she bears costs each investigator 1/1D4 Sanity points.

Each cage is foul-smelling because of closeness and lack of sanitary facilities. Buckets on the outside of each cage hold yams and other raw roots, and stale water and a dipper.

THE TOP FLOOR

Unless a quarterly cult ritual is taking place, which he always attends, Huston has a 75% chance to be here.

This large room is informally divided into sections for liv-

HUSTON'S HEADQUARTERS

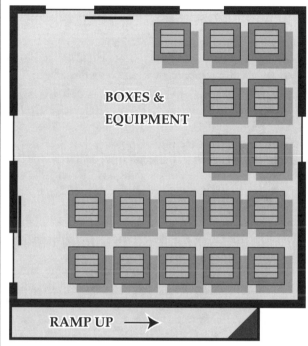

BOXES & EQUIPMENT

RAMP UP ➔

Ground Floor

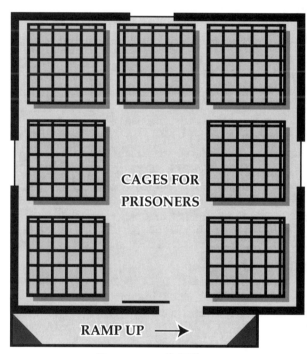

CAGES FOR PRISONERS

RAMP UP ➔

Second Floor

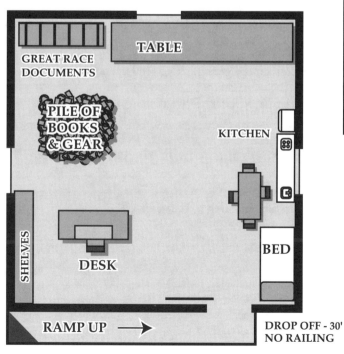

GREAT RACE DOCUMENTS

TABLE

PILE OF BOOKS & GEAR

KITCHEN

SHELVES

DESK

BED

RAMP UP ➔

DROP OFF - 30'
NO RAILING

Third Floor

ing, scientific experiment, and relaxed study. From one wall extends a large, firm bed. Not far away is a primitive electric kitchen. There are several long tables, and assorted decks and shelves. Hundreds of Great Race document cases are heaped against another wall. The cases mostly hold plans and formulae. The records are too alien for investigators to decipher.

The desk faces the doorway, which is closed only by heavy drapery. Huston is a moderate-sized graying man, neat in his khaki bush gear, pale from living underground. If Huston is here, his visitors surprise him. He graciously rises from his desk to greet them, his curiosity evident, but also a welcoming expression on his face. He asks after their health and offers them tea or coffee, then politely inquires for news of the outside world. After some time, he turns to the reason for their visit. He apologizes that he is busily engaged on vital researches—he would be pleased to chat away the day.

Underneath some papers on his desk a successful Spot Hidden notices a bulge about the right size for a .45 revolver. A lightning gun glints in plain sight on the desk, not far from Huston's right hand. Also on the desk is a copperish bowl etched with Mythos runes—this bowl is made of "copper from above", useful for the spell Send Dreams.

ROBERT HUSTON

Though normal-acting, a successful Psychology roll establishes that Huston is insane, He thinks of himself as a realist, but he is a megalomaniac who cannot resist trumpeting how he intends to conquer the world. He is a good psychologist yet has little sympathy for individuals, and inwardly he has always loathed the species' petty problems. He flatters himself that his scientific mind and his Jungian background meld together symbolic and physical relationships in a way which he alone is qualified to understand.

To Huston, the gods of madness are both the ultimate metaphor and the final reality. To protect his self-image and his genuinely powerful relation with Nyarlathotep, Huston kills without compunction. He will kill all the investigators if he can, though first he'll talk them to death with his theories concerning humanity, the unconscious, the Great Bank of Memory, the illogical link between racial memory and the return of the great old ones, etc.

In brief, Huston longs for the hour when the Gate can be opened, and a host of extra-dimensional horrors are returned to Earth. Huston feels safe about this prospect because he imagines that his own intelligence, dedication, and insight are without peer upon the Earth.

THE MIND CONTROLLER: A metal helmet with three protruding wires is in a corner, looking like a dunce cap. At the end of the wires are small triangular pads which are placed on the head of a victim, touching particular areas of the scalp. With a successful INT vs. INT roll on the Resistance Table, the operator activates the device and puts mental blocks in the mind of the target.

A target loses 1D6 Sanity points each time he or she is subjected to the controller. If the Resistance Table roll fails, the procedure does not work. Another attempt can be made the next day, when the mind of the target is sufficiently calmed. This Great Race device originally blocked memories of their possession from humans brought mentally up-time to the era of the Great Race.

With the device, Huston wipes out the long-term memories of captives, and implants instructions which are very difficult to resist. An investigator could figure how to use the device in a few hours, but could not determine its function and intent without experimenting with it.

Kakakatak, if the investigators mention it to him, can show how to reverse the zombification caused by this device.

A HAND-WRITTEN MANUSCRIPT: In a desk drawer are the six hundred neat sheets of manuscript, titled *Gods of Reality*. Huston has been writing this journal and extended essay since he entered the buried city.

It begins, "Madness is the mark of gods, the response to the whisper of ancient secrets, and the unseen hand that turns the world in its disordered course. With it, I have peered beyond mere dream and pattern, beyond childhood impetuosity and adult grief, beyond the analysis of which other men are capable. Accepting madness, I accept the gods and rule well with their gifts thereby."

The manuscript takes four hours to read, and conveys enough about human perception and the nature of reality to cost 1D3/1D8 Sanity points. The universe, Huston establishes, is so relative that no sane human can imagine it. In self-defense, humans teach themselves not to see evidence of this, but some truths seep into consciousness through what we understand as dreams.

The document mentions Gray Dragon Island and the Mountain of the Black Wind. It describes in detail what Huston must do on Jan. 14, 1926, at particular moments of Greenwich time, and relates the function of the storage statues in the purple temple. It also tells about the mind controller and how it works, about lightning guns and how they can discourage or sometimes kill random flying polyps, and how by Nyarlathotep's grace Huston was able to pull a Yithian (Kakakatak) forward through time.

Dr. ROBERT HUSTON (white), age 56, Cultist, Sorcerer, and Priest of Nyarlathotep

STR 10	CON 15	SIZ 12	INT 18	POW 35
DEX 13	APP 14	EDU 18	SAN 0	HP 14

Damage Bonus: +0.

Weapons: Fist/Punch 30%, damage 1D3
.45 Revolver 55%, damage 1D10+2
Lightning Gun 40%, damage 8D6/4D6/1D6
Cult Club 25%, damage 1D10

Spells: Call Yog-Sothoth, Contact Cthulhu, Contact Flying Polyp, Contact Nyarlathotep, Dominate, Mindblast, Send Dreams, Summon Haunting Horror, Time Trap.

Skills: Anthropology 40%, Archaeology 25%, Astronomy 15%, Bargain 30%, Chemistry 15%, Cthulhu Mythos 50%, Drive Automobile 30%, Electrical Repair 50%, Fast Talk 40%, First Aid 35%, Geology 25%, Kariera 15%, Library Use 60%, Listen 30%, Mechanical Repair 40%, Medicine 25%, Pidgin English 45%, Psychoanalysis 35%, Psychology 50%, Read Great Race 40%, Sneak 30%, Spot Hidden 50%.

Current Excavations

The miners work here when not resting at Huston's headquarters. If the miners are working, Huston is here 10% of the time. The zombified crew is opening a tunnel through a cliff of sand and cyclopean rubble. Their mindlessly patient excavations have nearly cleared the way. With a flashlight and a successful Spot Hidden, those risking the tunnel's creaking shoring see a head-sized hole to the other side, and through it glimpse a vast laboratory filled with strange artifacts. This hall is dust-covered and somewhat disturbed, but the things in it seem mostly to be intact.

Kakakatak's Chamber

A spur line from the northwestern chain of lights leads into three gray stone-lined rooms. Each is decorated with a few indecipherable Yithian symbols and described below.

THE FIRST ROOM

Through halls and long-empty rooms the straggling string of electric lights beckons into a room which is thoroughly lit. It is about twenty feet square. In it the investigators find a jumble of crates and parts. If they have been looking for spare parts, this is the place! A successful Electrical Repair roll shows that much of the gear is either of very advanced earthly manufacture, or of alien design and construction. Much is of no known commercial design, and bears no manufacturer's strike-mark. Some of the gear has been scrounged from the buried city. Some parts were made in Germany or Britain, and imported here at impressive cost. Here and there can be recognized transformers and power supplies, junctions and fuse boxes, and unorthodox vacuum tubes, but much more is inexplicable. The logic of the constructs would take weeks to work out. Investigator experts can only shrug their shoulders.

THE SECOND ROOM

The first room opens upon a second area forty feet across. In it stands an enormous and fashionably black control board covered with knobs, dials, gauges, handles, displays, and impressive sets of relays and junctions, and flanked by a few monitor lights and gauges. (Keepers who want to equip the place with spark gaps and cloud chambers meet no opposition, but they should be able to explain and rationalize whatever it is that they add.) One portion of the control board is open: conduits and connections simply dangle from the open panel. Plainly, a portion of the device is not in place.

At one point the long control panel is interrupted by a comfortable leather daybed (the sort of couch associated with Freudian analysts) built into it. An elaborate chromium headset and a series of hand-held controls connected to the control board and resting on the couch suggest that the couch's purpose is central to the device.

Nearby is an operating table equipped with hand, foot, and body restraints. A version of the same chromium headset rests there, and cables lead into the control board at a point close to that of the first headset.

This room has no meaning within the confines of this adventure. The keeper may create a use for it, let the players evolve one, or be content that it remains a passing mystery.

KAKAKATAK'S ROOM

An archway opens into the third room, one dimly lit, circular, and about fifty feet across. It is mostly empty. A long, high bench holds many alien artifacts and instruments. A successful Know roll identifies one large section as probably the missing panel from the control board in the Second Room, the room just visited.

Across the doorway to this room (in fact, through the walls, floor, and ceiling as well) is an invisible electrical field. Sensor holes can be seen on either side of the arch. The field does 3D10 damage. A human could crawl under the bottom sensor, but it's a tight squeeze requiring a successful DEX x4 roll to pass safely.

The force field can be turned off by throwing the knife switches in the fuse box on the right side of the doorway. Removing and hiding the huge cylindrical fuses would prolong the situation. Its cover is locked and the combination lock can be opened either by cutting the prongs of the lock, or by a successful Locksmith roll. Turning off the generator for this part of the city—it is not far away—is the simplest thing to do, but doing so draws immediate attention.

A successful Electrical Repair bypasses and isolates the fuse box without turning off the generator. A failed Electrical Repair sends a charge of 1D10+4 hit points through the unlucky electrician.

TIME TRAP, a new spell

Costs 100 magic points, 1D6 points of Power, and 1D8 Sanity points to cast. The ritual involves hours of uninterrupted meditation and a large quantity of human blood. To cast the spell, the caster must be able to visualize the target in its normal setting. For creatures of the past or future, this requires that the caster have access to a device that sees into the future or the past.

The spell is one-way. The trapped creature cannot be returned to its own time. The caster cannot use the spell to move himself or herself up or down the timestream. Per casting, only one creature is trapped.

When the spell is finished, match caster POW vs. target POW on the Resistance Table. If the roll succeeds, the snared creature appears anywhere within five miles of the caster, always on the surface of the earth and always in a location which does not harm the target. At that point the target is free and functions normally, though it is trapped in a new time. A creature requiring alien atmosphere or other absent conditions may well die before it can be recovered.

The spell only works through time, not through dimensions other than time. If the thing trapped may be angered at its condition, the caster should be suitably wary.

KAKAKATAK

In the shadows just to the left of the doorway rests a dark, motionless shape—Kakakatak, member of the Great Race. If someone steps into the force field, the lights in Kakakatak's chamber snap on, and the great intelligence wakes. The cost for seeing Kakakatak is 0/1D6 Sanity points.

If the investigators start shooting, Kakakatak protects himself as best he can.

When Kakakatak wakes, one of his claws picks up a blocky metal device, allowing it to communicate telepathically with mammalian minds (the investigators). Kakakatak picks the largest investigator first—if that one proves unsuitable, it'll keep trying, in order of lessening SIZ. The chosen investigator clearly feels the telepathic intrusion—a weird thrust at the edge of his or her mind.

KAKAKAKATAK

The investigator can try to resist the Yithian's magic points with his own on the Resistance Table. Failure means that investigator cannot block future telepathic contact from Kakakatak. If the target does not resist, or his or her attempt fails, the investigator loses 1 magic point and 1 Sanity point because of the intrusion. This happens when the dialogue ends for a while. State the communication in English.

Kakakatak's first message requests that the imprisoning force field be turned off. He provides succinct instructions for opening the fuse box.

Huston has brought Kakakatak out of the eons to force his participation on the mind controller and other projects. Already knowing the future, Kakakatak finds the tasks amusing and inconsequential, almost like using a bucket to help advance the sea. While he cooperates, he has been trying to meditate himself back to his original era or at least to contact another member of his species. So far he has been unsuccessful. If he can gain access to certain city libraries perhaps still intact, he thinks he can return himself using a reverse version of Huston's Time Trap spell.

Kakakatak bargains with the investigators in good faith. He feels no alarm about the impending opening of the Gate. If the investigators open the force field which imprisons Kakakatak without first asking for something in return, Kakakatak thanks them sincerely and majestically glides away, ending his participation in this adventure.

Among the things he might offer as a trade is to re-wire the mind controller so that the miners can be returned to themselves. Further, since he makes it a practice each day to read Huston's mind, scanning it as a human might a newspaper, he can also point out cultist connections to Ho Fong, Ahja Singh, and the Penhew Foundation. He also knows the general design of the conspiracy, and can recite all the important locations, how to best approach them, and who can be trusted and who cannot. As a scholar, he can telepathically impart 1D6 points of Astronomy, Biology, Chemistry, Cthulhu Mythos, Electronics, Geology, Physics, or Occult in a few hours, per investigator. (This is tedious to do, and he will not volunteer it, at least at first.) The keeper may think of other functions for Kakakatak, or knowledge that the investigators might wish to learn, such as practical tactics in fighting flying polyps.

When freed, the first thing Kakakatak does is to glide down several narrow, dusty ramps and enter an unexplored building. There he removes several fully charged (23-shot) lightning guns from a compartment in a seemingly blank wall. He explains their use to the investigators and takes one for himself. The investigator to whom he speaks telepathically understands that Kakakatak definitely does not want to meet a flying polyp without this weapon. He truly fears the polyp wind-attack.

Kakakatak knows the city and knows how to get where he wants. He is reluctant to share much information with the minimal intelligences who have freed him. He takes them along because he cannot climb rubble—the investigators must unclog areas so that he can cross. Kakakatak needs several weeks in order to locate or reach the archives he desires. He tries to keep the investigators with him throughout that period. Better motivated helpers would be hard to find.

KAKAKATAK, physical age 2644 years, Researcher of the Great Race

STR 40	CON 22	SIZ 60	INT 26	POW 13
DEX 13	MOV 7			HP 41

Damage Bonus: +5D6.

Weapons: Pincer 40%, damage 1D6+5D6
Lightning Gun 45%, damage 8D6/4D6/1D6

Armor: 8-point hide

Skills: Astronomy 90%, Biology 99%, Chemistry 85%, Cthulhu Mythos 30%, Electrical Repair 95%, Electronics 99%, Future of the Universe 70%, Geology 90%, History (Yithian) 90%, Library Use (Yithian) 90%, Mechanical Repair 95%, Natural History (Primordial) 95%, Occult 06%, Physics 90%.

Sanity Loss: 1/1D6 SAN.

Conclusion

As this chapter ends, the investigators are stranded in the desert, hundreds of miles from the nearest town. If the vehicles are useless, they can wait by Grogan's spring until a stock drive comes from the north, and then trudge with the drovers down to Wiluna. Or, faster, a prospecting or survey party might pass and head back to Cuncudgerie. Or perhaps the investigators still have vehicles and decide to head north to Darwin, then on to Hong Kong, Singapore, or Shanghai.

If the player-characters have done their job, Huston has been foiled or killed, Kakakatak freed, the miners dezombified, and the cultists crushed. Jeremy Grogan refuses to leave his camp, but is safe there from all but nature.

If the investigators eliminated Huston, grant each 1D8 SAN. He was a serious threat to the world. If Huston died without the help of the investigators, give them no Sanity points for him. If the cultists have been broken up or eliminated, grant the investigators an additional 1D4 SAN. If Kakakatak was dealt with fairly, grant 1D3 Sanity points for him. If the investigators were able to restore memory to any of the zombified miners, allow each a Sanity point for each miner. ■

SHANGHAI

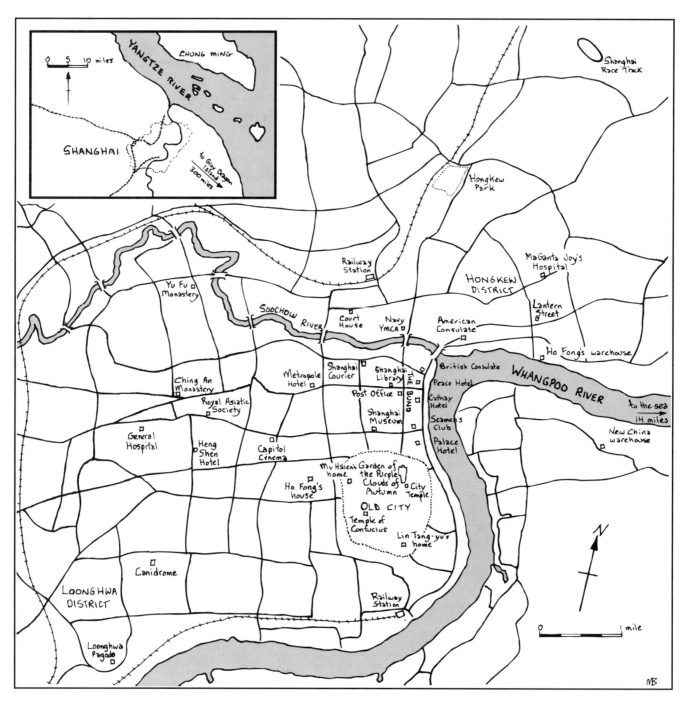

"I learned whence Cthulhu first came, and why half the great temporary stars of history had flared forth. I guessed—from hints which made even my informant pause timidly—the secret behind the Magellanic Clouds and globular nebulae, and the black truth veiled by the immemorial allegory of Tao."

—H.P. Lovecraft, "The Whisperer in Darkness"

Though Lovecraft never set a Mythos story in China, this chapter partakes of his imagination by using "The Colour Out of Space", the *Seven Cryptical Books*, the deep one crossbreeds, and so on. Another joy of *Call of Cthulhu* is to be able to explicate, elaborate, and expand upon the Cthulhu Mythos.

If the investigators come here first, rather than sailing to London, they'll find Shanghai difficult going, with its non-Mythos adversaries, radium poisoning, obscure Chinese cults, powerful sorcerers, and political fanatics. In compensation there are Jack Brady and his allies, and the *Seven Cryptical Books of Hsan*. Together they yield a way to stop the dire plan of Nyarlathotep, as well as provide useful information about the cults in Africa. If they survive, investigators who come first to Shanghai can emerge in good shape for tackling the other chapter locations.

Most investigators arrive in Shanghai at the beginning or the end of the campaign. If this is the conclusion of the campaign, strive to explain or to justify the handout clues which the players have been given, to leave them with the sense that all reasonable questions have been answered. Genuine mysteries, however, must be studied and pursued.

Unless the investigators somehow got Soviet visas and took the Trans-Siberia railway, they get to Shanghai by ship, by riding animal, or by foot. Investigators from New York take the train to Chicago, change trains for San Francisco, go by ship to Honolulu, on to Manila or Yokohama, and then board another ship for Shanghai. Investigators from Europe or Africa go by way of Singapore to Hong Kong, and then change ships for Shanghai.

Lacking other reason, keepers can summarize the travel and pass over it. Use the travel notes in the introduction to state a reasonable amount of time for the journey, and get on with the game.

If play is wanted, the appendix offers some guides to boosting investigator skills or sanity while aboard ship. Shipboard is an excellent arena for cult threats or attacks. Shipboard is also an excellent venue for discreet adventures or for meeting useful or interesting characters.

Empty-pocketed investigators stranded in London might consider stowing away aboard the *Ivory Wind*; see the London chapter for crew, captain, and cargo.

Several clues point to the presence of Jack Brady in Hong Kong. Brady has been there to visit Carlyle. If the investigators stop off in Hong Kong en route to Shanghai, they should find nothing unless they tour the sanitariums specifically looking for Roger Carlyle. If they find and identify Carlyle, he is able to tell them nothing. Brady gave an alias, Randolph Carter, for his friend, but Randolph Carter's home address is listed as Shanghai, in care of the Stumbling Tiger Bar.

In Shanghai, investigators will seek information about Jack Brady and Jackson Elias. If they saw the temple hemispheric map within the Bent Pyramid, they also will be looking for evidence of Nyarlathotep. Probably they have stumbled across the name of the exporter Ho Fong. In China the major cult of the dark god is the Order of the Bloated Woman,

Selected Connections for this Chapter

NP#	clue or lead	obtained from	leads to
13	matchbook cover	Elias' murder scene	Stumbling Tiger Bar in Shanghai
—	Fergus Chum	Stumbling Tiger bar	Jack Brady's location, Order of the Bloated Woman, Gray Dragon Island, the *Dark Mistress*
—	Isoge Taro	Stumbling Tiger bar	info, New China, Jack Brady, help from Imperial Japanese Navy
—	agents of Lin Tang-yu	Stumbling Tiger bar	they want Jack Brady and his Mythos tome; may lead to an interview with Mr. Lin
—	interview	Lin Tang-yu	Nyarlathotep, Bloated Woman, Gray Dragon Island, Ho Fong, Carl Stanford, powerful secret weapon, Jack Brady is alive, Congolese, cult of the White Gorilla
14	photo	Elias' murder scene	yacht *Dark Mistress* off Shanghai
—	map in sanctum	Bent Pyramid	vicinity of Shanghai
—	files and ledgers	Ho Fong Import	Penhew Foundation (London), Ahja Singh (Mombasa), M. Wycroft (Cuncudgerie)
—	room in Ho's warehouse	survey, forced entry	Sir Aubrey's rocket, plus suspect addresses world-wide
—	surveillance, forced entry	Ho Fong Import	Carl Stanford, Miss Choi
—	crates of parts	aboard *Ivory Wind*	rocket and warhead
—	Ho Fong's address	Gavigan's ledger	notes many shipments here
21	Nails Nelson	Elias' Kenya notes	Jack Brady in China
—	*Gods of Reality*	Huston's manuscript	Gray Dragon Island, Jan. 14, 1926
—	artifacts exported	Shakti's logbook	Ho Fong Import/Export
—	equipment invoices	Ho Fong Import	Mortimer Wycroft in Cuncudgerie
38	Seamens Club collapse	*Shanghai Courier*	Mythos influence, Jack Brady
39	fire on Ching-ling Road	*Shanghai Courier*	Jack Brady
40	"giant bat" in violence	*Shanghai Courier*	Miss Choi, Jack Brady
41	astrologer's ad	*Shanghai Courier*	Mr. Lung of Kaoyang Street
—	help in translation	Shanghai Museum	Mu Hsien
—	interview	Mu Hsien	Chu Min, Jack Brady, Order of the Bloated Woman
—	interview	Hsien, Brady	Firm Action's warehouse
43	Brady's statement	McChum, Hsien	role of Carlyle Expedition, Sir Aubrey, opening the gate
—	Gray Dragon Island	stow-aways	the cult activities there
45	diaries of Sir Aubrey	Gray Dragon Island	opening the gate

which worships yet another aspect of Nyarlathotep. The name Nyarlathotep means nothing in China, nor does the Bloody Tongue or the Brotherhood of the Black Pharaoh have significance there. As Jackson Elias wrote, "Many names, many forms, but all the same and toward one end." The dark god's intent becomes recognizable as the sessions are played.

JACKSON ELIAS IN SHANGHAI

Elias stayed at the Jin Jiang Guest House on Black Slipper Lane while in Shanghai. In Shanghai, he came to the attention of cultists, and magical attacks on his Sanity were begun. That is why his notes and speculations became bizarre and disarrayed. He learned nothing about Sir Aubrey's rocket, but he did see Sir Aubrey from a distance. Jack Brady did not then possess the *Seven Cryptical Books of Hsan*, so Elias knew nothing of them. He did hear Brady's story of the Carlyle Expedition, in the form that the handout "Jack Brady's Statement" gives it. Elias followed up the leads in Nairobi, and planned to in Cairo, but cult interference became substantial, and his research there could only verify that Brady's story was not disproved. Two days of inquiry among city offices establishes that Elias arrived in Shanghai in mid-September, and that he left on October 4. His destination was London.

Getting Around in Shanghai

As in Egypt, investigators must have a guide or be at the mercy of fate. Keepers are free to develop their own subplots here, emphasizing political, economic, or psychological reasons for being against the cult. Li Wen-cheng is offered as a guide typical of the times.

LI WEN-CHENG

Li comes from the Kiangsu countryside, the fourth son of a moderately wealthy farmer. In Li Wen-cheng's year of birth, the great imperial examination system of China was abolished. To obtain a Western technical education, Li converted to Christianity and attended a Methodist boarding school. When he announced his sincere conviction of Christ, his Confucian father tore Christ from a place of respect among the household gods and disowned his unfilial fourth son. Now Li Wen-cheng is without family, and serves as an impoverished library assistant at the Methodist university. He is known (to McChum for one) as friendly, intelligent, hard-working, and loyal. Li knows a good deal about Shanghai, though avoiding much of it as sinful and wicked. Counterpointing the investigators' need for information with Li's need to tread the straight-and-narrow could be amusing.

LI WEN-CHENG

LI WEN-CHENG, age 22, Youthful Christian and Librarian

STR 14	CON 13	SIZ 10	INT 14	POW 11
DEX 12	APP 14	EDU 13	SAN 65	HP 12

Damage Bonus: +0.

Weapons: naive faith; boundless energy, ever-renewing hope

Skills: Bargain 10%, Bible (King James) 60%, Biology 15%, Chemistry 15%, Climb 50%, Credit Rating 10%, Dodge 35%, English 35%, Fast Talk 25%, First Aid 35%, Jump 35%, Library Use 45%, Listen 40%, Mandarin Chinese 65%, Medicine 20%, Persistence 70%, Physics 25%, Sneak 25%, Spot Hidden 35%.

About Shanghai

Originally an undistinguished small city in Kiangsu province, the British opened Shanghai to occupation and trade as spoils from the Treaty of Nanking (1842), which put a humiliating conclusion to the piratical opium wars. British and American representatives took possession of certain areas adjacent to the Chinese city. These areas of extraterritoriality, within which no Chinese law pertained, became known first as the concessions and later mostly known as the International Settlement.

ORDER OF THE BLOATED WOMAN

大胖女人

This form of the dark god Nyarlathotep is that of a 600-pound, obviously female humanoid equipped with numerous tentacles in addition to two arms and two legs. The order's membership is almost exclusively Chinese. Rituals are practiced on several off-shore and unpopulated islands. The high priest is Ho Fong, a wealthy importer in Shanghai. The cult's main weapon is a sickle used to mutilate the trunk of the victim and then to sever the limbs. Cultists rarely use guns. The Order has links to a colony of deep ones in the East China Sea; human/deep one half-breeds are common in the cult.

Cultist ceremonial robes are of black and yellow silk, cut voluminously to ape the shape of the Bloated Woman. All cultists have a tattoo of the cult characters in their left armpits (this should identify any dead cultists left about). The cult characters are simply a version of the phrase "Bloated Woman".

The cult's minions have unsavory reputations among Shanghai's vast and cruel criminal underworld. The Order is vaguely known as well to the growing leftist and nationalist underground.

AVERAGE MEMBER, Order of the Bloated Woman (China)

STR 10	CON 09	SIZ 10	INT 09	POW 13
DEX 13	APP 04	EDU 02	SAN 0	HP 10

Damage Bonus: +0.

Weapons: Fist/Punch 60%, damage 1D3
Cult Sickle 50%, damage 1D4+3
Head Butt 50%, damage 1D4
Kick 50%, damage 1D6
Grapple 30%, damage special
Fighting Knife 25%, damage 1D4+2

Skills: Bargain 20%, Cthulhu Mythos 08%, Dodge 40%, English 10%, Fast Talk 25%, Hide 35%, Listen 50%, Mandarin Chinese (or Cantonese, Hakka, etc.) Chinese 45%, Martial Arts 30%, Shiphandling 30%, Sing 25%, Sneak 40%, Swim 65%.

The French concession, directly between the British concession and the old, original Chinese walled town, was never formally amalgamated. (When Japan later received a small concession in Shanghai, Chinese public opinion was much inflamed, for this opened the prospect of the further pillaging of the Middle Kingdom.)

Citizens of these treaty powers could not be tried under Chinese law, whether or not they were in the concessions. Though additional concessions at Shanghai were squeezed from a nearly prostrate China, the side-by-side French, British, and American zones formed the financial and industrial heart of the mushrooming city to come.

THE PEOPLE

Control and population do not mean the same thing, however. In 1923, out of 1.6 million Shanghai residents, slightly more than 20,000 were non-Chinese—mostly Japanese. (Cairo, in comparison, has 850,000 residents, of whom more than one-tenth are foreign.) In Shanghai the bosses may well be European, Japanese, or American, but everyone else—shopkeeper, cab driver, laborer, teacher, lawyer, etc.—is Chinese.

Unregistered American and European drifters and transients—Jack Brady is one—swell the occidental presence. The status, security, and trade advantages of the International Settlement also attracts propertied Chinese, some of whom are recently converted Christians.

The economy of China is in such ruins that foreigners of even moderate income can afford opulent possessions and princely living conditions. Millions of Chinese must work for almost nothing, and the cost of what they produce amounts to little more than materials plus the owners' profit. Many foreigners choose to continue to live in China though they could go home. In Shanghai and across much of Asia, the lowliest foreigner has servants, and wealthy foreigners live like kings.

AN ALTERNATIVE TO GOVERNMENT

Increasing poverty, overpopulation, lack of opportunity, and governmental neglect in Ching-dynasty China strengthened the traditionally strong family structure as well as the ubiquitous private associations. The associations in particular serve their members as clubs, insurance companies, pension funds, political allies, and more. What government later came to supply or to assure in the United States, the private association attempted to provide its members in China. An association might be a guild of thieves in one century, evolve to become a powerful political faction in another century, and form the basis of a revolutionary government in a third. The Chinese tongs were such a development.

In 1926, national central authority, never very strong, has long broken down. Innumerable regional and local rulers exist—cliques of men committed to maintaining their power by force. In Shanghai in the 1920s, there are more than one hundred powerful cliques, factions, and movements with pretenses to power, and it is unclear which will be the victor.

THE PHYSICAL CITY

Shanghai is built on the delta of the Yangtze River, with both the Grand Canal and the new railways at hand. The land upon which Shanghai stands is thus alluvial and nearly flat. Dikes and sea walls protect against flood, tide, and storm. Drainage is difficult. Shanghai is a low city. Only the largest city buildings are higher than three stories. The water table is very high. Obtaining pure water and disposing of sewage are recurring problems.

Everyone complains about heat and humidity in the summer and fall. Conditions resemble those of New Orleans, but Shanghai summers are wetter (3-5 inches of rain a month) and the winters are drier. Typhoons sweep in from the China Sea during the summer and fall, as do hurricanes from the Gulf of Mexico in the southern United States.

Throughout China, precautions against theft and banditry are routinely kept which would be astonishing in Western cities of the day. High blank walls and stout gates hide rich homes. Windows are universally barred. Everyone employs guards and watchmen. Large and profitable businesses operate in seeming squalor. At the office, wealthy bankers wear clothing worse than that of their clerks. Investigators must look closely and thoughtfully to know who is powerful, who is poor, and who pretends to one state or the other.

THE FICTIVE CITY

Though some mapped Shanghai locations in this adventure existed and are properly placed (the Seamens Club is one), keepers should not try to find most addresses in this scenario on a real map of Shanghai. The physical layout of the city and the city's social background are as accurate as humble writers who are not specialists in Chinese history are able to make them. As in the Cairo chapter, ficticious Chinese place names occur in English translation.

GENERAL HISTORY

Modern China was born accidentally, as a by-product of World War I. For its nominal assistance during the war, the Versailles conference generously gave Japan all of Germany's rights and possessions in China's Shantung province. Since China also was a nominal ally of the victorious side during WWI, this patronizing insult galvanized Chinese intellectuals. The Peking demonstrations of May 4, 1919, make May Fourth the general term for the nationwide outbursts that followed. The May Fourth movement launched the Chinese Communist party and revivified Chiang Kai-shek's Kuomintang party. These particular parties became implacable enemies as they grew in strength, and their internecine wars paralyzed China for the next half-century.

The investigators reach Shanghai in 1925 or 1926. In July of 1926, Chiang Kai-shek finishes intricate negotiations and officially launches the military Northern Expedition which is intended to vanquish local and regional warlords and to unify central China with Canton and the south. The effort meets considerable success, and Chiang takes Shanghai in March of 1927. Throughout 1926 and 1927 local fighting ravages Kiangsu province, and great strikes rage in Shanghai as well as in Hong Kong and Canton. In late 1927, Chiang attacks the Communist and leftist leadership, and executes many. Among those barely escaping Shanghai is Chou En-lai, a future premier of China.

HISTORY UP CLOSE

The colonial powers devoted themselves to making munitions during WWI, incidentally providing excellent business opportunities for Chinese manufacturers of all sorts of goods. Now the war is over, and renewed competition from the West has pushed Chinese industrialists to squeeze the wages of their workers again and again. It is perfectly likely and reasonable that investigators witness picket lines, rallies, roving mobs, and bloody worker-police-strikebreaker battles with stones, clubs, bottles, and swords.

Outside the International Settlement, without a Chinese-speaking guide to explain their presence, the investigators meet a confusion of excessive friendship, animosity, fearfulness, and servility. With an interpreter, they still must thread their way through very interesting times. The keeper has every excuse to litter streets with bodies, hustle troops or police across the stage, perform inexplicable assassinations, have consuls and police warn against provocation, and swing the gun turrets of destroyers and gunboats in the river—all against the drama lent by extreme wealth and hideous poverty.

LANGUAGE AND DIRECTION

English serves fairly well within the International Settlement, so long as the investigators keep questions to the "Where is—?" sort. The uniformed Chinese patrolmen are courteous and eager to please. There is a small phone book, and governmental buildings, better hotels, and prosperous businesses have copies, as well as possessing the only public pay phones. Local telegraph service and mails are reliable. Within the city, private couriers cost less than the price of a stamp, and are quicker.

Outside the Settlement, investigators must speak Mandarin Chinese or have interpreter-guides. Occasionally, missionaries, traders, and officials might be encountered who could be of help. Chinese officials and functionaries will be aligned with one or more warlords, political factions, bandits, underworld gangs, oligarchs, or tongs. There is no strong central government until the Communists solidify power in the early 1950s. Lacking the rule of law or custom, individual power and motive has become everything, whether for patriots, honest people, venal predators, or the cruelest cultists.

Chinese and Japanese convention causes the full name of an individual to be written or spoken with the family name first, followed by the given name. Thus the old scholar Mu Hsien is also called Mr. Mu—Mu is his family name. Similarly, Captain Isoge Taro's given name is Taro. If English-speakers used this convention, an identical formation would be Doe John rather than John Doe. Bureaucrats everywhere will understand the handiness of having personal names in ready-to-file order.

In principle, Chinese characters represent single syllables of meaning, without reference to an alphabet. In this adventure, Chinese names and places follow the Wade-Giles transcription system rather than the more accurate pin-yin now generally employed. Wade-Giles was used during the period, and reflects those times. With Wade-Giles, it is Chiang Kai-shek. Using pin-yin, the same generalissimo is Jian Jieshi.

The Stumbling Tiger Bar

Just northeast of the confluence of the Whangpoo and Soochow Rivers is a district of bars, gambling dens, and flower girl houses, convenient to the docks and factories of the American concession. At 10 Lantern Street is the Stumbling Tiger Bar, identified by both Chinese and English signs, and by the image of a drunken tiger tripping over a stone. Here Jackson Elias met Jack Brady, and learned the secret which eventually cost him his life. If the investigators did not get the match-cover clue leading to the Stumbling Tiger, the bar can be on a list of "puzzle talk" bars—places where information is regularly sold for money—which their guide gets from student friends in Shanghai's political underground.

The Stumbling Tiger is a single room plus a separate toilet. Both rooms are large, dark, and dirty. Lurid green and magenta posters of Chinese songstresses and film stars decorate the walls. The light is simultaneously harsh and inadequate. Decades of cigarette smoke and missed tries at spittoons give the air a heavy, damp, moldering quality. Doctors among the investigators will uneasily think of tuberculosis.

The owner-barman is a taciturn man, Fergus Chum, a squat Chinese-Scots whom the occidentals among his clientele know as McChum. He is a native of Shanghai. He keeps his eyes open and his mouth closed. His fingers, like those of his customers, are brown from chain-smoking cigarettes.

McChum is in debt to Jack Brady, because Brady once saved his life during a brawl in the Stumbling Tiger. McChum knows that Brady does not want to be found. He replies to anyone asking for Brady, "No see him for long time. Think maybe he leave Shanghai." If the questioner gently suggests that cash could improve McChum's memory, he seemingly agrees. But McChum doesn't come cheap—"Jack Brady once save my life," he swears, "right here in this bar. Yeah." To salve his conscience, 1D20+10 Mexican silver dollars helps. Lowering his voice, he says, "Jack Brady go to Rangoon. He have big deal there with Charlie Grey—they sell guns, I think. Charlie Grey a big money man—very important there."

FERGUS CHUM

The tale is convincing. Inquiries with the British consul in Shanghai, or telegraphic inquiries to British or American representatives in Rangoon, confirm that a Charles Grey Ltd. exists in Rangoon, and that the company handles arms. Mr. Grey, another friend who is covering for Brady, confirms by return wire that Brady worked for him for several months in late 1925. Grey believes that Brady then took some rifles to someone—Sacasa? Sandino?—in Nicaragua or Guatemala. Grey has no details. This convincing lie, adjusted to the year and situation, fended off a cultist probe if the cult took the Stumbling Tiger matchbook clue in New York. If cultists know of the significance of the bar, they still may be keeping watch—keeper's option here.

McChum does not know Brady's location, though he suspects the man is still in Shanghai, where he had many friends. Brady has kept his location from McChum more to protect his friend than to protect himself

HO FONG: McChum knows that Ho Fong leads the Order of the Bloated Woman in Shanghai, and perhaps throughout China. Ho is a very dangerous man. He has many contacts in the International Settlement, and is untouchable by local Chinese officials. His house is like a fortress.

GRAY DRAGON ISLAND: every few weeks junks sail from Shanghai to Gray Dragon Island, a coastal island unusual in the region because a dormant volcanic cone crowns it; the island is so called because grayish steam or smoke occasionally rises from the peak. Strange things are said to happen on the island. Fishermen dare death from storms rather than put in there. One of the vessels regularly visiting the island is Ho Fong's private yacht. McChum thinks that he goes there for cult rituals.

SCOUTING PARTIES: twice someone paid fishermen to survey the island. Both boats and their crews were lost, disappearing without a trace.

THE DARK MISTRESS: occasionally a large steam yacht, the *Dark Mistress*, pulls into Shanghai to load food, water, etc. Its crew is particularly depraved and degenerate-looking ("Like frogs, buddy, yeah"). McChum thinks this vessel is cultist-operated and that it comes from Gray Dragon Island, though it flies a Union Jack. The owner is an Englishman, Alfred Penhurst. No one ever has seen him. He must be very wealthy to own such a luxurious boat, and a very wicked man to hire such a terrifying crew.

CONSEQUENCES OF THE INTERVIEW

Once McChum tells the investigators what he knows, his life is in their hands. Though the cult is aware of McChum, they do not know that he is important. If they learn what McChum knows, the owner of the Stumbling Tiger dies that same day. Consequently, McChum makes a good ally, but is an ally who is hard to get. He hears everything, smiles thinly, lies like a trooper, and reveals nothing. He will aid his friend Jack Brady.

If the investigators are foolish enough to sail to Rangoon on the strength of McChum's story, be sure to make it plain to them once they are there that they've wasted several weeks and several hundred dollars. In pointing this out, let Charlie Grey sneer and condescend in an obnoxious manner.

Queries about Jackson Elias—even showing McChum a photo of Elias—bring nothing but shrugs. McChum did see Elias several times, but only as a patron who talked to Brady. "Lots of people come in here, friend. Sorry."

WHAT McCHUM ACTUALLY KNOWS

If the investigators dare to be honest with McChum, arranging a private meeting with him, showing him artifacts or tomes which cultists would never dream of exposing to strangers, and then sharing all they know about the murder of Elias, in return McChum may confide in them. McChum knows or guesses quite a bit. But it should not be easy to get McChum to talk—he risks his life if he talks; he lives serenely if he stays silent.

Questioning McChum may pique the interest of agents for Ho Fong, Isoge Taro, or Lin Tang-yu. For particulars, see the sections discussing those gentlemen. It is logical to assume, however, that these agents and henchmen notice each other, and that therefore corpses keep turning up where the investigators go. If the keeper wants to involve the Shanghai police, an ongoing murder investigation is an easy way to do it.

FERGUS "McCHUM" CHUM, age 40, Owner-Operator of the Stumbling Tiger Bar

STR 10	CON 11	SIZ 10	INT 13	POW 15
DEX 16	APP 12	EDU 04	SAN 35	HP 11

Damage Bonus: +0.

Weapons: Fist/Punch 70%, damage 1D3
Head Butt: 55%, damage 1D4
Fighting Knife 50%, damage 1D4+2
Kick 45%, damage 1D6

Skills: Accounting 25%, Bargain 65%, Credit Rating 20%, Cthulhu Mythos 05%, Drive Automobile 15%, Dodge 65%, English 25%, Fast Talk 75%, Japanese 20%, Law 20%, Listen 55%, Mandarin Chinese 65%, Occult 15%, Persuade 35%, Psychology 55%, Spot Hidden 35%, Swim 40%.

HO FUNG

Under his camouflage of a successful businessman,
Ho Fung's tentacles of terror reach around the globe.
Will the investigators comprehend his power before it is too late?

As well as in ten other locations across the Far East, importer Ho Fong maintains a large warehouse in Shanghai, on Kaoyang Street, not far from the Stumbling Tiger. Ho's public reputation is spotless and ultra-respectable. He deliberately accepts gratitude money and cheats a bit on his taxes, subscriptions, and contributions so that his peers will not think him a fool. Secretly the High

Priest of the Order of the Bloated Woman, he is one of the most dangerous men in the world.

His office is at his Shanghai warehouse. If the investigators ask for him, he is busy that day, but a subordinate makes an appointment for the investigators on the following day. If their reasons for wanting to see this important man seem inadequate to his aide, the aide has the investigators shadowed until they return the next day.

(For a description of Ho Fong's office, see that entry a few paragraphs further on. Statistics and notes for Ho Fong and his cultist henchmen are found at the end of this section.)

Ho is in his late 50s—short, fat, and apparently amiable. He wears a baggy white linen suit and smokes aromatic, dark-wrapped cigarettes. He offers the investigators tea, and cigarettes, and inquires after their comfort. He discusses Shanghai's weather, history, geography, and so on for several minutes, always in the most polite and non-controversial terms. If one of the investigators is obviously Christian, Ho echoes a similar faith-filled demeanor.

HO FUNG

His office is neat, large, and Spartan—this is a place for business. Noise from the surrounding warehouses and docks drowns out the soft whir of the overhead fans. One end of the office has a circle of comfortable armchairs with lace antimacassars. Low side tables for serving tea hold ashtrays and more doilies.

Ho never offers specific information. If asked about the destinations of shipments from the Penhew Foundation in London, or from Ahja Singh of Mombasa, he says that he can have a clerk look up those files, but wishes to know why this information is so important that the investigators would come such a distance to ask for it. Could not a cable or a letter suffice? "Come, gentlemen," he says guilelessly, "If I am to confide in you, breaking some small faith with my customers in doing so, you will admit—why, you must confide in me." A successful Psychology roll suggests merely that Ho's smooth questions indicate a cool customer.

If the spokesman for the investigators receives a successful Persuade roll, he or she might convince Ho Fong that the inquiries are above-board. Lacking conflicting evidence or information (such as them having been seen questioning McChum at the Stumbling Tiger), Ho Fong forgets about the investigators.

If the investigators decide to confide in Ho Fong, their lives are at risk once night falls. Ho gladly dispatches cultists night after night to kill whomever survived the night before. To escape his reach, the investigators must flee Shanghai, then return secretly if they wish to do more work there.

Ho Fong's home, his warehouse on Kaoyang Street, and his yacht (anchored at the warehouse) could interest the investigators.

Ho Fong's Shanghai Warehouse

The large brick building is on the north bank of the Whangpoo River. A successful Spot Hidden roll reveals that at least a portion of the warehouse is built on a wooden pier or wooden pilings. A stout peaked roof of tile fends off the rain. Five sets of large doors along the sides of the building give access to the high-ceilinged storage area, and two stories of low-ceilinged offices face the street.

All of the windows are at least seven feet from the ground, and iron grills (STR 35) cover them. At night, all the doors (uniformly STR 23) are padlocked. Their easily picked locks are STR 15 each. All doors are unlocked during business hours (6 a.m. to 6 p.m., and at other times to coincide with ship arrivals and departures). Every day but Sunday, thirty men work at Ho Fong's. All are Chinese, and all are members of the Order of the Bloated Woman. Normal work hours are 7 a.m. to 6 p.m.

When the warehouse is closed, six guards patrol the interior. They are expert martial artists. Captured intruders are kept for interrogation by Ho Fong or an aide, then sacrificed to the Bloated Woman—but nobody will care if one or two trespassers die during the fight. The leader (Number One Guard) has a key which unlocks the padlocks of the center-hasped rear warehouse doors.

HO FONG'S OFFICES: the entire second floor is utilitarian and contains nothing unusual. Though well made, the desks, side tables, and chairs are simple in design. If the investigators enter by means of the stairs, a successful Spot Hidden roll reveals that a section of them (point A on the plan) seems weak and loose.

In Ho Fong's private office, many rolled navigation charts (one is the best map available of Gray Dragon Island), railway atlases, gazetteers, shipping guides, tariff law compendiums, account books, ledgers, clipping books, and bound papers—mostly in Chinese—occupy the bookcases behind the table which serves as Ho's desk. Tall filing cabinets bulge with papers. A floor safe, STR 55, can be picked with a successful Locksmith roll. It contains 1D6 x100 Mexican silver dollars, 1D6 x100 five-pound sterling notes, two negotiable drafts for a total of 77,000 Japanese yen, and 30 U.S. 20-dollar gold pieces.

Investigators find little new evidence in the files and ledgers. Ho Fong has shipped to and received items from the Penhew Foundation (London) and Ahja Singh (Mombasa)—mostly "art objects", though books are referred to also. These sorts of shipments also are sent to points in Tokyo and Rio de Janeiro. In the same file are notations concerning shipments of mining equipment to Mortimer Wycroft of Cuncudgerie, who lives in Western Australia.

MAIN WAREHOUSE: this very large storage area is supported by several rows of wooden pillars. Archipelagos of salted fish, hemp cordage, copra, canned foods, bagged rice, chests and bricks of tea, porcelains, dried herbs, machine parts, hard woods, and yard goods mound across the floor. Reduce Spot Hidden rolls by 25 percentiles in this jumble. If it is raining, similarly reduce Listen rolls. At night, the dim overhead electric lights are turned off. The light stays on at the table just outside the special storeroom, where the six guards gossip and gamble at mah jong, craps, or fan tan. Every hour, two of them tour the warehouse with flashlights, examining the doors for signs of entry. They do check the front door, but Ho, fearing his safe may tempt even his cult fanatics, has forbidden them to go upstairs without clear reason or provocation.

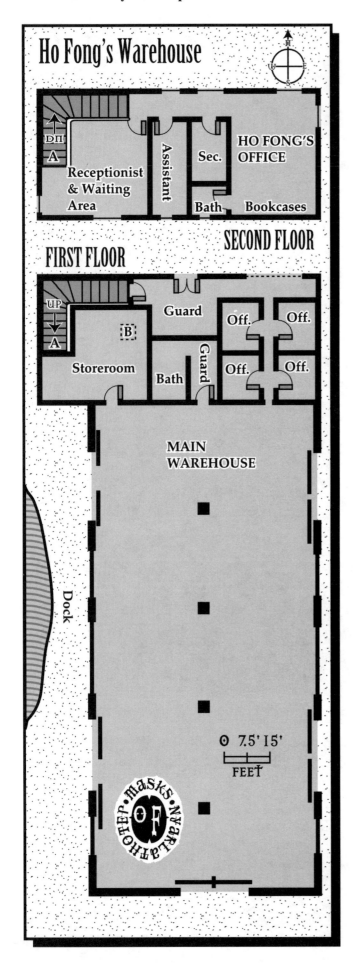

THE SPECIAL STOREROOM: here Ho keeps any Mythos artifacts passing through his hands. Apart from the sprawling, spitting, and snoozing guards, a stout iron door (STR 75) with a deadbolt lock blocks the way in. The excellent lock can be picked, with difficulty. Reduce any Locksmith roll by 25 percentiles.

From the inside, an Idea roll suggests that the weakened place on the stairs to Ho Fong's office may be part of some uncompleted carpentry repairs. If investigators move the stair runner aside and quietly pry up the risers, they can drop down into the storeroom and examine its contents at their leisure.

There is a third way out of the storeroom: point B on the plan consists of an iron hatch—two 3 x7-foot hinged doors (STR 55) can be pulled up and folded back to reveal the water and pilings below. Bolts lock this hatch; it can only be opened from above and inside. Depending on the tide, the surface of the water is a yard to five yards below. A hoist allows crates to be lowered to small boats tied beneath the pier. Ho chooses this method of transfer when he does not want a particular item to be seen leaving the warehouse.

A variety of artifacts are in the special storeroom—they can be anything the keeper wishes, including statues of deities, friezes from ruins, paintings done by artists under Mythos influence, etc. Paper items are securely insulated against Shanghai's humidity. Nothing is magical, nor are Mythos tomes present. Many artifacts are disturbingly repulsive, costing 0/1D4 SAN while viewing. Successful Archaeology rolls identify most items as ancient Chinese. There are also Japanese, Indian, African, and Polynesian pieces, as well as some which are unidentifiable.

Of interest are six small crates simply labeled AP. They contain extra parts for Sir Aubrey's rocket. If all are laid out and examined, a successful Physics roll reduced by 50 percentiles could define the intended use of the parts. Rocketry is an extremely esoteric study in the 1920s.

Most of the crates have addresses on them. Keepers may freely choose any destination and use those references as jump-off points for other scenarios. As examples, keepers might consider using H.A. Wilcox, 7 Thomas Street, Providence, Rhode Island, USA (see the story "Call of Cthulhu"); Mr. W. Whateley, General Delivery, Dunwich, Massachusetts, USA (see the story "The Dunwich Horror"); Mr. Herbert West, c/o Miskatonic University Medical School, Arkham, Massachusetts, USA (see the story "Herbert West—Reanimator").

HO FONG'S YACHT: This large, well-kept, motorized junk is moored near Ho's Shanghai warehouse. Ho has managed to get British registry for the vessel, the *Luxuriant Goddess*, effectively shielding it from inspection by any faction of Chinese government—a useful shield for a ship intended to ply only Chinese waters. Ho uses the yacht mostly for cult business. While moored, it carries nothing pertaining to Mythos matters. Ho keeps 1D4+2 cultist guards aboard the vessel. They (like their warehouse compatriots) are instructed to capture intruders for questioning, not to kill them automatically.

Ho Fong's Mansion

Ho Fong lives near the Old City, beyond the aegis of the relatively efficient International Settlement police. His compound walls are thirteen feet high, and his gates are strong (STR 95). Gates and walls are topped by spear points, broken glass, and barbed wire to stymie thieves and snoopers. Subtract 25 percentiles from investigator Luck or Jump rolls needed to clear these obstacles.

The mansion is built around two courts. The outer court faces the main gate, and houses kitchens, servants, storerooms, etc. Ho lives in the rooms of the inner court; they are luxurious. The mansion roofs are all of peaked red tile. All the rooftops are slippery and steep.

ROOMS OF THE OUTER COURTS: uniformly barren, these have only scraps of furniture and dribbles of possessions. Ho does not share his wealth with his cultist followers. At any time, 1D6+3 cultist servants are found working or sleeping in this part of the compound. In the rooms, Mythos statuettes or symbols, often the characters for the Bloated Woman, can be seen. Investigators managing to inspect this part of the mansion understand that the servants are cultists as well as the master.

THE DOORMAN'S ROOM: the doorman never gets a day off. His job is to admit or refuse entry to all who knock. If the investigators look shabby, he refuses the round-eyed bandits. If the investigators are well-dressed, the doorman has no choice but to admit them. Another servant hears their wishes and brings them to the luxurious outer sitting room (where they are carefully watched through tiny eye holes).

LUXURIOUS SITTING ROOM: the room is furnished with fine couches and chairs. A servant brings tea if the investigators have come in a legitimate fashion. Two fine screens grace one end of the room; behind each stands a guard. If an investigator looks around a screen and sees the guard, the guard smiles and bows.

THE DINING ROOM: A luxurious room. Light-fingered investigators could net 25,000 U.S. dollars just by selling the fine porcelains, screens, and tapestries here. A successful Archaeology roll establishes the authenticity and worth of the furnishings, which have no Occult or Mythos significance.

THE LIBRARY: about 4000 books are present, a few in English. Most are scrolls, in classical Chinese. They are valuable, being old, but are not magical or related to cult activity. There is a 20% chance that Ho has left one of his five Cthulhu Mythos tomes on the library desk. For particulars, see the section below dealing with the shrine to the Bloated Woman.

HO'S BEDROOM: fabulously-furnished, with rare silks, magnificently inlaid, hand-carved furniture, and an enormous bed. There are several white-jade Mythos statuettes, but amid the wealth of furnishings it takes a successful Spot Hidden to notice them, even though they're in the open, resting on a table.

CARL STANFORD'S ROOM: if the investigators have met Stanford in other adventures, they'll be dismayed by his presence here. Mighty Cthulhu has sent Stanford to acquire the *Seven Cryptical Books*—a degenerate scholar and collector, Lin Tang-yu, reportedly owned the scroll on which they were written. Jack Brady stole the tome before Stanford could get there. Now Stanford pursues both the scroll and Jack Brady. Having kidnapped Choi Mei-ling, a young woman who knows Brady's whereabouts, Stanford nears his goal.

CARL STANFORD

If the investigators stake out Fong's house, they have a 50% chance to spot Stanford coming or going. Assuming a discreet stake-out, Stanford has his normal Spot Hidden chance to detect the lurking investigators. If the investigators have not met Carl Stanford, they know no more than that an occidental is staying at Ho's.

THE ROOM OF HO TZU-HSI: Here lives Ho Fong's only child, Tzu-hsi. She is permanently insane, having witnessed the death of her mother during one of her father's obscene rituals. She never leaves this room. A beautiful young woman, she sits here every day, humming in a low voice. She now eats only living things, particularly earthworms, spiders, snails, and slugs which the gardeners catch for her. Entering investigators always see her eating these disgusting natural foods, which entails a 0/1D3 SAN loss to them. She no longer distinguishes anyone but her father, and gives no information of any kind.

HO TZU-HSI

INNER COURT: the garden seems innocuous. A successful Natural History roll identifies nightshade, peyote plants, etc., in the garden, and in the garden pool two blowfish and tiny blue-veined Australian octopuses, also exceptionally poisonous. These and many other natural things are handy sources for mind-altering drugs and poisons. This garden is one of Ho Fong's arsenals.

THE PAVILION: beneath the canopy of the pavilion is a bronze statue of the Buddha. A successful Spot Hidden roll reveals a thin seam around the statue's neck. If the Buddha's head is turned twice in a circle (it only moves clockwise), the entire statue slides out of the wall and to the right, disclosing a dark passageway. This is the entrance to Ho's shrine.

Shrine to the Bloated Woman

Iron grillwork (STR 35) guards the locked door (reduce chance to pick lock by 20%). Beyond the door is a small room about twelve feet square, with a ceiling ten feet high. This ceiling is Ho Fong's trap and recruiting device. Though Ho is already insane, he never watches the ceiling—even the permanently mad can't get back from where the ceiling takes them.

THE CRAWLING CEILING: the ceiling bears large luminescent brush strokes forming the Chinese characters for *bloated woman*. The shapes seem to shift slightly. The investigator can shift away at any time, but an investigator staring at the pattern for more than five combat rounds feels his or her mind being drawn out and into the pattern. The player may then attempt to roll D100 equal to or less then the investigator's INT+POW as a percentage; failing, the investigator's mind is lost to the pattern. The body of a victim continues to stand staring upward, and can be moved like a puppet. Moving a victim of the pattern out of the room is dangerous—while the victim is removed and not looking at the pattern, there is no way for a mind lost to the pattern to be regained.

The mind of a pattern victim understands what has happened, but can't quite get back into its body. It is staggered and bewildered by the avalanche of mental energy from the tormented collective minds—all insane—of everyone already captured. Such an experience is just the thing to drive the new captive insane. For every round within the pattern, the victim loses 0/1D4 SAN points (1/1D4+1 if the keeper is feeling stern). Reaching zero Sanity, the mind is forever captured.

Besides the D100 roll noted above, there is one other chance to come back. If one or several investigators became part of the pattern within a few rounds, their players may meanwhile attempt Luck rolls. Those receiving successful rolls can add together their Power characteristics. The sum represents the number which one of the players must roll equal to or less than on D100. If that roll succeeds, all the participants return to their bodies.

This rescue procedure can be tried just before the first Sanity loss roll. A successful Cthulhu Mythos or Idea roll is needed before the ploy can be attempted.

Though their minds are linked within the pattern, investigator Sanity losses remain individual and are rolled separately.

STATUE OF THE BLOATED WOMAN: Nyarlathotep in that aspect. The workmanship is exquisite and frightening, costing 1/1D4 SAN to view. The statue is eight feet high, and weights about 1000 pounds. Made of a bronze-colored alien alloy, it is impervious to physical damage. Magical attacks reasonably likely to damage an ordinary statue (Dread Clutch of Nyogtha isn't, for instance) can be attempted to damage this representation. The roll must match the statue's current magic points (40 is the maximum) versus the investigator's, on the Resistance Table. Ho knows a spell keyed to the statue which taps these magic points while he touches the idol. The statue regains 2 magic points per day courtesy of Nyarlathotep. It also absorbs the magic points of sacrifices made to it, to its maximum capacity of 40.

Before the statue lay the bone fragments and ashes of incinerated sacrificial victims.

THE TEAK CABINET: about five feet high, this Chinese case has hammered gold doors and is carved with strange monsters and alien inscriptions. The locked cabinet can be forced open (STR 10). Ho Fong always carries on his person the keys to both the cabinet and to the door of the shrine. A poisoned needle guards against lock pickers. Roll Locksmith or Mechanical Repair successfully and the door opens without tripping the defense. Failing the roll, the trap is sprung. Match the POT 15 poison on the needle against the target's CON on the Resistance Table. If the victim successfully resists the poison, he or she is temporarily blind for 1D6 minutes; if he or she fails, permanent blindness ensues. The poison is called Essence of Thoughtful Resignation.

The poison on the needle must be renewed daily, or it is ineffectual. Five sealed one-ounce vials of this poison are within the cabinet. Each vial holds twenty applications.

Also in the cabinet is a small flower press, from which Ho extracts fluids for Essence of Thoughtful Resignation and other poisons. If scrapings from the press are examined in a lab, a successful Natural History roll establishes what flowers are used.

Chinese scrolls and several Western-style books record the visitations of the Bloated Woman, monumental occasions in the cult's history. Sometimes the cult sinks ships, or arranges typhoons or earthquakes, plagues or famines. The Pale Viper—the cult name for Sir Aubrey Penhew—and his plan to blast the skies with far-flung poisoned metal is mentioned. Little more is directly said, but if the investigators penetrate and escape from this room, remind the players of these records if the investigators later need direction.

Additionally, there are five books: *The Goddess of the Black Fan*, commentaries on the *R'lyeh Text* and *The Tale of Priest Kwan* in Chinese, the *Livre d'Ivon* in French, and *True Magick* in English. The first two books are gifts from Carl Stanford to Ho Fong. There is an 80% chance that one or the other book has been left open in Ho's library.

LIVRE D'IVON: in French, +12 percentiles to Cthulhu Mythos knowledge, Sanity loss to read is 1D4/2D4 SAN points, spell multiplier is x2. As per the *Call of Cthulhu* rules.

TRUE MAGICK: by Theophilus Wenn, in English, +6 percentiles to Cthulhu Mythos knowledge, Sanity loss to read is 1D4/1D8 SAN, spell multiplier x2. As per the *Call of Cthulhu* rules.

THE GODDESS OF THE BLACK FAN: by Liu Chan-fang. Written on a scroll in classical Chinese, +5 percentiles to Cthulhu Mythos, Sanity loss to read is 0/1D4 SAN points. To learn the spell requires the ability to read the scroll plus a D100 roll of INT x5 or less. Spell: Contact Nyarlathotep.

The poems of this book tell how the monk Liu meets a goddess who hides her face behind a black fan. The goddess seduces the author, telling Liu her true name and how to call her from behind the fan. He follows her bidding, and is struck with horror when he sees the Bloated Woman. Losing all reason, he writes a last poem in his own blood after gutting himself with a sickle. This is the foundation for and the most sacred tome of the Order of the Bloated Woman. The cult will do anything and slay anyone to retrieve this book. Though he never mentions the name Nyarlathotep, one of the poems acts as the spell Contact Nyarlathotep in the aspect of the Bloated Woman.

R'LYEH TEXT COMMENTARY: in classical Chinese. Spells: Contact Cthulhu, Contact Spawn of Cthulhu, Grasp of Cthulhu, and Wave of Oblivion. The book also contains a sketch map of R'lyeh. +15 percentiles to Cthulhu Mythos

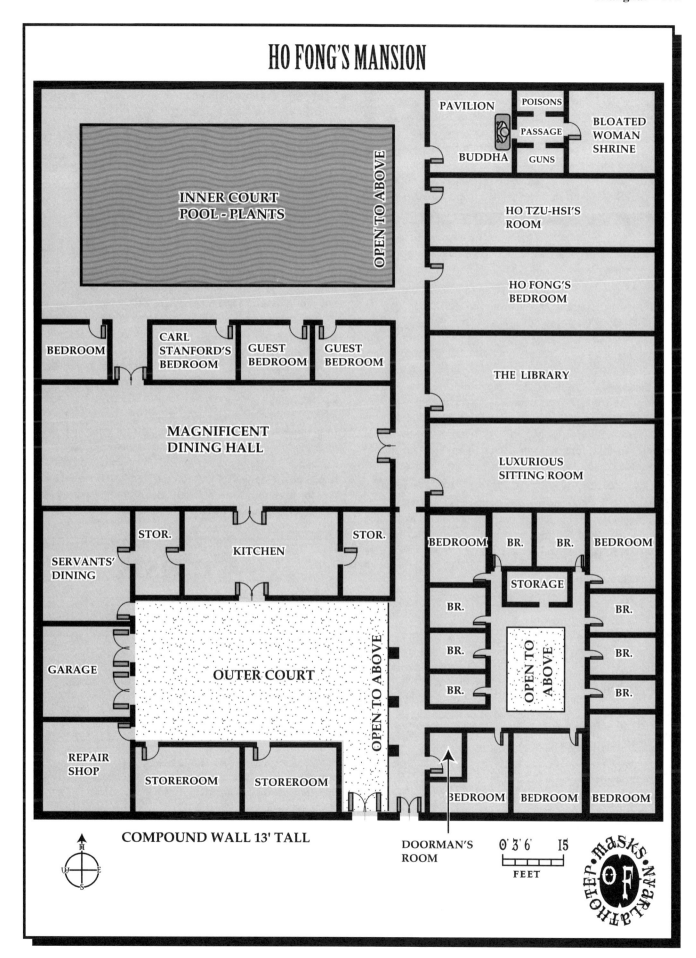

Tyuk

When mixed with liquid and swallowed, this greenish powder acts as a powerful hallucinogen. The target remains lucid, but for the next hour his or her senses have ten times normal sensitivity. Pain is especially overwhelming. One dose lasts one hour, two doses last two hours, and three doses kill outright. Made from a flowering plant known in Chinese as the Blue Petals of the Ineffable Paths, the preparation is rare. A successful Natural History roll locates the plant in Ho's garden.

knowledge, Sanity Loss to read is 1D8/2D8 Sanity points, spell multiplier x4.

THE TALE OF PRIEST KWAN: in classical Chinese, +5 percentiles to Cthulhu Mythos knowledge, Sanity loss to read is 1/1D6 SAN points, INT x1 to learn spells. Spells are partly in the form of poems, partly in the accompanying annotations: Grasp of Cthulhu, Power Drain, Shrivelling, and Steal Life.

This homily tells how, with pure faith, a priest of the Order of the Bloated Woman overcame and humbled a powerful noble. It graphically describes cult rituals, and mentions a powerful aide to the priest, a friend called the Great Faced Lion—a reference to the Black Sphinx and the cult of the Black Pharaoh (see the Cairo or London chapters).

OTHER CONTENTS OF THE TEAK CABINET: the black and yellow silk robe which is the ritual dress for priests of the Order, small torture implements such as needles of ascending gauge, a medallion bearing the cult characters, a kit holding several tattoo needles and some black and yellow dyes, the ritual sickle used in cult murders and sacrifices, and a small jar of a powder called tyuk.

THE SEVEN GATES TO HEAVEN: centered on the floor is a wide circle within which the cult characters have been inlaid in gold. Across this circle has been laid a coffin-like glass and steel box, three feet wide and six feet long. The box lies east to west; on its east end is a movable cage which holds two large, hungry, scaly Shanghai river rats. Choi Mei-ling lies naked within the box, her face directly beneath a thick glass plate—the only obstacle between her and the leering, salivating rodents.

The box holding Miss Choi is divided into seven compartments—the seven gates to heaven—by six yoke-like partitions sandwiching under and over her, both keeping her body immobile and the intervening spaces separate from one another. To torture her, the rat cage is moved to above one of the seven compartments, the clear glass bottom of the cage removed, and the hungry rats admitted. Earlier in the day, they were admitted to the compartment containing her feet and ankles, severely slashing and gnawing her before the gloved handler pulled the foul rodents back into the rat cage by their neck chains. No use to kill her by letting them chew her feet to the bone. After she talks there is plenty of time.

Miss Choi scarcely kept her sanity. Her screams tore

through the room. Carl Stanford smiled at her and said that, when he returned, he would select a new site upon which his pets could graze. Then he moved the rat cage to directly above her face. "Look upon them, my dear," he told her, "and try to find it within yourself to be more cooperative. Is Jack Brady worth such devotion?"

Mei-ling is a realist, however. She knows that Stanford will kill her once she tells him what he wants to know. Her remaining hope is that she can die before the pain betrays her. Even if rescued, she carries this death wish with her—she'll try to kill herself in some quick, painless way. A successful Psychoanalysis roll for a rescuing investigator or patient, friendly care alleviates her terror and depression, and she'll agree to tell them where Brady is.

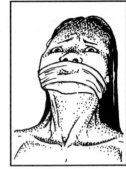

CHOI MEI-LING

The keeper decides if Mei-ling talks or dies bravely if the investigators fail to find her. It is suggested that her fate begin to be considered from the moment that the investigators learn of her disappearance. If the investigators never learn of her, the fate of poor Miss Choi is left to the kindly keeper.

Incidentally, anyone bitten by one of the rats must receive a successful D100 roll equal to or less than his or her CON x2, or contract a virulent disease. Symptoms appear in 1D4 days after the bite and, without bed rest and medical treatment, the disease will be fatal in 1D2 weeks. Blood poisoning or bubonic plague are obviously possibilities, but keepers may make it a more mysterious fever which comes and goes at awkward moments, palliated by successful Medicine rolls.

Cultists

HO FONG, age 57, High Priest of the Bloated Woman, Wealthy Merchant

STR 07	CON 13	SIZ 10	INT 19	POW 21
DEX 12	APP 14	SAN 0	EDU 12	HP 12

Damage Bonus: +0.

Weapons: Cult Sickle 85%, damage 1D4+3
Fighting Knife* 80%, damage 1D4+2
Fist/Punch 65%, damage 1D3

* Though Ho always carries a concealed fighting knife, he prefers slower, subtler methods. Adept with drugs and poisons, his cunning and intelligence are his most dangerous assets.

Spells: Contact Deep Ones, Contact Nyarlathotep, Grasp of Cthulhu, Hands of Colubra, Powder of Ibn-Ghazi, Summon Byakhee, Summon/Bind Hunting Horror, Wave of Oblivion.

Skills: Accounting 75%, Archaeology 25%, Bargain 80%, Classical Chinese 75%, Credit Rating 95%, Cthulhu Mythos 45%, Debate 50%, Dodge 80%, Dutch 30%, English 60%, Fast Talk 60%, French 30%, Hide 70%, Japanese 50%, Listen 65%, Mandarin Chinese 95%, Natural History 60%, Persuade 55%, Pharmacy 35%, Poisons 60%, Psychology 50%, Sneak 90%, Spot Hidden 70%, Swim 35%.

HO TZU-HSI, age 13, Insane Daughter of Ho Fong

STR 05	CON 07	SIZ 05	INT 10	POW 04
DEX 10	APP 11	EDU 07	SAN 0*	HP 06

Damage Bonus: -1D6.

Weapons: none

Skills: Catch Crawling Food 55%.

Permanently insane, poor Tzu-hsi is incapable of speech, reaction, defense, or attack, and is in no way dangerous. Kindly investigators who try to help her waste their time.

ASSORTED CULTISTS, Order of the Bloated Woman

Recall the bad guys in the worst kung fu movie you ever saw—here they are, bullies, cowards, and fanatics. Numbers One and Four can be leaders; Number Eight is the wily spy; Number Six is the fall guy. While in Shanghai, reuse these cultists as needed.

	1	2	3	4	5	6	7	8
STR	16	17	18	15	17	16	10	16
CON	13	10	12	14	16	09	10	08
SIZ	11	09	08	13	10	10	18	12
DEX	17	16	15	13	13	09	11	10
APP	03	03	04	06	05	07	04	70
INT	10	09	08	10	08	08	12	14
POW	09	06	13	04	15	09	10	14
HP	12	10	10	14	13	10	14	10

Damage Bonus: +1D4.

Weapons: Fist 70%, damage 1D3+1D4
Jo Stick 65%, damage 1D6+1D4
Cult Sickle 50%, damage 1D8+1+1D4
Head Butt 50%, damage 1D4+1D4
Grapple 50%, damage special
Kick 45%, damage 1D6+1D4

Skills: Cthulhu Mythos 08%, Dodge 65%, English 15%, Hide 60%, Jump 55%, Listen 65%, Mandarin Chinese 60%, Martial Arts 40%, Sneak 55%, Spot Hidden 35%.

	9	10	11	12	13	14	15	16
STR	07	10	08	11	11	13	15	12
CON	07	10	09	16	14	12	10	14
SIZ	09	10	08	10	13	08	08	12
DEX	16	16	16	13	13	13	10	10
APP	08	08	10	03	05	05	04	07
INT	11	11	12	08	09	05	08	13
POW	09	09	06	07	06	05	09	08
HP	08	10	09	13	14	11	09	13

Damage Bonus: +0.

Weapons: Fist 70%, damage 1D3
Jo Stick 65%, damage 1D6
Cult Sickle 50%, damage 1D8+1
Head Butt 50%, damage 1D4
Grapple 50%, damage special
Kick 45%, damage 1D6

Skills: Cthulhu Mythos 08%, Dodge 65%, English 15%, Hide 60%, Jump 55%, Listen 65%, Mandarin Chinese 60%, Martial Arts 40%, Sneak 55%, Spot Hidden 35%.

CARL STANFORD, may be immortal, Master Sorcerer and Mythos Fanatic

STR 14	CON 16	SIZ 12	INT 18	POW 40
DEX 14	APP 18	EDU 30	SAN 0	HP 14

Damage Bonus: +1D4.

Weapon: Sword Cane 95%, damage 1D6+1D4

Spells: all spells in the rulesbook, plus others the keeper may choose.

Magic Items: Sword cane stores magic points and currently holds 60 magic points. Magical gate box is linked to its twin in Hoosick Falls, New York State, USA.

Skills: Arabic 80%, Archaeology 75%, Astronomy 20%, Classical Greek 95%, Credit Rating 60%, Cthulhu Mythos 49%, English 95%. Fast Talk 85%, History 55%, Library Use 95%, Mandarin Chinese 80%, Persuade 90%, Sneak 80%.

INDEPENDENTS

*A captain in the Imperial Japanese Navy,
a degenerate mandarin from an inland city,
and reliable newspaper stories offer delicate opportunities.*

Isoge Taro

Captain Isoge was participating in the Imperial Japanese Navy's systematic survey of Chinese ports when he heard rumors of an awesome new weapon being developed by a Chinese faction. A member of the right-wing Kochisha and a protégé of Okawa Shumei, Isoge used his powerful connections to be assigned to investigate the matter. He has spent two months undercover, and has recruited several Shanghai-area Chinese as agents.

Isoge knows that Jack Brady is somehow involved. Along with other locations, Isoge has staked out the Stumbling Tiger. He knows that a fanatic militia is training in an empty ware-house on the south side of the river (on Chung-shan Road), and he knows that Brady has some connection to it, but he does not know that the New China group plans immediate action. (The existence of private soldiers is not news. Anyone who is anyone employs armed guards, perhaps hundreds of them, and most of these private armies in and around the city are intent on murdering each other. Isoge has contempt for the decadence which allows such disorderly conduct.)

The first time the investigators go to the Stumbling Tiger Bar, Isoge is there, dressed as a Japanese foreman and acting quite drunk. If an Anthropology roll is asked for by a player, it establishes that Isoge's actions are a bit too polished for his role. Likewise, a successful Psychology roll detects that

Isoge's reflexes have not been uniformly weakened by drinking, and that Isoge manages to spill most of his liquor, rather than drink it.

If Isoge overhears Brady's name mentioned to McChum, he'll shadow the investigators. The Spot Hidden chance to detect the tail is reduced by 25 percentiles.

Isoge knows nothing about the Order of the Bloated Woman. He fears that the new weapon is being assembled by Comintern advisors to the local Communists.

The investigators may be able to team up with Isoge. Even if they know that he is a Japanese agent, the effort might not be contrary to American national interests (like saving the world). Remember that Isoge can be deadly, and that he will not sell his honor and allegiance to Japan for the sake of momentarily friendly relations with a handful of Americans engaged in some mythological quest.

ISOGE TARO

Isoge is dedicated and formidable. He is perfectly willing to sacrifice himself to accomplish his mission of uncovering, destroying, or capturing the secret weapon. It is much more likely that he will announce himself to the investigators than that they ever will trap him into revealing himself.

ISOGE TARO, age 34, Agent of the Emperor and Captain in the Imperial Japanese Navy

STR 13	CON 16	SIZ 12	INT 18	POW 12
DEX 18	APP 15	EDU 16	SAN 60	HP 14

Damage Bonus: +1D4.

Weapons: 8mm Automatic Pistol (Pattern 14) 75%, damage 1D8
Fist 75%, damage 1D3+1D4
Head Butt 55%, damage 1D4+1D4
Fighting Knife 50%, damage 1D4+2 +1D4
6.5mm Rifle (Type 38) 35%, 2D8 damage
Samurai Ceremonial Sword 25%, damage 1D8+1+1D4

Skills: Bargain 30%, Climb 55%, Crack Cipher 25%, Credit Rating 25%, Disguise 45%, Dodge 65%, Drive Automobile 45%, Electrical Repair 50%, English 30%, Explosives 50%, Fast Talk 30%, Hide 50%, History 25%, Japanese 90%, Korean 15%, Library Use 35%, Listen 75%, Mandarin Chinese 55%, Martial Arts 70%, Mechanical Repair 40%, Persuade 45%, Psychology 50%, Sneak 60%, Swim 35%, Tagalog 15%, Throw 45%.

Lin Tang-Yu

The degenerate Mr. Lin, a resident of Kweilin, China, possesses an extensive Mythos library. By a stroke of luck (he always seems to be lucky), Jack Brady relieved Mr. Lin of a prized possession, the *Seven Cryptical Books of Hsan*, an important Cthulhu Mythos source. Mr. Lin wants the scroll back. He has come to Shanghai to get it. That is his motive. He knows of the Order of the Bloated Woman, and does not want trouble with it, though he would not be afraid to take advantage of the Order in certain circumstances.

Lin's cutthroats have been scouring the city. They watch McChum's, among other bars. They are very interested in the activities of the Order, and keep close watch on Ho's warehouse, yacht, and home. Occidentals visiting Ho, especially people asking for Jack Brady, draw Lin's attention and possibly his cruel questions.

In shadowing the investigators, Lin's agents are detectable by Spot Hiddens at a chance reduced by 15 percentiles. If the henchmen track the investigators back to their hotel, they soon ransack the investigators' rooms, stealing collectibles such as jewelry, old books, and statuettes.

Lin's agents can also be followed. Doing this leads the investigators to Lin's Shanghai headquarters, a large compound on Yu-yuan Road.

LIN'S SHANGHAI HEADQUARTERS

The house is well guarded, and those guards do their best to kill intruders. Additionally, Lin has two extraordinary guards—two large white apes, Tun-Tun and Ping—always hidden near him and controlled only by him.

The guards of the house take messages, and the investigators can make an appointment with Lin if they want. A letter handed to the doorman has the quickest effect. Fast Talks and Persuades have no effect on Lin's hand-picked guards.

Lin Tang-yu agrees to see the investigators if they possess the scroll of the *Seven Cryptical Books*, if the investigators seem likely to learn the scroll's location, if the investigators offer to sell to Lin some unique book or artifact for his delectation, or if one or more of the investigators is a good-looking female. Each possibility provokes a particular course of action by Lin, as summarized in a few paragraphs below.

The degenerate mandarin greets the investigators in his throne room, sitting formally on a magnificently carved chair. To his left a small table bears his opium pipe. His apes wait behind a curtain near the throne chair (a successful Spot Hidden tells the investigators that someone or something lurks there, but nothing more). At Lin's feet sits a beautiful woman in costly silks. Two more can appear from an adjoining room to do his bidding should he so desire. Soon after acquisition they all are silent—Lin severs the vocal cords of his women.

As he talks, a successful Psychology reveals that Lin is insane, though he gives the illusion of competency. He is an accomplished liar—reduce by 25 percentiles Psychology rolls to detect truths or falsehood. Even under the influence of opium, to which he may turn without apology, nodding in silence for a few minutes, Lin Tang-yu is cunning and dangerous, guided only by his own desires. If the investigators become his enemies, they should consider fleeing China.

If they show him the Eye of Light and Darkness (half was in Egypt, and the other half held by Jack Brady), Lin immediately recognizes it from the description in the *Seven Cryptical Books of Hsan*. Though he never reveals this to the investigators, he immediately wants the ward for his collection. He has no interest in trying to use it for anything, much less the benefit of mankind.

POSSESSION OF THE SEVEN CRYPTICAL BOOKS: Lin demands the scroll back. If the investigators do not yet possess it, he bargains with them to obtain it. Since the *Seven Cryptical Books* are Lin's property (sort of, since the scroll's

previous owner died suddenly), Lin will not pay for the scroll's return. He may say that he will, but he'll take the scroll by force instead. If the scroll is held by some third party, and can be taken only by assault, Lin may offer some of his men as shock troops. These bandits serve faithfully until the scroll is recovered, then do their best to kill the investigators and make off with the loot.

OFFER TO SELL AN ARTIFACT: if Lin's thieves do not manage to steal everything which the investigators have, Lin may be willing to bargain for some choice item. He may pay good money on the spot, but this is a ploy. That night he sends one or both of his killer apes to take back the money and silence the seller, and anybody else who may know of the transaction.

PRESENCE OF A GOOD-LOOKING FEMALE: as he makes small talk, Lin studies her. He pretends to consider whatever the investigators tell him or ask him, then says that he must consider what they say. He asks for quiet, then removes himself to another part of the room and there casts the yarrow stalks in the ancient ritual of the I Ching. "Hmm," Lin lies, "Hsiao Ch'u. Nine at the top." He takes up one of many ancient scrolls resting in a lacquer stand, and reads from it:

> *When rain comes, then comes rest*
> *as nature and character align.*
> *Only loud effort may endanger the superior woman,*
> *for she is strongest when the moon is nearly full.*
> *But should superior men persist,*
> *Misfortune follows.*

Lin says that the meaning is clear. To be aligned with destiny, he must follow the prescription of the trigram. "You, my dear," he says to the attractive female investigator, "must come here tomorrow evening. Try not to be seen. Here we two will complete the arrangements. Your friends may not come for, as the trigram states, their presence guarantees our failure." If the investigators protest, Lin remains adamant. The oracle must be followed, or all is lost. Nothing dissuades him.

If the female investigator returns to Lin's house as he asks, there she is drugged and flown in one of his planes to Lin's palace in Kweilin, and forced into his harem. Abducted women are usually hidden in large amphorae and taken away at night. A stake-out at the house sees several trips out and back by both a closed car and a truck. Unless investigators follow the truck, they'll never know where it took their friend. If she declines the invitation, Lin's henchmen try once to kidnap her, then give up.

If he successfully kidnaps the woman, Lin offers his consolations to the rest of the investigators. She slipped out a secret exit, as befitted the oracle, he says. He will have his men scour the city for her, he swears. A thousand regrets! But his men never find her. Then urgent business calls him back to Kweilin, from which he does not return.

Keepers might keep in mind that Lin Tang-yu has no aversion to working with the Order of the Bloated Woman if he can thereby achieve his end, and that this may entail a meeting with Ho Fong. But neither Lin nor Fong have reason to cooperate with Isoge Taro or his agents. The valiant Japanese is likely to conclude his investigation as a corpse.

WHAT LIN TANG-YU KNOWS

■ He is conversant with the pantheon of the Cthulhu Mythos. His Kweilin collection contains books pertaining to the Mythos, and his private intelligence corps keeps him informed about Nyarlathotep's cult in China.

■ He knows that the Order of the Bloated Woman holds rites on Gray Dragon Island, that they worship an aspect of the god whom the investigators know as Nyarlathotep, and that Ho Fong is High Priest. He knows that Carl Stanford is staying at Ho Fong's home, and that Stanford is a powerful magician. He knows nothing of Sir Aubrey Penhew.

■ A powerful machine has been whispered of as being built on the island, but Lin can learn nothing more, and has begun to discount the rumor as baseless.

■ He knows that Jack Brady stole the *Seven Cryptical Books of Hsan*, and knows that the Order also seeks Brady, though not why they want him. Jack Brady's girlfriend, Choi Mei-ling, has disappeared, but Lin does not know where she is.

Lin's knowledge of the occult and of the Mythos suffices to protect him. His knowledge of Asia is great. He raised his guardian white gorillas from their infancy, and may have some connection to the notorious Congo cult of the White Gorilla (see the Kenya Colony chapter and Neville Jermyn for a summary). Lin has an affinity with all simians and believes, given time, that he could command almost any ape. He is second brother to a notorious Kwangsi province warlord who has thrown in his lot with Chiang Kai-shek.

LIN TANG-YU, age 83, Wealthy Aesthete, Voyeur, Sadist, Addict, Murderer

STR 08	CON 15	SIZ 10	INT 15	POW 12
DEX 09	APP 08	EDU 20	SAN 0	HP 13

Damage Bonus: +0.

Weapons: none. The servants will do it.

Skills: Anthropology 35%, Arabic 35%, Archaeology 30%, Bargain 80%, Canton Chinese 75%, Classical Greek 20%, Command Apes 95%, Cthulhu Mythos 15%, English 45%, Fast Talk 90%, History 35%, Japanese 45%, Library Use 35%, Mandarin Chinese 90%, Occult 65%, Persuade 55%, Psychology 50%, Russian 20%, Sanskrit 40%, Sneak 60%, Spot Hidden 50%, Tibetan 40%.

LIN TANG-YU'S WHITE GUARDIAN GORILLAS

TUNTUN, The Larger Gorilla

STR 30	CON 15	SIZ 20	INT 07	POW 08
DEX 18	MOV 8			HP 18

Damage Bonus: +2D6.

Weapons: Bite* 65%, damage 1D6
Hand* 50%, damage 1D6+2D6**

Armor: 2-point skin.

Skills: Climb 99%, Dodge 95%, Hide 85%, Jump 95%, Sneak 75%.

PING, The Smaller Gorilla

STR 25	CON 17	SIZ 18	INT 03	POW 05
DEX 16	MOV 8			HP 18

Damage Bonus: +2D6.

Weapons: Bite* 45%, damage 1D6
Hand* 45%, damage 1D6+2D6**

Armor: 2-point skin

Skills: Climb 99%, Dodge 95%, Hide 85%, Jump 95%, Sneak 75%.

These gorillas can bite and attack with both hands in one round.

** *If one of these gorillas hits with both hands, it grapples its foe, doing the gorilla's damage bonus in damage to the victim in each successive round until the victim breaks the gorilla's grasp with a successful STR vs. STR roll on the Resistance Table, or until the target dies. A gorilla can bite while grappling. The grappled victim cannot melee with a weapon longer than a dagger or a hatchet.*

NEFARIOUS HENCHMEN OF LIN TANG-YU

Lin's men are trained in Monkey School gung-fu. Their hatchets bear the symbol of a monkey, and a Chinese sage such as Mu Hsien has a 35% chance of recognizing it as referring to Lin Tang-yu. These men are not too intelligent, but they're fanatically loyal. At least ten guard the Shanghai house at all times, while twice that many more ransack Shanghai for Jack Brady and the *Seven Cryptical Books of Hsan.*

NEFARIOUS HENCHMEN

	1	2	3	4	5	6	7	8
STR	15	14	12	16	13	13	15	14
CON	13	15	11	10	16	14	12	10
SIZ	09	10	11	08	11	10	09	10
DEX	15	14	12	13	16	10	09	12
APP	06	03	10	09	03	07	08	05
INT	09	08	10	10	10	10	11	12
POW	10	11	12	09	08	09	03	07
HP	11	13	11	09	14	12	11	10

Damage Bonus: +0.

Weapons: Fist/Punch 80%, damage 1D3
Monkey Hatchet 75%, damage 1D6+1, base range 8 yards
Head Butt 60%, damage 1D4
Kick 55%, damage 1D6
Monkey School Blackjack 50%, damage special*
Throwing Darts (ten per man) 50%, damage 1D3 each**
Grapple 35%, damage special

* *a hit means the target is knocked unconscious; this special blackjack used in melee does only 1D3 damage and is not a viable weapon.*

** *the darts may be tipped with poison or sleeping drug. The poison is POT 3D6, made from the venom of the krait snake; if it overcomes the target, he or she dies in a few minutes. If the POT does not overcome the target's CON on the resistance table, the target becomes extremely ill for several hours, halving all skill rolls. The sleep drug is Fragile Silver, POT 1D6+6. Overcoming the target's CON, it puts him or her to sleep in one minute; failing that, for 1D6 minutes it halves his or her DEX and leaves the victim groggy. Guards at Lin's home always apply sleeping drug to their darts; henchmen elsewhere have a 15% chance to have applied poison.*

Skills: English 20%, Fast Talk 45%, Hide 75%, Jump 70%, Listen 65%, Mandarin Chinese 55%, Martial Arts 50%, Sneak 80%, Spot Hidden 70%, Track 50%.

The *Shanghai Courier*

An English/Mandarin dual-language newspaper with a circulation of nearly 30,000 copies daily, it speaks for property owners and folk of financial substance—especially occidental Christians—but the accuracy and completeness of its reporting is respected throughout the Far East. It is a daily newspaper, usually of no more than twelve pages.

The files of the *Courier* are available at the Settlement public library, or at the *Courier* itself, in business libraries, educational institutions, and so on. It takes a day to research the back issues since 1919, the year of the Carlyle Expedition. Three recent articles catch the investigators' attention, because they all suggest "monsters".

ITEM. A news clipping from the *Shanghai Courier* (*Nyarlathotep Papers #38-40*).

Relevance of the Information: each clipping is a lead that, if followed up on, may direct the investigators to Jack Brady. The violent events discussed in the clippings should suggest that Brady is or recently was in great danger.

ITEM. Seamens Club Damaged, a story which appears in the *Shanghai Courier* six week before the investigators arrive in Shanghai (*Nyarlathotep Papers #38*).

Follow-up Information: (1) In surveying the scene of the damage, successful Geology or Mechanical Repair rolls indicate no apparent sign of an undermine. (2) A successful Luck roll uncovers one of the drunks in the story: he says that the creatures were like walking octopuses. (3) A successful Idea roll reveals that an American ("John Smith") was staying in the room directly facing the shattered wall; there is no trace of him. (4) If the investigators have a picture of Jack Brady, several of the Seamens Club staff identify him as Smith.

ITEM. Fire on Chin-lang Road, a story which appears in the *Shanghai Courier* four week before the investigators arrive in Shanghai (*Nyarlathotep Papers #39*).

Nyarlathotep Papers #38

Seamens Club Damaged

A portion of the Seamens Club was destroyed late last night, and inspectors report considerable damage to the river side of the institution "in excess of 8,000 pounds sterling," according to underwriters.

No injury or loss of life is reported.

According to unconfirmed though informed speculation, seepage undermined a portion of the embankment area upon which the famous club stands, causing the collapse.

Inebriates congregating along the bank swear that strange creatures emerged from the river shortly before the collapse. Their stories were a hearty momentary relief to the risky business of sorting through the rubble.

— *Shanghai Courier*

Nyarlathotep Papers #39

Fire on Chin-Ling Road

Three monks have been found dead in a pavilion fire in the Garden of the Purple Clouds of Autumn. They are thought to have died because of an overturned brazier.

The names of the deceased have not yet been released, but a reliable source indicates that all three were respected scholars of T'ang, Five Dynasties, and Sung literature, a profound loss to all who value China's great heritage.

Eyewitnesses remarked that the evening fire leapt in an uncanny fashion from one blazing structure to follow the fleeing monks into the second pavilion. "A floating cloud of fire followed them," according to Mr. Liu Chen-dai of Brilliant Poppy lane.

A European was seen leaving the vicinity of the conflagration. Police respectfully ask his assistance in their investigation.

—Shanghai Courier

Nyarlathotep Papers #40

Violent Incident on Lantern Street

Police report murders at Number 88 Lantern Street, "sometime after midnight" last night. The victims are identified as Miss Reparita Wong, resident at the address, and Mr. Chin Hsi-chou, address unavailable at the time of publication.

Police inspector Chong indicates that the slayings were unusually violent. He requests information from anyone with knowledge either of Miss Wong or Mr. Chin.

Even Lantern Street habitues, normally not noted for compassion, were taken aback by the cruelty of the crimes. One witness was so distraught that she identified the killer as a giant bat.

—Shanghai Courier

Nyarlathotep Papers #41

 THE STARS ARE RIGHT!

Do not allow dark fate to overwhelm you! Worry not that evil rivals seem to possess secret knowledge that you lack! The answer is in the stars! Consult the Heavenly Stem and the Earthly Branch for the answers. A most auspicious future is guaranteed! Contact Shanghai's Famous Astrologer, Mister Lung, 129 Kaoyang St. No appointment necessary. Any time before 10.00 P.M.

Follow-up Information: (1) An examination of the weather summary for this same day in the paper discloses that the entire day was unusually humid and windless—not likely conditions for a mobile fire. (2) The garden is just behind the Town Gods Temple. The bonze at the temple does not know why the monks had gathered in the garden, but he will recognize a photo of Jack Brady as the European who was also in the garden and who talked with the monks for some time.

ITEM. Violent Incident on Lantern Street, a story which appears in the *Shanghai Courier* two days before the investigators arrive in Shanghai (*Nyarlathotep Papers #40*).

FOLLOW-UP INFORMATION: (1) The building where the murders took place is just down the street from the Stumbling Tiger Bar. Inspection shows that it's a flower girl house, one of many in Hongkew. If they knock, several naughty ladies happily greet them; the manager of the house, a fierce woman named Madame Gee, condescends to talk with them if the investigators offer an amount in some currency equivalent to 1D10+10 Mexican silver dollars.

She'll show them the murder room—furnishings completely demolished and walls, floor, and ceiling splattered with blood. Anything else she doesn't know. She wasn't here, and she has things to do. She takes offers of additional money as insulting, and calls in two gigantic Korean bouncers who offer to neuter or otherwise alter the genetic destinies of insistent investigators.

(2) If any of the investigators receive a successful Idea roll, he apologizes profusely and requests meetings with the working women of the house. One of them, Quivering Jade, says that the girl who had lived in the room was sold to another house (140 Lantern Street) just the day before the murder, because she insisted on keeping an American in her room, a man whom Madame Gee disliked. Quivering Jade knew him only as "John", but she can identify Jack Brady from his photograph. The girl who was sold was Choi Mei-ling. Magenta Joy, the girl who said she saw a giant bat, is in the hospital in shock.

(3) The manager of Number 140 Lantern Street, a hokey Taoist "doctor" wearing a robe embroidered with meaningless symbols, is very interested if the investigators ask about Choi Mei-ling. "That whore escape!" he shouts. "I pay good money. I treat her right!" he swears. The investigators get no other information from this cad.

(4) Magenta Joy is in a nearby Chinese hospital. She is quite mad, and may be that way for months. An interview results in nothing but babble, unless an investigator shows her a representation of a hunting horror; then the poor woman begins to scream, and continues long after the investigators depart.

(5) A successful Idea roll causes an investigator to study the obituary notices in the *Courier* for the next few days. He or she will find a notice of Mr. Chin Hsi-chou's funeral, as well as his home address, a small apartment near the Old City. Questioning the neighbors about poor Mr. Chin, the investigators learn that he was liked and respected; everyone agrees that he had a hankering for flower girls and that he was just in the wrong place at the wrong time. They're right.

ITEM. A strange ad for an astrologer (*Nyarlathotep Papers #41*) which appears in the *Shanghai Courier* the day the investigators arrive in Shanghai. The advertisement runs in both English and Chinese.

Relevance of the Information: This advertisement is unrelated to either Nyarlathotep's plans, or Jack Brady's current location. However, the catch-phrases may attract the investigators. In addition, alert investigators will notice the address is close to Mr. Ho Fong's warehouse. If the players decide to investigate this ad, they will most likely become involved with "The Demon Cabinet of Mister Lung", below.

MORE *COURIER* MATERIAL

Additionally, the investigators notice the occasional mention of victims slain in identical fashion, their arms severed from their bodies. No sharp instruments were left at the scenes of the crimes. The victims were unrelated, except in their manner of death. A madman or a secret cult have been suggested. Recently, as many as two victims per month have been found. All the victims were poor and without influence.

Finally, about six months before the arrival of the investigators, a brief account tells of a huge wave swamping a trawler working near Gray Dragon shoals. The sole survivor swears that the wave struck without warning, on a calm day.

THE DEMON CABINET OF MISTER LUNG

*In which the investigators become entangled with
the powers of celestial retribution, and it is learned that
mere humans may never out-smart the wiliest of cats.*

This is a brief red-herring adventure, intended to contrast with the intensity of thwarting the dark god as well as to offer a fresh chance for investigators to be killed under unusual circumstances. Mistaken identities, slapstick reactions, and comical cats rub shoulders with traditional elements of Chinese mysticism, straight-forward murder, and sly treachery. Consider it a black farce.

Mr. Lung is a working astrologer and practitioner of the arts of Chinese magic. His indiscreet behavior and poor manners have got him into trouble with the Heavenly Powers. They have dispatched a demon to bring Mr. Lung to celestial justice. However part of the task of Chinese astrology is to determine those times in one's life when supernatural forces are

MR. LUNG YEN

ranged against one. Mr. Lung knows a demon or demons are coming today and is ready to meet them. He knows this visitor or visitors will take some outlandish form, probably that of weird human strangers. Unhappily for the investigators the day that has been foretold to Mr. Lung is the one on which they come to visit.

INVESTIGATOR'S INTRODUCTION

Only one opportunity exists for the investigators to encounter this adventure and that is Mister Lung's advertisement, which appears in the *Courier* (see *Nyarlathotep Papers #41*). If the investigators do not research old issues of the *Shanghai Courier*, or if they decide to ignore the advertisement, then the fate of Mister Lung is written only in the stars.

The House of Mr. Lung

Mr. Lung lives in a house on the north bank of the Whangpoo, two blocks east of Ho Fong's warehouse. It is small, the ground floor of a three-story building. It has five rooms: a front living area, a small office for astrological readings, a bedroom, a bathroom, and a back room at the top of a short flight of stairs. In the back room, junk and the demon cabinet are stored. This room is cluttered and smells of incense and burning slippers.

THE CAT ON THE THRESHOLD

Outside on the step a Siamese cat yowls to get in. It continues to appear at windows around the house, howling the whole time until someone lets it in. This could alert investigators to its demonic nature. It is pretty standard behavior for a Siamese cat. Mr. Lung has never seen the cat, but presumes it is a neighbor's animal, though the keeping of pets is relatively rare just now.

MR. LUNG

He is short, slight, and normally affable. Today, however, his looming fate leaves him demented and wild. When they arrive, he is convinced that the investigators are the demons sent to destroy him and escort his soul to the underworld. He believes their attempts to behave like curiosity-seekers simply display the usual cruelty of demons.

The investigators play with him, hoping to catch him off-guard and at the same time prolonging his agony. He maintains a desperate politeness towards the investigators even while he plots to destroy them. He talks with them about their interests in astrology and pretends to be willing to compile horoscopes for them—anything to stall their final attack and buy him time to annihilate them. If cornered or forced to confess, Mr. Lung accuses his demons of being especially cruel and blurts out the whole story, clinging fast to his belief the investigators are his tormentors. Only restraint or the appearance of the real demon (see below) will be sufficient against him.

MR. LUNG'S CRAFT

The notion of one's destiny fixed in the heavens from the moment of birth accords well with the fatalism of traditional Chinese beliefs. The twelve-year cycle of animals that is the most widely known facet of Chinese astrology bears as little resemblance to the real thing as newspaper astrological sections bear to the work of genuine Western astrologers. Mr. Lung's branch of astrology, Tzu Wei (Purple Star Astrology), is enormously complex and difficult to do. It takes into account the constellation animal of the hour, month, and day as well as the year of birth and the various mansions or palaces in which auspicious or inauspicious stars appear. Skilled practitioners are prized.

Mr. Lung's Defences

The mistaken astrologer will try several defenses against his demon enemies. He grows increasingly desperate as one by one his supernatural precautions fail. These are demons of the most powerful kind! The defenses appear below in Lung's order of preference. He resorts to each succeeding one with mounting bewilderment and anxiety as the investigators breeze past.

The keeper's difficulty here will be to introduce each defense clearly but casually, without so much emphasis that the players immediately understand that there must be meaning behind Lung's strange actions.

If the true demon, Wu the Demon-Cat, confronts these protections, it must resist the power of each on the Resistance Table or be driven squalling from the house. Otherwise it ignores the protections. Even if driven out, it prowls around doors and windows, sniffing audibly and growling sullenly, reluctant to report failure to the Celestial Court. It is a most persistent demon.

TIGER SCROLLS: Tigers offer good protection against demons whom the household spirits cannot repel. If the demons get this far they probably need a good dose of tigers. Tiger scrolls dangle about the front hall on strips like flypaper. Match Wu the Demon-Cat's POW against POW 14 on the Resistance Table.

FENG SHUI: The positioning of items in the room is crucial, not just for the good fortune this brings, but because many demons can only travel in straight lines and, finding themselves blocked, will be thwarted and must leave. Thus partitions and screens have been set up strategically, and chairs have been placed at odd areas around the rooms. Mr. Lung is especially appalled if those he believes to be demons casually move the furniture, showing utter contempt for the powers of his feng shui. Match Wu the Demon-Cat against POW 12.

AMULETS: Strategically around the room hang charms and amulets, usually of bronze. Mr. Lung tries to get the investigators to come near these or even to touch them. POW 11 against Wu the Demon-Cat.

COIN SWORD: A sword whose blade and hilt are of threaded Chinese coins hangs over the chair facing the table where Mr. Lung conducts his astrological questions. He lures the investigators here, sure the sword will send these arrogant demons running. During interviews conducted here it is hard for him to concentrate on anything but the sword, waiting for its powers to take effect. Match Wu the Demon-Cat against POW 15.

BRAZIER OF BURNING SLIPPERS: Usually better protection for infants, but Mr. Lung is using everything he can. The slippers are silk and have given good service. Their stench as they burn is overpowering. Mr. Lung won't light them until the previous protections have proven useless. POW 16 against Wu the Demon-Cat.

BRIBERY WITH HELL MONEY: Bundles of hell bank notes cost a few cents in the mundane world, but it is well known that their value to demons and spirits is inestimable. Mr. Lung casually drops fistfuls in front of the investigators. They may mistake it for real money unless they make a successful Spot Hidden or Idea roll. Imagine their surprise when Mr. Lung responds to their interest by burning up the bank notes, an act which renders the offering potent. POW 17 against Wu the Demon-Cat on the Resistance Table.

This tradition of the bank notes is still observed. Spurious bank notes of various denominations made out against the Bank of Hell are still sold in stores catering to Chinese customers.

THE CABINET: The demon cabinet is Mr. Lung's masterpiece, the result of many hours work and the tireless investment of hundreds of magic points. It is impossible to duplicate except by one steeped in Oriental occultism, hence its creation is ignored here. The downside of the cabinet is that the demon must be got into it by mundane means. Mr. Lung is not above using trickery, drugs (POT 15 to send the investigators to sleep, placed in tea) or force to get them inside.

The cabinet is constructed to trap and drain demons of their Power. It matches its POW 17 against their own magic points every minute, draining 1D3 magic points at each success. The inside of the cabinet is lined with mirrors, of which Chinese demons are very wary and which they will not break. Once drained to zero magic points, the demon must return to the underworld, never to bother Mr. Lung again.

Unlike most of Mr. Lung's demon traps, this one will harm human investigators. Humans suffer the same point draining, except it is from their Power and permanent. Once zero POW is reached the investigator is dead, shriveled to a dusty husk smelling of damp.

The cabinet is constructed of lacquered wood and jade and is quite solid with an outside latch that automatically locks. Mr. Lung has the only key, in his astrology desk. Both cabinet and lock are STR 25. (Humans don't have the same concerns about mirrors as do demons).

If investigators smash out of the cabinet, Mr. Lung might attack them, out of sheer terror, with his butcher knife.

Mr. Lung Yun, age 44, Demon-Haunted Astrologer

STR 09	CON 14	SIZ 08	INT 16	POW 19
DEX 13	APP 13	EDU 15	SAN 39	HP 11

Damage Bonus: none.

Weapons: Fist/Punch 52%, damage 1D3
Butcher Knife 40%, damage 1D6.

Spells: Repel Household Demon (see above), Create Demon Cabinet.

Skills: Art (Cast Horoscope)90%, Astrology 92%, Astronomy 40%, Chinese 90%, Dodge 35%, English 44%, Occult (Chinese) 70%, Sneak 86%, Spot Hidden 75%.

The Demon-Cat

The demon-cat enjoys watching Lung and the investigators interact. It tires of the fun once someone dies. It then acts. Use the true demon as a *deus ex machina* if one is needed, to save the party should catastrophe threaten. If the demon-cat is repulsed three times by the POW of Mr. Lung's defensive items, the demon is banished from the house and Mr. Lung is safe. By appearing to Lung and threatening him, then vanishing, the investigators are cleared of suspicion.

WU THE CAT-DEMON

The demon needs one of the investigators or Lung to let it into the house. It won't harm the investigators but doesn't mind watching Lung harm them.

WU THE CAT-DEMON, age 4, in Siamese Cat Form

STR 02	CON 08	SIZ 01	INT 12	POW 19
DEX 33	MOV 10			HP 05

Damage Bonus: -1D6.

Weapons: Bite 50%, damage 1D2-1-1D4
Claw x2 60%, damage 1D3-1D4

Armor: if injured, it changes instantly to cat-demon form even if injury is enough to kill a normal cat

Spells: none in this form

Skills: Cajole 72%, Climb 90%, Jump 90%, Yowl 99%.

Sanity Loss: none.

WU THE CAT-DEMON, Ageless and Cruel Servant of the Celestial Powers

In demon form, Wu is a 250-pound house cat with a big aggressive belly, gnarly glowing claws, and eyes that flash and smoke.

STR 40	CON 20	SIZ 18	INT 12	POW 19
DEX 11	MOV 6			HP 19

Damage Bonus: +3D6.

Weapons: Claws 55%, damage 1D8+3D6

Armor: ignores physical weapons and natural damage

Skills: Aplomb 90%, Art (Taunt Victim) 88%, Dodge 99%, Jump 99%, Land on Feet 100%.

Spells: none applicable

Sanity Loss: 1D3/1D10 SAN.

Rewards, Celestial and Otherwise

Seeing Mr. Lung receive his punishment at the hands of a demon servant of the Celestial court is sanity threatening, and not at all comforting. Helping Mr. Lung successfully dispel Wu restores 1D3 sanity points. Inadvertently or otherwise helping the demon dispel Mr. Lung costs 1/1D6 sanity points.

ALLIES

*Wherein thorough footwork by the investigators pays off
by leading first to Mu Hsien and then to Jack Brady,
to Chu Min, and to the Seven Cryptical Books.*

The Shanghai Museum

The museum has a fine collection of exquisite Chinese pottery, screens, statuary, and scrolls. It is a clearing house for information about pre-Manchu China. Mr. Mao, an assistant to the curator of the museum, can supply the names of Shanghai scholars who might be useful to the investigators as translators, evaluators, or sources of information. All expect pay for their labors; some live in poverty.

The list is thirty-four names long. It takes 1D6+2 man-days to locate and interview them all—longer if the investigators must work through an interpreter. Six of the men on Mr. Mao's list are authorities on Chinese occultism. Of those

six, five can be consulted easily. From them, the investigators learn some interesting facts if they ask about the Order of the Bloated Woman.

One of the most dread secret societies in China was the ancient Order of the Bloated Woman. The Order worshiped a dark god, and at one time was much feared throughout the coastal regions of China; the dread Fukien pirates were said at times to take instructions from the Order. The Order reputedly wielded powerful magic against its enemies. Authorities now doubt that the Order still exists.

The sixth and last reliable authority on the occult, Mu Hsien, is very busy. He will not see the investigators unless they mention the Order of the Bloated Woman or Jack

Brady's name. Keepers may ask for a Psychology roll here for the investigators to understand that Mr. Mu requires honesty of those who consult him. If the investigators make themselves plain, Mr. Mu alerts Chu Min, a friend of Brady's, who in turn has the investigators tailed until he figures out whether they're friend or foe. Since Mr. Mu is presently translating the *Seven Cryptical Books of Hsan*, and since Jack Brady is presently hiding in his house, the question must be resolved quickly.

MU HSIEN

Mu Hsien is a scholar, a specialist in Chinese history and traditional lore, an old man not up to fighting mad cultists and monsters, yet he is so shocked by what Brady has taught him that he cannot turn his back.

If Mr. Mu confides in the investigators, he can provide them with a number of pieces of information.

■ The Order of the Bloated Woman still exists, and that in the last few years it has grown very powerful.

■ Only a fraction of their victims have been found; in China, murder of the innocent has become simple.

■ Severing the arms of the victim is a cult trademark; they allow the victim to bleed to death.

■ The Order serves a dark goddess whom they believe is an aspect of a primal deity worshiped secretly in many forms all over the world. The Order knows the goddess as the Bloated Woman.

■ Mu believes that the Order wants to summon their goddess to Earth, and that the first step, a poisoning or rupturing of the sky, is planned to happen soon.

■ After the sky has been altered, about a year must pass before the world is tainted by these evil entities, when the stars themselves shift position and dread names of the dark goddess' pantheon—Cthulhu, Nyogtha, Yog-Sothoth, and Azathoth—are spoken in worship.

■ Mu hints that the use of ancient knowledge may prevent such dire events, but he supplies no details before Jack Brady meets the investigators.

If Mu Hsien concludes that the investigators are working against the Order, he warns them never to come to his house again, for it is far too dangerous. But they may leave messages for him at Shanghai general delivery under the name of Mr. Feng Wu-pei, and he will respond as he is able to such messages.

If the investigators inadvertently lead the Order to Mu Hsien, the Order will try to get the *Seven Cryptical Books*. Carl Stanford leads the attack. It is up to the keeper to decide when it takes place and how successful it is. If Stanford gets the scroll, he'll give it to Ho Fong (who puts it in his private shrine to the Bloated Woman). Stanford then leaves Shanghai on other errands for his god.

If the scroll is stolen, Brady quickly surfaces to try to get it back. Lin Tang-yu's men may also follow the investigators—that worthy sends apes and henchmen to retrieve the Books. If the investigators learn the location of the *Seven Cryptical Books*, and if they want the scroll for themselves, they'll have to break into Mu Hsien's house and find it.

In all of these cases, the house is physically stout and secure. If the keeper likes, Jack Brady has arranged some deadly surprises for clumsy intruders. There may be guards as well: take some Firm Action members and allow them to use handguns with silencers.

MU HSIEN, age 63, Wise Scholar of Traditional Classics

STR 05	CON 06	SIZ 10	INT 18	POW 15
DEX 09	APP 10	SAN 60	EDU 18	HP 08

Damage Bonus: -1D4.

Weapon: none

Skills: Astronomy 25%, Botany 30%, Brushwork 87%, Chinese History and Lore 90%, Confucian Tradition 75%, Cthulhu Mythos 15%, Debate 65%, Library Use 75%, Mandarin Chinese 95%, Natural History 35%, Occult 10%, Psychology 60%, Savor the Classics 85%, Taoist Magic and Tradition 80%, Tibetan 50%.

New China

Chu Min is a leader of a secret vigilante organization, New China, which consists of perhaps 200 youthful Chinese—males and females, students, vendors, shop attendants, day laborers, journalists, policemen, minor bureaucrats, and teachers. They are training to launch a campaign against Shanghai's most corrupt elements. Their techniques will be assassination by firearm or bomb.

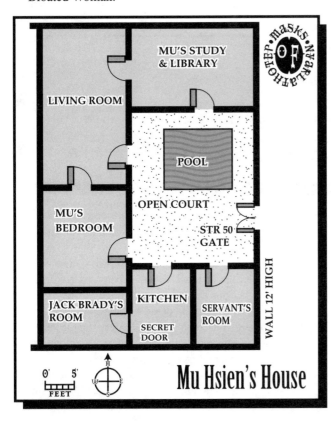

MU'S STUDY & LIBRARY

LIVING ROOM

POOL

OPEN COURT

MU'S BEDROOM

STR 50 GATE

JACK BRADY'S ROOM

KITCHEN

SERVANT'S ROOM

SECRET DOOR

WALL 12' HIGH

0' 5' FEET

Mu Hsien's House

Though factions within them sometimes commit acts of terror, formal political organizations have policies and goals which are impossible to achieve through terror, because such random activity becomes organization-threatening. Chu Min's group, however, is bankrolled by a rich radical, Sung Lee, and therefore does not need programs, plans, or compromises. The company's "four affirmations" slogan—Firm Study, Firm Belief, Firm Practice, Firm Action—is as subtle a statement as New China makes. New China's mass meetings denounce anyone and anything. Irritating people and groups are entered on an ever-lengthening hit-list of enemies, for ultimate retribution.

Some people are in New China to let off steam, but the Firm Action faction (led by Chu) is dedicated to violence, and its members tirelessly train in martial arts, small-unit tactics, and weapon use. This is the group in the warehouse on Chung-san Road watched by agents of Captain Isoge, and probably by other groups as well.

CHU MIN

On any day, Firm Action members at the warehouse consist of 1D20+5 men and women. To gain practical experience, some have hired out to local gangs and warlords for several months to a year, and already the group is well versed in brutality. Trained by a Whampoa graduate and by Jack Brady, and increasingly combat-experienced, Firm Action is formidable for its size, more representing a disciplined commando group than a clutch of dreamy anarchists. Along with plenty of rifles, submachine guns, and handguns, they have two .30 machine guns, cases of hand grenades, a 60mm mortar and plenty of shells, and as much dynamite and detonation gear as they want, all garnered from American sources in the Philippines black market. Statistics for Firm Action members and their weapons are found at the end of this chapter. Three warehouse guards are found below.

Ostensibly empty and next to a conveniently noisy foundry, the warehouse is boarded-up. Firm Action members routinely enter through a stoutly padlocked (STR 40) rear door, by ones and by twos. A standing guard of 1D3 members watches the entrance and the interior weapons vault. In an office, a desk holds records of arms shipments, a navigational map of the Shanghai approaches with a course marked to Gray Dragon Island, and a planning sheet noting likely tidal stages for various locations around the island. A file holds reports from scouting missions to the island. All are in military-jargon Mandarin. The only English words are on one sheet of paper.

ITEM. Casual handwriting in pencil on a crumpled sheet of white paper (*Nyarlathotep Papers #42*)

Relevance of the Item: establishes that the apparent assault on Gray Dragon Island will happen soon; also offers the likelihood that Jack Brady is participating.

When Brady asks Chu to contact him in"the usual manner", this refers to the fact that Chu goes to a certain teahouse each

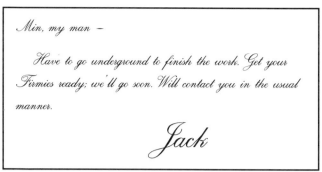

Min, my man –

Have to go underground to finish the work. Get your Firmies ready; we'll go soon. Will contact you in the usual manner.

Jack

Nyarlathotep Papers #42

morning, and orders tea and sweet cakes. If there is a message, it is on rice paper underneath the sweet cakes; then he eats the message along with the rest of the meal, and goes about his business. Isoge knows that the teahouse is part of Chu's routine, but does not know that it has other significance. If Chu contacts the investigators, he meets them at this teahouse, the Autumn Morning.

Chu maintains a cover identity as a warehouseman, but now is only on the Firm Action payroll. Originally a policeman, he and Jack Brady met years ago as minor opponents in an anti-corruption campaign. Later retiring from the police force, Chu was hired by Sung Lee. In turn, Chu recruited Brady—on the run, experienced, reliable, and not fussy about aims, means, or ethics. When Brady provided evidence of the Order's horrifying activity, he gained the pledge of the Firm Action faction to carry out an attack on the cult's headquarters. Neither Jack Brady nor the radicals truly understand what is at work on Gray Dragon Island, nor the awful forces which guard the place.

THREE FIERCE WAREHOUSE GUARDS

	1	2	3 *
STR	14	15	15
CON	13	11	14
SIZ	12	11	13
DEX	13	13	13
APP	09	10	11
SAN	65	50	45
INT	14	16	13
POW	14	13	16
HP	13	11	14

Damage Bonus: +1D4.

Weapons: Fist/Punch 80%, damage 1D3+1D4
Kick 70%, damage 1D6+1D4
Head Butt 60%, damage 1D4
Fighting Knife 55%, damage 1D4+2+1D4
Submachine Gun 50%, damage 1D10+2

Spells: none.

Skills: Mandarin Chinese 40%, Climb 55%, Dodge 85%, Firm Action Doctrine Drill 75%, Hide 65%, Jump 50%, Listen 70%, Martial Arts 80%, Past and Future Glories of the Han 70%, Sneak 65%, Spot Hidden 55%, Throw 60%.

* Guard 3 is a peasant woman whose husband was slain by the Order. She is tough and vindictive: merely surrendering will not be enough for her.

Jack Brady

Jack Brady lives in a secret room in the house of Mu Hsien. He rarely leaves this hideout, and only retiring scholar Mu and his ancient cook know that Brady lives in the small room, waiting for the right moment to act. Brady reveals himself when he is sure that the investigators are on his side, simply appearing some morning or afternoon at their hotel or restaurant—he has learned how dangerous it is to skulk about at night.

JACK BRADY

Though still sane, his manner is (justifiably) paranoid. He'll stick around long enough to tell his story and arrange further contact, then try to blend into the crowd (not an easy trick for an ex-Marine in Shanghai). Brady has disguised himself somewhat, but if the investigators are being watched, the keeper should make a Hide roll for Brady. If it fails, and if the watchers know who Brady is, then he has been spotted.

ITEM. Jack Brady's statement (*Nyarlathotep Papers #43*)

Relevance of the Information: the statement should answer most of the investigators' questions and determine their immediate course of action. Be prepared to expand on this information after the players read this handout.

When Brady finishes his tale, he tells them that the worship of Nyarlathotep is global, involving every class and every race. He knows about the Brotherhood of the Black Pharaoh, the Order of the Bloated Woman, the cult of Sand Bat, and of course the cult of the Bloody Tongue. But there also are cults to Nyarlathotep in India, Japan, South America, and Polynesia. Brady is able to name names, too: Omar Shakti, Edward Gavigan, Ho Fong, Tandoor Singh.

Brady had hoped that Jackson Elias would shed more light on some or all of these cults, since Brady knows himself to be no scholar. If one of the investigators is an author, he'll urge that investigator to tell the story.

Brady's goal is to learn the secret of the Eye of Light and Darkness from the *Seven Cryptical Books of Hsan*, which Mu Hsien is studying. Then he can replace the ward on Gray Dragon Island, foiling Nyarlathotep's opening of the Gate, and destroying Sir Aubrey and his slimy worshipers. Brady then plans to sail to Kenya, to destroy the Great Temple of Nyarlathotep, and to plant a second ward, then return to Australia and plant a third ward to protect the City of the Great Race from Mythos exploitation. The investigators are welcome to accompany him and help, but he cannot move until the *Seven Books* have been translated. The time is short—the gate will open soon.

Brady may or may not explain the details of the armed assault: those details are covered below, in a section titled "Attack on Gray Dragon Island" at the end of this chapter. Jack Brady's statistics are found there, as are those of Chu Min and other members of Young China.

BRADY AND CHOI MEI-LING

Brady advises the investigators to find someplace safe and wait. Someone will contact them when the time is right. But if the investigators tell him that Choi Mei-ling is missing, Brady reaches an immediate and angry conclusion—he'll raid Ho Fong's house to try and find her, thereby putting the Gray Dragon assault in jeopardy, and thereby setting the police after him as well as the cult of the Bloated Woman.

Chu Min angrily refuses to support a premature attack on Ho Fong, and Brady begs the investigators to help him. If they refuse, Brady goes by himself and never is seen again. Careful investigator negotiations with Firm Action might allow the Gray Dragon attack to continue.

From the time that the investigators meet Brady, it is 1D8+4 days until Mu Hsien completes the necessary translations of the *Seven Cryptical Books*.

BRADY NEVER MET?

If the investigators never meet Brady, the keeper has several options. The keeper can judge that Hsien does finish the translation, and that the investigators independently assault Gray Dragon Island. The keeper can decide that the Order of the Bloated Woman or Lin Tang-yu's men found Mu Hsien and retrieved the *Seven Cryptical Books* before the translation. The keeper could say that nothing critical happened during the visit to Shanghai, and that the investigators can take independent action against the cult based on what they uncover. The keeper also can separately connect Chu Min and the investigators after Brady's death, to continue with the planned assault on Gray Dragon Island.

THE SEVEN CRYPTICAL BOOKS OF HSAN

A single classical Chinese scroll organized into seven books. This particular copy is much more ancient and perfect than the usual copies: +11% to Cthulhu Mythos; x4 spell multiplier; spells include Contact Fungi from Yuggoth, Elder Sign, Eye of Light and Darkness, and Find Gate. This large scroll is always kept in a fitted scroll case bearing the Elder sign.

The passage concerning the Eye of Light and Darkness is in the fifth of the *Cryptical Books*. For information and procedures concerning it, see *Nyarlathotep Papers #44*. The method of creating the ward known as the Eye of Light and Darkness exists in only the particular copy being translated by Mu Hsien, and that is why the Order of the Bloated Woman so desperately wants this particular copy. The Order is several times referred to in the text, which remarks that the Bloated Woman is but one messenger of many.

Deciphering this scroll's idiosyncratic handwritten characters and understanding their portent is a lengthy task even for a fine classical scholar like Mu Hsien; on his or her own, an investigator must have at least 50% Mandarin Chinese to get started and, lacking outside help, stands only a 10% chance of success per year spent poring over the arcane scroll.

Jack Brady's Statement

"I'm Jack Brady. I hear you've been looking for me. I got a minute, and you got some questions. I gather you never got to talk to Jackson Elias. If it's all the same, I'll talk now, and you can ask your questions later.

"As far as I can make out, we're all in a lot of trouble. The more I learn about the situation, the scareder I get. When I spilled the beans to Jackson Elias, I figured people would read his book and do something about this cult. Sorry he ended up that way—you guys friends of his? All the same, I did warn him, and I didn't hold nothing back. I'm warning you guys, too: the cult plays for keeps. Or maybe mugs like you already know that." (He laughs.)

"Well, right from the start I knew that Roger's nigger-girl was trouble. She was as tough as they come, and she had him around her finger. He must have known she was trouble, too, because the more he saw her, the more crazy dreams he had. I thought it was great when he wanted to go to Egypt—that'd be the end of her, see, and things would get back to normal. I liked the guy, and I owed him a lot.

"It seemed for a while that everything would work out. London was a lot of fun, but once we got to Cairo, Roger started having dreams again about meeting a god, and crap like that. But now he wasn't drinking, and the girl wasn't around, and the gentlemen Roger had asked along started acting nuttier than Roger did, and so I said to myself, 'trouble is somewhere up the road.'

"After I paid Faraz Najir for his junk, Roger spent some time with it. He went off the deep end. There was a black kind of head-and-shoulder statue that he'd stare at for hours. And there was a map that he'd study and study, like a normal guy would check out a beautiful dame. He started telling me that we could meet the god as soon as he destroyed the eye and opened the path.

"That hotshot Dr. Huston should have talked Roger down, but he only encouraged him. So the first night that we were up the Nile at Dhashur, Roger snuck out and climbed up the Red Pyramid. Any of you guys ever climbed a pyramid? They're steep! Roger started up that pile like a monkey. Never looked back or hesitated once, which proved to me that the poor bugger was absolutely crazy. But I followed him up." (He laughs again.) "I was crazy, too.

"For about two thirds of the way up the Red Pyramid, you just climb up and over big blocks, sort of like something some dumb kid could make by piling up a million great big construction blocks. The pyramid builders filled in all the gaps with nice smooth stone, but then later people stole that nice stone from around the bottom of the pyramid—the high stuff was too hard to grab, and they couldn't finish the job. Well, Roger zipped right up this part, too, with me still behind, my eyes bulging out 'cause I could barely find handholds to keep from bouncing down the whole damn pyramid.

"There's a little flat place at the tip of the pyramid. When Roger reached the flat place, he put on some kind of robe and started making weird sounds, as though he had flipped for good. But then there was a hell of an explosion with all kinds of funny echoes and screams with it, and a big red flash of light. Well, I lay there for a minute until it seemed safe to go on. He looked at me and said, 'The eye is gone, Jack. Now we can be gods.'

"Well, that was just Roger talk, you know, but beside him there was a big patch ripped right out of the stone, and it looked fresh. When I went back the next day, the patch had been filled in, as though the pyramid had repaired itself. But near the base of the pyramid, I found part of a rock which looked like it could have been in that patch originally, and it had this sign on it." (Brady sketches a mysterious-looking sign; this is the strange symbol which appears in light grey to the top right of this handout..)

"Now I know what it was—its strong magic kept evil things away from us, and Roger deliberately broke its power.

"Two days later, the whole gang—Penhew, Roger, Huston, and Patty—gave me the slip and disappeared in the Bent Pyramid. Some of the messenger boys went to find them, and they came out shrieking that the pyramid had eaten the respected scientists, woe, woe, woe. Bingo, the workers run in all directions! The whole dig was deserted. In five minutes the only person left in the whole area was me. Well, I went in. Sure enough, nobody was inside. I was worried.

"But, a long time later, out come all the missing people from the pyramid. Roger says they'd been to Egypt, to the real Egypt. And that was about the most sensible thing he said. Penhew looked like he had lost about five years. And Patty and Huston both seemed somehow changed. Nobody would explain where they'd been, and nobody cared that after that it was hard to hire workmen.

"After that, when I'd wake up in the nights, the rest of the gang would be talking creepy lingo like I'd never heard before. Then one evening Roger said that he was going to show me the power of what they'd learned. We went out into the desert with a passel of Arabs. Everybody started screaming weird words and songs, and Penhew beat the drum that we got from Najir. When creatures started coming out of the ground and eating the Arabs, and Roger and the others started laughing, why I took my leave, as they say, and went on a real toot. Roger found me the next day, and warned me that I'd better change my attitude. Well, I owed the kid, and I wouldn't desert him, but after that I started thinking real good.

"Then we went to Kenya, and Roger filled me in during the trip. We had found a true god, he said, who would rule the Earth, and we would rule with that god, for we were the chosen of the god. The god had picked us to open the way for his return. And there was enough in what they said—and in what I saw—to make me listen. Every week, Penhew seemed a little younger and a little livelier. Patty was sick a lot. We were going to leave Nairobi from some place in the mountains where there was no river, no railway, no telegraph, no police, and nobody who looked friendly. I figured that Jack Brady wouldn't live very long there, so I made some arrangements. On the last night, in Nairobi, I drugged Roger, kyped the cash box (it was all Roger's money, anyway), and got me and them aboard an unscheduled deadhead freight to Mombasa.

"Later I read that my guess was right. The newspapers said a lot of people died, but Penhew, Huston and Patty Masters weren't among them.

"Anyway, my arrangements went off without a hitch—that happens when you think small and carry a lot of cash. When we got to Mombasa, we got off before the causeway and found a fisherman who was willing to go to Zanzibar for a few dollars. From there we hopped a coastal trader to Durban, and in Durban we dyed our hair, got some decent clothes, and sailed for Perth.

"Now, on the train to Mombasa, Roger got some sleep, and he seemed to wake up a different person. I guess that being away from the influence of those other people let him return to his old self. I told him we were in a lot of trouble, and that we needed to hide out, and reminded him about the Arabs being killed in Egypt, and the god stuff, and so on, and he could remember it all right, although it didn't seem very important, somehow. But he understood the logic of the situation. After a week or so, though, his nightmares started, and he began to go off the deep end. He was beginning to realize some of the things he had done.

"I was in Shanghai while I was in the Marines, and I had a fair number of friends here. By the time our ship put into Hong Kong, Roger could go no farther. He began shrieking at shadows and everything that moved. So I put him in a sanitarium there—I had to use up most of the remaining money to get him settled. Then I went on to Shanghai, believing that I'd never again see any member but Roger of that damned expedition.

"So I thought, until I looked through naval glasses at a certain yacht, and saw Sir Aubrey Penhew preening on the deck of the *Dark Mistress*."

ON THE EYE OF LIGHT AND DARKNESS

Once they have obtained the description given in the *Seven Cryptical Books*, investigators may attempt to ward one or more of the points of the triangle which influence the locus of the Great Gate. The passage must be followed precisely, and keepers should judge sternly the results.

The "blood of ignorance" means in this context the blood of someone who has no knowledge of the Cthulhu Mythos. The amount of blood needed for the entire procedure is no more than a few ounces. Idiot investigators who slaughter a dozen people to create a ward intended to save those people deserve to be apprehended and themselves slaughtered by society.

One hundred points of Power are permanently given to the ward, obtaining from and without the knowledge of the people creating the ward. Each hour of the chant, the Eye leeches 1D4 POW from each chanter in a random fashion until exactly one hundred points of POW have been absorbed. A character losing all of his or her Power drops dead. If one hundred points of POW are not accumulated between moonrise and moon-set, the activation of the ward fails, all leeched

Power is lost, and the procedure must be started from scratch if a ward is still to be created. Do not tell the players what is happening until the creation of the ward has succeeded or has failed—then they should be instructed to mark off the totals which the keeper has independently recorded until then.

Investigators know that the eye is active when the pupil of the symbol begins to glow. Once activated, the symbol disappears within the substance into which it has been etched, chiseled, or otherwise physically inscribed, and cannot then be removed by any physical agent or by any ordinary magical means. When nearby, those who created it (and only they) always are able to see the dim nimbus which the Eye emanates.

A working Eye is powerful. It weakens agents, monsters, and minions of the Outer Gods and Great Old Ones who enter the area it protects, at a rate of one magic point per hour. If they remain until their magic points reach zero, then they disintegrate. Further, Contact, Call, and Summon spells may not be cast within the ten-mile reach of the Eye.

Nyarlathotep knows how to destroy these wards, if they can be located, but each ward requires a separate spell, the

Nyarlathotep Papers #44

Translation from

The *Seven Cryptical Books* of Hsan

The ineffable Eye must be worked into natural substance which is naturally hard.

The unrivalled light of the marvellous Eye transcends taint if all evil presences have been dispatched or dispelled.

He who first chants must be able to create the gift of the Elder Sign.

"Of those signs effectively sealing the festerings of the dark god, the most potent is the *Eye of Light and Darkness*. Inscribed into the substance of a high place near the haunts of evil, and no further than 30 li from them, expels the evil strength for so long as the sign exists. The Eye must be created the afternoon before the full moon rises. At moonrise, the blood of an innocent must fill the pupil of the Eye once per drumbeat from then to moonset. As the first blood is given, chant the words 'sa-ma, sa-ma, te-yo, sa-ma,' and continue until the moon sets. When next the moon rises, the Eye opens to ward and to guard. Gather the friends of good to work this wisdom, for too few shall surely fail."

The wondrous Eye must not first burn where evil beings or creatures lurk.

Only one incorruptible Eye may guard a location.

The blood for the pupil of the winnowing Eye must be fresh.

All who chant must detest evil.

— Chou Teh

Along the edges of the scroll are written small red-ink commentaries signed by the monk Chou Teh

characteristics of which may take years to deduce. Further, those of the cults involved in the current plot know no procedures for detecting the wards. If they gain and learn to use the *Seven Cryptical Books of Hsan*, they get a spell, Find Gate, which allows visual inspection to find the exact spot, a simple process. But at present a naive agent of the gods must be sent to the suspect area, there to find and destroy the ward before it destroys him, as Roger Carlyle was sent to Dhashur in Egypt.

No one knows how many such wards still exist, who created them, or where they are located if more do exist.

GRAY DRAGON ISLAND

A cult stronghold, this ominous atoll plays a vital role in the opening of the Great Gate. Can the investigators both foil Nyarlathotep and survive the wrath of his minions?

Aboard the *Dark Mistress*

If the investigators found the photo of the Shanghai riverfront, a portion of the *Dark Mistress* appears in it. A 30% chance exists that the ship is in Shanghai when the investigators arrive; this chance improves by 5 percentiles for every day of their stay. With a successful Idea roll, investigators notice and recognize her. The craft never stays in Shanghai more than a few hours—coming in at dusk and leaving at midnight or thereabouts. She ties up along the bank, and boats bring supplies and special cargoes such as artifacts from Ho Fong's warehouse.

This information is available in the harbormaster's office, or from riverfront loungers for an insignificant amount of cash. If the harbormaster's office is consulted, records pertaining to the *Ivory Wind* (which the investigators may have visited in London), or that ship herself, also can turn up.

A check with the Shanghai central post office shows that none of the general delivery or boxholder clerks recognizes the name *Dark Mistress*, but the route carrier for Ho Fong's warehouse does recall occasional letters for Alfred Penhurst, aboard the *Dark Mistress*, c/o the warehouse address.

THE SHIP

The *Dark Mistress* is a trim, well appointed, ninety-foot yacht of British registry, her interior finished in dark varnished mahogany and yew wood. She has the sturdy, squarish lines typical of late-19th-century naval architecture, and her typical headway should be 8-12 knots. But secretly she has been rebuilt and strengthened internally. In calm seas, her unorthodox new power plant propels her at up to 45 knots, faster than any warship in the Pacific save for two experimental Japanese destroyers.

Except for the meteorite, any Mythos artifacts carried as cargo, and the curiously empty coal bin (see below), nothing is suspicious about the yacht. Captain Savoyard's room is dirty, littered with liquor bottles and crude pornography. The owner's suite, in which Sir Aubrey travels when he is aboard, is neat, clean, and locked. The light (STR 12) door can be forced or picked open. The crews' quarters are six cramped and filthy bunks in the foc'sle. There are several small storage lockers, a mid-ship wheel house, a lounge, a dining room, a galley, three small guest rooms, and three toilets. Only the unoccupied owner's suite offers a likely place to stow away aboard the *Dark Mistress*.

If the yacht is followed, a successful Spot Hidden by Savoyard detects the trailing craft. If Savoyard spots the pursuer, he radios Sir Aubrey when near Gray Dragon Island, and lets Sir Aubrey decide what to do.

THE CREW

The six crewmen of the *Dark Mistress* are despicable human/deep one half-breeds. For a detailed description of such folk, read Lovecraft's "The Shadow Over Innsmouth." Investigators who have met deep ones will recognize them as making up the crew. Jules Savoyard, a member of the Order, captains the yacht.

Captain and crew wear medallions bearing the Order characters. A successful Spot Hidden lets an investigator notice the medallions, and a successful Idea roll for the same investigators then allows the characters to be read or to be remembered for later translation.

Savoyard has a rubbery, degenerate look. His nose is partially eaten away, his eyes have yellowish veins, and bald patches spot his otherwise thick, greasy black hair. An investigator getting a successful Physics or Medicine roll suggests that Savoyard has radium poisoning.

Statistics for Savoyard and his bulgy-eyed crew appear at the end of this chapter.

THE DEADLY THING IN THE FIREBOX

Savoyard's poisoning comes from a chunk of glowing green stone hidden in the firebox of the engine room—masked by burning coal if a customs inspector comes aboard. The glowing stone is an unearthly meteorite. Its searing alien heat raises steam pressure far beyond what coal could achieve, hence the craft's rebuilt lines and boilers. Fire box and boiler are sealed off from the engine room by lead shielding, painted black to look like iron.

An investigator looking into the fire box notices the weird color within. Once the fire box door is open, the investigator and anyone else within twenty feet are exposed to its rays.

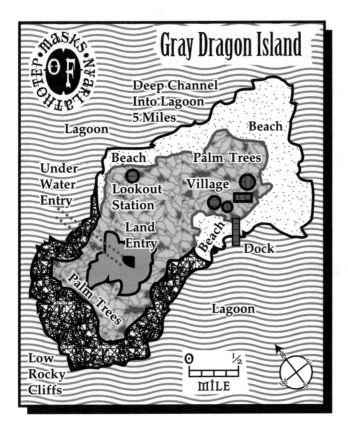

The meteorite's strange radiation is POT 15 to humans. Match it against the target's CON on the Resistance Table. If the radiation succeeds, in five hours the target weakens, has a headache and nausea, and his or her STR and DEX are halved, as are all his or her percentages for physical skills such as Climb, Jump, etc. This effect lasts twelve hours. For every additional exposure to the meteorite, call for another POT vs. CON, and for each additional successful attack double the extent of the radiation poisoning. For instance, the second exposure's symptoms would last twenty-four hours, the third for forty-eight hours, etc.

If in the opinion of the keeper someone spends an extended amount of time exposed to the rays of the meteorite, the poisoning becomes permanent. At some point the victim's hit points begin to decrease by one point per day, as the victim weakens and dies—unless daily blood transfusions are performed. No successful treatment is known, though hospitalization can indefinitely prolong remaining life. As long as the fire box door stays closed, everyone is safe from the effect of the meteorite.

Landfall

Three hundred miles southeast of Shanghai is Gray Dragon Island, a mere reef on most charts. It is in fact a dormant volcano, the major cone of which has been silent long enough to have eroded to a circular reef enclosing a broad lagoon. In turn, the lagoon surrounds a low secondary cinder cone, associated flat island, and a small vil-

lage. Only British and Japanese naval charts correctly represent this atoll, and they also label the entire vicinity as 'treacherous waters.' No country has bothered to claim such a worthless spot.

Into the Lagoon

The *Dark Mistress* moors at the rickety dock beside the village. About fifty deep one half-breeds live in the village. Several of them keep an eye on the channel through the reef in case intruders approach. Such reports reach Sir Aubrey in about ten minutes, the time it takes a deep one to swim from the camouflaged lookout station to the Chamber of the Bloated Woman, inside the cinder cone. A dry-land entrance to the Chamber also exists, as marked on the map.

The island is mostly cinders and sand. Stunted palm trees and sand crabs are its main residents. A dozen active steam vents dot the island, possibly giving the appearance of fires. The cinder cone topping the island is about five hundred feet high. Its upper reaches are steep but not impassable, requiring half an hour to negotiate. Keepers may want to request Climb rolls just before the top. There is nothing at the top but a jagged cup within the truncation of the cone, from which gentle steam emerges every few hours.

DEEP ONE COLONY: near the underwater entrance, but much deeper in the water is a small colony of deep ones. They can be called to the surface by chants from the lookout station, responding in 1D4+1 minutes. There is a 20% chance that a deep one out for a swim notices an intruding boat at night.

THE VILLAGE: a dozen thatched palm huts huddle among the trees, well enough into the island to be away from the worst of the sand crabs. There are no stores, radios, guns, or other useful gear. There are 1D10+10 Mythos statuettes in random huts, and many of the villagers wear the cult characters of the Bloated Woman on medallions, belts, and so forth. One hut contains dozens of extra yellow-and-black silk cult robes with which to outfit visitors.

THE DOCK: a simple wooden pier reaches far enough into the lagoon that ships of twelve-foot draft can tie up at low tide.

THE LOOKOUT STATION: a small tree-hut built thirty-five feet up between three close-growing palms. It is camouflaged well enough to remove 30 percentiles from any Spot Hidden directed toward it.

A normal Spot Hidden chance does detect the six steel cables anchoring the lookout station trees to the ground, to keep the position steady in the afternoon wind. The lookout station is purely a perch—it has no detection gear other than binoculars, and no signal gear other than messengers.

THE TRAIL TO THE VOLCANO: a clear trail winds from the village to a cave about one hundred and fifty feet up the side of the cinder cone. The entrance to the cave has been decorated with cult characters, dripping fangs, clutching tentacles, and other symbols which gladden the insane heart. Twisting stone stairs lead nearly two hundred feet down into the cone. Occasionally sulfur springs or noxious vents cloud and corrode the way. Investigators passing here may carry the reek for hours.

On ritual nights, the villagers and a handful of mainland visitors light torches and march chanting to this entrance. Investigators can join the parade if they disguise themselves by wearing cult robes.

Chamber of the Bloated Woman

The chamber houses both a shrine to the Bloated Woman and the device which Sir Aubrey has built to help open the Great Gate. The chamber is a rough cylinder 150 feet high, a cavern left when volcanic material retreated from the top of the cone to the magma pools below. Long steps lead down from the higher entrance. A hard orange light seems to emanate from the slimy fungi which liberally coat the walls and ceiling, but this actually is a reflection of the energies of the magma pit in the center of the chamber.

THE TRAIL TO THE VILLAGE: marked with an arrow and the word up on the map, the way to the surface of the island is decorated with incised outlines of Spawns of Cthulhu, deep ones, and shoggoths.

SIR AUBREY'S ROCKET: suspended above the magma pool on sturdy girders is a gleaming metal bullet about seventy-five feet high. Its alien metal gleams with a variety of oily colors never seen before by the investigators. Sir Aubrey also has worked into its hull small, stylish Art Deco motifs. The fin-like steering vanes of the rocket are also fanciful. Around this great bullet, cranes and platforms at various heights hold 1D6+10 cultists testing circuits, performing repairs, inserting wires, and making spot-welds. The nose of the rocket is currently not fitted to the rest of the vehicle.

A dozen inch-thick pipes lead five feet from the bottom of the rocket into the magma pit. Their white-hot glow is something like that of fluorescent bulbs, but of blinding intensity. All the workers wear goggles protecting against this light. These are devices from other worlds, conversion tubes that leech energy from the magma pit and store it for the moment that they drive Sir Aubrey's rocket across Southeast Asia and over the Indian ocean, there to open the way for fresh evil to corrode the world.

Often four or five deep ones shamble from the Bubbling Pool and plop bucketsful of a disgusting viscous substance into the magma pit.

PARTS STORAGE: a pile of tools, packing crates, raw materials, and many small cigar-shaped tanks studded with strange nozzles and harnesses. Several cultists working on the rocket wear these 15-pound units on their backs. The cigar-like tanks are welding devices emitting beams of scarlet light that sizzle and fuse metal surfaces. The tanks have batteries lasting 1D4+8 hours of continuous full-power use.

Though their flame reaches only five feet, within that range they also are formidable weapons, doing 2D10 damage at full power, and 1D10 at half-strength. Their principles of operation are completely unknown to present human science, though the tanks are obvious enough to use. Within the investigators' likely employment, the devices never need recharging or refilling.

THE QUIET POOL: this pool is the watery exit to the sea through which deep ones enter the chamber from their colony in the lagoon.

THE BUBBLING POOL: sloping steps lead into the uneasy watery murk. Five deep ones work here, commanded by a sixth. They herd a twitching, nervous shoggoth which lies almost invisible in the pool, and they collect from its tissue to add to the energies in the magma pit.

The head deep one is a *shoggoth-twsha*, or shoggoth priest, an important position in the society of the deep ones. The twsha holds buzzing blobs of quivering gray slime in his clawed webbed paws. Occasionally he gestures vaguely toward the pool, burbling fishy incantations.

THE CAGE: hapless sacrifices nabbed by the cult wait for their doom here. The pen holds 1D20+20 humans at any one time, mainly frightened fishermen and sailors. If a Brides-of-the-Deep-Ones ceremony is soon, the inmates mostly are female.

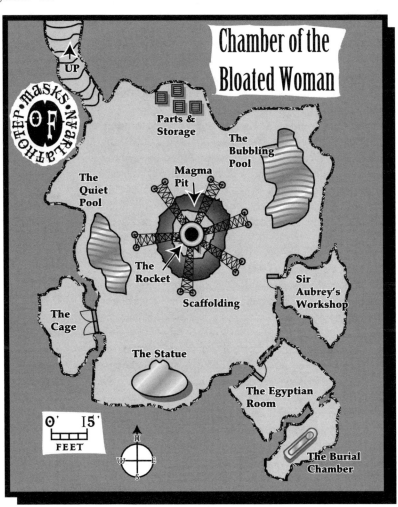

The rock ceiling of the cage is eight feet overhead; steel bars (STR 40) one inch apart barricade the front; the door (STR 35) is kept shut by a magnetic lock to which only Sir Aubrey has a key. The lock cannot be picked.

Since prisoners can watch through the bars, most of them are insane from the horrors they have witnessed, and may unwisely call out to or even try to kill rescuing investigators.

THE STATUE: an image of the Bloated Woman about ten feet high. As dreadful as is the image, the hundred severed human arms dangling from its outstretched tentacles in various states of decay are worse: lose 1D3/2D8 SAN. Now investigators know where the arms taken from the Shanghai corpses went.

A huge beaten-gold version of the cult characters decorates the floor before the statue, as do bloodstains.

The Shoggoth-Twsha

His slime blobs (called *mapulo* by the human/deep one hybrids) give him the power to control his shoggoth, if the controller gets a successful Resistance Table roll POW vs. POW of the shoggoth. Success causes the shoggoth to accept simple mental commands from the twsha. Such control lasts half an hour, and then a new POW vs. POW Resistance Table roll must be made. A twsha whose Power exceeds the shoggoth's by 10 or more automatically succeeds, and needs no roll.

If the roll to control a shoggoth fails, or if the monster is left uncontrolled for ten or more minutes, the shoggoth is free, and the mapulos (the slime blobs which the shoggoth-twsha holds) begin to attack the twsha, burrowing their way into his arms and causing 1D3 damage each, per round, unless they are excised or burnt off in some way. They stick like glue to the skin—they cannot be pulled off. And, of course, both must be removed to save the twsha.

While in contact with a shoggoth, a human controller loses 1D6/1D20 SAN per half hour. A person who goes mad while controlling a shoggoth can still control that shoggoth, though he or she may do so in an insane manner.

A given shoggoth-twsha only controls one shoggoth with his mapulo. If the shoggoth is killed, the mapulo attacks the wielder as described previously. Murder of the controller enrages the shoggoth even as the thing is made free. Death of the twsha also allows the mapulo to activate and begin devouring the corpse.

A few deep ones always protect a shoggoth-twsha. He cannot attack physically, but may use magic if he is shocked or annoyed. Since the shoggoth-twsha can spare no more than ten minutes from control of his charge, he attacks as lethally as possible. The shoggoth is usually the best weapon available.

Shoggoth-twshas usually are superior members of the deep one race. Other species can become controllers of shoggoths by using the mapulo, but once in command, must succeed in Luck rolls (96-00 always fails) once a week or so to remain in control and uneaten by the mapulo. Only deep ones can become genuine shoggoth-twshas, and a deep one controller need only receive a roll of less than 00 on percentile dice to remain in control.

A shoggoth-twsha remains with his charge until the day the mapulo eats him. The usual trance of the shoggoth-twsha is restful, and the mapulo processes the user's fatigue poisons, so that the shoggoth-twsha never need rest nor sleep and, in fact, dares not.

Once the mapulo has activated and begun to devour a controller, it becomes useless for control purposes, and the deep ones usually feed it to a shoggoth. Mapulo is created by a deep one process taking several seasons to complete.

SHOGGOTH-TWSHA, Deep One Priest of the Shoggoth

STR 24	CON 18	SIZ 24	INT 18	POW 24
DEX 18	MOV 6/10 swimming			HP 21

Damage Bonus: +2D6.

Weapons: commands a shoggoth
Claw 25%, damage 1D6+2D6
Trident 25%, damage 1D6+2D6
Grapple 25%, damage special

Spells: Contact Father Dagon, Contact Mother Hydra, Contact Spawn of Cthulhu, Grasp of Cthulhu, Summon Deep Ones, Wave of Oblivion.

Skills: Climb 10%, Cthulhu Mythos 22%, Deep One 70%, Dodge 40%, Listen 40%, Sneak 10%, Spot Hidden 40%, Swim 90%.

THE SHOGGOTH

STR 65	CON 46	SIZ 89	INT 7	POW 14
DEX 1	MOV 10 (rolling)		HP 68	

Damage Bonus: +9D6.

Weapon: Crush 100%, 9D6 sucking damage

Skill: Find Prey 70%, Lift Big Things Then Put Them Down 90%.

FIVE WORKER DEEP ONES

	1	*2*	*3*	*4*	*5*
STR	15	15	13	14	20
CON	08	14	09	14	11
SIZ	21	22	24	22	19
INT	12	15	15	13	13
POW	08	08	15	14	08
DEX	15	14	11	14	10
HP	15	18	17	18	15
MOV	8/10 swimming				

Damage Bonus: +1D6.

Weapons: Trident 25%, damage 1D6+1+1D6
Claw 25%, damage 1D6+1D6

Spells: Deep One #3 knows Contact Cthulhu and Contact Spawn of Cthulhu; Deep One #4 knows Contact Cthulhu.

Skills: Deep One 55%, Dodge 45%, Hide 35%, Jump 30%, Listen 40%, Sneak 35%, Spot Hidden 45%, Swim 95%, Throw 25%.

The alien matter of the statue is immune to most forms of destruction. A million tons of TNT probably could destroy it; any force much less strong would not.

If an investigator uses the Find Gate spell, he discovers that the statue is a gate—one through which Nyarlathotep, in the aspect of the Bloated Woman, appears when summoned.

THE EGYPTIAN ROOM: this is Sir Aubrey's place to relax, a living room loaded with Egyptian artifacts from every dynasty. The stuff is almost priceless—one-of-a-kind and never-seen statues, artifacts, necklaces, etc., with a nominal cash value of 1D3 million U.S. dollars. The room is entered through an open doorway in the cavern wall. A successful Spot Hidden notices a slot running all the way around the doorway—when dropped, a steel panel (STR 100) seals off the Egyptian room from the rest of the complex. The panel is raised and lowered by a pull-cord hanging from beside Sir Aubrey's throne chair.

SIR AUBREY

Behind the throne chair is another, smaller doorway leading to an Egyptian-style burial chamber. An ornate sarcophagus waits there, made of marble and decorated with about three hundred pounds of hammered gold and uncut precious stones. The face of Sir Aubrey decorates its askew lid. When the lid is closed, a vial strapped to the inside of the coffin expels gas which puts the person in the sarcophagus into suspended animation for eight months. If the lid is opened, the gas dissipates in 1D6 minutes. Breathing it for a little while causes slight dizziness.

If he is not leading a ritual, there is a 50% chance that Sir Aubrey will be in this room.

SIR AUBREY'S WORKSHOP

Two thick lead doors seal off this area. They are unlocked but interlock so that one will not open unless the other is closed. Shelves, tables, parts, and papers crowd the workshop interior. If he is not leading a ritual, there is a 50% chance that Sir Aubrey will be in the workshop.

THE TRIGGER: on the center table in the workshop is a large unit resembling in shape the detached nose of the rocket. An easy deduction establishes that this unit goes in the nose of the rocket. The assembly is crammed with strange little wheels and multi-colored wires and tiny little panels with strange, minute geometric designs etched on them. The electrical portion of the unit baffles even the best scientist among the investigators (no one is likely to be able to duplicate even three-quarters of a century of electronics advances in an afternoon). Nevertheless, enough can be deduced that a successful Electrical Repair roll suggests that the device is some sort of positioning and triggering mechanism. A successful Mechanical Repair or Physics roll tells the user that the trigger is to do something after reaching a particular combination of time and atmospheric pressure.

THE WARHEAD: the smaller cylindrical space in the center of the trigger might be where a warhead could go. A search of the workshop turns up a lead casket containing a metal cylinder which fits precisely in the space provided by the large unit. The warhead is a radium bomb, intended to scatter murderous radiation over a hundred square miles of ocean in welcome to those returning. The main explosive power of it, just enough to break momentarily the fabric of space, comes from the mysterious meteorite power source, quantum-excited when smashed against the radium core. Once the warhead has been removed from its shielding, the warhead emits dangerous radiation, in about the same amount and under the same conditions as did the power chunk in the fire box of the *Dark Mistress*, which see further above.

Connecting the warhead to the arming mechanism is simple—three bolts, two pistons, two electrical leads, and a safety wire. To arm the warhead, the top of the cylinder is rotated a half-turn to the right, and the safety wire inserted into a catch. The warhead cannot explode by itself. If the trigger housing is destroyed, building a new one requires most of a year. A separate section below discusses ways to stop the launch.

THE PLANS: strewn around the table are many blueprints concerning the bomb and the rocket. The writing and associated mathematics are in the script of the Great Race of Yith, translatable in 1D10+4 weeks by someone of at least INT 18 and 80% Physics. The plans obviously resemble the rocket and the warhead. Any investigator can deduce that the war departments of many nations would lovingly examine this material, among them the Japanese Army and Navy, whose respective agents already suspect this strange weapon exists.

THE CHRONOMETER: in a fitted wooden case is an ordinary marine chronometer, the same double clocks used by ship's navigators all over the world to establish daily positions at sea. Though the minute and second hands agree with investigator watches, the hour hands are set eight hours earlier. A successful Astronomy roll, or a successful Idea roll lowered by 25 percentiles, suggests that all navigational instruments keep Greenwich meridian time, and that eight hours is about right for the difference between GMT and East China time.

THE TOOLS: the hand tools in the workroom are shaped oddly, as though for hands other than human, and most functions of the tools are unfathomable. The elegance of their form and finish suggests that they represent a technology far in advance of 1925.

ITEM: Pertinent entries in the diaries of Sir Aubrey Penhew, Viscount Pevensey. (*Nyarlathotep Papers #45*)

Relevance of the Information: in Sir Aubrey's handwriting, in books dated from 1921 through 1925. Roger Carlyle is mentioned once, Jackson Elias not at all. Robert Huston frequently appears. If the investigators already have witnessed the birth of the Spawn of Nyarlathotep in Kenya, that event is mentioned; if they haven't gone to Kenya, the event isn't mentioned; if they went to Kenya, missed the great event, but might go back, then it's keeper's choice. One passage mentions the "Children of Great Cthulhu"—this refers to the spawn of Cthulhu who were sent after Jack Brady at the Seamens Club in Shanghai (Brady is the traitor referred to in

Nyarlathotep Papers #45

Hail Pharaoh of Darkness, Hail Nyarlathotep, Cthulhu fhtagn. Nyarlathotep th'ga, shamesh, shamesh, Nyarlathotep th'ga, Cthulhu fhtagn!

13th June, 1921: At last I have arrived to begin the task of my lord and master, the Black Pharaoh. He has given me my dreams, given me Egypt, and I will duly repay him by giving him the world of men. The power, the beauty, none cannot appreciate who do not witness. I know the power, the beauty; I bear the beauty of a life devoted to him ....

30th August, 1921: Huston has at last sent the plans. Very complex and fascinating. It will take some time to grasp their meaning and begin building. I have been promised the knowledge necessary, and my faith is strong ....

7th September, 1921: The first shipments have arrived. All of us know great joy. The deep ones have arrived to stay. The work begins ....

15th January, 1922: The first phase is complete. Shipments are arriving more quickly now. I must begin work on the warhead soon ....

8th April, 1923: The rods have been drawn, but more knowledge is needed. Huston is worthy—I never would have thought it possible ....

4th October, 1923: Work on the guidance system has halted. Huston must open a deeper level, and that will take time. Our Master has promised to aid him by bringing one of the Great Race. How I long to speak to one of those ....

19th January, 1924: With joy we begin work again. Soon is the day ....

29th September, 1924: The missile is complete, but the warhead baffles me. I must pray for guidance. Ho Fong warns of someone who knows our plans—is that nursling Carlyle still alive? Will Our Master deign to tell me?

11th February, 1925: All is ready. Now we simply await the Great Day When the Great Gate Opens. None can baffle His will. Nyarlathotep th'ga, Cthulhu fhtagn!

several entries). This diary directly links the schemes of Nyarlathotep and Cthulhu. If the investigators can steal it, keepers can use its existence to create new clues in this or succeeding campaigns. Reading the entire diary costs 1D6 SAN.

RADIATION IN THE CHAMBER

Low radiation from the magma pit infests the chamber. Much of the magma is a Lovecraftian substance left otherwise undefined. If the keeper likes, he may inflict some health penalty on everyone spending time in the chamber, but keep in mind that Sir Aubrey has worked here for years, and is still in good health. Perhaps Nyarlathotep protects him.

If the keeper wishes radiation to be a factor, try the following. After a day of constant closeness to the edge of the magma pit, living things exhibit symptomatic sickness and tissue degeneracy 1D6 days later. The powerful rays are uniformly deadly, and no treatment can cure the victim, though hospitalization and rest can prolong life. When the symptoms of exposure begin, halve the STR and DEX of the victim, and halve all of his or her physical skills. The victim loses 1 hit point daily until death occurs. Keepers should embroider the situations with blotching skin, skin cancers, disgusting eruptions, sprouting appendages, hair loss, etc.

At least half of the work force suffers from such exposure; as they die, the workers are replaced. Seeing such victims of advanced exposure costs 0/1D4 SAN.

Rituals of the Order

Reflecting the cult's narrow range of interests, the Order normally holds only death rites and breeding rites—keeper's choice as to what the investigators find. The chamber is irregular enough and shadowy enough that investigators have a 90% chance to view a complete ritual without discovery unless they deliberately betray themselves.

On ritual nights the island approaches are left unwatched. After such a big party, the cultists are exhausted, and the entire chamber is cleared, with the exception of the shoggoth-twsha, who remains to control the shoggoth. The shoggoth is not part of any ritual. It is fed victims every few days.

These rites are held for the island's cultists, and any visitors. Other locations of the Order hold their own ceremonies. Ho Fong's rituals in Shanghai, for instance, are much larger, but much the same.

DEATH RITES

Following several hours of mad chanting and dancing, sacrificial victims are slaughtered. Their arms are severed and they are bled to death. Counting the deep one colony, fifty to two hundred cultists may attend this sort of ritual. These rites are episodic, but typically conform with the lunar calendar at the dark or the full of the moon.

With banging gongs and wailing bamboo flutes, the cultists dance in voluminous black and yellow silk robes far too big for them, symbolizing the glorious cosmic bulk of the Bloated Woman. The robes slow cultists by one MOV per round, and uniformly decrease their effective DEX by 2 points each.

©1989 NICK SMITH

The rites always end in the summoning of the Bloated Woman, who appears amid a choir of maddened singers, devours the sacrifices, and then in elegant Mandarin delivers a short homily encouraging self-sacrifice and blind obedience. Witnessing the death rites exacts a small Sanity loss for each corpse, plus normal cost for the Bloated Woman.

BREEDING RITES

These rites are held irregularly, when a priest or priestess requires, but always including observances at the beginning and the end of the typhoon season. They involve the ravishment of humans by deep ones. About a third of the females involved (deep one females also take an active role) become pregnant and successfully come to term. Investigators who thoroughly spy out the island may notice an unusual number of pregnant villagers.

The breeding dances are uninhibited and copulatory. Investigators whose natural senses of decency are outraged lose 1D3 SAN; jaded investigators lose nothing.

THE SPECIAL RITUAL ON THE DAY OF OPENING

On January 14, 1926, the island holds as many members of the Order of the Bloated Woman as can get there: this is a great day for the cult, and everyone wants to participate. (In consequence, murder and other crime decrease for a few weeks all over the Far East.) The number of attending cultists might vary from 250 to 25,000, as the keeper desires. If there are a lot of people, hold the ritual outside the volcano. Perhaps the palm trees are chopped down so that everyone can see. All captured investigators are in chained teams and involved in this—it's a handy way to justify keeping them alive this long.

Carl Stanford will not be on the island. That powerful sorcerer is elsewhere, already performing new wickedness and cruelty for his evil master. Unless business presses, Ho Fong and many other Order notables will be on the island to share in the great event.

After two hours of solemn chanting, Contact Nyarlathotep is cast, the god appears as the Bloated Woman, and her followers grovel. Sir Aubrey then dedicates the assembly's collective will to the god, and all rejoice in the existence of the outer gods and the great old ones. The goddess aspect then freezes, not to move again until the opening of the Gate. Sir Aubrey then begins, at a calculated second, to intone the awful phrases of the ritual opening. When the Gate opens, the Bloated Woman wakes, roaring a horrible triumph.

Some twenty-five minutes before the Gate must open, Sir Aubrey instructs hand-picked cultists to use their welders to cut through the rocket's supports. Working to a precise timetable, the rocket sinks into the magma to a depth of ten feet, welling hot magma up over the edge of the pit and incidentally killing everyone who worked to free the rocket from its supports. Now appropriately blooded and complete with nose cone and warhead in place, the rocket begins to develop power. At fifteen minutes before the scheduled opening of the Gate, explosive charges blow away the cap of the cinder cone, and the vehicle launches upward toward the Indian Ocean, to the oohs and ahhs of happy cultists. At the proper moment, Sir Aubrey intones the final terrible words,

as do his cohorts on other continents. The rocket explodes and the way is opened. Nyarlathotep screams out his triumph. The world is one step closer to ultimate destruction.

At the height of the celebration, Sir Aubrey goes to his sarcophagus for a well-earned rest. Months later he awakes refreshed, ready to perpetrate new horrors upon the world.

FOILING THE RITUAL OF OPENING

A host of ways exist to foil the Great Gate ritual. Obvious possibilities are set forth below. Players undoubtedly will think of more.

The simplest and seemingly most effective way would be to set Sir Aubrey's chronometer 10-20 minutes ahead or behind, making both his spellcasting and his rocket out of phase with the rituals on other continents. The chronometer is the one from the *Dark Mistress*. An invocation and explosion missing the central totality of the eclipse are of no help in opening the Gate, and likely doom the ritual's effect.

Unfortunately, far-seeing Nyarlathotep is also likely to mention the ploy while Sir Aubrey winds the chronometer, which the sorcerer does daily after breakfast. The investigators have to be lucky. For this scheme to work, each must receive a successful Luck roll.

If the keeper wishes, Sir Aubrey's diary can make clear the need for split-second coordination at the sites. If the chronometer is destroyed several days ahead of time, the *Dark Mistress* can fetch another, which will be guarded by dozens of cultists, but destroying the chronometer on the morning of the ritual leaves Sir Aubrey helpless unless Nyarlathotep interferes.

If the warhead were thrown into the magma pit, the intense heat and the pressure trigger it in 1D4 minutes, blowing up the island and leaving the area radioactive until the 1970s. Though the investigators might die, so would many cultists and the rocket with them, decisively smashing Nyarlathotep's scheme.

If the girders supporting the rocket above the magma were severed (STR 50, three minutes for one man to make the needed cuts), the rocket would fall into the magma and launch itself against the stone ceiling, ruining the missile. The destruction of the rocket decreases the chance for a successful ritual, but Nyarlathotep still has a chance of winning. The explosion and splattering magma kill everyone within the chamber.

If the girders were part-way cut through, the rocket would slump into the magma in four minutes, thereafter following the course just above.

The trigger of the rocket could be physically smashed with a hammer, or altered internally with a successful Mechanical or Electrical Repair roll, making its flight impossible.

Enough chemical explosives could blow up the volcano, but this would take 1D10+15 tons of dynamite, or eight tons of nitroglycerin, an inconvenient amount. If the investigators could lay naval guns on the target, they could do the job from a distance, since the shells will be able to penetrate: the effort requires 60 14-inch, about 300 8-inch, or approximately 1000 5-inch shells. Only Captain Isoge is in a position to quickly arrange such a strike. As the island is unclaimed, only permission of his superiors would be required.

No effective bomber strikes could reach Gray Dragon Island in that day, and no usable aircraft carriers exist. Planted explosives or ranged bombardment by naval gun could trigger Sir Aubrey's radium bomb, blowing the island sky.

The New China Assault Force

Ideally the assault comes on a calm, overcast night with a rising tide, after Ho Fong's yacht has gone to the island, a sign that some ritual may soon take place. Mu Hsien believes that few or no cultists will be on guard during or just after a ritual.

If the number of cultists on the island visibly increases, Chu and Brady try to deal with anyone who can supply reliable fighters. Brady will not hesitate to offer the *Seven Cryptical Books* to Lin Tang-yu in return for aid; if he knows about Captain Isoge, he'll give the Japanese every scrap of military information found on the island. If Isoge can be convinced of the honor of Brady and Chu, he is in a position to offer considerable aid, should the keeper so desire.

But keepers should be wary of pitched battles with mercenary Chinese, fanatical cultists, and Japanese marines, supported by broadsides from heavy cruisers and featuring destroyer-chewing shoggoths. Such a presentation might require a coordinated timetable and several assistant keepers!

Here is the likeliest scenario. Scouting missions to the island indicate a steady increase in cultist numbers—so many cultists that a thorough survey of the island becomes impossible. With so many people present, the scouts have all they can do to land, spend a few terrifying minutes in the scrub, and then leave again. But they are able to capture a few degenerates, and learn by stern interrogation that the great machine is within the volcano and will soon fly.

Chu and Brady decide to land several independent commando teams, who are to find and destroy Sir Aubrey and his rocket. Guns are to be used only as a last resort; with unhappy candor, Mu Hsien says that guns will not be much use anyway against the awful monsters that wizards can raise. "Be as stealthy as the tiger," he says, "and spring as decisively." Chu leads six men, Brady leads six, and the investigators can form up their own commando team, perhaps with a few weapons experts or martial artists to bolster their combat punch.

Conclusion

If the investigators are reasonably lucky and make no silly moves, they can prevent the opening of the Gate. Some Sanity gain, about 1D10, should be given, mostly for knocking off sundry human foes and not for spoiling a scheme which the investigators probably grasp incompletely.

If they manage to ward any of the three parts of the triangle forming the Great Gate, give each of them 1D20 SAN for each place warded. But do not allow them to rest on their laurels. They have dared too much, and their enemies are too powerful. Surely surviving cultists will dog them, desperate to know just where the wards have been planted. Once delving so far into the Mythos, the investigators must bid goodbye to personal peace and comfort, and find lonely contentment in great deeds achieved for the good of all mankind.

Statistics

GOOD GUYS

JACK "BRASS" BRADY, ageless Soldier of Fortune and Last Sane Member of the Carlyle Expedition

Brady is violent and instinctual. His Sanity is perilously low for the task before him—he likely will die soon. He is a killer, a dangerous man to cross. If he goes insane, he'll attack everything which seems to him Mythos-related.

STR 17	CON 16	SIZ 17	INT 13	POW 16
DEX 18	APP 08	SAN 20	EDU 05	HP 17

Damage Bonus: +1D6.

Weapons: Fist/Punch 80%, damage 1D3+1D6*
Head Butt 75%, damage 1D4+1D6
Thompson Submachine Gun 60%, damage 1D10+2
Fighting Knife 70%, damage 1D4+2+1D6
Nightstick 50%, damage 1D6+1D4
Kick 40%, damage 1D6+1D6

* *If he has a moment to slip on his brass knuckles, Brady does 1D3+2+1D6 damage with Fist/Punch.*

Magic: the brass plate given to Brady by his mother has an 85% chance to attract and deflect one impaling weapon attack per combat round, but the attack must come from the front, not his back.

Skills: Arabic 15%, Climb 70%, Cthulhu Mythos 45%, Dodge 95%, Drive Automobile 50%, Explosives 85%, Fast Talk 60%, First Aid 65%, Hide 75%, Jump 70%, Listen 75%, Mandarin Chinese 35%, Operate Heavy Machinery 50%, Psychology 35%, Sneak 85%, Spot Hidden 85%, Swim 65%, Throw 75%, Track 50%, Turkic 22%.

MORE FIGHTERS FOR THE NEW CHINA TO COME

	1	2	3	4	5	6	7	8
STR	14	13	15	14	15	12	13	14
CON	13	11	14	12	10	15	09	10
SIZ	12	13	13	11	12	15	14	13
DEX	13	13	13	13	12	12	12	12
APP	09	10	11	12	11	08	05	10
SAN	65	50	45	49	35	30	95	80
INT	14	16	13	13	12	13	15	14
POW	14	13	16	11	10	09	17	08
HP	13	12	14	12	11	15	12	12

Damage Bonus: +1D4.

Weapons: Fist/Punch 80%, damage 1D3+1D4
Kick 70%, damage 1D6+1D4
Head Butt 70%, damage 1D4+1D4
.45 Automatic Pistol (with silencer), damage 1D10+2*
Fighting Knife 55%, damage 1D4+2+1D4
Nightstick 50%, damage 1D6+1D4
Thompson Submachine Gun 45%, damage 1D10+2

At the keeper's option, Firm Action handguns may be silencer (suppressor)-equipped; these halve handgun base ranges but anyone over 30 feet way must get a successful Listen roll to hear the shot.

Spells: none.

Skills: Climb 55%, Dodge 85%, Hide 65%, Jump 50%, Listen 70%, Mandarin Chinese 60%, Martial Arts 80%, Sneak 65%, Spot Hidden 55%, Throw 60%.

The Bloated Woman

*"Behind the black fan
the soul-twister simpers,
snake-armed and slickened,
inflated with blood fat.
The dragon-toothed feaster
gluts down gray lilies, the
gracious donation
of children left twitching...."*
—"Goddess of the Black Fan"

"...a form most majestic appears before proud Hun Tao—the goddess Herself come to humble him! Her graceful tentacles embrace his mealy-fleshed followers. Her dragon fangs test the milksops' shrieking throats. Her sickles reap frantic limbs wherever She will! Her five mouths chant victory, while Hun Tao weeps and shivers in his empty hall!"
—The Tale of Priest Kwan

This particularly disgusting form of Nyarlathotep is known on Earth only among the Order of the Bloated Woman, which is centered in Shanghai.

She appears as a 600-pound, seven-foot-tall female horror, with tentacles in place of arms, and more tentacles sprouting from rolls of sickly yellow-gray flesh. Below her eyes another tentacle waves, and below and beside that are lumpy chins, each sporting a mouth, each mouth a perfect rosy bow made hideous by clusters of fangs. She wears a yellow-and-black tunic of fine silk.

She crudely resembles a human woman. Multiple smaller tentacles sprout from the rest of her body. Six sickles hang in the belt of her tunic. Also in her belt is the magic black fan which, when held just under her eyes, permits her to take on the appearance of a slim and beautiful Chinese maiden. The fan pulls all attention to the eyes and somehow conceals the avatar's bulk and its true form—everything but those lovely eyes. When the fan is removed, its full monstrousness is gruesomely apparent.

Assisted by the Black Fan, the Bloated Woman may seduce men, giving victims unearthly and degenerate pleasure before smothering them in flabby bulk.

If killed as the Bloated Woman, Nyarlathotep becomes a mass of reflexively writhing tentacles which bore into the earth and there disintegrate. The Bloated Woman will rise again from this tentacular ruin in 1D6+2 months. This apparent death and eventual rebirth has no bearing on Nyarlathotep or his other avatars.

THE BLOATED WOMAN, an Avatar of Nyarlathotep

STR 31	CON 44	SIZ 26	INT 86	POW 100
DEX 19	MOV 12			HP 35

Damage Bonus: +3D6.

Weapons: Arm Tentacle 85%, damage 3D3 + hold for Kiss
Small Tentacle 50%, damage 1D4+3 each—the small tentacles wield sickles in combat
Kiss 100%, damage destroys 1D6 INT

Spells: she knows all Mythos spells. She can summon monsters at the rate of 1 magic point per POW point of the monster. She may summon shantaks, hunting horrors, or Servitors of the Outer Gods at the cost of a single magic point per entity.

Sanity Loss: 1D10/1D100 Sanity points.

Attacks: the Bloated Woman has two arm tentacles and can attack with both each combat round. When first grabbed by one of these tentacles, the victim takes 3D3 points damage.

On subsequent rounds, he is gripped by the tentacle and mouthed by one of the slobbering maws. This mouthing, the Kiss of the Bloated Woman, destroys 1D6 INT of the victim per round, permanently. As long as the victim has INT remaining, he can try to escape by overcoming the Bloated Woman's STR with his own. When a victim's INT is reduced to 0, his skull bursts open under the Woman's slobbering lips and the entity slurps down his living brains (the 'gray lilies' of the poem).

The Bloated Woman has a thicket of smaller tentacles with which it can also attack. Each round roll 1D10 for the number of smaller tentacles which can attack, each wielding a small sharp sickle.

CHU MIN, age 31, Leader of the New China to Come

STR 15	CON 18	SIZ 13	INT 13	POW 8
DEX 16	APP 12	EDU 16	SAN 55	HP 16

Damage Bonus: +1D4.

Weapons: .45 Automatic Pistol 90%, damage 1D10+2*
Thompson Submachine Gun 75%, damage 1D10+2
Fist/Punch 75%, damage 1D3+1D4
Fighting Knife 70%, damage 1D4+2+1D4**
Head Butt 55%, damage 1D4+1D4
Nightstick 50%, damage 1D6+1D4
Kick 40%, damage 1D6+1D4
* he has a silencer, or suppressor, for this weapon.
** Chu always carries the fighting knife in a forearm scabbard.

Spells: none

Skills: Climb 70%, Dodge 90%, English 10%, Explosives 30%, Fast Talk 40%, First Aid 55%, Hide 75%, Jump 65%, Listen 75%, Mandarin Chinese 65%, Martial Arts 75%, Mechanical Repair 45%, Persuade 25%, Sneak 65%, Spot Hidden 65%, Swim 65%, Throw 55%.

BAD GUYS

SIR AUBREY PENHEW, appears 55, Peer of the Realm, Egyptologist, and Callous Sorcerer

Sir Aubrey now has the physical capacities of a 20-year-old, though he looks 55. If the island seems doomed, he flees aboard the Dark Mistress. *It is possible for him to operate the craft by himself, and he can cast off and get beyond the reef in 1D4+3 minutes after he reaches the yacht. If investigators are captured on the island, Sir Aubrey will interrogate them thoroughly before sending the meddlers to their doom.*

STR 15	CON 18	SIZ 12	INT 18	POW 21
DEX 16	APP 18	EDU 18	SAN 0	HP 15

Damage Bonus: +1D4.

Weapons: .38 Revolver 30%, damage 1D10
Cult Sickle 25%, damage 1D8+1+1D4

Spells: Contact Deep Ones, Contact Nyarlathotep, Contact Sand Dwellers, Dread Curse of Azathoth, Fist of Yog-Sothoth, Shrivelling, Steal Life, Wave of Oblivion, and others as desired.

Skills: Anthropology 55%, Arabic 40%, Archaeology 75%, Astronomy 25%, Cthulhu Mythos 20%, Deep One Speech 35%, Dodge 35%, Egyptian Hieroglyphs 85%, Egyptian History 75%, Occult (Egyptian) 50%, Electrical Repair 35%, Great Ones Written Speech 40%, Hide 50%, Mandarin Chinese 50%, Mechanical Repair 45%, Persuade 75%, Physics 35%, Psychology 50%, Sneak 40%.

DIRE DEEP ONES

	1	2	3	4	5	6	7	8
STR	10	13	11	12	13	16	20	16
CON	06	17	14	07	11	16	15	11
SIZ	19	15	21	16	19	12	10	15
INT	13	13	09	16	11	11	16	15
POW	06	14	10	08	09	13	11	09
DEX	16	15	15	14	12	10	08	05
HP	13	16	18	12	15	14	13	13

MOV 8/10 swimming

Damage Bonus: +1D4.

Weapons: Trident 25%, 1D6+1+1D4 damage
Claw 25%, 1D4+1D4 damage

Spells: Deep One #2 knows Shrivelling

Skills: Dodge 45%, Hide 35%, Jump 30%, Listen 40%, Sneak 35%, Spot Hidden 45%, Swim 95%, Throw 25%.

VILLAGER HALF-BREEDS on Gray Dragon Island

Reuse the villagers if the investigators put ashore a strong force. If the opening of the Gate is at hand, vast numbers of cultists could be present on Gray Dragon Island. All of these are half-breed humans who will soon degenerate into deep ones. They ferociously attack intruders upon sight. All are thoroughly insane.

	1	2	3	4	5	6	7	8
STR	11	10	08	07	11	14	12	11
CON	09	08	10	07	15	12	10	09
SIZ	12	12	10	09	11	09	12	13
INT	09	09	08	08	08	08	09	09
POW	05	04	13	08	07	10	11	06
DEX	13	12	12	10	09	09	09	08
APP	04	04	05	03	03	03	06	08
HP	11	11	10	08	13	11	11	11

Damage Bonus: +0.

Weapons: Cult Sickle 35%, damage 1D4+3
Small Club 25%, damage 1D6
Fist/Punch 20%, damage 1D3

Skills: Boating 40%, Dodge 45%, Fishing 65%, Listen 45%, Sneak 55%, Spot Hidden 45%, Swim 90%.

JULES SAVOYARD, age 39, Ship's Captain and Minor Priest of the Order of the Bloated Woman

STR 08	CON 10	SIZ 15	INT 10	POW 16
DEX 09	APP 03	EDU 10	SAN 0	HP 13

Damage Bonus: +0.

Weapon: .45 Automatic Pistol, damage 1D10+2

Spell: Wave of Oblivion

Skills: Mandarin Chinese 20%, Cthulhu Mythos 15%, English 35%, French 75%, Law 20%, Navigation 45%, Shiphandling 60%, Sneak 40%, Spot Hidden 50%.

CRAZED HALF-BREED CREWMEN OF THE *DARK MISTRESS*

These half-breeds eventually degenerate into deep ones. They attack intruders upon sight, and fight ferociously; they are all thoroughly insane. On board ship, there is not much for them to do, and they imitate their drunken captain in endless bouts of drinking and sleeping. They will not be much more alert at sea than at anchor.

	1	2	3	4	5	6
STR	10	11	09	09	11	13
CON	09	08	10	07	15	12
SIZ	12	13	10	09	11	09
INT	09	09	08	08	08	08
POW	05	04	13	08	07	10
DEX	13	12	12	10	09	09
APP	04	04	05	03	03	03
HP	11	11	10	08	13	11

Damage Bonus: +0.

Weapons: Cult Sickle 35%, damage 1D4+3
Small Club 25%, damage 1D6
Fist/Punch 20%, damage 1D3

Skills: Boating 40%, Fishing 65%, Listen 45%, Spot Hidden 40%, Swim 90%. ■

Appendix: Shipboard Activities

The following are simply ideas concerning ocean voyages during the campaign. There can be a lot of them, depending on investigator decisions. Some keepers will summarize and otherwise ignore them; others may construct additional small adventures to vivify a shipboard passage. Keepers who perceive the need may also use voyages to help restock investigator SAN levels, and perhaps to train investigators in skills suddenly perceived as valuable.

LIKELY PASSAGES

The following passages may occur in a *Masks of Nyarlathotep* campaign:

■ New York to Southampton

■ Southampton to Alexandria or Port Said

■ Port Said to Mombasa

■ Mombasa to Singapore

■ Singapore to Darwin, Port Hedland, or Perth

■ Singapore to Hong Kong or Shanghai

■ Shanghai or Perth to San Francisco

■ by rail, New York / Chicago / San Francisco

SOME HANDY SHIP NAMES

The following merchant and passenger ships may be used to transport the investigators across the world in the *Masks of Nyarlathotep* campaign: the *Laurentides*, an Atlantic-run passenger vessel, British registry; the *Snohomish*, a U.S. merchantman with passenger space; the *Ivory Wind*, a cultist merchantman running between London and China; and the *Ineluctable*, an older passenger liner running between Britain and India

MINOR INCREASES OF A SKILL

For the purposes of this adventure, one limited skill roll might be possible per investigator at the conclusion of a passenger liner voyage. To increase a skill while on a pleasure voyage, first roll POW x3 or less to demonstrate enthusiasm and willpower. Failing, the investigator is too distracted (or too relaxed) to concentrate fruitfully. To increase a skill, choose from one of the following:

■ daily skeet-shooting from fantail gives +1D4-1 to Shotgun skill

■ daily saber class practice gives +1D4-1 to Saber or other sword skill

■ daily handgun practice below decks (if available) gives +1D4-1 to chosen Handgun skill

■ daily gymnastics practice gives +1D4-1 to Dodge or Jump skill

■ daily swimming practice gives +1D4-1 to Swim skill (if swimming pool is available)

■ daily wrestling practice gives +1D4-1 to Grapple skill

■ daily boxing practice gives +1D4-1 to Fist/Punch skill

Investigators traveling first class can increase their Credit Rating skill. To add +1D4-1, total Credit Rating, Fast Talk, Listen, and Psychology, then roll D100. If the result is equal to or less than the total, increase Credit Rating. This increase requires daily contact in the cocktail lounge, and extended card playing and gossip.

If an investigator's skill is 10% or less in Occult, Navigate, or an Other Language, one of those skills might be increased by +1D4-1 points. On a large ship, the Purser's Office would arrange such studies as part of the ship's services. Any of the following languages have a 50% chance of being available: Arabic, French, German, Hindi, Italian, and Spanish. Any of the following are plausibly available, at 25% chance each: Bengali, Cantonese, Dutch, Greek, Japanese, Latin, Mandarin Chinese, Parsi, Polish, Russian, Swedish, Turkish, or Urdu. Additional modern languages by arrangement with the keeper, each with a 10% chance of being available.

Language lessons would simply be extended conversations with some bored passenger, but daily application could pick up something useful. INT x5 or less roll to learn enough to be worth remembering. The Occult skill lessons are imparted by a traveling Theosophist or other student of the Beyond. The Navigate lessons would be taught privately by a ship's officer, for some arranged sum of money.

A few skill gains aboard a passenger-carrying freighter might be possible:

■ Operate Heavy Machine +1D4-1

■ +1D4-1 to Navigate skill if Navigate is 10% or less.

■ dominant language of crew: +1D4-1 if present skill of investigator is 10% or less.

Highly intellectual skills require more skill to impart and more time to acquire than an ocean voyage affords.

SANITY GAIN FOR A VOYAGE

Doctors in the 1920s frequently prescribed ocean voyages to their patients, an excellent idea for this campaign. Allow an automatic Sanity gain of 1D4-1 SAN if no adventures occur aboard ship on that voyage, or if the investigator is able to ignore the significance of the adventures.

THE NYARLATHOTEP PAPERS

In which the handouts are reprinted,
so that the Keeper may easily replicate them.
Permission given to photocopy for personal use only.

HANDOUT INDEX

Nyarlathotep Papers #23

Main Points of Prof. Anthony Cowles' NYU Lecture

ONE A bat cult once existed among the Aboriginals of Australia. It was known across the continent, and the god of the cult was always known as the Father of All Bats. Adherents believed that by making human sacrifices to their god they themselves would become worthy enough that the Father of All Bats would appear to them. Once he was enticed to appear, he would conquer all men. Sacrifices were run through a gauntlet of worshipers who struck the victims with clubs embedded with the sharp teeth of bats. The teeth were coated with a substance derived from rabid bats. The poison was quick-acting, but victims apparently went mad before they died. Leaders of the cult reputedly could take the forms of bat-winged snakes, enabling them to steal sacrifices from across the land.

Cowles believes that this cult became dormant or extinct hundreds of years ago. Its former existence is the reason that he became interested in Jackson Elias' books about present-day cults.

TWO An Aboriginal song cycle mentions a place where enormous beings gathered, somewhere in the west of Australia. The songs say that these gods, who were not at all like men, built great sleeping walls and dug great caves. But living winds blew down the gods and overthrew them, destroying their camp. When this happened, the way was open for the Father of All Bats, who came into the land, and grew strong.

THREE Cowles shows the investigators a set of four over-exposed glass slides. Each shows a few sweating men standing beside enormous blocks of stone, pitted and eroded but clearly dressed and formed for architectural purposes. Dim carvings seem to decorate some. Billows of sand are everywhere. Though he did not bring the book with him, Cowles says that the discoverer, one Arthur MacWhirr of Port Hedland, kept a diary in which he records several attacks on the party by Aboriginals. MacWhirr reportedly records deaths to victims from hundreds of small punctures, reminiscent of the earlier bat-cult.

FOUR Cowles tells finally of a tale he collected from near the Arafura Sea in northern Australia. In it Sand Bat, or Father of All Bats, has a battle of wits with Rainbow Snake, the Aboriginal deification of water and the patron of life. Rainbow Snake succeeds in tricking and trapping Sand Bat and his clan into the depths of a watery place from which Sand Bat can only complain, and is unable to return to trouble the people.

Nyarlathotep Papers #1

What You Know About Your Friend, Jackson Elias

Jackson Elias is 38, of medium height and build, and dark-complexioned. He has a feisty, friendly air about him and, as an orphan in Stratford, Connecticut, he learned to make his own way early in life. He has no living relatives, and no permanent address.

You like him, and value his friendship, even though months and sometimes years separate one meeting from the next. You'd be upset and probably crave vengeance if anything happened to your friend. The world is better for having Jackson Elias in it.

His writings characterize and analyze death cults. His best-known book is *Sons of Death*, exposing modern-day Thuggees in India. He speaks several languages fluently and is constantly traveling. He is social, and enjoys an occasional drink. He smokes a pipe. Elias is tough, stable, and punctual, unafraid of brawls or officials. He is mostly self-educated. His well-researched works always seem to reflect first-hand experience. He is secretive and never discusses a project until he has a final draft in hand.

All of his books illustrate how cults manipulate the fears of their followers. A skeptic, Elias has never found proof of supernatural powers, magic, or dark gods. Insanity and feelings of inadequacy characterize death cultists, feelings for which they compensate by slaughtering innocents to make themselves feel powerful or chosen. Cults draw the weak-minded, though cult leaders are usually clever and manipulative. When fear of a cult stops, the cult vanishes.

[Snapshot given to you by Jackson Elias, pictured on the right.]

Skulls Along the River (1910)—exposes headhunter cult in Amazon basin.

Masters of the Black Arts (1912)—surveys supposed sorcerous cults throughout history.

The Way of Terror (1913)—analyzes systematization of fear through cult organization; warmly reviewed by George Sorel.

The Smoking Heart (1915)—first half discusses historical Mayan death cults. Second half instances present-day Central American death cults.

Sons of Death (1918)—modern-day Thuggees; Elias infiltrated the cult and wrote a book about it.

Witch Cults of England (1920)—summarizes covens in nine English counties; interviews practicing English witches; Rebecca West thought some of the material trivial and overworked.

The Black Power (1921)—expands upon *The Way of Terror*; includes interviews with several anonymous cult leaders.

All of these books are published by Prospero Press of New York City, and all were edited by owner/editor Jonah Kensington. Kensington is a good friend of Jackson Elias, and knows you well.

Nyarlathotep Papers #2

World-Wide Telegraph Service

HUDSON TERMINAL, 30 CHURCH STREET
NEW YORK, USA

```
HAVE INFORMATION CONCERNING CARLYLE EXPEDITION STOP NEED
RELIABLE INVESTIGATIVE TEAM STOP ARRIVE JANUARY 15 STOP
SIGNED JACKSON ELIAS
```

Nyarlathotep Papers #3

Big Apple Dateline

ROGER CARLYLE, the playboy whom everybody knows—or knows about—is quietly leaving New Yawk tomorrow to check out the tombs of Egypt! You've seen the cuties ROGER has found in the nightspots. Who can doubt he'll dig up someone—er, something—equally fabulous from the Egyptian sands?

—*NEW YORK PILLAR/RIPOSTE, April 4, 1919*

Nyarlathotep Papers #4

CARLYLE EXPEDITION EMBARKS FOR ENGLAND

Led by the fabulously-wealthy playboy Roger Carlyle, the Carlyle Expedition departed this morning for Southampton aboard the crack British steamship *Imperial Standard.*

Contrary to earlier reports, the expedition will perform researches in London under the auspices of the Penhew Foundation before continuing to Egypt next month.

Readers may recall the enormous party which Mr. Carlyle, now 24, gave at the Waldorf-Astoria Hotel upon reaching his majority. Since then, scandals and indelicate behavior have become Carlyle's trademark, but he never has become tarnished in the eyes of Manhattanites.

Members of the expedition have been reluctant to reveal their purpose in Egypt.

OTHER EXPEDITION MEMBERS

Renowned Egyptologist Sir Aubrey Penhew is assistant leader of the team, and in charge of excavations.

Dr. Robert Huston, a fashionable 'Freudian' psychologist, accompanies the expedition to pursue parallel researches into ancient pictographs.

Miss Hypatia Masters, linked in the past to Carlyle, will act as photographer and archivist.

Mr. Jack Brady, intimate to Mr. Carlyle, accompanies the group as general factotum.

Additional members may be secured while in London.

—*NEW YORK PILLAR/RIPOSTE April 5, 1919*

Nyarlathotep Papers #29

Dear Aubrey,

Elias has been dealt with in New York. You must stop Brady. It is stupefying that he has evaded us for so long. This man may become an obstacle to our Great Lord. If you wish, I will ...

Nyarlathotep Papers #12

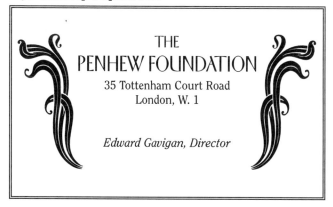

Nyarlathotep Papers #13

Instructions: Cut on the dotted lines. Fold on the solid lines. Use Piece A to form the inside box and Piece B to form the outside box. Box A should slide cleanly into Box B. Afterwards, glue the Stumbling Tiger wrapper to the outside of Box B.

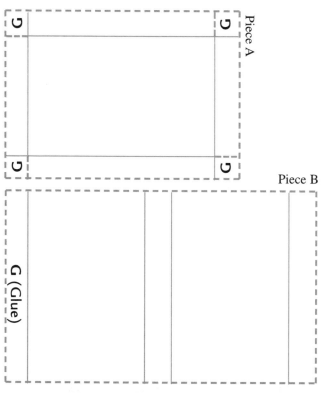

Nyarlathotep Papers #5

CARLYLE DEPARTS EGYPT

CAIRO (AP)—Sir Aubrey Penhew, temporary spokesman for the Carlyle Expedition, indicated Monday that the leaders are taking ship to East Africa for a 'well-earned rest.'

Sir Aubrey debunked rumors that the expedition had discovered clues to the legendary wealth of the lost mines of King Solomon, maintaining that the party was going on safari "in respite from our sandy labors."

Roger Carlyle, wealthy New York leader of the expedition, was unavailable for comment, still suffering from his recent sunstroke.

Discussing that unfortunate incident, local experts declared Egypt entirely too hot for Anglo-Saxons at this time of year, and suggested that the young American had not been well-served by his democratic enthusiasm, rumored to have led him to personally wield pick and shovel.

—*NEW YORK PILLAR/RIPOSTE, July 3, 1919*

Nyarlathotep Papers #7

CARLYLE EXPEDITION FEARED LOST

MOMBASA (Reuters)—Uplands police representatives today asked for public assistance concerning the disappearance of the Carlyle Expedition. No word of the party has been received in nearly two months.

The group includes wealthy playboy Roger Carlyle and three other American citizens, as well as respected Egyptologist Sir Aubrey Penhew of the United Kingdom.

The expedition left Nairobi on August 3, ostensibly on camera safari, but rumor insisted that they actually were after legendary Biblical treasures.

Carlyle and his party reportedly intended to explore portions of the Great Rift Valley, to the northwest of Nairobi.

—*NEW YORK PILLAR/RIPOSTE, Oct. 15, 1919*

Nyarlathotep Papers #8

ERICA CARLYLE ARRIVES IN AFRICA

MOMBASA (Reuters)—In response to clues, Miss Erica Carlyle, sister to the American leader of the lost Carlyle Expedition, arrived in port today aboard the Egyptian vessel *Fount of Life*.

Several Kikuyu-villager reports recently have been received concerning the putative massacre of unnamed whites near Aberdare Forest.

Miss Carlyle declared her intention to find her brother, regardless of the effort needed. She brought with her the nucleus of a large expedition.

Detailing agents to coordinate supply and other activities with Colony representatives, Miss Carlyle and the remainder of her party depart for Nairobi tomorrow.

Her companion, Mrs. Victoria Post, indirectly emphasized Miss Carlyle's purposefulness by recounting the rigors of the voyage aboard the Semite ship.

—*NEW YORK PILLAR/RIPOSTE, March 11, 1920*

Nyarlathotep Papers #6

IMPORTANT VISITORS

MOMBASA (Reuters)—Leading members of an American archaeological expedition arrived here on holiday from digs in Egypt's Nile Valley.

Our Under-Secretary, Mr. Royston Whittingdon, held a welcoming dinner for them at Collingswood House, where the wit of Sir Aubrey Penhew, expedition co-leader, was much in evidence.

Accompanying Sir Aubrey are two Americans, youthful financier Roger Carlyle and medical doctor Robert Huston.

The party leaves inland tomorrow, for Nairobi and hunting.

—*NEW YORK PILLAR/RIPOSTE, July 24, 1919*

Nyarlathotep Papers #9

CARLYLE MASSACRE CONFIRMED

NAIROBI (Reuters)—The massacre of the long-missing Carlyle expedition was confirmed today by district police representatives.

Roger Carlyle, New York's rollicking playboy, is counted among the missing.

Authorities blame hostile Nandi tribesmen for the shocking murders. Remains of at least two dozen expedition members and bearers are thought found in several concealed grave sites.

Erica Carlyle, Roger Carlyle's sister and apparent heiress to the Carlyle family fortune, led the dangerous search for her brother and his party. She credited Kikuyu tribesmen for the discovery, though police actually found the site.

Among other expedition members believed lost are Sir Aubrey Penhew, noted Egyptologist; New York socialite Hypatia Masters, and Dr. Robert Huston. Many bearers also are reported dead.

—*NEW YORK PILLAR/RIPOSTE, May 24, 1920*

Nyarlathotep Papers #10

MURDERERS HANGED

NAIROBI (Reuters)—Five Nandi tribesmen, convicted ringleaders of the vicious Carlyle Expedition massacre, were executed this morning after a short, expertly-conducted trial.

To the end, the tribesmen steadfastly refused to reveal where they had hidden the bodies of the white leaders of the expedition. Mr. Harvis, acting for the Colony, cleverly implied throughout the trial that the massacre was racial in motivation, and that the fair-skinned victims were taken to a secret location, there to suffer the most savage treatment.

Miss Erica Carlyle, defeated in her efforts to rescue her brother, left several weeks ago, but is surely comforted now by the triumph of justice.

—*NEW YORK PILLAR/RIPOSTE, June 19, 1920*

Nyarlathotep Papers #11

Cairo, Egypt
3 January 1919

Dear Mr. Carlyle,

I am informed that you seek certain knowledge of our land and can perhaps aid you in this. In my posession are singular curios which I most happily believe of interest. These I willingly send for your consideration, if a price can be agreed upon. Naturally they are ancient and must command a goodly sum. I will arrange matters to your satisfaction when your agent calls at my shop, in the Street of Jackals in the Old Quarter.

Until then I remain your most humble servant,

Faraz Najir

Nyarlathotep Papers #17

Tonight Only

"The Cult of Darkness in Polynesia & the Southwest Pacific"

a two-hour lecture with slides delivered by Prof. Anthony Cowles, Ph.D.

of the University of Sydney (Australia), and presently Locksley Fellow of Polynesian Esoterica at Miskatonic University (Arkham)

Schuyler Hall, NYU
8 PM

Tonight Only

Nyarlathotep Papers #16

Nov. 7, 1924

Mr. Jackson Elias
c o Prospero House Publishers
Lexington Avenue, New York City

Dear Mr. Elias,

The book about which you inquired is no longer in our
collection. The information you seek may be found here
in other volumes. If you will contact me upon arrival,
I will be most happy to further assist you.

As Always,

Miriam Atwright

Miriam Atwright

Nyarlathotep Papers #14

Photograph

Blurry and grainy, it shows a large yacht at anchor surrounded by Chinese junks.
Only part of the name of the yacht is visible: the first three letters are DAR.

Nyarlathotep Papers #18

Nyarlathotep Papers #15

Emerson Imports

648 West 47th Street
New York, New York
Telephone: HA 6-3900

Silas N'Kwane

Reverse of Emerson Imports card is in Elias' handwriting. Cut out, fold on dotted line, and tape or glue together.

Nyarlathotep Papers #19

Life as a God

excerpt from the handwritten diary of Montgomery Crompton

Its angles were magnificent, and most strange; by their hideous beauty I was enraptured and enthralled, and I thought myself of the daylight fools who adjudged the housing of this room as mistaken. I laughed for the glory they missed. When the six lights lit and the great words said, then He came, in all the grace and splendour of the Higher Planes, and I longed to sever my veins so that my life might flow into his being, and make part of me a god!

Nyarlathotep Papers #22

Many names, many forms,
but all the same and toward
one end—
need help—
Too big, too ghastly. those dreams,
—Dreams like Carlyle's—
Heard that psychoanalyst's files—
All of them ~~[illegible]~~ writing!
They'll open the gates. Why?—
so the power and the danger is
real. They —
many threads beginning—
The key one in Carlyle's safe—
Coming for me. Will the case
protect?—
[illegible]
and make [illegible] Desire. Should
I scream for them? Let's
scream together

Nyarlathotep Papers #20

August 8, 1924
Nairobi

Dear Jonah,

Big news! There is a possibility that not all of the members of the Carlyle Expedition died. I have a lead. Though the authorities here deny the cult angle, the natives sing a different tune. You wouldn't believe the stories! Some juicy notes coming your way! This one may make us all rich!

Blood and kisses,
J.

P.S. I'll need advance money to follow this one up. More later.

Nyarlathotep Papers #28

"IT ALMOST HAD ME!"

by Alan Groot, Victim

It was like turning suddenly, knowing something was there, only to find nothing — a nothing possessing hideous life! The dank water smell of the cloying fog was replaced by a foul scent of smouldering hair which somehow reached out and filled my lungs, driving itself deep into my body. I began to choke. It meant to kill me. I cannot describe the terrible feeling of invasion by those foggy tendrils. And still I could see nothing!

– excerpt from longer article ghost-written by Mahoney months before the investigators arrive.

Nyarlathotep Papers #30

My Dear Omar,

The scarab is magnificent. If the matching pieces could be found, I would be most appreciative.

A.P.

Nyarlathotep Papers #24

```
First Meeting Jan. 11, 1918
Reference: Erica Carlyle
Closest Relative: Erica Carlyle


        At his sister's insistence, Mr. Roger Vane Worthington Carlyle visited me
this morning.  He deprecates the importance of his state of mind, but concedes
that he has had some trouble sleeping due to a recurring dream in which he
hears a distant voice calling his name.  (Interestingly the voice uses Mr.
Carlyle's second given name, Vane, by which Mr. Carlyle admits he always thinks
of himself.)  Carlyle moves towards the voice, and has to struggle through a
web-like mist in which the caller is understood to stand.
        The caller is a man--tall, gaunt, dark. An inverted ankh blazes in his
forehead. Following the Egyptian theme (C. has had no conscious interest in
things Egyptian, he says), the man extends his hands to C., his palms held
upward. Pictured on his left palm C. discovers his own face; on the right palm
C. sees an unusual, asymmetric pyramid.
        The caller then brings his hands together, and C. feels himself float off
the ground into space.  He halts before an assemblage of monstrous figures,
figures of humans with animal limbs, with fangs and talons, or of no particular
shape at all.  All of them circle a pulsating ball of yellow energy, which C.
recognizes as another aspect of the calling man.  The ball draws him in; he
becomes part of it, and sees through eyes not his own.  A great triangle
appears in the void, asymmetric in the same fashion as the vision of the pyra-
mid.  C. then hears the caller say, "And become with me a god."  As millions of
odd shapes and forms rush into the triangle, C. wakes.
        C. does not consider this dream a nightmare, although it upsets his
sleep. He says that he revels in it and that it is a genuine calling, although
my strong impression is that he actually is undecided about it. An inability to
choose seems to characterize much of his life.

September 18, 1918.  He calls her M'Weru, Anastasia, and My Priestess.  He is
obsessive about her, as well he might be--exterior devotion is certainly one way
to ease the tensions of megalomaniacal contradictions.  She is certainly a rival
to my authority.

December 3, 1918.  If I do not go C. threatens exposure.  If I do go, all pre-
tense of analysis surely will be lost.  What then will be my role?
```

Nyarlathotep Papers #25

Shocking Canvases Bring Recognition

Local Artist's Monstrous Scenes Mock "Surrealists"

NOW COLLECTORS CAN BUY savage scenes which rival or surpass the worst nightmares of the Great War, but which are far more exotic than that grim business.

London artist Mr. Miles Shipley's work is being sought out by collectors, who have paid up to £300 for individual paintings.

This correspondent has seen dozens of the works of artist Miles Shipley, and finds them repulsive beyond belief. Maidens ravished, monsters ripping out a man's innards, shadowy grotesque landscapes, and faces grimacing in horror represent only a fraction of Shipley's work.

Withal their repellent content, these works are conceived and executed with uncanny verisimilitude, almost as though the artist had worked from photographs of alien places surely never on this Earth!

The artist reportedly is in contact with "other dimensions" in which powerful beings exist, and says he merely renders visible his visions.

Mr. Shipley is a working-class man without formal artistic training, who has nonetheless made good where thousands have failed.

Art critics say that Shipley provides an English answer to the Continental artistic movement of "surrealism," whose controversial practicioners have still to convince John Bull that the way in which a thing is painted is more important than what is painted.

A tip of the hat to Miles Shipley for exposing those frauds!

—THE SCOOP

Nyarlathotep Papers #26

POLICE BAFFLED BY MONSTROUS MURDERS!

Inhuman Killer Shot But Still Alive?

VALLEY OF THE DERWENT RESIDENTS, shocked several months ago by two murders and a serious assault on a third victim, are still without explanation or perpetrator of the dreadful attacks.

At that time, Lesser-Edale farmer George Osgood and resident Miss Lydia Perkins were torn to shreds in apparently-unrelated murders on consecutive nights. On the third night, wheelwright Harold Short was nearly killed but managed to drive off a grisly creature which he swore to be man-like but not human.

Constable Tumwell, also of Lesser-Edale, believes that he shot and killed the beast on the night Mr Short was attacked. Other residents of the region have claimed to have seen the thing since.

Reportedly, Lesser-Edale endures to this hour the bizarre wailings of the beast on nights near the full moon.

Readers of *The Scoop* are reminded of their esteemed journal's long-standing Danger Protocols, and are advised that the picturesque cloughs surrounding The Peak have been declared by *The Scoop* to be a Zone of High Danger!

Residents of the Midlands are advised to remain indoors at night, and to report all mysterious happenings to the police and to *The Scoop*.

—THE SCOOP

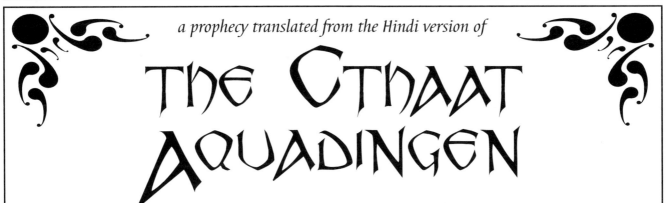

a prophecy translated from the Hindi version of

THE CTHAAT AQUADINGEN

And then shall the gate be opened, as the sun is blotted out. Thus the Small Crawler will awaken those who dwell beyond and bring them. The sea shall swallow them and spit them up and the leopard shall eat of the flesh in Rudraprayag in the Spring.

Nyarlathotep Papers #27

SLAUGHTER CONTINUES!

Scoop Offers Reward!

AN UNIDENTIFIED FOREIGNER was found floating in the Thames this Tuesday, the 24th victim in a series of bizarre slayings.

Though Inspector James Barrington of the Yard had no immediate comment, sources exclusive to *The Scoop* agreed that the victim had been beaten severely by one or more assailants, and then stabbed through the heart.

This series of murders has continued over the space of three years, to the bafflement of our faithful Metropolitans. Must we hope that Mr. Sherlock Holmes, though reported by Mr. Doyle to be in retirement, will one last time rise to the defense of our majestic isles?

Readers of *The Scoop* are reminded that this esteemed journal has a standing reward for information leading to the apprehension and conviction of the perpetrators, in an amount now risen to £24 with the latest death. Be on guard!

—THE SCOOP

Nyarlathotep Papers #32

Tragedy at the Mosque of Tulun

Six of Ibn Tulun's most respected scholars died last night in the collapse of the ceiling of their study room.

The cause of these tragic deaths is being investigated.

Still missing, but presumed dead, is Nessim Efti. The nazir of Ibn Tulun, Achmed Zehavi, survived, but was taken to hospital in shock.

The collapse occurred in a building adjacent to Ibn Tulun itself; the historic structure is undamaged.

Nyarlathotep Papers #33

Nyarlathotep Papers #36

Mar. 7—Jock Kuburaga says that abos are following us. Most unusual if true. Primitives have every reason to fear guns—and our bush ranger predilection for using them. In the past, I have always known them to head the other way as soon as they sight white men.

Mar. 21—We are about equally distant from Joanna Spring and Separation Well, east of an awful line of dry lakes. The heat is terrible. Our hopes are low—there is nothing here, certainly not quartz reels! L.'s notations are in systematic error. He is a complete duffer as a surveyor.

Today we sighted several enormous birds flying lazily far above us. How did they get here, and where can they be going?

Mar. 22—At about noon today we found Jock, partly buried in a gully. His body was scoured and covered with hundreds of small punctures, as though somebody had sandblasted him, We buried him, of course. I shall miss his counsel, and he was an excellent hand with the camels.

Mar. 23—We have discovered what appears to be remnants of an ancient city, rising from the shifting sands! I believe I have secured several good photographs of this amazing find, though the heat has ruined all but six of my photographic plates. By the pitting of the stone, the blocks and pillars appear to be more than 10,000 years old! Incredible!

Mar. 24—Four camels killed in the attack last night. I saw at least two abos, and more must have been skulking out there. I'm sure I hit one. That ends this trip—we'll have to head back to Cuncudgerie and report this incident.

More than men were out there last night. I saw shapes much bigger than men during the attack. My evidence is the body of Old Sam the camel, punctured and scraped is the best way I can described the remains, just like poor Jock. Since the attack lasted only a couple of minutes, it's hard for me to believe that anything human could have done so much damage so quickly. But then what was it?

Nyarlathotep Papers #34

Sgt. Bumption's Statement

SGT. BUMPTION

"It were right 'orrible. I seen nothin' to match it. Bodies every-where—not bodies, mind, but bits o' bodies. An 'ead 'ere, an arm there, torn to shreds like you would a newspaper. Something grabbed those poor blokes and chewed the 'ell out of them, beg-gin' your pardon, ma'm. You woulda thought the jackals and buzzards woulda et 'em down to the bone by the time we arrived, but the niggers said the animals shied off and wouldn't touch the free meal. Even animals get bad feelin's, I'm thinking. Well, I never want sight o' such a thing again."

Nyarlathotep Papers #38

Seamens Club Damaged

A portion of the Seamens Club was destroyed late last night, and inspectors report considerable damage to the river side of the institution "in excess of 8,000 pounds ster-ling," according to underwriters.

No injury or loss of life is reported.

According to unconfirmed though informed speculation, seepage undermined a portion of the embankment area upon which the famous club stands, causing the collapse.

Inebriates congregating along the bank swear that strange creatures emerged from the river shortly before the collapse. Their stories were a hearty momentary relief to the risky business of sorting through the rubble.

— *Shanghai Courier*

Nyarlathotep Papers #31

Warren Besart's Statement

"A lawyer contacted me. I agreed to act as purchasing agent for Mr. Roger Carlyle of the United States, who was represented to me as a wealthy American. On written instructions from Mr. Carlyle, I purchased certain artifacts from Faraz Najir, an antiquities dealer, and illegally shipped them out of Egypt to Sir Aubrey Penhew in London. I know the artifacts were ancient, but nothing more.

"When the Carlyle Expedition came to Egypt, I arranged for all their equipment and permits. Their main site was at Dhashur, in the area of the Bent Pyramid.

"One day at Dhashur, Jack Brady came to me and told me that Carlyle, Hypatia Masters, Sir Aubrey, and Dr. Huston had entered the Bent Pyramid and then vanished. Brady was excited and suspected foul play, since the diggers already had fled the site and work had come to a stand-still. We did not know what to do, so we drank.

"The next morning, Carlyle and the others reappeared. They were excited by some tremendous find, but what it was, they would not say, nor did I learn, for Sir Aubrey was a fiend for secrecy. All of them had changed in some inexplicable way, and a way not for the better; I did not ask further.

"That evening, an old Egyptian woman visited me. She said that her son had been one of the diggers. She said the diggers had fled because Carlyle and the others had con-sorted with an ancient evil, the Messenger of the Black Wind. She said that she could recognize that the souls of all the Europeans but Brady and myself were lost. If I wanted proof, I should go to the Collapsed Pyramid at Meidum at the time when the moon is slimmest—the night before the dark of the moon. God help me, I went!

"I took one of the trucks, pretending to leave for a night in the pleasure quarter of Cairo. But instead I drove the twenty miles south to Meidum, and secreted myself where she advised. There in the midnight blackness I saw Carlyle and the others disport themselves in obscene ritu-als with a hundred madmen. The very desert came alive, crawling and undulating toward the ruins of the pyramid. To my horror, the stone ruins themselves became a skele-tal, bulging-eyed thing!

"Strange creatures emerged from the sands, grasped the dancing celebrants, and, one by one, tore out their throats, killing all until only the Europeans (and one other robed celebrant) remained.

"Something more loomed out of the sand, the size of an elephant but with five separate shaggy heads. Then I realized what it was—but it is madness to speak it! I saw it rise and in a great ravening swallow as one all the torn corpses and their hideous murderers, leaving alive only five people amidst the stench of the blood-soaked sands.

"I fainted. When I recovered, I wandered into the desert. There further horrors awaited me. Stumbling up a rise before dawn, I saw beyond hundreds of dark sphinx-es, rank upon rank drawn up and waiting for the hour of madness when they will spring to devour the world! I fainted again, and this time I left the world for many months.

"A man found me; for two years he and his mother cared for me—me, a man mindless and returned, I came back to Cairo. But I began to dream! Only hashish helps now, or opium if it can be found. My supply is low again, and my life is intolerable without it. Will you gentlemen please contribute? Only strong drugs keep me from insan-ity. Everything, gentlemen, everything is lost. There is no hope for any of us. Everywhere they wait. Perhaps you will join me in a pipe?"

Nyarlathotep Papers #39

Fire on Chin-Ling Road

Three monks have been found dead in a pavilion fire in the Garden of the Purple Clouds of Autumn. They are thought to have died because of an overturned brazier.

The names of the deceased have not yet been released, but a reliable source indicates that all three were respected scholars of T'ang, Five Dynasties, and Sung literature, a profound loss to all who value China's great heritage.

Eyewitnesses remarked that the evening fire leapt in an uncanny fashion from one blazing structure to follow the fleeing monks into the second pavilion. "A floating cloud of fire followed them," according to Mr. Liu Chen-dai of Brilliant Poppy lane.

A European was seen leaving the vicinity of the conflagration. Police respectfully ask his assistance in their investigation.

—*Shanghai Courier*

Nyarlathotep Papers #40

Violent Incident on Lantern Street

Police report murders at Number 88 Lantern Street, "sometime after midnight" last night. The victims are identified as Miss Reparita Wong, resident at the address, and Mr. Chin Hsi-chou, address unavailable at the time of publication.

Police inspector Chong indicates that the slayings were unusually violent. He requests information from anyone with knowledge either of Miss Wong or Mr. Chin.

Even Lantern Street habituÈs, normally not noted for compassion, were taken aback by the cruelty of the crimes. One witness was so distraught that she identified the killer as a giant bat.

—*Shanghai Courier*

Nyarlathotep Papers #41

Nyarlathotep Papers #45

Hail Pharaoh of Darkness, Hail Nyarlathotep. Cthulhu fhtagn, Nyarlathotep th'ga, shamesh, shamesh, Nyarlathotep th'ga, Cthulhu fhtagn!

13th June, 1921: At last I have arrived to begin the task of my lord and master, the Black Pharaoh. He has given me my dreams, given me Egypt, and I will duly repay him by giving him the world of men. The power, the beauty, none cannot appreciate who do not witness. I know the power, the beauty; I bear the beauty of a life devoted to him ....

30th August, 1921: Huston has at last sent the plans. Very complex and fascinating. It will take some time to grasp their meaning and begin building. I have been promised the knowledge necessary, and my faith is strong ....

7th September, 1921: The first shipments have arrived. All of us know great joy. The deep ones have arrived to stay. The work begins ....

15th January, 1922: The first phase is complete. Shipments are arriving more quickly now. I must begin work on the warhead soon ....

8th April, 1923: The rods have been drawn, but more knowledge is needed. Huston is worthy—I never would have thought it possible ....

4th October, 1923: Work on the guidance system has halted. Huston must open a deeper level, and that will take time. Our Master has promised to aid him by bringing one of the Great Race. How I long to speak to one of those ....

19th January, 1924: With joy we begin work again. Soon is the day ....

29th September, 1924: The missile is complete, but the warhead baffles me. I must pray for guidance. Ho Fong warns of someone who knows our plans—is that nursling Carlyle still alive? Will Our Master deign to tell me?

11th February, 1925: All is ready. Now we simply await the Great Day When the Great Gate Opens. None can baffle His will. Nyarlathotep th'ga, Cthulhu fhtagn!

Nyarlathotep Papers #43

Jack Brady's Statement

"I'm Jack Brady. I hear you've been looking for me. I got a minute, and you got some questions. I gather you never got to talk to Jackson Elias. If it's all the same, I'll talk now, and you can ask your questions later.

"As far as I can make out, we're all in a lot of trouble. The more I learn about the situation, the scareder I get. When I spilled the beans to Jackson Elias, I figured people would read his book and do something about this cult. Sorry he ended up that way—you guys friends of his? All the same, I did warn him, and I didn't hold nothing back. I'm warning you guys, too: the cult plays for keeps. Or maybe mugs like you already know that." (He laughs.)

"Well, right from the start I knew that Roger's nigger-girl was trouble. She was as tough as they come, and she had him around her finger. He must have known she was trouble, too, because the more he saw her, the more crazy dreams he had. I thought it was great when he wanted to go to Egypt—that'd be the end of her, see, and things would get back to normal. I liked the guy, and I owed him a lot.

"It seemed for a while that everything would work out. London was a lot of fun, but once we got to Cairo, Roger started having dreams again about meeting a god, and crap like that. But now he wasn't drinking, and the girl wasn't around, and the gentlemen Roger had asked along started acting nuttier than Roger did, and so I said to myself, 'trouble is somewhere up the road.'

"After I paid Faraz Najir for his junk, Roger spent some time with it. He went off the deep end. There was a black kind of head-and-shoulder statue that he'd stare at for hours. And there was a map that he'd study and study, like a normal guy would check out a beautiful dame. He started telling me that we could meet the god as soon as he destroyed the eye and opened the path.

"That hotshot Dr. Huston should have talked Roger down, but he only encouraged him. So the first night that we were up the Nile at Dhashur, Roger snuck out and climbed up the Red Pyramid. Any of you guys ever climbed a pyramid? They're steep! Roger started up that pile like a monkey. Never looked back or hesitated once, which proved to me that the poor bugger was absolutely crazy. But I followed him up." (He laughs again.) "I was crazy, too.

"For about two thirds of the way up the Red Pyramid, you just climb up and over big blocks, sort of like something some dumb kid could make by piling up a million great big construction blocks. The pyramid builders filled in all the gaps with nice smooth stone, but then later people stole that nice stone from around the bottom of the pyramid—the high stuff was too hard to grab, and they couldn't finish the job. Well, Roger zipped right up this part, too, with me still behind, my eyes bulging out 'cause I could barely find handholds to keep from bouncing down the whole damn pyramid.

"There's a little flat place at the tip of the pyramid. When Roger reached the flat place, he put on some kind of robe and started making weird sounds, as though he had flipped for good. But then there was a hell of an explosion with all kinds of funny echoes and screams with it, and a big red flash of light. Well, I lay there for a minute until it seemed safe to go on. He looked at me and said, 'The eye is gone, Jack. Now we can be gods.'

"Well, that was just Roger talk, you know, but beside him there was a big patch ripped right out of the stone, and it looked fresh. When I went back the next day, the patch had been filled in, as though the pyramid had repaired itself. But near the base of the pyramid, I found part of a rock which looked like it could have been in that patch originally, and it had this sign on it." (Brady sketches a mysterious-looking sign; this is the strange symbol which appears in light grey to the top right of this handout..)

"Now I know what it was—its strong magic kept evil things away from us, and Roger deliberately broke its power.

"Two days later, the whole gang—Penhew, Roger, Huston, and Patty—gave me the slip and disappeared in the Bent Pyramid. Some of the messenger boys went to find them, and they came out shrieking that the pyramid had eaten the respected scientists, woe, woe, woe. Bingo, the workers run in all directions! The whole dig was deserted. In five minutes the only person left in the whole area was me. Well, I went in. Sure enough, nobody was inside. I was worried.

"But, a long time later, out come all the missing people from the pyramid. Roger says they'd been to Egypt, to the real Egypt. And that was about the most sensible thing he said. Penhew looked like he had lost about five years. And Patty and Huston both seemed somehow changed. Nobody would explain where they'd been, and nobody cared that after that it was hard to hire workmen.

"After that, when I'd wake up in the nights, the rest of the gang would be talking creepy lingo like I'd never heard before. Then one evening Roger said that he was going to show me the power of what they'd learned. We went out into the desert with a passel of Arabs. Everybody started screaming weird words and songs, and Penhew beat the drum that we got from Najir. When creatures started coming out of the ground and eating the Arabs, and Roger and the others started laughing, why I took my leave, as they say, and went on a real toot. Roger found me the next day, and warned me that I'd better change my attitude. Well, I owed the kid, and I wouldn't desert him, but after that I started thinking real good.

"Then we went to Kenya, and Roger filled me in during the trip. We had found a true god, he said, who would rule the Earth, and we would rule with that god, for we were the chosen of the god. The god had picked us to open the way for his return. And there was enough in what they said—and in what I saw—to make me listen. Every week, Penhew seemed a little younger and a little livelier. Patty was sick a lot. We were going to leave Nairobi from some place in the mountains where there was no river, no railway, no telegraph, no police, and nobody who looked friendly. I figured that Jack Brady wouldn't live very long there, so I made some arrangements. On the last night, in Nairobi, I drugged Roger, kyped the cash box (it was all Roger's money, anyway), and got me and them aboard an unscheduled deadhead freight to Mombasa.

"Later I read that my guess was right. The newspapers said a lot of people died, but Penhew, Huston and Patty Masters weren't among them.

"Anyway, my arrangements went off without a hitch—that happens when you think small and carry a lot of cash. When we got to Mombasa, we got off before the causeway and found a fisherman who was willing to go to Zanzibar for a few dollars. From there we hopped a coastal trader to Durban, and in Durban we dyed our hair, got some decent clothes, and sailed for Perth.

"Now, on the train to Mombasa, Roger got some sleep, and he seemed to wake up a different person. I guess that being away from the influence of those other people let him return to his old self. I told him we were in a lot of trouble, and that we needed to hide out, and reminded him about the Arabs being killed in Egypt, and the god stuff, and so on, and he could remember it all right, although it didn't seem very important, somehow. But he understood the logic of the situation. After a week or so, though, his nightmares started, and he began to go off the deep end. He was beginning to realize some of the things he had done.

"I was in Shanghai while I was in the Marines, and I had a fair number of friends here. By the time our ship put into Hong Kong, Roger could go no farther. He began shrieking at shadows and everything that moved. So I put him in a sanitarium there—I had to use up most of the remaining money to get him settled. Then I went on to Shanghai, believing that I'd never again see any member but Roger of that damned expedition.

"So I thought, until I looked through naval glasses at a certain yacht, and saw Sir Aubrey Penhew preening on the deck of the *Dark Mistress*."

Nyarlathotep Papers #44

Translation from
The *Seven Cryptical Books of Hsan*

The ineffable Eye must be worked into natural substance which is naturally hard.

The unrivalled light of the marvellous Eye transcends taint if all evil presences have been dispatched or dispelled.

The blood for the pupil of the winnowing Eye must be fresh.

Only one incorruptible Eye may guard a location.

"Of those signs effectively sealing the festerings of the dark god, the most potent is the *Eye of Light and Darkness.* Inscribed into the substance of a high place near the haunts of evil, and no further than 30 li from them, expels the evil strength for so long as the sign exists. The Eye must be created the afternoon before the full moon rises. At moonrise, the blood of an innocent must fill the pupil of the Eye once per drumbeat from then to moonset. As the first blood is given, chant the words 'sa-ma, sa-ma, te-yo, sa-ma,' and continue until the moon sets. When next the moon rises, the Eye opens to ward and to guard. Gather the friends of good to work this wisdom, for too few shall surely fail."

The wondrous Eye must not first burn where evil beings or creatures lurk.

He who first chants must be able to create the gift of the Elder Sign.

All who chant must detest evil.

— Chou Teh

Along the edges of the scroll are written small red-ink commentaries signed by the monk Chou Teh

Nyarlathotep Papers #42

Min, my man –

Have to go underground to finish the work. Get your Firmies ready; we'll go soon. Will contact you in the usual manner.

Jack

Nyarlathotep Papers #37

TO: All Acolytes
SUBJECT: Learning Magic
DATE: - - 1925

MESSAGE: Acolytes are reminded that their duty to their god includes the prompt and persistent practice of necromantic gestures and intonations necessary to spell-casting. A test of your Shrivelling abilities takes place two weeks from today.

R.H.

TO: All Acolytes
SUBJECT: Our Recent Hunt
DATE: - - 1925

MESSAGE: We still have not found our last "2-legged deer." There is utterly no excuse for not being able to find an unarmed human who has neither food, nor water, nor magic.

Remind the line-walkers to be alert.

R.H.

The Nairobi Notes of Jackson Elias

Sheets of plain paper, each covered on one side only with Elias' neat printing, and paperclipped together into sets by Jonah Kensington. They are reasonably well-organized, and seem in many ways complete, yet are remarkable for the absence of conclusions, connections, and clearly-defined themes. The hand is strong and bold.

SET ONE of the Nairobi notes sets forth the offices, officials, and tribes which Elias visited, searching for material concerning cults and cult rituals. Nothing conclusive was learned, though Elias discounts the official version of the Carlyle massacre.

SET TWO describes his trip to the massacre site. He notes particularly that the earth there is completely barren, and that all the tribes of the region avoid the place, saying it is cursed by the God of the Black Winds, whose home is the mountain top.

SET THREE is an interview with a Johnstone Kenyatta, who says that the Carlyle murders may have been performed by the cult of the Bloody Tongue. He says that the cult reputedly is based in the mountains, and that its high priestess is a part of the Mountain of the Black Winds. Elias is politely skeptical, but Kenyatta insists upon the point. In quotes, Elias records that regional tribes fear and hate the Bloody Tongue, that tribal magic is of no protection against the cult, and that the cult's god is not of Africa.

SET FOUR follows up on the Kenyatta interview. Elias confirms from several good sources that the Bloody Tongue exists, though he finds no first-hand evidence of it. Tales include children stolen for sacrifice. Creatures with great wings are said to come down from the Mountain of the Black Winds to carry off people. The cult worships a god unknown to folklorists, one fitting no traditional African pattern. Elias in particular cites "Sam Mariga, rr-sta."

SET FIVE is a single sheet reminding Elias that the Cairo-based portion of the Carlyle itinerary must be examined carefully. He believes that the reason which prompted Carlyle's Kenyan sidetrip is on the Nile.

SET SIX is a long interview with Lt. Mark Selkirk, leader of the men who actually found the remains of the Carlyle Expedition, and a Kenya hand since the Great War and the fight against the resourceful von Lettow. Importantly, Selkirk says that the bodies were remarkably undecayed for the length of time which they lay in the open—"almost as if decay itself wouldn't come near the place." Secondly, the men had been torn apart, as if by animals, though what sorts of animals would pull apart bodies so systematically he could not guess. "Unimaginable. Inexplicable." Selkirk agrees that the Nandis may have had something to do with the episode, but suspects that the charges against the ringleaders were trumped-up. "It wouldn't be the first time," he says cynically. Finally, Selkirk confirms that no caucasians were found among the dead—only corpses of the Kenyan bearers were scattered across the barren plain.

SET SEVEN is another single sheet. Elias ran into Nails Nelson at the Victoria Bar in Nairobi. Nelson had been a mercenary for the Italians on the Somali-Abyssinian border, and had escaped into Kenya after double-crossing his employers. Nelson claimed to have seen Jack Brady alive (March of 1923) in Hong Kong, less than two years before Elias was in Kenya and long after the Kenyan court declared that Brady and the rest of the expedition were dead. Brady was friendly, though guarded and taciturn. Nelson didn't press the conversation. From this report Elias deduced that other members of the expedition might still live.

SET EIGHT discusses a possible structure for the Carlyle book, but is mostly featureless, with entries like "tell what happened" and "explain why."

Index

By no means is this index a complete list of references in this book. However, it is a listing of all the important references for the items included. When looking up Characters & Groups, also see the character listing on pp. 13-16.